A HISTORY OF ART

BY GERMAIN BAZIN

CONSERVATEUR-EN-

CHEF OF THE LOUVRE

TRANSLATED

BY FRANCIS SCARFE

A

from PRE

668 ILLUSTRATIONS

BONANZA BOOKS

NEW YORK

to

HISTORY OF ART

HISTORIC TIMES

THE PRESENT

(I)

PREFACE

ANYONE trying to write a short history of the arts is liable to find his work being compared with Salomon Reinach's famous *Apollo*, which served as a manual for several generations of students. Perhaps it was a mistake on my part to yield to the friendly but insistent pressure of Messrs. Garamond, who urged me to undertake this handbook of art history. At all events the task has become remarkably more complicated since the time when Reinach wrote his Manual in 1905. Since then many civilizations have been more fully explored or even freshly discovered. The great Hellenist scholar confined himself to the art of the West, and as his title *Apollo* suggests, his chief purpose was to expound the "Greek Miracle" with all its antecedents and consequences. Reinach's work covered mainly the ancient Mediterranean and the Renaissance. But since then we have discovered another "miracle" which might well be called the "Barbarian Miracle," taking the word *barbarian* in the same sense as the Greeks and Romans did. The primitive civilizations are now admired as they could not possibly have been fifty years ago, and since then we have also discovered the arts of the East. Moreover, we now recognize certain other values to be as fertile as the classicism to which Reinach devoted his researches, in particular the baroque, which in his day was still ignored or condemned as a sign of decadence.

The reader may be surprised to find certain variations in the way the different chapters of this book are planned. All those dealing with

ancient civilizations or with Pre-Columbian archaeology or the Far East
contain a historical introduction which appeared superfluous in the case
of the Western civilizations, whose history is sufficiently well known.
In the case of the Far East, it appeared advisable to add some account
of the religions of the countries concerned, without which it would be
hard to understand the artistic works of races whose outlook is so unlike
our own.

This book is a historical work, designed to give the uninitiated
reader as many precise ideas and established facts as possible. The
remarks which introduce each chapter may be read separately, but in
each case they contain a short critical and aesthetic survey. In the
Conclusion the reader will find an outline of the various ways in which
the *work of art* has been interpreted, from the time when modern man
first turned his eager attention to this particular product of human genius.

The illustrations were chosen to accompany the text, but occasionally they diverge from it, especially those accompanying the prefatory
remarks and the conclusion: in such cases the plates are intended to
bring out resemblances or historical perspectives, and offer the reader
the most direct evidence of whatever unifies or distinguishes the characteristic forms of different civilizations.

The author's aim has been to consider the work of art from a
genuinely universal, impartial point of view, as something which transcends the limitations of time and place. While he does not claim to
have succeeded, he will feel rewarded if his efforts in that direction are
recognized. But unless he has no roots at all, who can hope to escape
from his own time, or ignore the claims of the civilization in which he
was reared?

GERMAIN BAZIN

CONTENTS

vii

LIST OF COLOR PLATES

A HISTORY OF ART

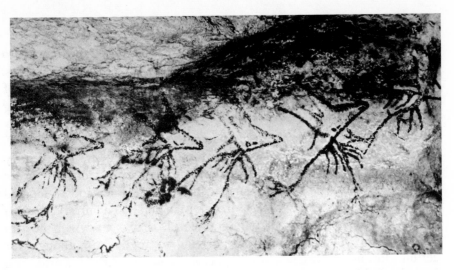

1. The Frieze of Stags. Drawn on rock in Lascaux Cave, Dordogne.

CHAPTER I

THE ORIGINS OF ART

THE EARLIEST KNOWN products of human genius enable us to grasp the creative impulse behind works of art at the very source. The perfection of the statuettes of the Gravettian hunters and the masterpieces of Magdalenian cave art show that primitive man had no inner urge to express some preconceived notion of "beauty" through the medium of forms. Art is only one of the many expressions—though perhaps it is the most specific—of the unique genius which drives man to repeat the creative act of the demiurge in everything he does, so that he must needs excel himself from century to century. If the Gravettian carvings have such a dynamic sense of form, and if the animal figures painted in the French and Spanish caves are perfect works of naturalism that no later civilization could surpass, it is because primitive man, in making them, was convinced that he was genuinely *creating*. For him the image was no mere imitation. It had the same living faculties as the being of which it was a model, a double. It was thus a work of magic by which man asserted his mastery over the world. We know that our ancestor of the Old Stone Age (the Palaeolithic) painted or carved natural forms with no intention of making a

I

"work of art": he intended, rather, to ensure the fertility of his prey, to entice it into his traps, or to acquire its strength for his own purposes. The primitive artist was a magician whose drawing had all the virtue of a magic spell, an incantation. If he gave so much attention to the living truth, it was in order to make shapes as lifelike as possible and endow them with the actual qualities of the *creature*. Thus the vivid naturalism of those early images can be traced to that desire to identify himself with the world, which distinguishes man from all other forms of life. The animal is bound to the natural order and is doomed to be merely one of its blind forces. Man, on the contrary, has an innate awareness of the surrounding world, thanks to which he can break free of it while ceaselessly striving to rejoin it in thought or action. Primitive man was deeply involved in the natural world, and lost none of its inherent energy. Not a thought or deed of his failed to make contact with some power in the universe. Man's entire activity was aimed at skillfully intervening in the play of natural forces, in the hope of preserving a balance, attracting "good" and repelling "evil" powers.

If works of art appeared so late in Palaeolithic times, it was by no means because man was incapable of making them. The earliest Palaeolithic "industries" of the Chellean, Acheulean and Mousterian

2. Map of prehistoric Occidental cave art sites. *After Frobenius, Geschichte der afrikanischen Kultur.*

periods show a craftsmanship that could well have been applied to art. But a long period was no doubt necessary before man could acquire a creative grasp of the forces underlying the world. The discovery and evolution of language, in itself, is an artistic operation in which verbal forms have to be invented and perfected. Naming things is the first creative act. To the primitive mind, the name has a magic power which identifies it with the object. Thus man had slowly to bring his mental picture of the world into focus before he could make his inner vision even more effective by reproducing the shapes he saw in nature. But at last certain "magicians," who were no doubt of a race with an exceptional plastic sense, thought of extending their verbal spells, and giving them more evocatory power, by first of all painting images of the things or creatures they wanted to control. The profound knowledge of nature that can be seen in these works was not the result of the artist's disinterested contemplation, but was drawn from an intimate acquaintance with animal life, learned in the daily drama of the hunt. Perhaps this explains why human images were so few and relatively crude: the drawing of the human figure was not an integral part of the primitive system of magic. As these paintings, drawings and engravings were executed without a model, often in the depths of gloomy caves and by the light of the feeblest of lamps, the primitive artist needed a marvelous memory to inform his creative imagination with such a power of synthesis. The artist-magician had to enter into a ritualistic trance, during which he "emptied" his own soul by an act of intense mental concentration: he then evoked the supernatural powers which identified him with the bison, mammoth, horse or deer, until he was possessed by the soul of the animal itself and could then portray its image on the wall of his cave.

The study of the origins of art has a surprise in store, for the highest level of art was reached when man was living in this primitive state of the Old Stone Age, at a time when conditions had been made arctic or subarctic by the advance of the glaciers. From the Neolithic period onward, civilization tended to become almost entirely material-istic in its outlook. There was a gap of several thousands of years between the cave art of the Magdalenian era (the final era of the Old Stone Age) and the first great civilizations of southwestern Asia and the Nile Valley.

PREHISTORIC AND PROTOHISTORIC CIVILIZATIONS

Though its chronology is not firmly established, it is safe to say that
the long prehistoric era during which man left little or no account
of himself lasted for hundreds of thousands of years—perhaps about
500,000. In the Palaeolithic phase, the largest part of man's prehistorical development, men existed by hunting and fishing, making most
of their tools by chipping stone (especially flint). They lived in
isolated tribes always in close contact with animal life. In the final
most recent periods (Upper Palaeolithic) men built summer huts and
also, in regions where rock shelters were not available, winter houses
half dug into the ground. Men's elementary equipment did not change
drastically in the Mesolithic phase (Middle Stone Age). In the Neolithic phase (New Stone Age), the age of the greatest refinement of
stone tools, there were swift changes in man's development, and toward 5000 B.C., in the Near East, human effort was increasingly and
ever more rapidly directed toward civilization, that is to say the
framework of an organized society; industrial specialization involving
endless improvements in tools; the emergence of new techniques such
as pottery and mining (for flint); the development of trade; the discovery of agriculture; the domestication of animals; and permanent,
collective settlements on land or lake.

THE UPPER PALAEOLITHIC AGE

The oldest examples of art date from the first millennia of the Upper
Palaeolithic Age, a long period of the east-west migration of *Homo
sapiens* into Europe, where he replaced less advanced stocks. His
rupestral art in the naturalistic style, consisting of carvings, drawings,
paintings and engravings on rock faces, is found concentrated in the
southwest of France and in northern Spain, and is therefore known
as Franco-Cantabrian.

Aurignacian invaders and settlers (named after the French site
at Aurignac, Haute-Garonne) first evolved drawing, engraving and
painting. In early cave works (for example, La Pileta cave, Malaga)
animals are silhouetted in "absolute profile," with only one leg to represent a pair and no indications of detail.

Gravettian mammoth hunters from Russia and eastern Europe
(named after the rock shelter of La Gravette, Dordogne) carved,

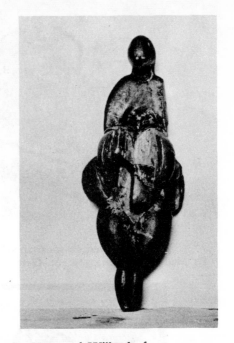

3. Female figure, known as the Venus of Willendorf.
Vienna, Kunsthistorisches Museum.
4. Statuette, known as the Venus of Lespugue (reconstructed).
St.-Germain, Musée des Antiquités Nationales.

especially out of mammoth ivory, small figures which have been found over a wide area in Eurasia. Some are of women apparently suffering from the fatty degeneration known as steatopygia still found among remnants of the bushmen in South Africa. While some of these statuettes tend to be representative (Willendorf, Austria, pl. 3), others (Lespugue, France, pl. 4) are almost geometrically stylized. It is not known whether this three-dimensional vision came before or after the portrayal of shapes on a flat surface. In southwestern France and northern Spain the Gravettians developed Aurignacian traditions of painting, their pictorial art reaching a climax in the admirable paintings of the Lascaux cave in the Dordogne (pl. 1), discovered in 1940.

The ill-defined Solutrean period (named from the site at Solutré, Saône-et-Loire) is known for leaf-shaped flint tools of astonishing refinement, and for a very few carvings of animals in relief on rock faces (the frieze of horses along the rock shelter of La Chaire-à-Calvin, Mouthiers; frieze of horses, ibex, and others, at Roc de Sers, Charente). Such sculpture was continued in the Magdalenian period (named after

5. Bison, carved on spear thrower. From the rock shelter of
La Madeleine, Dordogne. *St.-Germain, Musée des Antiquités Nationales.*

6. Reindeer and salmon engraved on reindeer antler, from cave at Lortet
(Hautes-Pyrénées). *St.-Germain, Musée des Antiquités Nationales.*

7. Leaping bison, painting in the cave at Altamira, Spain.
Taken from Fauconnet.

the rock shelter of La Madeleine, at Les Eyzies, Dordogne), for example in the splendid equestrian frieze of Cap Blanc, in the Dordogne, and the frieze of bison, horses, ibex, human female torsos, of Angles-sur-l'Anglin (Vienne). The 30,000 years or thereabouts of the Magdalenian period (to be compared with a probable span of 50,000 years for the preceding Aurignacian and Gravettian periods) were rich in artistic expression. Sculpture ranged from the large (originally colored) friezes to small objects in reindeer horn (pl. 5). The same material was also engraved or incised (pl. 6). However, the pictorial arts became dominant, reaching their peak in the polychrome animals of the famous caves of Altamira (pl. 7) and Castillo (Santander, Spain), Font-de-Gaume (Dordogne) and Marsoulas (Haute-Garonne).

The Abbé Breuil's investigations enable us to trace the evolution of this mural art from the simple line drawing of Aurignacian times to the final polychrome painting, which is late Magdalenian. Whether incised on rock surfaces naturally covered in soft clay or drawn (with the finger or "brush"), the line was at first of even thickness, and was only modulated later. Next a tinge of red ocher or black manganese was added, silhouetting the outline of the animal's body. At a later stage the brush or graving tool would be run over all the finer points in order to bring out the movement, the pelt, or details of anatomy—always, though, without the slightest hint of the picturesque. In the advanced Magdalenian technique the painter finally blended his tones to reproduce the graded coloring of the hide or fur. All these various stages were dictated by a growing urge toward naturalistic truthfulness, yet such a virtuosity was achieved that the painter's hand marked the line down as boldly as a Pisanello, seeking and finding the clear-cut elegance of the arabesque. This thoroughbred art, the product of thousands of years of evolution and intense research, vanished from the Franco-Cantabrian areas while it was still at the height of its perfection, and with hardly a sign of any fall in quality. This may be explained by the amelioration of the cold climate of the Ice Age and the consequent disappearance of the hunter's quarry, which had occasioned Upper Palaeolithic art in all its remarkable forms.

During the Capsian period (named after the site at Gafsa, the Capsa of antiquity, in Tunisia) which began during the later Palaeolithic Age and continued into the Mesolithic, the Hamitic peoples of Africa produced a rock art comparable with that of southwestern

Europe. Our present inadequate knowledge of the geology and prehistory of Africa makes it hard to settle the time scale of the engravings
and paintings of the Atlas and Sahara regions, or of Egypt, Libya, Nubia
and Rhodesia (pl. 8). However, this art seems to have extended into
the historic period. Here we find two distinct styles. In addition to
the naturalistic manner, not unlike the Magdalenian, there was also an
expressionistic and schematic form of art in which human and animal
figures were grouped in dramatic actions. In Magdalenian art, the
figures were usually separate, and no such complexity of action was.
attempted. Drawings of the human figure, similarly grouped, are
plentiful in the above regions. For the first time the artist had set
himself the task of mastering the fundamentals of dramatic composition, and in this he succeeded all the more impressively as his dia-
grammatic treatment avoided the picturesque: the artist created the
impression of whirling vectors of movement, pushing his systematiza-
tion almost to the point of abstract draughtsmanship, the magical
figures becoming pure "signs." The peculiar Upper Palaeolithic
rupestral art of eastern Spain (pl. 9) is to be related to this aspect of
Capsian art, rather than to the developed Magdalenian art, although
it was influenced by art north of the Pyrenees. Thus, from very
ancient times, man found a source of artistic inspiration in abstract
art as well as in naturalism.

8. Rock painting
(tracing) in Rhodesia.

9. Bowmen in battle. Drawing on rock face. *Morella la Vella, Castellón, Spain.*

THE NEOLITHIC AGE

Though it survived in Africa and Scandinavia, the early naturalistic art came to an end in the Franco-Cantabrian region in the Mesolithic Age (about 10,000 B.C.) in the Azilian phase. The painted pebbles of the great cavern of Mas d'Azil (Ariège) are evidence of an art verging on the abstract, which was to prevail throughout the Neolithic period. Ceramics, which appeared in early Neolithic times, developed rapidly with the later (Bronze Age) invention of the potter's wheel and was no doubt favored by the expansion of agriculture.

In the Neolithic and Chalcolithic stages (the latter being so named because during it metals were first used), mankind developed a rudimentary form of architecture which was sometimes impressive in its effects. Such *megalithic* (large stone) monuments were usually constructed with colossal, unwieldy pieces of stone, and were intended for burial or for ritualistic purposes. The burial chambers consisted of upright stones weighing several tons each, serving as supports for slabs that were laid across them, the whole being finally covered (though not in all cases) with a mound of earth or small stones. They are of three main types, *dolmen*, a table arrangement of stones with

9

10. Ritual circle. *Stonehenge, England.*

no passage leading in; *passage grave*, a rectangular or more or less circular tomb approached through a narrow stone passage; and *gallery grave* (covered passage serving as a long burial vault). These underground tombs spread from the eastern Mediterranean in the third millennium and second millennium B.C. to France, Spain, Portugal, Great Britain and northern Europe.

Huge arrangements of standing stones, whether set in straight lines as at Carnac in Brittany, or grouped in circles as at Avebury, Arbor Low and Stonehenge, in England, formed impressive sanctuaries which must have required enormous human effort and, at the same time, a fairly advanced social order.

THE PROTOHISTORIC PERIOD

A major event in the history of human techniques was the discovery and use of metals. These seem to have been valued at first for their preciousness. After learning how to obtain gold and silver, and then copper in the raw state (Chalcolithic period), man shaped them with hammers before he discovered the art of casting. The discovery of the blending properties of tin so as to form alloys enabled him to harden copper, making possible its industrial use in the form of brass and bronze.

The eastern regions of the Mediterranean made the greatest creative contribution. In the third millennium the rise of the Elamite, Sumerian and Aegean historical civilizations coincided with the development of bronze metallurgy, which itself began about 3500 B.C. The peoples of central, western and northern Europe now emerged from their prehistorical stage to enter what is called the protohistorical phase; for although they left no written records of their history, certain echoes of it survive in the traditions handed down by the peoples of the Near East. In any case, so far as metallurgy was concerned they depended on the Mediterranean, for merchants of the eastern Mediterranean not only exported bronze articles to the West, but imported eastward from Spain to England the tin they needed for its production. Metallurgical techniques also found their way into central Europe through the Caucasus route by which the Near Eastern empires went in search of ore. It is not easy to give any strict chronology of the diffusion of metals, for although a relative time scale may be clearly distinguished, there are no definite, epoch-making dates for the earlier periods. Copper side by side with tools of polished stone was widely in use in the second half of the fourth millennium B.C., while the same phenomenon is to be found in the Aegean area at the beginning of the third millennium, and in the western Mediterranean by about 1900 B.C. Bronze was in common use in the Near East in the first half of the third millennium; in the Aegean about 2300 B.C., and in the West about 1500 B.C. As for iron, this was still a rare metal in the Near East in the first half of the second millennium; by 1400 B.C. ironworking techniques were evolved, nevertheless, in Asia Minor, the center of dispersion. In the West the Iron Age, which lasted for two thousand years, falls into two periods: the Halstatt period, taking its name from a site in Austria, which lasted roughly from 1000 to 500 B.C.; and the La Tène period (named after a site in Switzerland) from 500 B.C to the Christian era.

The protohistoric Bronze and Iron civilizations extended over a considerable area, notably Italy, Spain, Gaul, the British Isles, central and northern Europe, Scandinavia, the Urals and the Altai Mountains. The epoch of La Tène corresponded with the westward expansion of the Celts. Although some anthropomorphic sculptures of this period have been found (in France, at Roquepertuse and Entremont; in Czechoslovakia at Msecké-Zehrovice), the artistic activity of the above peoples showed itself mainly in domestic articles such as terra-cotta vessels (pl. 11), gold vases and jewelry. Whereas the creative imagination of the Mediterranean and Asiatic races found an endless source of inspiration for their plastic art in nature itself, the peoples of central and northern Europe seem to have derived more satisfaction from the abstract. The decorative range of their weapons and pots did not go beyond a few non-representational signs, such as the sacred horns of the bull, the double axe symbolizing thunder, the solar disk and its many derivatives—the wheel, the rowel, the star, the S, the spiral and double spiral (pl. 648), the swastika, the symmetrical cross, and protomic emblems of the horse and swan which were also solar symbols.

11. Burial urn. Halstatt period, about 7th century B.C.
Stuttgart, Landesmuseum.

CHAPTER II

PRIMITIVE ARTISTIC CIVILIZATIONS

THE ARTISTIC MATURING of the Magdalenians was an isolated phenomenon. For thousands of years the people of northern, central and western Europe, plunged in the obscurity of prehistory until our era, remained static in simple tribal groupings with not a glimmer of political or cultural genius. This entirely materialistic civilization spread as far as the Bosporus, where the seven superimposed cities of Hissarlik in Troas (unearthed in the 1870's by the German scholar Schliemann—one being the site of Homer's Troy) reveal a striking poverty of the artistic instinct at a time which saw the rise of great neighboring civilizations.

It was in the Mediterranean area that man made his first great efforts to emerge from his natural state. By inventing systems of politics, culture, religion, industry and commerce, he considerably extended both his practical and intellectual progress. Three great centers of civilization may be distinguished from the Neolithic period onward, before 3000 B.C. These were in the Nile Valley, Mesopotamia (Tigris and Euphrates basins), and the Aegean. All these civilizations were inspired by a heroic resolve to embody their idea of the world in enduring works. The various races who created them seem to have been blessed with a marvelous plastic imagination, and there is nothing —not even the most abstract of concepts—to which they failed to give a concrete form, a figure.

The magical, unorganized setting in which primitive man had lived was now set in order. Man became immune from the elemental powers he so much feared, by personifying them. He worshiped gods: he was no longer in contact with mere things, but with beings he could name, pray to and evoke. Beneficent and maleficent things now tended to crystallize into the abstract qualities of good and evil. The medicine man gave way to the priest, an intermediary between man and God. Man's relationship to the visible or invisible world became regulated by a code of doctrines and practices; that is to say, religion.

Meanwhile the countless figures with which the Egyptians and Mesopotamians covered their monuments still remained profoundly imbued with the sense of the supernatural which had guided the hands of Magdalenian artists. No civilization carried to a higher point than did the Egyptian the belief in the identity of the image with its original. The host of illustrations, through which we can learn the smallest details of Egyptian life, were meant to add the support of reality itself to the objects and people who had to accompany the dead so as to allow them, in the afterlife, to lead the same kind of existence as in their earthly state. These images are replicas, doubles of the articles and beings they represent, and on which magic formulas conferred all the properties of the original model. The invention of images was then, properly speaking, a creation; so that in the Nile Valley the sculptor was known as "He-who-keeps-alive." In Mesopotamia this faith in the power of the image did not result in such a coherent system of imitation, but it was none the less present to the mentality behind the civilizations which succeeded each other in the Tigris and Euphrates Valleys. Why did conquering princes so carefully cut the heads off the statues of defeated kings, if not to rob them of that power of survival after death which in those days was guaranteed by an effigy? At the beginning of the Sumerian civilization in the first Ur dynasty, apparently it was not enough to paint or sculpture the likeness of a dead man's friends on the walls of his tomb, as was the custom in Egypt: they were actually put to death in the course of bloody funeral rites—wives, princes and servants followed their overlord into death, complete with their weapons, jewels, chattels and chariots of war. Belief in the replica later put an end to such holocausts.

This faith in the realness of images brought in its train a whole system of plastic conventions which, more or less empirical in Mesopotamia, assumed in Egypt a rational and sacred character. In order to have the maximum of real power, the image had to reproduce the model in its entirety and not with the incompleteness of our normal vision. The parts on the second and third planes which remained hidden owing to the foreshortening of perspective were therefore reproduced with the same fidelity as those which were fully visible. This explains the strange canon of the human figure, observed in religious art in Egypt for thirty centuries, by which a head in profile, but with one eye full-face, is planted on a trunk whose upper part is seen from the front, the trunk set on profiled legs shown in walking position (pl. 13). Thus all parts of the human body were represented

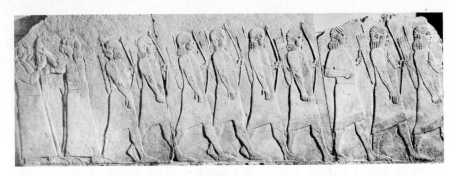

Primitive vision: The figures, which in reality are in a row and thus hidden by each other, are portrayed in file as though following one another.

12. Warriors. Low-relief. Assyrian art, early 7th century B.C.
Paris, Louvre.

from the angle at which they appeared most complete. Figures of men who in reality were *seen* in depth, one behind the other, were portrayed each one complete, either in Indian file (pl. 12) or superimposed in ranks (pl. 15). The herdsman milking a cow was represented next to the animal but not against it, so as not to hide its body:

Primitive canon: Front view of eye set in profiled head; front view of upper trunk, set on profiled legs.

13. Panel of Hesy-ra from Saqqara. Wood. 3rd Egyptian dynasty, about 2700 B.C.
Cairo, Museum.

Primitive vision: The winged bull has five legs, so that it will appear equally complete from front or side.

14. Winged Bull of Khorsabad. Assyrian art, 7th century B.C. *Paris, Louvre.*

in the same way offerings brought to a king by slaves would be portrayed *above* the basket supposedly containing them. At Khorsabad
the famous winged bulls of the palace are shown with five legs, so as
to appear equally "complete" from both front and side (pl. 14). These
mighty figures, like some of the sacred cows of Hathor in Egypt,
are not properly speaking built in the round, but are no more than
a profile and a frontal view put together. The artists of those early
civilizations had no spatial conception of objects. The sense of depth
was as alien to them as the idea of perspective; some objects were
portrayed flat while the profile of others was reduced according to the
composition; the composition being dictated according to a moral

*Primitive vision: presented in
profile on a horizontal plane, the
figures and objects are placed in
layers and not shown in perspective.
Interiors are shown.*

15. Plan, section and elevation of a fortified town. Assyrian bas-relief.
After Layard, Monuments.

16. Portrayal of a garden. Scroll of the Dead, Egyptian papyrus.
London, British Museum.

hierarchy in which no account was taken of the relative sizes of the things themselves. Thus a man was always bigger than a tree, and even too big to enter his own house (pls. 15 and 16). Integral realism, dictated by the needs of magic, obliged the artists to defy appearances; they did not see things from a distance as they appear to us, but saw them only as they knew them to be: the object they portrayed was not a spectacle for them; they identified themselves with it by a process of empathy. Following their hand, their eye rested simultaneously on all the object's planes; they deliberately ignored the fact that certain parts of a thing were farther away than others. Statuary was therefore usually presented face-on, with none of the play of line or forms that would give it spatial life (pl. 69). The name "law of frontalism" has been given to this slavish convention which makes the statue completely static, giving it the inertia of mere architectural material.

In the images imposed on surfaces—bas-reliefs, paintings—the works were based on the side view, silhouetted shadow fashion against the wall; the details of the model were indicated diagrammatically by the chisel, rather than sculptured. The main outline thus kept all the expressive strength that was characteristic of the cave art of earlier times.

The architecture of all the primitive civilizations aspired to the colossal. It would appear that from the beginning, thanks to the multiple and combined efforts afforded by slave labor, man intended his creations to rival those of nature itself. The Egyptian, in the same way as the Mexican or the Hindu, built mountains of stone in the form of pyramids, while the colossi of the Nilotic sculptors are rocks given forms and faces. All of them, Egyptians, Mycenaeans and Peruvians, exploited gigantic materials, while the Mesopotamians, for whom stone was in short supply, built their palaces on artificial hills of dried clay. It seems as though the poorer man was in technical resources, the more he tried to persuade himself of his own supernatural strength. In the art of bonding materials several races—such as the Mycenaeans and some Peruvian tribes—used stones of unequal sizes and shapes which they assembled as in a jigsaw puzzle (pls. 49 and 59). The Greeks called this the Cyclopean style of building. However, at a very early stage the Egyptians and Sumerians developed a regular style, which the Romans later called *opus quadratum;* this notion of a wall made of

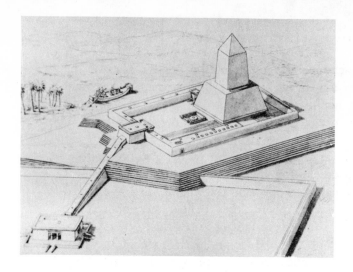

17. Sanctuary of the Sun, built by Neuserre at Abusir. 5th Dynasty. *Drawn by L. Borchardt, after Schaefer and Andrea, Kunst des alten Orients.*

identical and interchangeable parts (bricks and stones) implies a great effort of reasoning.

The image maker of the Nile Valley, like the Sumerian, carefully polished the hardest of stones, as once the artist of the New Stone Age had done. Till the decline of the ancient world Egypt prolonged Neolithic art in the manufacture of vases of hard stone, in which Egyptian craftsmen had excelled from the outset.

All Egyptian art may be seen emerging from that technique. Nilotic sculptors first extended their activities from vases to steles (needles) which they erected over royal tombs. They then took to polishing granite doors for their brick sanctuaries. It was at the beginning of the Memphitic period that they first dared to set up temples and tombs entirely of stone which they used in enormous slabs. These obelisks were honored as images of the deity in the Temples of the Sun during the Memphitic empire (pl. 17). The *menhir* had the same function among the western barbarians, and we know that in Sumeria they worshiped *bétyles*, perhaps symbols of the earth-mother in her least perishable form, stone. This explains why these artists often showed a religious respect for the original shape of rough stones, which they simply improved with a little abrasion (pls. 18, 19).

It might be asked whether the inclination for mural art, so pronounced in Egypt but also found in the post-Sumerian civilizations of Asia, was a continuation of prehistoric cave art. Do not the mastaba and the pyramid artificially reproduce the prehistoric cave inscribed with images? The second Theban empire in its turn began to seek subterranean shelter for its tombs, and certain Asiatic civilizations

18

(Hittites and Persians) showed a particular interest in carving live rock faces in the same way that the prehistorical civilizations of the Fezzan and the Sahara had done earlier.

The Egyptian technique of hollow-relief recalls that of engraving in caves, and in both cases before becoming an independent art, painting was used only as an auxiliary to the carved outline. There is a thread of continuity between the cave art of Africa—which, unlike that of Europe, was pursued well into the historic period—and the mural art of Egyptian civilization, which without doubt had its roots in prehistoric Africa.

The significance given to animals in religion, and consequently in art, is another characteristic which links the first civilizations to prehistoric times. To primitive man, brute strength seemed to be an

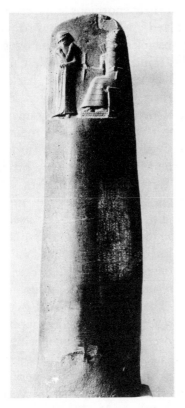 

18. Hammurabi's Code. Babylonian, about 1700 B.C.
Paris, Louvre.

19. Menhir from Maurels (Tarn). Barbarian art. Aeneolithic epoch.
Rodez, Museum.

attribute of divine power. The lion, the eagle, the bull and the snake played an outstanding part in primitive mythologies. They are to be found in Egypt (at first totemistic) as symbols or, rather, as incarnations of gods. In Mesopotamia they were closely identified with the divinities of the heavens or the underworld. The artists of the Nile, Tigris and Euphrates therefore became adept at the portrayal of animals, like their Magdalenian predecessors. Moreover the bodies of animals, fused in daring syntheses, gave rise to what amount to theological and plastic speculations.

This chapter, in which we have tried to discount geographical and temporal factors so as to give a proper assessment of a primitive stage in the history of forms, must also include some study of the so-called Pre-Columbian civilizations. In the strictest sense some of these remained at the Stone Age: others discovered bronze but none of them iron, and the Mexicans erected their enormous stone structures with stone implements. No other evolved civilization shows so pathetically the material and psychological obstacles that had to be overcome by primitive man in order to raise his standard of life. We can only admire how those mysterious races, notwithstanding their backwardness which was no doubt caused by their isolation, managed in spite of their crude technical development to create civilizations superior in some respects to what the *Conquistadores* were to build on their ruins.

As for the Bronze and Iron Ages, which in western Europe are shrouded in the mist of prehistory, in the Mediterranean they produced historical civilizations rivaling those of Egypt and the Chaldees. While we recall that iron was imported from Asia, we are still at a loss to say who invented the alloy of tin and copper—in itself too pliable—which resulted in a much tougher metal, bronze, easier to work, moreover, since it has a much lower melting point. No doubt it was via southwestern Asia that bronze slowly reached the Mediterranean, where local absence of tin deposits made its use costly and confined it to articles of luxury. For a long time in Egypt and Sumeria it was used only sparingly for statuary, being applied in the form of thin foil on a wooden core, the head alone being cast. The Indo-Europeans who toward 2000 B.C. invaded the Mediterranean basin, and fought and conquered the great powers of the period, no doubt owed their victory to their superior bronze and iron weapons, together with the domestication of the horse. During those ages of metal, the most skillful and highly evolved form of civilization was the Aegean, which developed in Crete and later in Argolis from 3000 to 1130 B.C. It produced no statues, preferring personal articles to durable creations in stone. It excelled in making weapons, jewelry and pottery which were exported all over the East and to some parts of the West. This civilization recalls—though this time it was by the sea—the nomadic habits of those mounted tribes, who were rearers of horses. Metal was better adapted than stone to the conditions of a wandering existence that encouraged them to produce only small objects such as jewelry, personal finery and trappings for harness. It was during the second millennium, well before historic times, that these nomad races entered the history of art. In certain sites of central Asia we are beginning to find the oldest specimens of what is now termed Steppe Art, which after absorbing the influence of the zoomorphic style from Chaldea was to invade the whole of northern Europe, where it held sway until something like A.D. 1000. In style and spirit this art, which gave exclusive attention to the portrayal of animals, must be studied as a rival to the primitive artistic civilizations rather than—as is usually done—as a prelude to the Middle Ages of the West.

The spirit of the Stone Age and the Ages of Metals is not dead today. It continues to inspire certain communities in Africa, Oceania and America, whose way of life (though degenerating all the time) perpetuates that of prehistoric man. The artistic output of these peoples will therefore take its proper place at the end of this chapter.

EGYPTIAN CIVILIZATION
HISTORICAL BACKGROUND

Invulnerable on account of its position, with its desert hinterland and the redoubt in the Upper Nile which thrice in the course of history enabled its national unity to be restored, Egypt developed a highly skilled civilization which for thirty centuries maintained a political, cultural and artistic tradition unique in the history of the world. This unshakable tradition, almost devoutly preserved, accounts for its strength and greatness but at the same time for its monotony, though in those long centuries its subtle variations do show a gradual evolution.

The first artistic manifestations of Egyptian civilization—those of the pre-dynastic era (before 3200 B.C.) and the early dynastic era

(1st–3rd Dynasty, after 3200 B.C.)—show its close relationship to the neighboring Sumerian civilization; perhaps because Egypt fell under its influence or because they both sprang from some common source. The Old Kingdom (4th to 7th Dynasty, 2680 to 2258 B.C.) carried out in the Delta region the most grandiose constructions to be found in Egypt: the Pyramids which are the burial places of the Pharaohs Cheops, Chephren and Mycerinus (4th Dynasty, 2680 to about 2565). At that time art was exclusively funerary, while domestic buildings were made of perishable materials, crude bricks of sun-baked clay, or wood. Statuary, relief and painting appear to have been already properly established. After a period of anarchy (First Intermediate Period, 7th–10th Dynasty, 2258 to 2052 B.C.), Egypt was formed anew in the Middle Kingdom (11th, 12th Dynasties, 2052 to 1786 B.C.). The great architectural projects largely disappeared with rebuilding done in the New Kingdom. Funerary architecture continued to predominate. The Second Intermediate Period (13th–17th Dynasty, 1786 to 1570 B.C.) was a time partly of foreign domination (Hyksos invasion), ending with the Theban princes in control.

20. The Sphinx and the Pyramid of Cheops at Giza.

They founded the New Kingdom (18th–20th Dynasty, 1570–1085 B.C.), which was the most brilliant phase of Egyptian art. In this period the wealthy pharaohs, the lines of Amenhotep and Rameses, built imposing temples (Luxor and Karnak, near Thebes), while there was a tendency to hollow out tombs in hypogeal form in the cliff face of the Valley of the Kings. Painting developed and became a completely independent art tending to take the place of low-relief in funerary works. The decorative arts were flourishing, as we can see from the tomb of Tutankhamen. In the first millennium Egypt was several times invaded and lost its independence. Only the dynasties established in the Delta at Saïs managed to maintain Egyptian civilization (Saïte period, 26th Dynasty, seventh to sixth century). Conquered by the Persians in 525 B.C., then by Alexander, who established the reign of the Ptolemies (Ptolemaic period, 332–30 B.C.), Egypt, although open to Hellenic influence, never ceased to develop its native art, which, though it never regained vitality, was piously respected by the Romans, who were the last conquerors of the Nile Valley in ancient times.

ARCHITECTURE

The Nile Valley was the cradle of mankind's earliest social syntheses, and witnessed the first great human endeavor in the art of building. The country's wealth in stone materials, as well as the determination to make the dwellings of the dead last forever, favored the birth and progress of architecture. The longing for immortality inspired the first of these works, the Ancient Empire tombs called *mastabas* (shaped like the *frustum*—horizontal section—of a pyramid), and *pyramids* (pl. 20). The pyramid is, indeed, the most elementary architectural form, the one which most suggests stability and durability. Egypt had inherited from primitive times the taste for the gigantic which stresses the mightiness of man's creations (the Pyramid of Cheops, the largest of all, now measures 450 feet high, and 746 feet wide, its base covering about 13 acres). On the outside there is a chapel in which the priest celebrated the funeral rites: it is decorated with mural images, carved or painted, and with a "false door" *stele* ostensibly leading into the *serdab* containing the numerous "doubles" which were intended as material sustenance for the deceased king's soul in the afterlife. The corpse, embalmed in the form of a mummy, was deposited in a crypt hollowed in the soil or built into the main structure.

21. Pylons of the Temple of Khonsu, at Karnak. 11th century B.C. *After Jéquier, Les Temples ramesséides et saïtes.*

After many experiments, the Egyptian temple took its final form in the New Kingdom (pl. 22). It was nothing less than a stone replica of the royal palace, which was made of wood and clay. Like the palace itself, it comprises three sections, the first reserved for introduction, the second for reception, the third for private life (*harem*). The stone temple was built inside an enclosure of crude brick. There were two monumental "pylons" or towers (pl. 21), themselves preceded by two obelisks (monolithic needles of stone), leading to a courtyard sur-

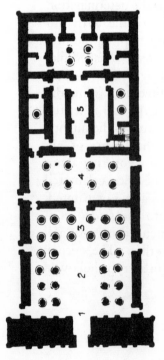

22. Ground plan of the Temple of Khonsu at Karnak. (1, Pylon; 2, courtyard; 3, vestibule; 4, pillared hall—hypostyle; 5, sanctuary)

23. Processional Colonnade of Horemhab and Forecourt of Amenhotep III. Temple at Luxor. Begun about 1375 B.C.

rounded by colonnades (pl. 23); the great pillared hall was a sort of throne room in which the image of the god was shown to the crowds when it emerged in its galley on feast days; behind it the private quarters were composed of treasure rooms, sacristies, grouped round the *naos* or sanctuary which enveloped in secrecy and darkness the statue which was the god's "double."

Egyptian architecture was hindered in its development by its underestimation of the arch (vault): though it was not totally unknown or ignored, it was exploited only rarely and incidentally. Nilotic building was based on the system of flat arching, which consists of holding roofs by means of slabs laid on supports. The solidity of the whole rested on the inertia of horizontally superimposed materials; and as stones, unlike wood, cannot take great weights without breaking, the Egyptian had to add the numerous supporting struts which encumber the interiors, in order to be able to roof spaces of any size (pl. 22). As was later the case with Christian churches, though not with Greek temples, the Egyptian temple was essentially an enclosed space; closed from the outside and partly covered in from above, it hid its mystery behind long blank walls, keeping all its wealth of effects for the inside. The lighting of hypostyle chambers was supplied diagonally by skylights or lantern lights obtained by giving extra height to the central naves. Its dominant feature of horizontality gave full expression to the notion of stillness to which all Egyptian art was devoted. The stones, well cut, were assembled by means of internal or flush jointing: by a careful coursing which hid the joints, the Egyptians strove to give the effect of monolithic blocks. Owing to his urge for strength and his desire to build for all time, the Nilotic architect also made liberal use of massive materials sometimes weighing as much as 500 tons (as in the high temple of Chephren's pyramid). Though he created the art of building in stone, his imagination, always after realism, stopped the Egyptian from inventing abstract forms that would have suited the raw material which he was the first to exploit in a rational manner: he contented himself with transposing into harder materials those earlier forms of architecture—in wood, compressed earth or clay—which remained in use for domestic purposes. The walls and towers, or pylons, kept the sloped shape which was given to mud or brick walls to prevent them from falling; the corners were decorated with a stone beading reminiscent of the sheaves of rushes used for binding dwellings of

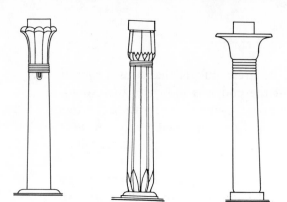

24. Types of Egyptian column (palmiform, lotiform, campaniform or "papyrus").

beaten earth, while the cornices had that splayed form characteristic of the tops of palm trees. As for the columns themselves, whether lotus-shaped, palm-shaped or bell-shaped (pl. 24), their structure was that of the ancient supports made of sheaves of reeds or rushes, tied together and crowned with floral devices.

STATUARY

The Egyptian sculptor rarely made use of soft stone such as limestone. He preferred the hardest of materials such as granite, basalt and porphyry which endure longest and are polishable. During the thirty centuries of Nilotic civilization statuary never managed to break free from the law of frontality. With the head always on the axis of the bust, and the arms glued to the sides, the statue has all the appearance of being an accessory or organ of architecture. Under the Old Kingdom, sculpture showed a powerfully synthetic modeling and an intensely realistic vision which inspired the greatest masterpieces of that art (pls. 25 and 69). But this experimental movement was checked during the first Theban empire when it gave way to a classicism rejecting individual characteristics and inclining more toward an ideal of impersonality. This evolution was very much accentuated until the academicism of the second Theban empire, when an ideal of ease and gracefulness admirably expressed the peaceable nature of the race (pl. 26). The initiative of a heretical pharaoh, Amenhotep IV, or Akhenaten (about 1380–1363 B.C.), brought about a revolution in the figurative arts that almost freed Egyptian art from the static style to which dogma had hitherto condemned it.

Challenging all previous sacred conventions, the sculptors and painters of Tel el-Amarna (Amenhotep IV's new capital) tended to portray forms according to expressionist and mannerist principles

26

25. Seated Scribe. 5th Dynasty, before 2400 B.C. *Paris, Louvre.*

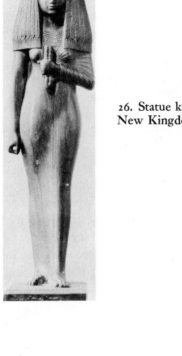

26. Statue known as the Lady Toui. New Kingdom. *Paris, Louvre.*

27. Royal head. Hard wood. Amarna style. End of 18th Dynasty, about 1360 B.C. *Paris, Louvre.*

27

(pls. 27 and 641). Unfortunately this movement was stifled. The accession of the weak pharaoh Tutankhamen, who at once restored the traditional religion and power to the priests of Amon, reduced art once again to a theological convention. The ephemeral restoration of the Saïte period breathed new life for a short time into moribund Egyptian sculpture, when it passed through a phase of archaism, renewing the elegant tradition of the New Kingdom and drawing some inspiration from the realism of the Old.

MURAL ART

This title covers sculptures in low-relief, as well as paintings, which are only an economical imitation of them. The term low-relief does not apply very well to mural sculptures, especially in the Middle Kingdom period, when by making a deeply incised outline the Egyptian sculptor produced a flat sculpture which did not project beyond the wall's surface and on which he then chiseled minor detail. The conventions governing such figurative compositions have been described in the introductory pages of this chapter. In portraying human beings the face, always impersonal, played no part in the movement, while gesture was always subordinated to a rhythmic cadence that gave it a priestly solemnity (pl. 28). In portraying animals the artist, no longer inhibited by the same theological discipline, could give free rein to his genius for observation (pl. 28). Curiously enough, the female figures were always more supple and alive than the male: alone of all the pre-Hellenic peoples, the Egyptians succeeded in expressing the voluptuous grace of the feminine body. The execution of low-reliefs by specialized teams of workers who carved the details, once the overseer had worked out the general composition, explains many an imperfection. The coloring of the paintings was extremely sober: red or yellow ocher, a little green or blue. Following a convention established in the infancy of Egyptian art, masculine bodies were painted red, and feminine ones yellow.

THE MINOR ARTS

The dry Egyptian soil, preserving whatever sank into it (except iron, owing to the presence of silica), has yielded thousands of specimens of domestic objects, many of them executed in luxurious style by the artists of the Nile Valley and destined for the afterlife of important personages. The treasure-trove of the intact tomb of the pharaoh

28. Hunting water fowl, fragment of a fresco from a Theban tomb.
17th Dynasty. *London, British Museum.*

Tutankhamen (pl. 29) has yielded us a royal suite of incredible wealth.
The Egyptians had good taste in finery, the men even more than the
women adorning themselves with costly ornaments which often had
some magic property or showed their social status. Artists excelled in
the working of such jewels, using hard gems set in gold or sometimes
in silver, which was both rarer and more valuable. But the purely realistic imagination of the Egyptians hampered them in the invention of a

29. Funerary mask of Tutankhamen. Enameled gold.
18th Dynasty. *Cairo, Museum.*

30. Breast ornament in the shape of a tower.
Paris, Louvre.

decorative system: they reproduced the forms of animals and human beings and even those of architecture; breast ornaments, for instance, taking the shape of a temple tower or pylon (pl. 30), and earrings that of the lotus-type column. This grip of architecture on all the other arts is typical of highly organized communities in which artists work in teams under the supervision of a foreman or chief who, in his turn, has to carry out the instructions of the priesthood.

THE CIVILIZATIONS OF WESTERN ASIA[1]

While Egypt was working out its unchanging destiny, Mesopotamia, a frontierless region exposed to envious neighbors on account of its wealth, suffered many historical and ethnical vicissitudes which now make it hard to follow the histories of the successive civilizations in those parts. None the less, the creative impulse of the Sumerians was so strong that we can trace its development through the numerous feudalities and empires of which this "land of two rivers" became the theater.

As for the most part these peoples took little care of their burial places, archaeological evidence remains scarce. The earliest artistic works of this civilization go back to the Aeneolithic Age and are to be found on the site of Susa in Elam (now Iran) and at Tel el Obeid in Mesopotamia (fourth millennium). Under the name of Chaldean civilization scholars used to imply the "high period" of Mesopotamia, comprising: the first Ur dynasty in Sumeria (about 2700 B.C.) which left admirable specimens of the goldsmith's craft in its tombs; the Semitic dynasty of Akkad set up by Sargon the Elder toward 2450 B.C., who united the land of Sumeria with the Semitic land of Akkad (in Syria), and who also founded Babylon (about 2450 B.C.); the period of the Guti invasions (about 2250 B.C.) when the Shepherd King (*patesi*) Gudea (pl. 40) held court at Lagash—a city whose site has yielded important works now to be seen in the Louvre; the third Ur dynasty, destroyed by Elamite invaders toward 2000 B.C.; the first Babylonian dynasty (1830–1530 B.C.) which with Hammurabi represents perhaps the peak of Chaldean civilization. Many people imagine that the

---

[1] I have adopted the short chronology (brought forward by about 300 years) established by Dr. Contenau.

Assyrian Empire with its seat at Nineveh (beginning of first millennium down to 612) embodies Mesopotamian civilization, on account of the important remains which have been unearthed and its reputation for cruelty; it is on the contrary no more than the expression of its decadence. Achaemenian Persia (sixth to fourth century) was the political and artistic successor of the Assyrians. In Persia, Mesopotamian art was to lose something of its origins by imbibing the classical Greek influence. Moreover, the principles of Chaldean art nourished more or less all the peoples of western Asia, both Semitic and Aryan. Having little gift for artistic creation, the latter turned to it for inspiration and at the same time helped to sustain it in their periods of success (Hittites, Kassites, Kingdom of Mitanni). The radiation of Mesopotamian civilization spread very far afield, since towns of the third millennium, showing a distinctively Sumerian character, have been found in the Indus Valley (excavations at Mohenjo-Daro and Harappa).

THE CHALDEAN GENIUS

Whatever may be the attributes common to the two civilizations of the Nile and the Euphrates, and of which much has been made by historians, the genius of the Mesopotamian peoples is strikingly opposed to that of Egypt. An agricultural nation, peaceful in outlook, the Egyptians lived in close contact with the out-of-doors world; the beneficent action of the Nile waters inspired them with an optimistic notion of natural powers, which gave them a belief in the immortality of the soul as well as a deep love of nature, both of which informed their art. Positivistic and with little bent for abstraction, they delighted in the reproduction of natural forms. Egyptian art is one of observation.

Although the flooding of the Tigris and Euphrates, which man learned to control, gave Mesopotamia at that time a social structure not unlike that of the Nile, yet for reasons which perhaps have something to do with ethnical factors of which we know nothing, the races who first occupied these regions did not adopt the same naturalistic optimism. If they recognized the benefits of nature—and worshiped it in Ishtar, their goddess of fertility—they considered human life to be threatened by demonic powers that had to be exorcised with the aid of magic. Little given to realism, which would have encouraged them to imitate their neighbors, they had an extraordinary gift for abstraction which made them arithmeticians and astronomers. The genius of each

31. Hieroglyphs of the Old Kingdom. Wood. 5th Dynasty. *Cairo, Museum.*

32. Cuneiform writing: Hammurabi's Code.
About 1700 B. C. *Paris, Louvre.*

of these two peoples was perfectly expressed in their technique of writing (pls. 31, 32). Egyptian hieroglyphic writing was only an abridged transcription of the forms of natural things; the belief in the identity of the "double" obliged Egypt right through its history to cling to this cumbersome pictographic method, which in any case was primarily reserved for sacred use. On the other hand, at an early stage, in their cuneiform script the Mesopotamians worked out a syllabic system of abstract symbols, intended for everyday use, and this rapidly made their tongue the language of diplomacy in the East. Art itself became for them a "script"; that is to say, not a collection of naturalistic shapes, but a system of signs. The Mesopotamian artist imposed a series of schematizations and metamorphoses on the elements he borrowed from nature, creating purely imaginary forms which, compared with the supernatural powers they evoked, had a sign-value rather than a replica-value as in Egypt.

The oldest expressions of this faculty for abstraction are the admirable prehistoric funerary vases found at Susa and Elam (pl. 33). The animal shapes on the vases from the oldest stratum, called Susa I, are geometrically stylized and thus achieve a most elegant decorative effect,

33. Goblet in terra cotta, decorated with ibex, hounds and ibis, from Susa.
End of 4th millennium. *Paris, Louvre.*
34. Imprint of a Sumerian cylinder seal. Detail.
End of 4th millennium. *Paris, Louvre.*

comparable with the Rhodesian cave paintings (pl. 8) or the first Greek vases (pl. 101). But the real source of this art is to be found in glyptics. For writing purposes the Mesopotamians used cylinders covered with hollowed-out carvings which, when rolled on a slab of damp clay, gave an imprint in relief. These cylinder seals, which were signets or else magic formularies, were used for all kinds of business or religious purposes. Unlike the monuments of the major arts they have survived in large numbers, and their study can teach us the entire evolution of the Mesopotamian aesthetic. From the beginning of Sumerian art these cylinder seals reveal, already highly organized, the whole formal system of Mesopotamian art.

By skillfully combining animal forms suggested by the ibex, ass, lion, bison, eagle, snake and other beasts the artists invented monsters, that is to say imaginary compositions (pl. 34). While Egyptian monsters remain mere composite designs of architectural quality, those of Mesopotamia have an astonishing unity as though dynamized by the artist's own nervous energy, and these imaginary creatures are strangely alive. Associating these monstrous shapes with each other by superimposition,

fusion, antithesis, symmetry and synthesis, the Sumerians in their compositions created what amounted to a plastic language capable of infinite
variation. This vocabulary of forms was to have important repercussions in the history of mankind, whereas Egyptian art reached a dead
end and had no successors, a fate quite usual with naturalistic art that
can only prolong its own perfection by sterile imitation.

This play of metamorphoses on animal themes, invented by the
Mesopotamians, was to prove an excellent source of training for others
and to be most fertile imaginatively. Iranian, Scythian, Sarmatian,
Turanian, German, Viking and Byzantine, and finally Roman artists,
were to delve freely into this mine of ideas, enriching it with endless
original variations.

In architecture, by their use of vaulting the Mesopotamians were
to give the world a principle infinitely richer in possibilities than the
flat arching of the Egyptians. The Sumerian scientific mind was needed
in order to dare project a keyed arch into space, with its radial
arrangements of wedge-shaped stones coursed in converging layers, and
its stability assured by nothing more than the force of gravity. From
the time when it was to be applied with all its implications by the
Parthian and Sassanian builders, this principle was to revolutionize architecture and dominate building throughout the West, from Roman times
to the Christian Middle Ages.

The Mesopotamians were thus great innovators, great imitators
of artistic culture, and no doubt the Egyptians themselves were indebted
to them in the initial stages. But whereas Egyptian art was ultimately
to become a dead letter, the Mesopotamian plastic code was to remain
a living language for many centuries.

ARCHITECTURE

The scarcity of wood and stone obliged the Mesopotamians to build
in baked brick—or often merely sun-dried brick—for which the silt
from rivers gave them plenty of excellent material. Softened by centuries of rain, these great heaps of clay now form hillocks (called *tells*
by Arabs) which alone serve to break the monotony of the plains.

The most important invention of the Mesopotamians was the
vault. If like many primitive peoples they also made it with superimposed horizontal layers, each jutting out further than the ones below

(corbeling)—which results in a false vault—they more frequently built
it on the radial principle: tunnel vaults bonded in this way have survived
from the Sumerian period (tomb of king at Ur). Assyrian low-reliefs
give evidence of the use of the semicircular and elliptical cupola, but
as no such domes have come down to us we cannot say whether the
corbel or radial system was used.

Vaulting increases the possibilities of clearance without recourse
to detached struts to ease the overhead weight; but on the other hand
it puts a lateral strain on its supports and thereby demands strong
shoring, which the Mesopotamians usually effected by the enormous
thickness of their brick walls. For the stability gained from mere
weight and mass in the flat-roof or lintel system, the vault substitutes a
system of counterstrains which makes the structure an active organism.
If the Mesopotamians did not take this principle to its obvious conclusions, none the less they deserve credit for its invention.

Unlike the Egyptians, with their spiritual preoccupations, the
Mesopotamians gave their architectural skill mainly to temporal under-

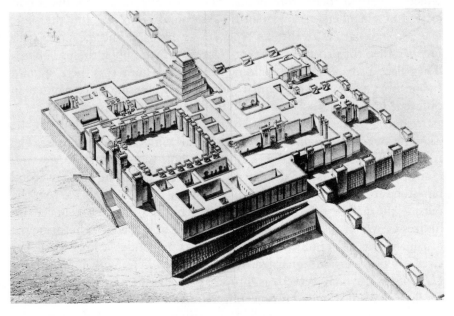

35. Aerial view of Sargon II's palace at Khorsabad. 713–707 B.C.
After Perrot and Chipiez.

36, 37. Ishtar Gate at Babylon, with polychromic low-reliefs.
7th and 6th centuries B.C.

takings. As well as fortresses they built grandiose palaces that were practically royal cities, as proof of the monarch's power (Sargon's palace at Khorsabad covers almost 25 acres). Mesopotamian architecture impresses us as monarchic and military, whereas the Egyptian was entirely religious.

The royal palaces were built on hillocks some 30 to 50 feet high which protected them from floods. They form a rather confused collection of chambers, grouped in blocks round courtyards in the same way as Arab palaces to this day (pl. 35). First came the reception halls (*serail*), then the private apartments (*harem*), then public rooms (*khan*). The palace also contained a building for worship known as the *Ziggurat*. It consisted of seven rectangular stories of decreasing size, painted in different colors and surmounted by a chapel which also served as an astronomical observatory. The corners of the palace, like those of the Ziggurat, were set according to the cardinal points of the compass. The rooms, though numerous, were of small dimensions—for the Mesopotamian made little use of detached pillars because he had neither wood nor stone to spare. The interiors were lit only by the door. From the outside the palace offered nothing but blank walls, often relieved by buttresses which produce some play of light and shade. The principal ornament was a monumental gateway, opening under a long vault between two towers and guarded by two winged bulls with human faces (*kheroubin*) which served as propitiatory geniuses (pl. 14). These porchways were also used for meetings. In Assyrian and Neo-Babylonian days they were decorated with compositions in low-relief or painted ceramics (pls. 36, 37), making a plinth course round the base of the walls.

36

The Mesopotamians also discovered the principles of military architecture which, passing from the Arabs to the Byzantines and thence to the Crusaders, survived until the introduction of gunpowder. For the simple passive resistance obtained by the mere thickness of walls, which the Egyptians relied on, the Mesopotamians substituted active resistance. The square towers jutting into the compounds enabled connecting walls to be covered by crossfire: they were decorated with merlons—embattled parapets between embrasures—which could shelter watchmen who fired from the space between the battlements. A series of courtyards each commanding the other increased the obstacles to be overcome by the attacker, who could never turn an overrun enclosure against the garrison. Finally the complex internal communications, with numerous narrow defiles and tortuous passages, further delayed the besieger's progress. The Hittites improved on this system by building round keeps, better protected from the flanks and more difficult to sap, and with walls sloping at the foot so that projectiles hurled from the battlements would rebound on the enemy (Zinjirli fortress, pl. 38).

SCULPTURE

The oldest works of sculpture of the first Ur dynasty (low-relief of Ur-Nina, vulture stele, Louvre) are still close to the graphic technique of the cylinder seals. On the low-relief of Ur-Nina and his family the figures, all alike and with their names carved on their skirts to identify them, are little more than calligraphic symbols (pl. 39). Realism is to be found in the Naram-Sin stele (Louvre, Akkad Dynasty) in which the artist skillfully portrayed different actions in a battle. The excava-

38. Hittite military architecture. Fortress at Zinjirli. *After Koldewey, Ausgrab in Sendschirli.*

39. Detail of low-relief of Ur-Nina. About 2400 B.C. *Paris, Louvre.*
40. Statue of Gudea. About 2250 B.C. *Paris, Louvre.*

tions at Lagash have revealed the only great works of Chaldean sculpture in the round that is so far known to us, for instance, the figures of the Shepherd King Gudea (pl. 40). Carved in diorite and carefully polished, works such as this reach a degree of perfection, a synthesis, which must have been the result of a long evolution, of the terms of which nothing is yet known. The squareness of the statue is concentrated within itself; its muscular vigor gives an impression of power never achieved by the sculptors of the Old Kingdom in Egypt, in whose works the expression of energy was tempered by serenity and spiritual detachment. Scarcely emerging from the block of stone of which it was made, the Sumerian statue retains all the crude power of rock; it is a menhir in human form. This menhir quality is even more noticeable, and was no doubt intended, in the famous *Hammurabi Code* (Louvre, 1st Babylonian Dynasty) in which we can also see writing mixed with sculpture as in certain statues of Gudea (pls. 18, 32).

ASSYRIAN ART

The Hittite low-reliefs (at the sites at Boghazkeui and Carchemish) are transitional between Chaldean and Assyrian art. Long series of figures are shown in low-relief on the palace walls of the Assyrian kings, and displayed at the foot of the wall and not as friezes at the top. This arrangement seems to have first occurred to the Mitannites, who in Upper Mesopotamia had unlimited supplies of rock, so scarce in Chaldea. The abundance of this material (a gypsum-like alabaster, unsuitable for building but soft and very easy to shape) allowed the Assyrians full scope for low-reliefs, as we see from the excavations on the site at Nineveh. Reliefs from the palaces of Assurnazirpal (883–859 B.C.) and Sennacherib (705–681 B.C.) can be seen in the British Museum, from the palace of Assurbanipal at Khorsabad in the Louvre and British Museum. The Assyrian kings' custom of abandoning their predecessor's palace and building one of their own favored the development of sculpture. It has been calculated that if they were placed end to end, the panels discovered at Assurbanipal's palace at Khorsabad would stretch for one and a quarter miles (pl. 41).

The great Assyrian compositions are, in historic times, the first examples of artistic undertakings of a purely monarchical character, in other words exclusively devoted to the glorification of a ruler. The art of the Egyptian pharaohs, even at the time of the Rameses, was always conditioned by a religious outlook. The Assyrian kings made images neither for temples nor for tombs, but for their own palaces in the same way that Louis XIV was to do in modern times. Those long monotonous processions in which the king made such a frequent

41. Army of Assurbanipal (669–626 B.C.) on the march.
London, British Museum.

42. A worshiper. Low-relief from the palace of Sargon II at Khorsabad. 8th century B.C. *Paris, Louvre.*

appearance were intended to stress the wealth, warlike qualities, hunting prowess and cruelty of the sovereigns who for centuries imposed their reign of terror over all western Asia, and whose refinements of torture were surpassed only by the civilizations of the Far East. Technically these low-reliefs, whose very number suggests that they must have been hastily carried out, show a profound decadence, especially in the portrayal of the human figure. They reduced this to a play of arbitrary forms with none of the power and noble significance of the Egyptian canon. The limbs are badly articulated, the gestures mechanical and lacking in truth, the faces set like masks; the sculptors always sacrificed life to their cherished notion of superhuman strength; their instinct for abstraction led them to treat details as decorative themes (beards, curling hair, the folds of clothing, jewels) elaborated for their own sake (pl. 42). All these elements were assembled without being brought into harmony with the main composition, which makes the whole thing a kind of puzzle. Here we see in embryo all the characteristics of the hieratic style typical of the Asiatic monarchies and which were later adopted in Byzantine art. The principles of the composition of animated scenes followed the conventions described at the beginning of this chapter: it is to be noted, however, that in Assurbanipal's time a certain sense of perspective began to emerge. The different features of the composition were sometimes arranged in depth, each hiding something

40

43. Wounded lioness. Low-relief from Nineveh, period of Assurbanipal, 669–626 B.C. *London, British Museum.*

of the other; but this progress toward optical truth remained unusual and was not part of general practice.

The real distinction of Assyrian art was in the representation of animals. The Assyrians' innate love of hunting and cruelty (being a people who by comparison with the Sumerians show a relapse into barbarism) helped them to understand the secret workings of animal psychology, much as primitive man had done. The intense truthfulness to life of their animal figures contrasts with the conventional style in which they portrayed human beings (pl. 43). All the expressions of the hunted animal, as it flees or stands at bay or roars with pain under the arrow or spear, were rendered by Assyrian sculptors with a savage vitality unknown to the Egyptians. The peaceful, pastoral Egyptians were too used to the company of domestic animals, which they painted and sculptured so admirably, to have as much understanding of the ways of wild beasts.

THE ART OF ACHAEMENIAN PERSIA

Political successors to the pharaohs and to the kings of Nineveh and Babylon, the Achaemenian Dynasties (539–331 B.C.) inherited a mixed tradition. These kings of the greatest empire of antiquity prior to Rome built castles in keeping with their wealth, such as those at Pasargadae (Cyrus, 539–529 B.C.), at Persepolis (Darius, 521–486 B.C., and Xerxes,

41

44. Capital from the palace of Artaxerxes II at Susa, Achaemenian Dynasty, early 4th century B.C. *Paris, Louvre.*

486–465 B.C.), and at Susa (Artaxerxes II, 404–358 B.C.). For the first time in Asia, these palaces were built of stone, though brick was used with it. They consist of an extraordinary number of rooms all built on a colossal stone foundation, the finest rooms being called *apadanas*, or throne rooms, in the hypostyle manner borrowed from Egypt. The apadana of Artaxerxes II at Susa, which covered nearly 8375 square feet, rested on thirty-six columns 63 feet 3 inches in height: these columns were in the form of a fluted shaft topped with a double series of scrolls, bearing a capital made of two bulls back to back, borrowed from Assyrian art (pl. 44). Other forms such as palm-shaped cornices were taken from Egypt. The Achaemenian buildings were all for secular purposes: the highly spiritual character of the Mazdean or Mazdakite religion forbade the use of temples and considered them as pagan. The fire cult was celebrated on simple open-air altars or pyres (*pyrea*). The "kings of kings" also had luxurious tombs built in their honor, some of them being hollowed into rock after the manner of the Egyptian hypogea (tombs at Persepolis and Naqsh-i-Rustam).

The figurative and decorative art of the Persians devolves directly from Assyrian art, of which it retains all the monarchical character, much modified however by an element of placidity in keeping with the spirit of Persian civilization, which was one of the most humane of ancient times. At Persepolis and Susa we find the same long rows of soldiers and subject peoples as in Nineveh. The Persians made low-reliefs in stone or enameled terra cotta (friezes from Susa palace, in the Louvre, pl. 133) which the neo-Babylonian Empire (625–539 B.C.) had already used with great effect. Here the realistic portrayal of animals begins to disappear: the winged bulls and Achaemenian gryphons assume more heraldic, emblematic characteristics. The style of these sculptures has lost the barbarous strength of Assyrian works, and, already influenced by the Greek plastic arts, tends toward a decorative elegance.

THE AEGEAN CIVILIZATIONS
HISTORICAL BACKGROUND

We call those civilizations "Aegean" which from about 3000 B.C. to about 1130 B.C. flourished on the shores of the Aegean Sea, in the island of Cyprus, the Cyclades, Crete and the Peloponnesus, where the Achaeans, after conquering Crete, continued its tradition for some time. This civilization was essentially based on the industry and commerce of metallurgy, and the Aegean invaders, who came from Asia Minor, brought copper with them from about 3000 B.C. and by about 2300 managed to perfect its use by alloying it with tin, thereby producing bronze. While the Cyclades islanders were beginning to experiment with sculpturing in marble, the Cretans, who began to rule the seas from an early date, created a highly skilled civilization comparable to those of the same period in Egypt and Mesopotamia, but one which had an extraordinarily modern flavor, for this nation of seafarers, merchants and industrialists seems to have been singularly free from that obsession with the deity which governed every thought and act of the Egyptians and Mesopotamians.

MINOAN ART

The Minoan civilization, so named by Sir Arthur Evans who discovered it in Crete, flourished on that island from roughly the end of the fourth millennium till 1400 B.C. It was destroyed by the Achaeans, who came from Argolis (Peloponnesus), people of Indo-European stock who inherited the Aegean love of the sea and for a short time only (1400–1200 B.C.) imposed themselves on the semi-barbarous "Mycenaean" civilization which the German Schliemann discovered in the Peloponnesus.

45. Gold drinking vessels from Vaphio. Cretan art. Late Minoan I,
1580–1450 B.C. *Athens, National Museum.*

As with most of the peoples of the Bronze Age, they made few
images of the deity—from which sculpture draws its chief inspiration—
and busied themselves mainly with industrial products.

Ceramics and the working of metals were the principal occupa-
tions in Crete. They excelled in the working of precious metals as well
as bronze, and exported silverwork, gems, gold, weapons, bronze ingots,
to Asia Minor, Egypt, Peloponnesus (see the gold vessels found at
Vaphio, south of Sparta, pl. 45), and also to the West. With the
Cretans, ceramics had none of the crude industrial character it had
with the other Bronze Age peoples (Hissarlik pottery): the prestige

46. Rhyton (drinking horn) with nautilus decoration.
Cretan art. Late Minoan I, 1580–1450 B.C.
Herakleion, Museum.

of metal was so great that potters began by imitating bronze vessels, giving the pots slim or gracefully curved shapes and covering them with a dark glaze. Artists prized elegance of contour and relied on painting for decorative purposes (2400–2200 B.C.). The vases of the Kamares style (about 1800–1700 B.C.) bear geometrical patterns: among the finest are the vases of the Middle Minoan III period (1700–1580 B.C.) and those of the Late Minoan I (1580–1450 B.C.) in which realistic motifs are used (pl. 46), taken from floral or marine forms (cuttlefish, octopus, coral, nautilus, sea urchin, anemone, actinia); but the geometrical impulse took over again in the Palace style (Late Minoan II, 1450–1400 B.C.).

The art of painting, probably begun on terra cotta, found free expression in the frescoes adorning Cretan palaces. The imagery is borrowed from everyday life (dancing, bullfighting), from nature (dolphins, flying fish, flowers) and from more conventional designs (double-spiral, pl. 47). The bull, which left evidence of its importance in the Greek legend of the Minotaur, figures very frequently. The style is one of great ease, full of lively realism. Inspired by Egyptian and Sumerian art, it is none the less more subtle and worldly; its jovial expressionism, its humorous, worldly realism foreshadow the hedonism of the Greeks, who were to deliver mankind from its fear of supernatural powers.

47. Fresco from the palace at Tiryns. Late Minoan III, 1400–1200 B.C.
Athens, National Museum.

48. Faïence figurine of a Snake Goddess, from Cnossus. Middle Minoan III, 1700–1580 B.C. *Herakleion, Museum.*

Cretan art has left no large-scale sculpture. The only works in the round, and which are well executed, are earthenware figurines (snake goddesses—see pl. 48) and figures in bronze or carved in hard stones. These were all for domestic decoration.

After the year 2000 the Minoans built great towns and palaces (Cnossus, Phaestus, Hagia Triada, Mallia) where a very carefully planned system of sewers and canals and the size of storerooms and cellars show an awareness of town-planning problems. The Minoan palace, composed of suites of rooms grouped round inner courts, was no doubt influenced by Mesopotamian palaces. The complexity of the layout of the chambers was perhaps responsible for the Greek myth of the labyrinth. These buildings were made of stone and wood, while numerous isolated supports were used. The column appeared about 2000 B.C., with its shaft narrower at the base than at the top. The cushioned capital is thought to be a forerunner of the Doric style.

MYCENAEAN ART

The Achaeans who destroyed Cretan civilization inherited its might, but unlike the Minoans these hardy pirates were of a quarrelsome and warlike temperament, as Homer reminds us in the *Iliad*. Their warlike instinct led to the construction of the strongholds at Mycenae and

46

49. Lion Gate at Mycenae. Perhaps Late Minoan III, 1400–1200 B.C.

Tiryns (pl. 49). Thanks to their colossal stonework, made of irregular blocks (what the Greeks called the Cyclopean style), these buildings belong even more to megalithic architecture than they do to the Cretan palace style, although their masonry is more regular. Their tombs—the Treasury of Atreus at Mycenae (pl. 50) and the tomb at Orchomenus—like certain Celtic burial places (pl. 51), consist of a covered passage leading to a burial chamber, the latter being hutlike in shape and topped with a sort of cupola made of slabs superimposed corbel-wise.

The decorative art of the Achaeans, so far as we can see from what has survived, appears to have been inspired by the Cretan, of which it is a degenerate form. Like the Cretans they knew the crafts of metal-work and had a great taste for silver and gold trinkets.

THE ART OF THE NOMADS

Central Asia, an immense reservoir of human energy, has never ceased pouring hordes of nomads into Eurasia. They were always ready to swoop like birds of prey on the pastoral settlers who built up the great historical civilizations of China and southwestern Asia. These mounted barbarians had a vast territory to overrun in every direction. In the wide strip of the steppes from Budapest to Mongolia every race was

47

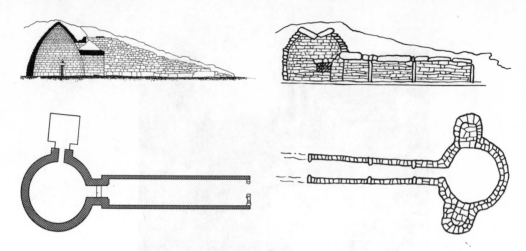

50. Section and plan of the Treasury of Atreus at Mycenae.
After Perrot and Chipiez.

51. Section and plan of a neolithic tomb in Portugal.
After Déchelette, Archéologie celtique ou protohistorique.

represented with all its tribes: in the eastern steppes there were the Turco-Mongols (Ordos, Avars, Huns, Turks), while the western steppes were inhabited by peoples of Indo-European stock, Scythians, Sarmatians of southern Russia, Satians (Saces) and Sogdians from Turkestan. But whatever their origins, their similar way of life imposed similar characteristics both in space and time on their chosen forms of artistic expression. As their nomadic habits restricted them to making small chattels, such as carpets (almost all of which have disappeared), gold ornaments and trinkets (buckles, sword hilts, brooches, disks and badges for sword belts), harnessings for chariots and horses, they perpetuated the customs of the Bronze Age. As with the Magdalenian hunters, the animal represented the primordial power of nature for these tribes of hunters and shepherds: they gave something of the living suppleness of the animal to their ornamentation, which was all composed of curves and countercurves to which the malleability of metals, whether gold, silver or bronze, readily lent itself. However, if their imagination was capable of creating an original style, their ornamental and zoomorphic art derives from the more civilized arts of Mesopotamia. It was by way of Iran, the great historic point of focus and communication between southwestern Asia and the steppes, and the melting pot for so many races, that the tribes of the steppes came to know the ornamental style of Sumerians and Elamites.

48

53. Gilded bronze plaque, Scythian art.
Leningrad, Hermitage.

52. Bronze funerary statuette from Luristan. *Paris, Louvre.*

Excavations in the Luristan mountains, which form the frontier between Mesopotamia and Persia, have done much to enable us to understand how this intricate compounding of forms came about, by revealing to us the art of the earliest Iranian settlers who had formed communities by the eleventh century B.C. After their nomadic phase they still retained their skill in the arts of metalwork: in their standards and their trappings for harness they transposed into bronze, with wonderful elegance, the monstrous, intertwined heraldic forms of the Chaldean cylinders (pl. 52). Among these tribes of the steppes (Ordos, Huns, Scythians), in daily contact with animal life, the zoomorphic style lost its monstrous character and showed a renewal of realism, though this was soon affected by the passion for ornament which filled the barbarians with a longing for fantasy, their nomadic way of life luring their imagination into a perpetual, onward flux.

It is their tombs which have revealed this art of the steppes. Graves were covered by mounds called *kurgans*, in which the tribal chiefs were buried with their wives, servants, horses, chariots and jewels in the same way as in the oldest Ur dynasties, which they were no doubt imitating. These have been examined especially in the steppes of Siberia and southern Russia, which were inhabited by the Scythians some centuries before the Christian era. The Scythians created a dramatic art in which animals are entwined together in furious combat, such violent

49

54. Detail from a wooden staff or prow (?) found in a
Viking death ship at Oseberg. About A.D. 820–850.
Bygdøy (near Oslo), Viking Ship House.

themes resulting in fine modulations of pattern (pl. 53). While Scythian
art became debased by its contact with the Greek goldsmiths of the
Black Sea region, a new zoomorphic art began to appear in central
Asia: that of the Sarmatians, which spread as far as China in the Han
period (202 B.C. to A.D. 220), and which appeared in graves in South
Russia in the Christian era. Sarmatian art spread to other hordes which
were to invade the West, notably the Germans, Huns, Goths and
Franks. Among these latter races this form of art tended to become
increasingly aniconic (imageless) and abstract, losing sight of the
animal realism of its origins. They favored interlaced patterns, a kind
of indecipherable ornamental knot, as well as cloisonné work in gold,
the setting of glass beads or gems (garnets, sapphires, emeralds) in

55. Plaques of cloisonné gold work with gems. Detail of trimmings on
a purse, found in the grave of a Saxon chief at Sutton Hoo.
About A.D. 650. *London, British Museum.*

gold, and inserting gold filigree into another metal (known as dama-skeening). They might well have been influenced by the fine gold craftsmanship of the Sassanians or Sassanids (A.D. 227–641), who came to Persia after the Seleucids. However, the jewelry of the Ordos and Scythians seems to suggest that the steppe tribes knew this technique earlier. These Nordic barbarians made much use of an ornamental system derived from the circular motif (wheels, helices, spirals, roses, six-petaled marguerites, swastikas) which the Sumerians had invented. This abstract art, which consists of handling any living form as a purely ornamental motif, was to flourish once more among the Scandinavian Vikings until about A.D. 1100 (see the Death Ship of Oseberg, pl. 54). It also gave vitality to the first artistic productions of the chris-tianized West, those of the Franks, Merovingians and Saxons (pl. 55) and more especially the Irish monks of the seventh and eighth cen-turies (pl. 650). It was one of the sources of Romanesque art, and, as such, of fundamental importance in the advance of the arts in the Western World.

THE PRE-COLUMBIAN CIVILIZATIONS
THE PRE-COLUMBIAN MENTALITY

The "civilizations" which flourished on the American shores of the Pacific Ocean before the voyages of Columbus were historically con-temporary with our own Christian era, and yet even more than the older civilizations of Egypt and Mesopotamia they remained deeply enslaved to the primitive mentality. In no other part of the world did any civi-lized race remain longer at the mercy of terrifying supernatural powers: nowhere did man have a more tragic awareness of his fragility in a hostile world. He imagined he was on earth only to pay blood tribute to deities lusting for death and murder, and the sun itself had to be fed its daily ration of human blood in order to continue on its course. The terrors of the Millennium left a memorable scar on our own civilization, so that we can only imagine what the psychology of such a race as the Aztecs must have been, who were plunged every fifty-two years into despair lest the world come to an end. The ritual sacrifice of young women, children or captured enemies—for warfare often had no other purpose than to replenish the altars—has left the Aztec civilization with a disgusting reputation.

Although they were more humane, the civilizations of Peru and Bolivia also practiced, though with a little more restraint, similar liturgical sacrifices. But no other evolved civilization made death the very principle of a cosmological, magical or religious system. As though the survival of the species in a terrifying universe could be ensured only by the sacrifice of an enormous number of its members, those who were privileged to live had themselves to pay the horrible levy, being obliged for instance to make blood gush from their ears, or to draw a string covered with thorns through a hole pierced in their own tongues.

The works of the Peruvians are certainly imbued with some humane spirit, but this was never the case with the images made in Central America. The gods represented by the Mayans, the Toltecs and Aztecs are all monsters, while the men are in the image of their gods. No art has ever symbolized so dynamically the inhumanity of a hostile world, no race ever erected such figures as these of the demoniacal powers that primitive man imagined to govern the world.

The strange formal structure of these Pre-Columbian works—whose only parallel is to be found in old Chinese bronzes—is made up of a jumble of features all imbricated without the slightest continuity (pl. 56). The introduction of some unifying principle, of some consecutive order in the chaos of appearances, is the very hallmark of rational thought, which has the capacity of projecting intellectual,

56. Detail of the Plumed Serpent Frieze, from the temple of Xochicalco (Tetecala), Mexico. Aztec art.

guiding lines into the manifold discords of the world. The Egyptians and Sumerians had this gift, which expressed itself in their art through the still entirely intuitive conception—of which the Greeks became fully aware—of the unifying principles that govern the various elements of which a work is composed by subjecting it to the laws of rhythm, cadence and proportion. In an Egyptian composition all the gestures are interrelated with the continuity of an arabesque (pl. 28). Sharp breaks constantly disturb the unity of Aztec reliefs, which have a chaos of forms taken from all the kingdoms of nature, the only rhythm relating them with one another being something like what is found in savage dances consisting of a series of frenzied shudders. It is a kind of seismic rhythm, crude energy in action, uncontrolled by any intellectual power.

These races are the only ones to have knowingly given artistic expression to the mentality of primitive man, hurled into a universe whose powers he had no idea of harnessing, through works which for grandeur and beauty invite comparison with those of Sumeria and Egypt. They show us the highest level of civilization that is attainable by mankind without the aid of reason, without that marvelous instrument of the mind, which in different ways made possible the scientific and philosophical awakening of India, China and the Mediterranean peoples. They were also retarded perhaps by their isolation on a continent cut off from the great centers of the world's civilizations. Yet with no more than the most rudimentary tools, the Pre-Columbians sought and contrived to overcome by energy alone a universe that appeared more hostile to man there than in any other part of the globe.

HISTORICAL BACKGROUND

The two empires of the Aztecs and Incas, which dominated the greater part of civilized America at the time the Spaniards arrived there, succeeded for a long time in concealing the rich complexity of the civilizations they had enslaved. In fact these two empires were both agents of political unification (like the Roman Empire) which were creative mainly at the material level and in spiritual matters depended on the conquered races.

Pre-Columbian America may be divided into two main spheres of influence: parts of Central America and the Pacific side of South America. Central America in this sense covered present Mexico and the republics of Honduras and Guatemala. The numerous civilizations that flourished in this region had several elements in common, notably the use of the terraced pyramid as a base for the sanctuary; the ritual game of *pelota;* the frequency of human sacrifice; the use of hieroglyphic writing; the calendar based on eighteen months of twenty days, making cycles of fifty-two years. The two most creative races of this region were the Toltecs and the Mayans. The birthplace of the Mayans, who seem to have reached the higher degree of culture, was in Honduras and Guatemala, where in the early centuries of our era they built numerous townships which are now being unearthed in the forest by archaeologists (Uaxactún, Palenque, Quiriguá, Copán). After a time of decadence the Mayan Empire revived toward the sixth or seventh century in the Mexican peninsula of Yucatán, and its greatest period lasted for two hundred years (987–1191, cities of Uxmal, Mazapa, Chichén Itzá, Kabah). The empire fell owing to civil war: in the eleventh and twelfth centuries the neighboring Toltecs seized Chichén Itzá and created a mixed art, Maya-Toltec, which shows a great profusion of forms.

The high plateau of Mexico was a very active center of civilization right from early times. Several peoples settled on the shores of Lake Texcoco, now dried up, the site of Mexico City. Several centuries before our era, one of these tribes founded the city of Teotihuacán which fell into decay in the tenth century, about the time when the invading Toltecs built the city of Tula. The Toltecs paid particular honor to the god Quetzalcoatl, the green-plumed serpent, who was god of the wind, then later god of the arts and of civilization (pl. 56). It is not certain at what date (perhaps the thirteenth century?) the Aztecs, coming from the north, settled on the central plateau: the date when Mexico City (Tenochtitlán) was built is variously put at 1325 or 1370. Their principal deity was the cruel god of war, Huitzilopochtli, whose thirst for human blood surpassed all others'.

On the two ocean slopes of Central America lived satellite peoples of the Toltecs, Mayans and Aztecs: on the Atlantic shore were the Zapotecs (city of Monte Albán), the Mixtecs (city of Mitla, founded in the fifteenth century), while on the Gulf of Mexico were the Totonacs (sites of Tajin, Cempoala, between the sixth and twelfth centuries).

The civilizations of South America are less known owing to the absence of written evidence, since the peoples there had no system of writing. They have been revealed mainly by burial places containing excellent pottery and utensils. Their chronology is still obscure. It is usual to distinguish between the pre-Inca and Inca civilizations. The Andean plateau (Peru and Bolivia) was the birthplace of American metallurgy, gold, silver, copper, then bronze. The Aymaras built the gigantic monuments of Tiahuanaco to the south of Lake Titicaca. On the Peruvian coast, several peoples succeeded each other in an order which is difficult to establish chronologically: in the north, the Chimú (site of Chan Chan); in the center the builders of the city of Pachacamac near Lima; in the south, those who modeled the fine works in terra cotta since discovered on the sites of Ica and Nazca. In the twelfth century the Kichuas appeared, sun worshipers who established, over different races occupying a region over 2500 miles long, a vast empire with a very advanced material civilization: the empire of the Incas which was to be destroyed by the Spaniards.

ARCHITECTURE AND SCULPTURE

The architecture of the Pre-Columbian peoples has dimensions which strive after great monumental effects, but its range of expression is limited by the absence of the vault and the rarity of the disengaged pillar. The tribes of Central America, Aztecs, Toltecs, Mayans, Zapotecs, erected their monuments on artificial terraced mounds, and, for religious structures, high pyramids built stepwise and with tiled facings (pl. 57). The summit was reached by way of four steep staircases, giving access

57. Temple of Kulkulcan, called "El Castillo,"
at Chichén Itzá, Mexico. Mayan art.

58. Monument called the Governor's Palace at Uxmal, Mexico.
False arch. Mayan art.

to the sanctuary containing the idol and the sacrificial altar. These monuments were often on a colossal scale: the Pyramid of the Sun at Teotihuacán still measures 212 feet in height and covers an area of 53,820 square yards, with a frontage of 700 feet. The largest of these remains yet found, the Pyramid of Quetzalcoatl at Cholula, 1463 feet wide, has a far greater volume than the Cheops Pyramid in Egypt. The architects who built the palaces show a preference for long halls in order to limit the bridging of beams and slabs for roofing. The most highly developed and richest architecture was that of the Mayans, who were the only ones who dared build corbeled false vaults (pl. 58) and made frequent use of the detached support.

The Andean region has kept intact a much larger number of civil and military buildings. The monuments of the Peruvian coast, built in adobe (dried clay), have left very few remains (Chan Chan). On the plateau, on the contrary, are to be found enormous works dating from the pre-Inca and Inca periods: paved roads, huge walls crossing the mountains, strongholds, palaces and temples. The city of Cuzco (in Peru) stands to this day on the foundations of the Inca city (pl. 59). The pre-Incas made free use of colossal monoliths (Tiahuanaco, Gate of the Sun). Both polyhedral and regular stonework was so carefully assembled that today it is impossible to insert a pin between the interstices. The stones were often bound with copper cramps.

Sculpture was rare with the Peruvians, but the Central Americans made considerable use of it both in isolated carvings and for facing walls. The figures are ferocious, composite monsters, of which the best known is Quetzalcoatl, the plumed serpent (pl. 56). In sunken reliefs they are accompanied by a background of geometrical patterns. The finest school of monumental sculpture was that of the Mayans (pl. 60). Whereas the Toltecs and Aztecs followed the ideographic conventions common to primitive peoples, only the Mayans came anywhere near optical truth in their construction of the human figure: the rhythmical beauty of their works sometimes recalls Greek art.

THE MINOR ARTS

The Pre-Columbian peoples excelled in the minor arts such as textiles, the working of hard stones and precious metals, which they lavished on their monuments (Temple of the Sun at Cuzco), and especially ceramics (pls. 61, 62). The finest Central American ceramics are the burial urns of the Zapotecs, with their statuesque lines and flamboyant ornamentation, and the smiling heads of the Totonacs: these works witness the domination of sculpture over the other arts, which is normal in an artistic society governed by its feeling for the monumental. The Peruvian potters, on the other hand, sought curves better adapted to the needs of the vase, of which numerous specimens have been preserved

59. Inca wall at Cuzco, Peru.   60. Stele at Piedras Negras, Guatemala. Mayan art.

61. Proto-Chimú vase, Peru. *Paris, Musée de l'Homme.*

62. Nazca vase, Peru. *Paris, Musée de l'Homme.*

intact in tombs. In polychromatic tones, on red or black slip, the Ica pots are adorned with a geometrical pattern, and those of Nazca with a demoniacal symbolism not unlike that of Central America. The anthropomorphic Chimú pottery perfectly adapts realistic observation to the curve of the vase, and these works are the only human representations to be found in the Americas. The Chimú potters, and above all those who made the earlier Proto-Chimú or Mochica pots, with their red foundation, left some admirable portraits. The later Chimú pots, with their black ground, show a withering of realistic inspiration.

THE ARTS OF THE UNCIVILIZED PEOPLES

In the tropical zones, far removed from the great centers of civilization, peoples of negroid race who go about naked under the hot sun, living a primitive kind of existence, still give the work of art the sacred and magical meaning that it had in earliest times. These peoples form two great cultural groups, dispersed across Africa and in the chain of islands scattered across the Pacific, from Australia to Madagascar and Easter Island.

Though these races have no known historical relationship, they hold in common an aesthetic notion which exalts the painted or sculptured form into a revelation from the Beyond, a *sign* fraught with supernatural powers. This is true not only in the case of ancestral images, fetishes and totems evoking beneficent spirits and evil demons, or the masks used for ritual dances and ceremonies, but also in the case of objects of everyday use whose stylized patterns have symbolic value (for instance figureheads on Polynesian canoes); for primitive man lives at all times in contact with the beyond. The attitude of the Negro or Oceanic artist is thus anti-realistic. When he evokes the form of a bird, a crocodile or a human being he is pursuing an idea, not an image, accentuating some traits, stylizing the lines and volumes: the visual truth of the object is profoundly affected by his sense of magic and mystery. Contrary to the practice of primitive or barbarian peoples of the white race, in Negro and Oceanic art the human figure plays a preponderant role because of the ancestor worship they have in common. The mask is the essential object of these civilizations: the wearing of the mask produces a veritable transfer of personality in the man who assumes it. In funeral or ritual ceremonies, which are masked dances, the primitive man ensures the passing over of the deceased ancestor, or else possesses himself of his virtues.

This art is also characterized by having no *history*. Objects collected by explorers before the contact of modern civilization caused rapid decay in native cultures are objects in actual use whose origins have long been forgotten. Only some parts of Africa are able to provide a historical perspective. The African continent, cut off like an island, seems to have had no communication worth mentioning with the Medi-

63. Bronze plaque from Benin, Nigeria. 16th century. *Paris, Private Collection.*

64. Wooden statuette from the Belgian Congo. *Tervueren (near Brussels)*,
Musée Colonial.

65. Sarcophagus from Waato Tarani (New Zealand). *Paris, Musée de l'Homme*.

terranean civilizations or with those of Asia, except in the North, which
was conquered by Islam, and in Egypt where a highly skilled civilization
developed, and in Abyssinia which, converted to Christianity, pursues
to this day the primitive Christian art from Egypt known as Coptic
art. Cave paintings whose traditions go back perhaps to a period contemporary with those of France and Spain have been discovered in the
northwestern Sahara and in Rhodesia. In the latter region ruins of towns
have been discovered, such as Zimbabwe, which was built by the Bantu
probably between A.D. 459 and 689. Finally, the ancient kingdom of
Benin, on the Ivory Coast, whose zenith seems to have been in the sixteenth and seventeenth centuries, produced—no doubt under certain
Mediterranean influences—admirable anthropomorphic and zoomorphic
objects in bronze and ivory (pl. 63). The most productive Negro artistic
civilizations at present are to be found in Central Africa, in the Sudan,
on the Guinea coast and in the Congo. African art, which devoted itself
chiefly to wood-carving, is full of grandiose and tragic meaning that
shows itself in a harsh and dry stylization, giving priority to the straight
line over the curve, and the whittling down of the statue into clear-cut
geometrical volumes (pl. 64). It is these characteristics which appealed
to the Fauve and Cubist painters of our own period.

Oceania has produced works which are more suggestive, less elementary and with a more mystical and poetical meaning. The Oceanic
native has a particular bent for whorls of curves and spirals (pl. 65) and
on this basis makes very subtle formal patterns, whereas the forms of

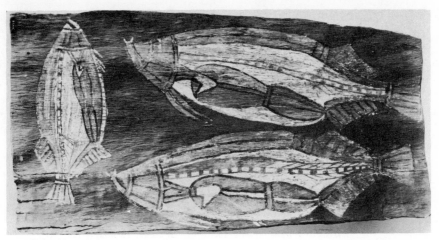

66. Painting of fish on bark, from New Guinea. *Paris, Musée de l'Homme.*
An integral realism makes the artist show the animal's internal organs.

African art are always dramatically isolated from each other. These patterns are, incidentally, not unrelated to those of Pre-Columbian art. The stylistic interpretation of the Oceanic artist is even farther from nature than that of the African. He is a sculptor, but he also has the painter's temperament, which expresses itself in paintings on bark (pl. 66) and in the colorings of masks and statues. The art of the Pacific offers great variety from island to island. The finest works are to be found in Melanesia, New Caledonia, the Solomon Islands, the New Hebrides, New Zealand and the Marquesas. Easter Island, the last link in the chain of islands stretching toward America, has some five hundred monolithic statues of unknown origin in the human image.

The Red Indians of North America show no signs of the same artistic gifts as the peoples of the same race in the center and south of the continent. In the Rio Grande, in New Mexico, the Pueblo civilization is a derivative and provincial center of the aristocratic civilizations of Central America. These peoples have left towns built in stone on a semicircular plan, sheltered under rocks or at the foot of cliffs. Farther to the north the Indians have remained in the nomad state, and they are painters rather than sculptors, making colored patterns in feathers or paint.

In South America, in the upper Amazon as well as on the Atlantic coast, primitive peoples carried on a degenerate form of Pre-Columbian art, sometimes mingled with influences that appear to have come directly, across the chain of islands, from Polynesian art.

67. Assurbanipal lion-hunting. Cyzicus. Low-relief.
London, British Museum.

CHAPTER III

THE CLASSICAL CIVILIZATIONS
OF THE MEDITERRANEAN

THE EGYPTIAN, Chaldean and Aegean civilizations are the work of the
Semitic and Asiatic peoples who had settled in the Mediterranean basin
or in western Asia long before 3000 B.C. The Indo-Europeans who
gradually infiltrated the Mediterranean, mainly after 2000 B.C., spent
a long period as parasites of the civilizations they came to overthrow.
For over ten centuries neither the Mitannites and Kassites nor the Hittites made anything really original. The Achaeans battened on the cultural remnants of the Cretans, and later the Persians, on whom the
mantle of the Assyrians fell, made little more than a pale imitation of
the royal art of Nineveh.

However, in the course of that protohistorical phase of the Aryan
peoples, a slow assimilation was being accomplished, a blending of elements that was to produce the miracle of Greece. Whether they were
pushed back by the Dorian invasion which was the last wave of Aryan
migration to penetrate Greece proper toward the year 1200 B.C., whether
in the preceding centuries they had fled from the misery caused in their
own cities by social crises of their own making; whether they came
from the North, or rather, as some now think, from the Middle East,
the Hellenes, who almost immediately proved to have great talent for
trading, gradually established colonial centers in both the eastern and

68. Chariot race from Cyzicus, Ionia.
End of 6th century B.C. *Istanbul, Museum.*

western Mediterranean and as far north as the Hellespont. They settled more especially in Asia Minor where they founded the numerous cities of Ionia which, succeeding to the Aegaean "thalassocracy" or maritime state, gradually supplanted the Phoenicians' hegemony of the seas and by way of reaction excited the rivalry of the mother cities, Athens and Corinth.

Compared with the ancient great powers, now in ruin, of Egypt and Mesopotamia, or with the Iranian empires of the Medes and after them the Persians, who took up all their traditions, the Hellenes, who were produced by the ferment of successive migrations, represented all the youthful energies of the universe in the seventh and sixth centuries. In them the Aryan genius emerged from its long obscurity, to accomplish one of the most vital revolutions of mankind and lay the foundations of the modern world.

The Greeks broke with the magical bond which had made man, ever since his origins, a power inseparable from the world about him. However mature they were, both Egyptian and Chaldean still had the feeling of being no more than a cog in the immense mechanism of the cosmos, so that man's intelligence, the privilege of his species, could do no more than propitiate the play of occult forces by bringing some divine power into action. In order to rise above nature, man has to identify himself with God: the pharaoh assured life and afterlife to his subjects by uniting the human and divine in his own person.

We shall never be able to fathom the tremendous effort human genius had to make to upset a scheme of things based on traditions

63

thousands of years old in order to stand alone, aware of his new-found strength, face to face with the universe. From then on man no longer tended toward self-identification with the spirit of nature, but tried to transcend it by means of reason, so that he could draw knowledge and power from its laws. The creative act, carried out by primitive man only when he believed himself possessed by some demiurge, was now to become pure creativity. Man stopped being the creature of God, and began to create God in his own image. The Greek Pantheon brought under its roof all the personifications of the faculties and attributes of the human soul: intelligence (Athena), sensibility (Aphrodite), the aggressive instinct (Ares), the genius of trade (Hermes), the creative gift (Apollo), lyric power (Dionysus). Even the cruder instincts which subconsciously still link man with the beasts found an idealized image among their demi-gods. Everywhere man began to project his own dimensions into a world suddenly reduced to a new scale. Order was brought into chaos, for human intellect thought it could discover some law of harmony in the world, some pre-established system. Foreshadowing the spirit of modern discoveries, Pythagoras saw the essence of things in a mechanics which reduced all phenomena to the norm of numbers.

Man's freedom from those shackles which had enslaved him to the laws of the universe broke out somewhat naïvely in archaic statues, evoking a psychological expression which was hitherto unknown to the art of mankind—the smile, a symbol of euphoria, the "hieroglyph of happiness" as it has been called, which expresses the joy of pure creation and of free discovery (pls. 77, 78).

The magic touch now gave way to rational knowledge, but the latter had not yet felt that austere renunciation which is characteristic of modern times. The Greek did not reject the supernatural but transposed it into images and mythology. There is as much difference between mystery and myth as between night and day; not that myths entirely stopped being objects of belief (though for enlightened minds this was to be the case, and the gods of Olympus quickly became the divinities of Fable); but such belief was no longer placed in blind powers as though they were universal data, but rather in concepts. Primitive religions were born of fear. Greek religion, or rather mythology, sprang from the union of reason with poetry which is perhaps the very essence of the Greek miracle. It was as much through the songs of poets as through theological speculation that the confused legends of primitive times gradually syncretized into cycles of anthropomorphic myths. Eager to pour the world's every aspect into the mold of ideas, the Greek imagination personified everything, the most abstract concepts as well as nature's material forms, all the data of the mind, of history and natural philosophy; and, what is more, all these allegories were given a human face. The Greeks thought of everything as either concepts or figures. Any study of man's historical evolution will show that there is not a human attitude, whether of the senses or intellect, whether personal or social, that did not find its first representation in some Greek myth. The universe crystallized itself for them in shapes, in a vast system of anthropomorphic images which became an endless source of speculation for the plastic arts, poetry and drama.

The artists of that civilization saw before them an immense field of activity unknown to the Mesopotamians and scarcely touched by the Egyptians: the discovery of man. The human figure was about to dethrone the animal from the sway it had held so long over the imagination and works of the first civilizations. Conscious of his physical weakness, man had at first worshiped the unerring mechanism of instinct to be found in the beasts, and he gave it all his admiration although he alone enjoyed the privilege of intellect. Formerly man had had to borrow some animal attribute in order to become godlike; but now it was the animal that was translated into man, and the monsters of Greek mythology—centaurs, sirens, satyrs—are all animal forms promoted to the human plane, the plane of intelligence.

This discovery of man was made in two stages, first physically, then morally. It took no less than three centuries to gain experience of the human body as such: the sixth and fifth centuries B.C. for male anatomy, the fourth century for the female. After the stadium the artists went on to explore the gynaeceum. Then, having painfully mastered the knowledge of the body, they applied it to expressing the soul. This great investigation into the passions which they began in the fourth century ended in the Hellenistic period in an inquiry which, passing beyond Greek man, was directed on to the yet-uncivilized world.

The work of art was delivered from that bondage to magic which had made it the slave of narrow conventions by turning it into a means of compelling the supernatural powers. It became a simple illustration of myths, then very soon an end in itself. The image emerged from the

EVOLUTION OF
THE ATHLETE

69. Egyptian art. Statue of Mycerinus. 4th Dynasty. *Boston, Museum of Fine Arts.*

70. Youth. Statue signed "[Poly]medes, the Argive." First half of 6th century B.C. *Delphi, Museum.*

71. "Apollo" of Tenea. First half of 6th century B.C. *Munich, Glyptothek.*

72. Apollo. End of 6th century B.C. *Athens, National Museum.*

sorcery of the temple's darkness to glitter in the sunshine, and as an ornament of cities offered itself as a spectacle to all and sundry, and not only to a few initiates. Costly to produce and carried out by free and paid men, it escaped that obsession with the gigantic that had been served so well in Egypt and Assyria by hordes of slaves. It was now made to the scale of cities and not of empires: not that it stopped aspiring to grandeur, but this quality was now sought by the Greeks in matters of proportion and not of dimension.

IN SCULPTURE

73. Cassel Apollo (after Phidias?). 2nd half of 5th century. *Cassel, Museum.*

74. Replica of the Diodumenos of Polyclitus. 5th century B.C. *Athens, National Museum.*

75. Agias. School of Lysippus. 4th century B.C. *Delphi, Museum.*

76. Borghese Gladiator, by Agasias of Ephesus. Early 1st century B.C. *Paris, Louvre.*

The conventions which for thousands of years had paralyzed the free portrayal of the forms in nature had therefore no excuse for survival. There was no longer any question of endowing the image with the maximum magical power by giving it the largest possible number of attributes of the model. Any resemblance was drawn from mere external appearance. For the first time natural forms were represented as they are seen by the eye; that is to say in their spatial truth, with the foreshortening which deforms them and in the perspective which hides

77. Head of Apollo of Thasos. 6th century B.C.
Copenhagen, Ny Carlsberg Glyptotek
78. Head from the pediment of the Temple of Aphaia at Aegina.
Early 5th century B.C. *Munich, Glyptothek.*
79. Polyclitus. The Doryphorus. After a replica.
5th century B.C. *Naples, National Museum.*

them or reduces their size. The Greeks' great plastic discovery was that of depth. After defining plane geometry they laid down the principles of stereometry. Their rationalistic turn of mind was necessary to understand that unlimited space could be reduced to a three-dimensional system.

The intuitive naturalism which prevailed in primitive times became, in Greek art, a rationally planned realism; but it found its own limits in the idealism which led the Hellenes to see an expression of universal order in everything. The Greeks rigorously defined all the ideas of proportion, measurement, composition and rhythm which shape every form—whether abstract like a temple or realistic like a statue—according to the laws of number. In their aesthetic all the parts of a whole are in keeping with each other, proportioned according to a common scale, what we call a relationship and what the Greeks called a *canon*, meaning a rule. This canon or standard is the formal principle from which component elements may be deduced according to a series of interrelationships: for instance the statue was based on the *dactyl* or width of the finger; while the entire temple depended on the width of the column. This secret order which governs the world and which constitutes Beauty had to be reflected externally in art, while the philosopher strove to

FACE IN SCULPTURE

80. Style of Praxiteles. Head of Hermes. *Olympia, Museum.*

81. After Scopas. Head of Meleager. 4th century B.C.
Rome, Villa Medici.

82. Agasias of Ephesus. Head of the Borghese Gladiator.
Early 1st century B.C. *Paris, Louvre.*

define its principles. Freed from the magical or theological bondage of its origins, art at last drew its whole mission from itself, much as science did, each of them aiming at the discovery of harmony; that is to say ultimately, and beyond all accidental discords, the pursuit of unity.

The name *classicism* has been given to this realism, which tended toward abstraction and was governed by a philosophy that reduced all things to the measure of man. It had such a universal validity that Greek civilization has remained alive while all its predecessors have long since been extinct.

Hellenism emerged from and returned to the East. The Greek genius was born in Asia Minor. Rich from the start, though still bearing traces of the experiments of the Egyptians, Cretans and Mesopotamians, it quickly shed them and expressed itself in all its purity in the fifth century, in a few cities of the Greek mainland and particularly Athens, that tiny strip of land which will always glitter like a diamond on the map of the world. Perhaps it was an increased infusion of Hellenic blood, from the ethnical contribution of the Dorian invasions, which produced this crystallization. Once rigorously defined, this philosophical and plastic culture was to become the ferment from which future civilizations were to rise. In the Hellenistic period Ionia again took the

69

first place, while Greece, fertilized once again from contact with the East, came into contact with Asiatic mysticism, and brought the speculative and rationalistic instrument it had created to bear on alien metaphysical systems: a synthesis from which Christian dogma was to emerge. The Greek plastic code, conceived in order to express the serenity of deified man, showed its adaptability by conforming to the new spiritual disquiet. Greece gave Rome the spiritual support which enabled it to base its material empire on the foundation of a powerful culture. Rome turned the classical sense of unity into the tool of politics, borrowing from Asiatic Greece that imperial spirit which the latter had inherited from the earlier monarchies. Even Rome's genius for engineering (its main claim to greatness in the domain of the arts) derived from the wealthy cities of Ionia, which the Arabs so thoroughly destroyed that nothing was left but a few bones.

The powerful impulse of Greek genius remained active in time and space. It went to enrich the complexity of Byzantine art. In the West it still remained an unseen presence until it brought about the dawn of the Renaissance. Recent excavations have shown the astonished world that Hellenism spread as far as the Indus, and that Indian art received a definite impetus from the example of Greece.

GREECE
THE EVOLUTION OF GREEK ART

The evolution of Hellenic art has been divided into three periods: archaic, classical and Hellenistic. Its beginnings and maturity were dominated by two rival principles, the Dorian and Ionian, in which the Ancients themselves saw the virile and feminine principles of Greece. The Ionian, springing from the contact of Asian Greece with the East, favors grace, elegance and wealth of ornament; while the Dorian, which originated in Greece proper and in western Greece, tends toward severity and rigorous observance of proportions.

1. *The Archaic Period*, during which Greece emerged from the protohistorical period and slowly developed toward maturity, covers a period of several centuries (1200–450 B.C.) and has been subdivided as follows:

(a) *The geometric phase* lasted from the fall of Mycenae to the

83. The three Greek styles: Doric, Ionic and Corinthian.

eighth century—five hundred years of darkness which have been called the Greek Middle Ages, during which art and civilization languished as a result of the Dorian invasion. It has been called geometrical owing to the decorative pattern found on ceramics discovered in Attica, Boeotia, Laconia and in the Archipelago, and also the "cubist" style of carved idols found in the Cyclades. The temples at that time were built in crude clay and wood, with architectonic patterns in modeled and painted terra cotta.

(b) *The archaic phase*, which lasted from 700 to 500 B.C., showed the preponderance of the Asian Greeks, which is very marked in ceramics (workshops at Rhodes, Cyclades, Corinth and Attica) as well as in sculpture and was already developed by the early sixth century in the form of statuary and monuments (Naxian Sphinx, Cnidian Treasury, at Delphi; Temple of Artemis in Corfu; painted limestone relief of the Hecatompedon in Athens). The same century witnessed the first stone temples: the Doric style developed in Magna Graecia (Sicily and southern Italy, sites of Selinunte, Syracuse and Paestum), at Corinth (Temple of Apollo) and in the Peloponnesus (Heraion at Olympia). Though few traces of the Ionic style remain, we know that it developed contemporaneously in the cities of Samos, Miletus, Ephesus in Asia Minor.

(c) *The pre-classical phase* (500–450 B.C.). The conquest of Ionia by the Persians was to bring about a momentary eclipse there. Architecture flourished in southern Italy, then called Magna Graecia (Selinunte, Paestum, Segesta, Agrigentum in Sicily) and in the sanctu-

71

aries of Greece itself (Delphi, Olympia): this was the great period of the archaic Doric, yet the Ionic spirit still inspired such monuments as the Treasury of the Siphnians at Delphi, while the Corinthian style appeared in Sicily. The workshops of Attica took the lead in ceramics. Then, in the course of the sixth century and the first half of the fifth, masculine and feminine types of statuary began to develop, inspired respectively by the Dorian and Ionian principles. In the first half of the fifth century monumental sculpture broke free from archaism with the pediments of the Temple of Aphaia at Aegina, the Auriga at Delphi and the decoration of the Temple of Zeus at Olympia, which is the triumph of the Dorian spirit.

2. *The Classical Period* (second half of fifth century to the fourth century) was the period of equilibrium and maturity, dominated entirely by Greece proper. Toward 450 B.C. the Attic Myron and the Argian Polyclitus brought the athletic type to its perfection, the one in the expression of movement, the second by establishing the canon of athletic proportions. The great initiative of Pericles, who, with Phidias as his master-of-works, undertook to rebuild the Acropolis from its ruins after

84. The Parthenon, by Ictinus and Callicrates.
Northwest view. Begun 447 B.C.

it had been burned down by the Persians, was to make Athens the artistic center of the Greek world. The Doric style found its perfect expression in both architecture and sculpture with the Parthenon, which was dedicated in 438 B.C. and of which Ictinus and Callicrates were the architects and Phidias the sculptor. The Propylaea (437–432 B.C.) combines the Doric and Ionic styles, but the Temple of Athena Nike by Callicrates (dedicated 421 B.C.) and the Erechtheum (425–406 B.C.) are in the Ionic.

The Athenian hegemony emerged shaken from the Peloponnesian wars. In the fourth century the great architectural undertakings were already shifted to Asia Minor, which cultivated the Ionic style and showed an Asiatic taste for the colossal (the Artemisium at Ephesus, Temple of Apollo at Didyma (Miletus), the Mausoleum at Halicarnassus). A new architectural form appeared transposed into wood, that is to say the theater (Epidaurus and Athens). Meanwhile Greece kept its pre-eminence in sculpture with Scopas of Paros, Praxiteles of Athens and Lysippus of Sicyon. The arrival of Polygnotus of Thasos in Greece gave great impetus to painting, the imitation of which led to the decadence of the art of ceramics which had been flourishing.

85. Temple of Athena Nike on the Acropolis,
by Callicrates. 427–424 B.C.

3. *The Hellenistic or Alexandrian Period* (third century till the Christian era) dates from the dismembering of Alexander's empire (323 B.C.), which created great prosperous kingdoms in Asia while transferring the seat of Greek art to the East. New cities such as Pergamon in Anatolia, Alexandria in Egypt, Antioch in Syria, all of which were cosmopolitan in character, furthered the fusion of Hellenism with the East which is peculiar to the Hellenistic period of this civilization. The Doric decayed, and the Corinthian took the lead. From the third century we see the development of official architecture, colonnades, meeting rooms (*bouleterion*), libraries, museums, while large urban works were built of which the thoroughly explored ruins of Pergamon give us a fair idea. Sculpture derived from Lysippian expressionism, which developed toward pathos and realism. The frieze of the Altar of Zeus at Pergamon (pl. 99) of the second century encouraged the "pathetic" style which was further exploited by the Rhodes school (second and first centuries B.C.). The city of Pompeii, submerged A.D. 79 by the eruption of Vesuvius, reveals an Italian reflection of Hellenistic art at the domestic level. The only surviving paintings of ancient times come from this site, and from Delos and Rome.

ARCHITECTURE

The Greeks inherited flat-roof building. They knew nothing of the possibilities of covering great spaces by means of the vault; and yet they accomplished a profound revolution in monumental art. A slave to massive walls, the architecture of previous civilizations had to limit itself to such expression of mere strength as could be obtained by colossal dimensions: the monuments of the Nile and the Euphrates were still little more than buildings coated with decoration; they were closely derived from the mud wall which remained the basis of Mesopotamian building until the end, and which the Egyptians continued to imitate in stone even after they had abandoned it. The Greek temple, on the contrary, had its origins in the wooden edifice, wood being a material allowing of large gaps in construction: the column of the hypostyle chambers of the Nile was a fragment of wall, whereas that of the Greeks derived from the stake. Building in stone, the Greeks had the idea of masking the nakedness of the full wall with a colonnade, which looked far less heavy and broke the monotonous surface of blank walls by vertical effects that were further accentuated by fluting. They thus invented a gamut of monumental expression, by alternating solids and spaces, carried and carrying parts; while by bringing relative dimensions into play (height, width, thickness) in the component elements such as the support (column), the interval (between columns) and the carried surface (coping, and so forth), their genius was able to achieve those effects of rhythm and harmony which properly constitute architecture in the real sense; that is, something the Hellenes thought of as a science of numbers.

All Greek monumental art derives from the column. The entire proportions of the temple depended on its strength and slimness, and the relationship between the diameter and height of the column—a relationship known as the "module"—thus governed the entire edifice. With their scrupulous love of clarity and unity the Greeks reduced the expressions of architecture to three, nobility, grace and sumptuousness, to which corresponds the three "orders," the Doric, Ionic and Corinthian (pl. 83). These orders differed the one from the other in their proportions as well as in certain elements in their decoration: the Doric capital, with its unadorned molding, frankly and robustly expressed the architectonic function of the strut or support (pl. 84), while the fluting of the Ionic capital suggests an elegant impression of elasticity (pl. 85). The acanthus flowers decorating the vase of the Corinthian column contribute an element of ornamental luxury. Originating in Asia, which always favored serial decorations (Assyrian and Persian friezes), the Corinthian and Ionic orders always have, on their entablature, a sculptured frieze showing a continuous pattern. The Doric order best corresponds with the Western mind, which inclines toward sharpness of definition: the rhythm of the columns and intercolumniation is repeated in the entablature by the alternating of fluted triglyphs and sculptured metopes. The Parthenon is the most perfect of all Greek temples, representing the golden mean between the somewhat heavy strength of the first Doric temples and the fragile gracefulness of the Ionic. It is 238 feet long and 110 feet in width, built according to the Doric order; but the frieze is to be seen *inside* the portico, at the top of the walls, as in the Ionic order.

The Greeks further enriched the expressive range of architecture by creating a system of ornamental molding which was extremely simple and logical, dispersed about the monument in such a way as to underline its divisions and define the proper function of each element. Greek

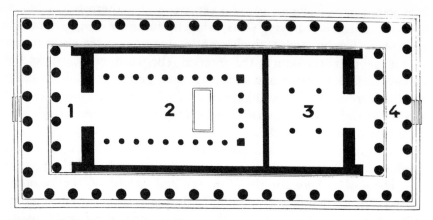

86. Plan of the Parthenon: 1, pronaos; 2, naos; 3, opisthodomos; 4, peristasis.
After François Benoît, L'Architecture: Antiquité

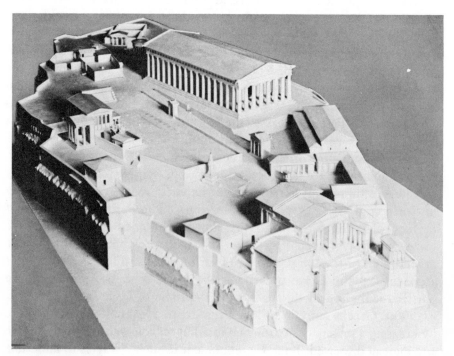

87. Reconstruction of the Acropolis. *Model by Gorham P. Stevens.*

monuments were constructed with the greatest care in moderately sized
materials, hewn in marble and assembled with scientific skill. The walls
were entirely ashlar masonry without the use of cement, solidity being
guaranteed by sheer weight, though the blocks were often bound with
bronze clamps. Greek temples delight us now by the beauty of their
marble which glitters in the sunshine, but their architects often embellished them with effects of coloring. This polychromy, applied to all
the adornments of the archaic temple constructed in limestone, was
more discreetly done when they adopted marble, and was used only to
emphasize the main members of the edifice.

The essential monument of Greek architecture was the temple
(pl. 86). Temples were every city's pride, and were often built either
alone or in groups at the highest point in the city, where stood its earliest center, the Acropolis (pl. 87). The Greek temple, of much smaller
dimensions than the Egyptian, usually comprised a blank rectangular
wall, with a single or double colonnade (*peristasis*) running all round.
Inside, the image of the god was kept in the *naos* or *cella*, which was
frequently divided into three naves: this was preceded by a vestibule
(*pronaos*) and followed by a sacristy or treasury (*opisthodomos*). The
rooms were all somewhat feebly lit through the roof. At the front and
back (façades) the gently sloping gable roof made two triangular sections, the pediments, which were decorated with sculptures. All the
other monumental undertakings of Greek architecture such as the meeting room, the market (*agora*), the portico (*stoa*) incorporated colonnades. The house consisted of a number of rooms grouped round a
peristyle containing a garden (pl. 88): unlike the temple, which was a
public monument, the house was conceived from the inside, centering
on the interior. The Greeks also invented the theater, built with an
extraordinary simplicity and economy of means (pl. 89). Backing
against a hill, the theater as it finally developed had three main parts:
a large segment of a circle with tiers of seats for the spectators, a circular
orchestra or dancing-place for the chorus, a proscenium in front of the
skene or decorated back wall for the actors.

The drawback of Greek architecture is its monotony. The monumental perfection attained in the fifth century left little scope for invention in the following centuries. Like all those forms of architecture that
lack the arch or vault, Greek architecture could only exploit a limited
number of possibilities both at the structural level and by way of har-

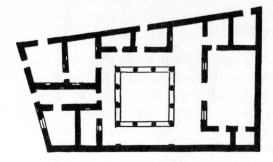

88. Plan of a house at Delos.
After François Benoît,
L'Architecture: Antiquité

89. The Theater at Epidaurus (Peloponnesus). 4th century B.C.

monic effects. By their use of the arch the Romans were able to give the architect a far wider field of action.

SCULPTURE

Greek sculpture evolved in such a logical way, and with such a complete exploitation of its plastic and human potentialities, that it is rightly considered the most perfect example of the creation of a style.

After the abstract idols sculptured in marble in the Cyclades in the Bronze Age (pl. 90), and without showing any obvious connection with them, in the seventh century sculptors began to raise the problem of the male type (*kouros*) and the feminine type (*kore*). The votive and religious statues gave them the pretext for "still" statuary. Starting from Egyptian frontality, in the course of the sixth century they loosened its stiffness and began to animate their works by exploring ana-

90. Woman performing on the lyre. From Amorgos. Marble.
Bronze Age. *Athens, National Museum.*

tomical truth as well as volume and movement. Modeling at first showed
a geometrical tendency which had little relationship to internal structure, then gradually it began to express what was beneath the surface.
Originally the statue was thought of as a front and profile, symmetrically
assembled on a strictly vertical axis: then by degrees it became a volume
turning in space. Workshops all over the Hellenic Mediterranean contributed their share to this slow apprenticeship. The Peloponnesus seems
to have played a major part in perfecting the naked athlete, a most austere expression of concentrated strength (pls. 70 to 76). It was Ionia
that created the feminine type, with a rather affected charm, whose
transparent linen drapery (*chiton* and *himation*) hints at the body's
lines. The naked kouros served as an experiment for the discovery of
anatomical modeling, whereas the kore was the basis for discovering
draped modeling. At first incised schematically over the body, gradually the folds of the dress began to be modeled in hollows and con-
vexities and gave vigorous expression to the reliefs of the figure. The
preference given in the fifth century to the monumental *peplos* of Dorian
wool, replacing the Ionic linen garment, was to advance this evolution
which was completed by Athens. Overcome toward the year 550 by
the "Levantine" grace of the emigrant Ionians, Athens absorbed this
influence and at the beginning of the fifth century created the grave
but unsevere style which was to become its own.

79

The evolution of still statuary found its perfect fulfillment in the fifth century with the Peloponnesian Polyclitus, who, about 445–440 B.C., expressed the Dorian ideal of the athletic figure in his bronze *Doryphorus* (lance bearer), which the Greeks called the "canon" because the sculptor executed it according to the proportions which he himself had described in an aesthetic treatise of that name. In this work, conceived as the expression of the ideal beauty of the human body, all the problems of volume and anatomy were solved scrupulously but without the slightest stiffness, the harmonious composition of the gestures giving the impression of living suppleness (pl. 79).

It was in monumental sculpture in low-relief that "mobile" statuary seems to have developed, and it sprang from the need for learning how to group together several figures participating in some common action. Sculpture had been distributed as a uniform adornment but with no particular order, on mural surfaces in Egypt and Assyria; but now it was to become closely involved in the rhythm of the architecture. It was set at vantage-points in which architectonic expression demanded balance of relief such as the metopes between the triglyphs of the Doric temple, the pediments of the façades, the continuous frieze of the Ionic order. The pediments of the Temple of Aphaia at Aegina (about 500–480 B.C., Munich Glyptothek) were the first victory over monumental expression, but still show no more than independent or juxtaposed statues, conceived on the frontal or profile plane (pl. 78). But in the metopes and pediments of the Temple of Zeus at Olympia (472–456 B.C.) the figures are associated one with the other by the rhythm of the action and the cadence of the total composition: they attempt the three-quarters stance, but not without constraint from recent memories of Egyptian frontality, which curbs the natural swing of the torso in its rotation. On the western pediment, in Apollo checking the struggle of the Centaurs and Lapithae, the Olympian quality appears for the first time: Olympia is the culminating point of the Dorian spirit.

The sculpturing of marble in low-relief had encouraged a freer expression of gestures, because the forms remained attached to the background or were applied to it as in the case of the pediments. It was the use of bronze which, being both stronger and less heavy, was to help the statue in the round to solve the problem of movement. A gesture like that of the outstretched arms in the *Zeus* or *Poseidon* (about 470 B.C., Athens Museum), could never have been thought of in marble (pl. 91).

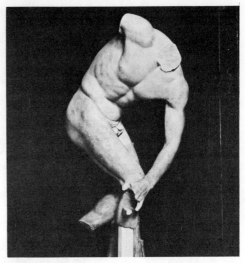

91. Zeus (or Poseidon). Bronze found at Artemision. About 470 B.C.
Athens, National Museum.

92. Style of Myron. The Discobolus. About 460–450 B.C.
After an ancient replica. *Rome, National Museum.*

In his famous *Discobolus* (toward 460–450 B.C.) Myron contrived the canon of movement just as Polyclitus in his *Doryphorus* had expressed the canon of repose. A synthesis between the contraction and relaxation of muscular effort at speed, this work finds the principles of its harmony in the balance of opposites (pl. 92).

All these efforts converged toward Phidias, who from both the moral and plastic point of view represents the supreme expression of the Greek spirit. It was he who gave the most perfect form to that Greek notion of divinity which is known as Olympian, a kind of superhumanity whose serenity is untouched by earthly cares. In his famous religious statues in gold and ivory, called for that reason "chryselephantine"— Zeus at Olympia, and Athena in the Parthenon—the colossal dimensions (the Zeus being 45 feet 6 inches in height) as well as the precious sheen of the material still contained something of the old, magical notion of the deity. But in the monumental sculptures of the Parthenon, the divinity is conceived of in terms of heroic man. In this group (447–432 B.C.) in which Atticism brings together Dorian gravity and Ionian grace, Phidias achieved a perfection of harmony which no artist has ever surpassed. Each item, taken by itself, is a fluid composition of happily counterbalanced volumes, while the twist of the bodies in space is accomplished with all the ease of real life. At the same time the figures

81

93. Phidias. Persephone, Demeter and Artemis (?).
About 438–432 B.C. Statues from the east pediment of the Parthenon.
London, British Museum.

are related to each other according to the principles of a harmonious rhythm. The two pediments (*Birth of Athena*, pl. 93, and *Dispute between Athena and Poseidon*) and the ninety-two metopes contain restricted compositions which had to conform with geometrical requirements. The frieze which unfolds at the top of the walls under the colonnade, on the other hand, is a continuous pattern of related forms, developing like the theme of a melody in music (pl. 94). This is one of the greatest undertakings in all sculpture: 350 human figures, 200 animals (horses and beasts of sacrifice) portray in heroic style the procession of the Panathenaea. Composed of youths on horseback, magistrates, musicians, Athenian maidens, every four years such a procession came to offer the statue of Athena, protectress of cities, a new veil which had been woven specially for her.

The late fifth century lived on the strength of the Phidian aesthetic, which was observed particularly by the sculptors of grave columns at the Cerameicus cemetery (reserved for heroes). The anonymous author of the caryatids of the Erectheum (between 420–413 B.C.) subjected the *korai* (maidens) to the architectonic expression of the support. The sculptured parapet of the Temple of Athena Nike at Athens (toward 410 B.C.) accentuates the Ionian gracefulness of feminine figures. Paeonius achieved for the Temple of Zeus at Olympia, probably

94. Phidias. Fragment of the north frieze of the Parthenon.
Panathenaic procession.
London, British Museum.

after 421 B.C., an instantaneous glimpse of movement in his Nike (Victory) caught in full flight as she descends from Olympus (original still at Olympia, pl. 95). This effort toward expression of motion had been made earlier by the anonymous author of the Nereids dancing on the sea, discovered at Xanthos (now in the British Museum). With his bust of Pericles, Cresilas created the heroicized type of portrait, reduced to the head and bust.

Of the great masters of Greek sculpture, only Phidias is known to us by original works, for, like the masterpieces of Myron and Polyclitus, those of the fourth century were pillaged by the Romans and have disappeared, while scholars have great difficulty in identifying later copies by which they are known.

Between the idealism of the fifth century and the naturalism of the Hellenistic period, the fourth century came as a period of crisis in Greek sculpture. It marks the transition from the mythological to the human. Scopas (very damaged remains of the Temple of Athena at Tegea, in the Peloponnesus, begun about 360? B.C.) accomplished a revolution by introducing into the Greek plastic code the portrayal of passion violently affecting the body and filling the face with anguish, which hitherto had remained imperturbable even in the moments of action, grief or death (pl. 81). Praxiteles, who first dared to portray the feminine body

83

95. Paeonius. Victory. Originally mounted on a pillar before the east front of the Temple of Zeus at Olympia. Probably after 421 B.C. *Olympia, Museum.*

96. Style of Praxiteles. Apollo Sauroctonus (or The Lizard Slayer). Bronze, about 350 B.C. After an ancient replica. *Rome, Villa Albani.*

entirely naked (the *Cnidian Aphrodite*), was the refined product of the Athenian decadence. He transformed the athlete into the adolescent: moreover the hips of his adolescents, who appear somehow lethargic, destroy the statue's proper balance and drive the sculptor to the use of supports (*Apollo Sauroctonus*, pl. 96; *Lycian Apollo;* the *Resting Satyr*). An overanxiety for gradation, no doubt to be blamed on the influence of painting, weakens the modeling, which becomes too smooth and fluid, as can be seen from the Hermes of Olympia, no doubt made later (pl. 80). In the time of Alexander, the bronze smith Lysippus, born at Sicyon in the Peloponnesus, kept a taste for athletic figures, characteristic of his Dorian origins: but, obeying the spirit of his age, he debased the Polyclitian squareness by lengthening the proportions (making the body eight times the head, instead of seven). He upset the firm stance of the statue with unstable postures, caught or snapped with a suddenness which twists the bust and gives the whole body an angular uneasiness (*Statue of Agias*, pl. 75; *Resting Hermes; Athlete with the Strigil*). Forgetting the support which the wall formerly afforded, the statue was now fully modeled from all angles, three-dimensionally, the overanalysis of the anatomy giving the modeling a knotty and episodic appearance

84

97. The Venus of Milo. Detail. Early 3rd (?) century B.C.
Paris, Louvre.

detracting from the expression of strength. In the Ionian tradition, which was increasingly active, the Asiatic background seems to have inspired artists to a luxurious fleshiness, well expressed in the statue of the king (from *Mausoleum at Halicarnassus*, British Museum, about 350 B.C.) and the *Venus of Milo* (Louvre, beginning of third century?), the latter being one of the most sensual marbles left to us by Greek art (pl. 97).

In the Hellenistic period the Greek plastic code sacrificed every effect of harmony to expressionism and naturalism. The sculptor began to explore the whole gamut of human expression, suffering, death, sleep, laughter, voluptuousness, tenderness, instinct, physical infirmity, old age and infancy. In Alexander's time portrait sculpture became more individualistic under the influence of painting, while landscape found its way into relief and sometimes became its sole theme (pl. 98).

Hellenistic art glorified brute strength. It created the type of Hercules, a circus athlete with overgrown muscles, and also showed an interest in types of long-haired Barbarians (statue of *Dying Galatians* or Gauls). The beautiful athletes of the classical period now became professionals of the stadium (in the Louvre: *Running Athlete*, or the *Borghese Gladiator*, first century, pls. 76 and 82). Sometimes, on the

98. Dionysus visiting Icarus. Low-relief.
After a Greek original of the Hellenistic period.
London, British Museum.

other hand, they became effeminated to the point of hermaphroditism. The largest group of work surviving from that period was the altar built at Pergamon for Eumenes II (197–159 B.C.) on which a frieze of 390 feet, arranged as a plinth in the manner of the Persians and Assyrians, portrayed a *Gigantomachy* (Battle of Gods and Giants). This work was returned to the Pergamon Museum in 1958 (pls. 99 and 643). The projection of the forms, excessively emphasized, and the chaotic movement of the attitudes, the draped form pronounced to the point of inflation, the melodramatic play of muscle, and the convulsed faces, express all the passions of strife, suffering and death. The taste for pathos led to the composing of groups of statuary bringing together a number of figures in some violent action (group called the *Farnese Bull*, Naples Museum). The school of Rhodes carried on the traditional theatrical style of Pergamon, which was still very much alive in the famous *Laocoön* group (about 50 B.C.)—the last great work of Greek plastic art. Discovered in Rome in the sixteenth century, it then had a profound influence on Michelangelo (pl. 645).

PAINTING AND THE MINOR ARTS

If mutilated remains help us to reconstitute the history of Greek sculpture, though with many gaps, painted works of art have equally disappeared, apart from a few specimens of the later decadent period at

86

99. Detail of frieze of the Altar of Zeus at Pergamon.
Athena fighting the giants. Between 180 B.C. and 159 B.C.
Berlin, Pergamon Museum.

Pompeii, Delos and Rome (pl. 100). The latter are extremely beautiful
in spite of their clumsiness which was due to mediocre executants. We
will thus always remain ignorant of the art of the great painters of
antiquity: Polygnotus, Zeuxis, Parrhasius, Apelles. However, we can
gain some idea of what the general evolution of Greek painting was
like from the mark it left on an industrial art, that of painted ceramics.
The considerable number of specimens (found in tombs) of these

100. Mural painting in the Villa of the Vettii at Pompeii.

101. Large krater, Geometric style. From the Dipylon, Athens.
Attic, 8th century B.C. Detail. *Paris, Louvre.*

102. Oenochoë (vase). Corinth, late 7th–early 6th century B.C. Detail.
Paris, Louvre.

products, which were exported all over the Mediterranean, amounts
to an enormous collection of forms which, better than any other figurative art, enables us to reconstruct the life, customs and general evolution
of styles in Greece. Study of the vases shows us that painting was freed
from primitive constraints earlier than sculpture, and this increases our
regret for the loss of so many great works.

Before the seventh century the enormous Attic vases of the Dipylon
(gate near one of the cemeteries of Athens) shows ceramics to have been
under the same influence of the geometric style (pl. 101) as were the
temple idols of the Cyclades. The triangular stylization of the human
body recalls that of the ceramics of Susa in the fourth millennium and
certain cave paintings of prehistoric Africa. This bent for rectilinear
stylization, so unlike the fluid formalism of the Cretans, appears therefore to have been the manner of the Dorian primitives. We have already
seen from sculpture that the Dorian spirit always maintained a tendency
toward squareness (Polyclitus and Myron). More clearly than sculpture, ceramics prove that the curvilinear style came from Asia by way of
Ionia. The pots made in the workshops of Rhodes, Boeotia and Corinth
in the eighth and seventh centuries were decorated with dark figures on
a light ground, set out in a continuous frieze and composed of animals
seen either naturalistically or with a touch of fantasy, and of Phoenician
or even Assyrian origin (pl. 102). The seventh century introduced

88

scenes from everyday life which at first were mingled with animal adornments. The growing influence of Athenian ceramics which was to flood markets hitherto in the hands of the Corinthians freed vases from Oriental influences.

Athens used a process of black figures on a red ground (650 to 530 B.C. approximately) and, abandoning the layout according to zones, adopted the metope style of composition; that is to say rectangular panels blocked out in light red, to take the mythological scenes which were introduced at that time. The lines of the drawing were incised on the black surface of the figure with no attempt at modeling. The beauty of arabesque and elegance of silhouette, the lifelike gestures, show that painting was already far in advance of sculpture which was still under the tyranny of the block's mass. A demonic life animates these figures, which suggest the vitality of the Homeric poems (pl. 103).

The potter Nikosthenes or his colleague Andokides is credited with the invention of the process of depicting red figures on a black ground, toward the end of the sixth century. The light tint of the figures enabled the painter to work them with the brush, to analyze the modeling, perspective, foreshortening, lights and shades. The increasing influence of painting pushed the artist toward naturalism at the cost of beauty in

103. Achilles and Ajax Playing Dice. Detail of a black-figured amphora by Exekias. Second half of 6th century B.C. *Rome, Vatican.*

104. Bottom of drinking vessel, figures in red, by the Brygos Painter. About 490–480 B.C. *London, British Museum.*

105. The Death of Talos. Detail of bowl from Ruvo. First half of
4th century B.C. *Ruvo di Puglia, Iatta Museum.*

decorative style, the figure being no longer conceived as a silhouette
but according to the inner modeling. The finest red-figure vases are
those of the so-called "severe" or "archaic" period (late sixth century
to 460 B.C. approximately). Euphronios, the potters Brygos and Douris
signed some magnificent pieces in which the balance between realism
and style anticipated the harmony of Phidias (pl. 104). Naturalism was
stressed after the arrival in Athens in 470 B.C. of the painter Polygnotus
of Thasos, who introduced perspective effects and psychological expression into his painting. About 450 B.C. saw the beginnings of the "fine
style" period in ceramics: the aesthetic of Phidias made itself felt in
painting and led to a certain degree of academicism. During the period
of the ornate style which began in about 420 B.C., its chief exponent
being Meidias, ceramics was invaded and led astray by the imitation of
painting: compositions included too many figures and became confused,
the modeling suggested volumes (pl. 105) and, emulating the painter,
the potter began to transgress the decorative laws of his medium—all
these defects being further accentuated in the ceramics of southern Italy,
whose development coincided with the decadence of Athenian pottery
after the Peloponnesian War. The Greek ceramic works nearest to
painting that have survived are the funerary *lekythos* or oil jars which
had a white ground: drawn in firm outline on a limewash background,
the figures must have been made in imitation of those found in stucco

90

106. Attic krater (mixing bowl). *Paris, Louvre.*

107. Drinking vessel. *Paris, Louvre.*

108. A lekythos (narrow-necked vessel). *Paris, Louvre.*

109. Gold plaque found at Delphi. Detail. Second half of 6th century B.C. *Paris, Bibliothèque Nationale.*

paintings. The beauty of design of some of the fifth century lekythos only increases our regret for the loss of works by the great masters themselves, since so many of those known to us were from the hands of humble craftsmen.

The Greeks had a particular bent for the monumental arts and produced little in the way of the minor arts, with the exception of pottery, for which they invented some admirable forms, peculiarly suitable for the various functions of the vase, and a decorative style of considerable beauty. The Greek disregard for comfort did not encourage the making of everyday things and furniture, except in the Hellenistic period. Miniature sculpturing on bronze was only a reflection of large-scale sculpture, but their bronze mirrors have some beautiful incised drawings. Sober in their tastes, the Hellenes paid little attention to finery, at least in the classical period. Some fine examples of silverware

91

110. Decadrachm from Syracuse. End of 5th century B.C.
Paris, Bibliothèque Nationale.
111. Greek cameo. 4th century B.C. *Paris, Bibliothèque Nationale.*

have survived from the Hellenistic period. The Hellenic artists made some excellent intaglios from hard gems for use as seals, and in Alexander's time they invented cameos, onyx stones cut in relief in which the different-colored layers of the material are skillfully exploited. Their genius for sculpture also came out in their minting of coinage, the best specimens of this art being produced not at Athens but at Syracuse (pl. 110).

112. Two huntsmen. Bronze tablet, cut-out. 7th century B.C. *Paris, Louvre.*
113. Figurine of man with rickets. Terra cotta.
Hellenistic period. *Paris, Louvre.*

THE ROMAN WORLD
HISTORICAL BACKGROUND

In the central region of Italy (Tuscany and Latium), Etruscan art, which came before that of Rome, was a kind of provincial extension of Greek art. It sought and found its happiest inspiration in Ionia during the archaic period (late seventh century to the first half of the fifth). The classical stream (second half of fifth century to fourth) was more banal. The rapid degeneration of this art from the third century produced neo-primitive forms heralding the plastic style of the late Empire, that of the early Middle Ages, or certain aspects of modern art.

The Etruscans imported a great quantity of Attic vases, and imitated the designs on them in the frescoes of their own underground tombs. This they did with a primitive touch, but with a narrative sense remote from the classical spirit which has something of the Asian sensibility while foreshadowing Roman realism. The Romans were to inherit some of their gift for portraiture. The Etruscans also left some fine archaic bronzes (pl. 114). The few structures of theirs that are known to us (city walls, municipal works) are interesting because they show a very precocious use of the arch of wedge-shaped stones when it was still unknown to the Greeks.

114. Chimera of Arezzo. Bronze. Etruscan art, about 500–475 B.C.
Restored by Cellini.
Florence, Archaeological Museum.

The Roman art of the Republican period saw a slow infiltration of the Greek aesthetic into Etruscan models. This carried all before it in the last years of the Republic, when the Roman aristocracy were fired with enthusiasm for conquered Greece and vied with each other for originals or copies of the masterpieces of Greek art. Caesar began the great transformation of Rome into the imperial capital, by enriching it with great monuments: a forum, a theater, the Aemilia and Julia basilicas, the Curia Julia. What is called "Augustan" art emerged from a great Greco-Roman synthesis of political theory; for Augustus wanted to found a Roman classicism in both literature and art which would be worthy of its Hellenic example and which would become the typical culture of the Empire. The architect Vitruvius Pollio condensed the principles of this classicism in a treatise on architecture written between 25 and 23 B.C. Augustus had numerous monuments erected in Rome: the Forum, gates, the Theater of Marcellus, several temples including that of Mars the Avenger, and the Ara Pacis (pl. 120). This was the beginning of that great period of building which was to spread all over the Empire and bring to so many peoples the benefits of Roman government, peace and comfort. The burning of Rome in A.D. 64 enabled Nero—whether he was responsible for the disaster or not—to make the city more healthy and build himself an immense palace (the Golden House). In the first century of our era Vespasian founded the amphitheater later called the Colosseum, which was finished by Titus and had a story added by Domitian. The Antonine period was one of active building all over the Empire. Hadrian, thoroughly steeped in Greek culture, tried to perpetuate the images of the finest Hellenic works of architecture in his Villa at Tivoli (A.D. 127–134) and rebuilt the Pantheon (A.D. 115–125). His enormous Mausoleum was later incorporated in the Castle of Sant'Angelo. A further great fire in Rome in A.D. 191 enabled Septimus Severus and Caracalla to undertake among other things the Baths of Caracalla (A.D. 212–216), one of the masterpieces of Roman architecture. This activity continued until the fall of the Empire (Basilica of Constantine or Maxentius, A.D. 310–312). The whole of the Roman world was covered with monuments. Provence has some very fine ones dating from the first and second centuries (arch and theater at Orange, amphitheaters at Nîmes and Arles). Africa has ruins of fine buildings at Timgad, Sbeitla and El Djem, while on the confines of the Empire, Asiatic Baalbek was enriched with colossal monuments. As for Pompeii and Herculaneum, the two cities of the campagna which were buried by Vesuvius in A.D. 79 and rediscovered in the eighteenth century, they are a western offshoot of Hellenistic rather than of Roman art.

ARCHITECTURE

It was in the domain of architecture that the genius of the Romans found its most powerful expression. Prolonged peace, the wealth accruing from intense commercial activity, the public works commissioned by an administration anxious for the public welfare combined with the Roman taste for comfort, all created an enormous demand for building all over the Empire.

For religious undertakings the Romans drew inspiration from the Greek temples and from certain Etruscan traditions, showing a preference for the "Corinthian order." They also used the "Tuscan order" which was an Etruscan interpretation of the Greek Doric. They innovated especially in civil engineering, making buildings which were functionally perfect. The adoption of the arch facilitated the creation of new types of monuments called into being by the development of public ceremonies and social needs; the possibilities of spanning gaps with arches and vaults, which they made with remarkable skill and science, allowed them to make buildings with the immense roofed spaces required for holding large meetings. Abandoning the Greek manner of building with blocks of dressed but uncemented stone, they adopted a system of building in brick or rubble, having invented a cement of exceptional firmness. This base of brick or rubble they overlaid with marble facings, superimposing the Greek orders one on the other just as they wished, and giving no thought to relating decoration to structure as the Greeks had done. On their strong supports of brick or cement they set huge arches and vaults: domes, tunnel vaults and cross arches or groined vaults. All these principles seem to have come from Asia Minor, and a better knowledge of the Hellenistic cities would perhaps reduce the number of Roman inventions, most of them being of Greek origin.

For ceremonial purposes the Romans took from the Hellenistic culture the memorial column and triumphal arch with anything from one to three arcades (pl. 115). For public works they also took the *basilica* from the East; this was a building with a nave or a nave and

115. The Arch of Titus, erected about A.D. 81 in the Forum, Rome.

116. The Colosseum (elevation). Begun about A.D. 80.
After Guadet, Etudes sur le Colisée.

aisles, often ending in an apse, which they perfected and used as an exchange, a covered market or for the magistracy. The *forum* was a public place surrounded by arcades used for business purposes, and decorated with memorials and works of art. They took the theater from the Greeks, but transformed it by building it on open ground, the hemicycle being held and framed by tiers of arched galleries. By putting together two theaters they invented the amphitheater (pl. 116) which was built in an ellipse and used for circus performances. This is a masterpiece of practical planning. The circuses or *hippodromes* came from the Greek stadium: they were usually made of wood and have left few remains. The *thermae*, one of the Roman's monumental inventions, contained public baths, game rooms, all kinds of rooms used for the recreation of the body and the mind (promenades, gymnasiums, libraries, lecture rooms). Provided with a central-heating system of hot air which flowed under the floor and between the walls, the bathing places comprised a *caldarium* (room for hot baths), a *tepidarium* (a room heated with warm air to induce perspiration) and a *frigidarium* (for the cold bath). The ruins of the Baths of Caracalla in Rome, with their enormous arches, are the most grandiose of the Empire. Anxious also to supply their towns with abundant water, the Romans tapped springs at great distances away, conducting the water by means of enormous aqueducts

96

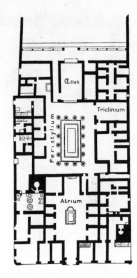

117. The peristyle of the Villa of the Vettii at Pompeii.

118. Plan of a Pompeiian house (Villa of Pansa).
After François Benoît, L'Architecture: Antiquité.

made of superimposed rows of arches to water towers in the city. Domestic architecture consisted of blocks of apartments as well as private villas. These latter combined the old Etruscan with the Greek form of house (pls. 117 and 118). Round a court or *atrium,* in the middle of which was an open tank or cistern (*impluvium*), were grouped the service quarters, the public rooms, the master's office or *tablinum;* then behind this part, which was of Etruscan origin, came the private quarters which were exactly the same as the Greek house, set round a garden fringed with columned arcades (peristyle, pl. 117).

The Romans had a splendid sense of monumental grandeur, as can be seen from their amphitheaters and aqueducts. They obtained excellent effects from a combination of straight lines, vertical or horizontal (columns and entablatures) and curved lines (arches and vaults). The great height of some of their structures did not favor the adoption of one particular "order" throughout; so Roman architects made it a rule to superimpose the three orders, the Doric, Ionian and Corinthian, one on the other. From the combination of the Ionic and Corinthian they made a fourth order, the *composite* (often called Roman). Except in religious monuments they usually omitted fluting from their columns, leaving them smooth. The shafts, instead of being set up in segments, were usually cut from a marble monolith. The Romans unfortunately

119. Decorative fresco from Boscoreale, near Pompeii.
New York, Metropolitan Museum.

120. Group of senators and priests. Detail of north frieze of the Ara Pacis
Augustae, Rome. Dedicated in the year 9 B.C.

indulged a taste for the picturesque which diminished the grandeur of their loveliest monuments, and only their later ruin, which stripped them of ornament, was to reveal their honesty and strength of structure.

They made a considerable use of polychromy in their building, combining marbles of different colors which were brought from all over Europe.

Generally speaking, they sought effects of luxury and strength, calculated to impress the mob's imagination; whereas Greek buildings, intended for a more cultured public, were primarily addressed to the intellect.

SCULPTURE, PAINTING AND THE LESSER ARTS

The interiors of Roman houses were covered with paintings representing decorative architectural themes (pl. 119) and arabesque, with panels showing scenes from mythology (pl. 100).

The Roman contribution to sculpture was less outstanding. They admired the Greek plastic achievement, but did little more than painfully copy it. Augustus' initiative resulted in the creation of an official style, nobly dignified, with conventional drapery effects and formal gestures (pl. 120). The practical Roman mind transformed the pathos of the

Hellenistic relief into a historical and narrative genre (*Arch of Titus; Trajan's Column*, pl. 121). Their most original creation was the portrait which, unlike the Greek portrait, reproduced the model without idealizing him, with an exact physical truthfulness (pl. 122): this was the revenge of the old indigenous stock over the Greek aesthetic. In the minor arts the Romans followed Hellenistic models, and made some fine bronze articles, of which many were found intact in the ruins of Pompeii and Herculaneum. Pottery, on the other hand, assumed a purely industrial character.

EASTERN RESISTANCE

Alexander had pushed the frontiers of the Greek world as far as the Indus. The dynasties which succeeded him in Iran and Mesopotamia carried on a superficial Hellenism which stifled native art. After the Seleucid kings, the Parthian Dynasty of the Arsacids, who described themselves on their coinage as "Phil-Hellenes," remained attached to Greek culture. But the revolution of the Sassanians (A.D. 227 to 641) represents a return to the national tradition of Achaemenian Aryanism, based on the restoration of the Mazdakite religion. The Sassanians,

121. Detail of Trajan's Column, Rome. Early first century.

122. Bust of Lucius Caecilius Jucundus, a Pompeiian banker. Bronze. About A.D. 50. *Naples, National Museum.*

123. Palace of Shapur I (A.D. 241–272)
at Ctesiphon, Persia. *An old view, after
Dieulafoy, L'Art antique de la Perse.*

124. Plan of the palace at Sarvistan.
Sassanian period. *After François Benoît,
L'Architecture: L'Orient médiéval et
modern*

conquering the Romans and Byzantines, drove Hellenic civilization
back to the coast, at the moment when they themselves were overcome
by the Moslems. Turning their back to the Mediterranean, they developed an art which was to be the basis of the invasions of the West by
the East in the form of Islamic and Byzantine art.

In the domain of building, the achievement of the Sassanians is
more or less parallel with that of the Romans, substituting for Greek
architecture with its columns and coursed lintels a system of massive
brickwork to serve as buttressing to take the thrust of arches. Inheriting

125. Detail of stucco low-relief from a Sassanid palace at Veramin, Persia. Mid-4th century. *Philadelphia Museum of Art.*

Mesopotamian building methods they perfected the science of constructing arches, barrel vaults and domes, using the latter with a daring unsurpassed even by the Romans (the great elliptical barrel vault at Ctesiphon is 84 feet 6 inches across, 123 feet 6 inches high, and 156 feet deep, pl. 123). They managed the transition from the square plan to the circular plan of the cupola by means of squinches thrown over the corners, or large curvilinear inverted triangles called *pendentives*, and contrived to set the vault strains one against the other. The plans of their palaces (at Ctesiphon; Sarvistan, pl. 124; Firuzabad; Taq-e-Eivan) tend to focus round a higher vault, an idea later adopted by the Byzantines. This vault crowns the throne room or *divan* which is open at one side, an arrangement which the Moslems followed. Inside, the masses of brick were covered with plates of painted stucco or enameled terra cotta in the Achaemenian manner: the Romans likewise covered their walls with inlaid decorations of this kind; but in their case it was used to hide the structural basis and was borrowed from the Greek "orders." The monotheistic religion, which had no idols, did not inspire the Sassanians to any great architectural undertakings as was the case in Persia.

Sculpture spread round the walls like a tapestry was a conception foreign to Greek plastics but was characteristic of the Assyrians and

126. Statue of the Parthian period found at Shami. *Teheran, National Museum.*

127. Sacrifice to the Palmyran gods.
From the temple at Dura-Europus in Syria (upper Euphrates). About A.D. 70.

Achaemenians. On the walls of palaces or ossuaries of Naqsh-i-Rustam, Taq-i-Bustan, warlike or hunting scenes were depicted in tiered rows comparable with the oldest notions of perspective (pl. 125). Although, under Greek influence, the relief was more vigorous than among the Assyrians or Persians, the frontal and profile positions inhibit the free expression of volume. Statuary was rare and anti-classical in spirit (pl. 126).

The Sassanians had a considerable influence over Islamic and Byzantine art, and even on Roman art, through their handicrafts (silverwork and textiles) which carried on the Mesopotamian tradition of zoomorphic imagery, whether naturalistic or fantastic, and it was through them that this fund of imagery, created by the Sumerians as long ago as the second millennium B.C., was passed on to the Middle Ages.

Recent researches are revealing in upper Mesopotamia, Syria and Palestine traces of monuments built by pagan communities, either Jews or pre-Islamic Arabs. These show, in the early centuries of our era, a widespread revolt against Hellenism. At Dura-Europus, in the upper Euphrates Valley, paintings were recently found in a temple dedicated about A.D. 70 to the Palmyran gods. These show already all the attributes of Byzantine hieratic art (pl. 127). The transition toward early Christian art is demonstrated at Dura-Europus itself, by the paintings of a synagogue and in a Christian chapel of the third century. In Egypt, during the Roman period, panels painted in wax or distemper now replaced the masks of mummies in the sepulchers of Fayum and in the region of Thebes. The evolution of these from the first century B.C. to A.D. 300 shows the progressive orientalization of the Hellenic type (pl. 582).

The spirit of the ancient East persisted in the castles, vaulted in the Sassanian manner and no doubt built by the first Omayyad Caliphs, which have been found in the Syrian desert. One of them, at Mchatta, had a great continuous frieze running round the lower part of the external walls, reproducing the Iranian theme of animals and birds sporting among sprigs of vine, of which the early Christians made a eucharistic symbol (pl. 236).

CHAPTER IV

EARLIEST FORMS OF CHRISTIAN ART

THE DECAY of the plastic arts of the Ancients, which shrank progressively under Oriental influence from A.D. 200 onward, is one of the most remarkable phenomena in the history of art.

For the first time in the history of world civilization, Greece had given pride of place to all that was *temporal* in human life: the lucid speculations of thinkers, even those of a Plato, projected the light of reason into the dark places of the soul, and the relationship between the soul and the beyond became a matter for pure dialectic and not an article of faith. Once man was delivered from his obsession with the deity, religion gave way to metaphysics.

The religions of the East, which at the end of the ancient world began their onslaught on paganism, reforged the chains of man's submission to God; but by means of initiation they offered the believer a form of participation which united him with the person of a redeeming God. It was by an intuitive and mystical knowledge, and no longer a rational form of it, that man was able to cross the gap separating the world of appearances from the Beyond. Of all the religions which were struggling between themselves to take over the Empire, Christianity, which triumphed, was the most spiritual: it submitted human destiny to a future life, as was the case with the ancient Egyptians, who had some influence on early Christianity.

The pure spirituality which Christianity had inherited from Judaism was to lead its first followers into an aversion to art, which had served the worship of idols only too readily. When the new religion broke new ground and attracted the pagan masses, it had to come to terms with the mind of the illiterate classes who needed images to guide their belief. Having allowed such imagery against its inclination, Christianity had to purge it of that physical emphasis which, ever since the Greeks, had made it a reflection of earthly things. If it was to be no longer an object of worship, but only a means to it, the image was none the less to play a part in the new faith very like the one it had held in the old religions of the East. It was an instrument of theology, the figurative intermediary on which faith leans in order to appreciate the dogma of which the image is only the garment and representation. While it was an intermediary shorn of that reality which had given it magical power in the ancient religions—though perhaps secretly the laymen never stopped believing in that magical property—the image was to enter a new phase by becoming a *symbol:* and art is a language which translates the truth of dogma into forms, *parlar visibile,* as Dante put it.

All that was foreign to the clear transcription of the symbol was eliminated. Landscape was replaced by a few guiding accessories. Some compositions were reduced to a few forms linked together like words in a statement, reminding us of hieroglyphs (pl. 128).

Images were now unreally suspended as though in flight, against an abstract golden background: the line of the horizon disappeared, together with the earth itself. Events no longer took place on earth or in the sky, but in the abstraction of an ideal universe. The various features in the composition no longer had the relative sizes that would be theirs in concrete reality, but their size was now determined by the idea behind them: as in the early Egyptian and Mesopotamian arts, the principal person in the composition towered over all the rest, who were grouped like dwarfs at his feet. The composition of landscape was

Abstract composition without ground line or horizon.
The elements of the setting are schematic, while the figures
are proportioned according to their rank in the moral hierarchy.

128. The Temptation of Christ. 12th-century mosaic in the Basilica of St. Mark, Venice.

The Sta. Maria Maggiore angel, seen in semi-profile, still
follows the classical canon, conceived spatially; the features
of the S. Vitale head are leveled down and are without volume.

129. Detail (reversed) of a Pompeiian fresco. Head of Achilles.
Naples, National Museum.

130. Detail from a mosaic (Abraham and the Three Angels). Angel's head.
Basilica of Sta. Maria Maggiore, Rome. A.D. 352–366.

131. Detail from a 6th-century mosaic (Theodora's Offering)
in the Basilica of S. Vitale, Ravenna. Head of one of Theodora's attendants.

treated with the same severity, a mountain becoming a mere mound of
sand, or a building no larger than a footstool (pl. 128). A purely moral
hierarchy replaced the material order of things.

This entirely spiritual interpretation of objects, according to which
temporal existence is a delusion and the only reality is in the timeless,
was to destroy the Greek plastic arts just as it destroyed the Greek
aesthetic itself. The Greeks must have seen everything from the corporeal point of view, and this gave all their creations, even in philosophy,
the sharp edges and the clarity of geometrical forms. Their essential
concern was the definition of objects and concepts in their proper
dimensions and limits, so we can understand why their plastic creations were as exactly circumscribed as solids in the three dimensions
of space, and why sculpture was for them the major art. The Christian
aesthetic was to abolish sculpture, reducing forms to an unreal flatness
of surface. The half profile, or three-quarter view so dear to the Greeks,
disappeared and gave place to frontality and to the profile (pls. 129
to 131). Modeling was flattened into calligraphy. The artist deliberately avoided any expression of movement, which would be guilty of

Byzantine art returned to the traditional Oriental composition, in which figures are shown in an endless series.

132. The Martyrs. Mosaic frieze in S. Apollinare Nuovo, Ravenna. 6th century.

imitating life. He fixed his figures in eternal attitudes and gave his compositions the strictest symmetry. The repetition of figures in endless series, so much liked by the ancient East (pls. 132 and 133), symbolizes that oneness to which the deceptive variety of appearances is reduced in eternity.

133. Frieze of Bowmen. Palace at Susa, Persia. Polychrome glazed relief. 5th century B.C. *Paris, Louvre.*

Typical composition showing figures one above the other. Their dimensions have no relation to reality: the man is larger than the elephant.

134. Adam in the Garden of Eden. Detail of an ivory diptych. 4th century. *Florence, Bargello.*

As the sense of volume died out, that of perspective, which the Greeks had intuitively discovered, also vanished, and early Christian art returned to the old mode of perspective used in primitive cultures: composition in superimposed layers or rows (pl. 134). To this was added radiating composition in which all the elements are arranged round a center (pl. 135). Applied to building methods this radial form gave rise to the central plan, which was an outcome of architectural

RADIATING COMPOSITION

135. The Last Supper. Miniature from a Syriac New Testament. 12th century. *London, British Museum.*

136. Christ, with Angels and Prophets. Mosaic, 12th century, in the Palatine Chapel of the Royal Palace, Palermo.

speculation among the Byzantines. On a centered monument the roundness of the cupolas reinforces the idea of gravitation round a given
point, and this became a striking symbol of monotheism (pl. 136).

The whole gamut of primitive conventions, now directed against
Greek art, replunged the Greco-Roman world into a type of vision
that it had left behind for eight centuries. The eye no longer saw things
in an order whose hierarchy was dictated by their true proportions in
reality. As in the primitive cultures, everything was now seen for its
own sake, in its essence, with the result that the details on a figure were
out of proportion, out of scale with the person, who was, so to speak,
"blazoned" or emblematized by the accessories of his clothing or equipment. The tendency toward series is to be found even in the stylization
of draperies and the handling of hair and beards as decorative motifs.
Such was the avoidance of the notion of space that very often the perspective was reversed, the figures in the middle ground being larger
than those in the foreground, while the lines of objects converged toward
the spectator and not toward the background (pl. 137). This aesthetic
system reflects a kind of thought which seeks to identify itself with
things in their entirety, by an intuitive sense like that of touch, whereas
the Greek vision set objects in a perspective comparable with that which
the analytic operations of reason impose on ideas.

*Example of reversed perspective: the table is elongated,
the small sides coming together in the foreground.*

137. Abraham and the Three Angels. Mosaic, A.D. 352–366.
Sta. Maria Maggiore, Rome.

This conception is so Oriental that the earliest Christian art produced in Rome still knew nothing of it. Without Byzantium it might have seemed that the classical plastic code was going to be changed only as regards meaning (pl. 130). Quickly developed in Byzantium in the fifth and sixth centuries, the new aesthetic quickly spread over the entire Mediterranean, then to the still barbarous peoples of the West: the poverty of these latter peoples as regards any artistic tradition made them welcome the Byzantine example only too greedily, without in the least understanding its lofty implications of dogma. For them, it was only a matter of being given a repertory of forms, which they used much as children repeat parrotlike the sounds of a foreign language. Obstinately hostile to the portrayal of the human figure, even in this conventional form, for several centuries they pursued the purely imaginative speculations they had inherited from their nomadic ancestors, seeing in Byzantine art no more than a vehicle of those Oriental forms which reminded them of their own origins; and all this at a time when Byzantium itself was undergoing a serious disturbance of conscience.

A survey of the Western World and the Mediterranean basin in the seventh and eighth centuries would show, indeed, such a complete regression from the Greek plastic arts that the human person and the figure in general tended to disappear from art entirely, being reduced to a purely ornamental expression. Islam, established on the southern and eastern fringes of the Mediterranean, imposed in those regions an outlook hostile to images, strictly observing the spirit of the Koran and opposed to the portrayal of anything human or living. In Byzantium a great movement—the iconoclastic crisis—which sprang partly from Islamic influence tended to forbid the worship of images as being idolatrous, and to suppress the figurative portrayal of holy personages. In the West, the impulse toward ornamentation thrived and encroached on even the few representations of sacred art that were attempted.

However, just when it might be expected that a kind of artistic puritanism was finally about to dominate the world, a simultaneous reaction in East and West restored form and shape to the figure. In the ninth century the Macedonian renaissance in Byzantium and the Carolingian renaissance in the West both aimed at redirecting art toward the spirit of the classical arts. Under this influence the Byzantine hankering after orientalism was profoundly shaken as it began to long for the harmonious rhythms of ancient Greece. As for Charlemagne, wrapped in his northern mists and far removed from the home of classicism, he received the classical influence only at second hand, by way of Byzantine art which was fortunate enough to thrive on the very soil on which the Ancients had labored.

The Macedonian and Carolingian revivals, both of them intellectual undertakings brought about by the heads of states, were purely formalistic in character. It is true that they created masterpieces, but a genuine revival cannot spring from such unspontaneous movements. In eleventh century France and thirteenth century Italy, the West, finally emerging from its protracted childhood, was to create a mode of expression as complete and as original as Greek art itself.

East and West: these three plans developed one from the other.

138. Plan of the Church of SS. Sergius and Bacchus at Constantinople. First third of 6th century. *After Lasteyrie.*

139. Plan of S. Vitale at Ravenna. Begun between A.D. 526 and 534, consecrated in 547. *After Holtzinger.*

140. Plan of the Palatine Chapel (Carolingian parts) at Aix-la-Chapelle. Late 8th century. *After Lasteyrie.*

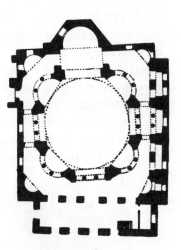

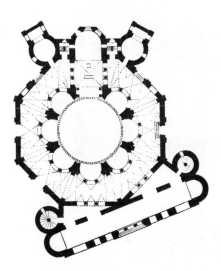

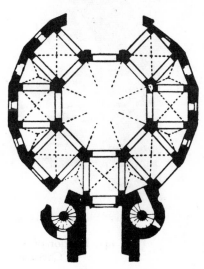

EARLY CHRISTIAN ART IN ROME
THE ART OF THE CATACOMBS

While in the East some figures, though still pagan, already contained elements of the aesthetic which was to triumph with Christianity, in the West the first Christian art was no more than the last phase of ancient art. The earliest images of the new cult are to be found in the catacombs, underground cemeteries made by the Christians during their secret life in the first three centuries of our era, down in the chalky subsoil of Rome. In the walls of long passages (*ambulacra*) which were practically subterranean towns, the sepulchers (*loculi*) were set in tiers, closed with stone slabs bearing the names of the dead. Occasionally a more imposing tomb cut in the shape of an arch (*arcosolium*) was the resting place of some notable or martyr, while clearings in the gallery containing *arcosolia* served as funeral chapels (*cubicula*, pl. 141). The chapels were often decorated with stucco or mural paintings, very fragile because they were executed straight on the unprepared wall, in the manner of the Egyptians or Etruscans. The dominant idea in these decorations was the future life to which the Christian soul was called after shedding its earthly trammels (of which the symbol was the figure of the *orante*, thanks to the redemption brought by Christ). Subjects taken from the

141. Interior of a catacomb: *Cubiculum* and *loculi*.
Christian. 4th century. Rome.

142. The Good Shepherd.
Mural painting in the Catacombs of S. Calixto in Rome.
3rd century. *After Wilpert, Roma sotterranea.*

Old and New Testaments were rare and without any historical significance, being used as apologetic evidence of divine mercy. For the most
part the Christians contented themselves with pagan legends and images
to which they gave a new meaning. Thus Aristaeus, the god of gardens,
with a lamb on his shoulders, became the Good Shepherd, a symbol of
Christ (pl. 142). The amorous shepherds and harvesters of the vine
found in the villas of Pompeii end their career by symbolizing Paradise
and the Eucharist, respectively. Orpheus charming the wild beasts pre-
figures Christ, while the pagan myth of Eros and Psyche becomes a
symbol of the trials undergone by the human soul before entering
heaven. Going even farther in their passion for cryptograms the
Christians, in order to portray Christ, his Passion and the Redemption,
created a whole system of picture puzzles—and no doubt the persecu-
tions had something to do with this esotericism. Findings in the catacombs also include funerary lamps, and gold-bottomed flasks in which
the blood of martyrs was kept. A fine bronze medallion of the second
century, buried in the Domitilla catacombs, shows the oldest portraits
of St. Peter and St. Paul, which set standard types for the Middle Ages.

ART AFTER THE TRIUMPH OF CHRISTIANITY

The early Christians had no interest in forms themselves and were
content with the models they borrowed from Hellenistic plastic conventions: all they cared about was the idea behind them. This state of affairs

continued until Christianity came out of hiding and became the official religion of the Roman Empire, when it celebrated its victory in an ostentatious way, for which reason the art of the Christian Empire may be called Triumphal art (from A.D. 313 to the fifth century).

The most noticeable result of this victory was the creation of an architecture to house the new religion. The inconvenience of the Greco-Roman temple as well as its idolatrous associations led the new cult to reject it as a possible form. The temple with its porticoes was conceived from the outside, being the house of God to which only priests could have access, whereas the church (*ecclesia*, meaning assembly) was a place for the meeting of all the faithful, who were called without distinction to participate in the Deity. Thus it had to enclose an immense space. The Christians found a ready-made form for this in the Ancients' repertory of architectural inventions—the *basilica*, a long rectangle with a nave and aisles, which used to serve as a meeting place, a tribunal or a closed market. To this they added only a transept or transverse nave, to give it the shape of the cross. The apse, containing a bench (*presbyterium*), was reserved for the priests. The altar was at the crossing of the transept, and the ceremonies took place in the main nave, the faithful standing, men to the left and women to the right in the single or sometimes double aisles, which at times had a gallery. The church was entered by a *narthex* in which the catechumens met, and a courtyard surrounded by four colonnades (the *atrium*), which was the origin of the cloister of the medieval monasteries. In the center of the atrium stood the *cantharus*, a fountain for ablutions which was the origin of our stoup for holy water (pl. 143).

The Roman basilica, like that of the Ancients, was timbered over, all but the apse which was vaulted with a semi-dome (half sphere). The pillars separating the nave from the aisles were surmounted by architraves, or more frequently arcades (pl. 144).

Symbolic of the Christian soul, which should be completely turned toward the inner life, the brick-built basilican church appeared from the outside as an unadorned structure. Inside, on the contrary, luxurious adornment was spread everywhere to give the faithful the impression of some supernatural place. The columns were of marble, the lower walls were covered with decorative mosaics in precious marble, to which were often added porphyry, mother-of-pearl, onyx and other rare materials. In the upper parts, above the arcades, on the triumphal arch

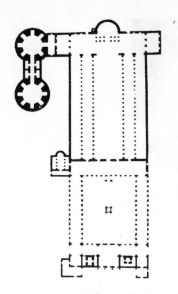

143. Ground plan of Constantine's basilica of St. Peter, Rome,
with the atrium and baptistery. *After a plan by Alfarano.*

144. Section of the old Constantine basilica of St. Peter, Rome.
After a fresco in the Vatican Grottoes of the 17th century.

separating the nave from the transept, and in the apse, were frescoes
of scintillating mosaics, showing the main figures in scenes from the
Testaments. The altar was surmounted by a canopy in worked gold
or marble (*ciborium*), while the choir was surrounded with an incrusted
marble screen (chancel) containing the *ambons*, or pulpits for the reading of the Epistle and Gospel.

The principal basilican churches still standing today are, in Rome,
San Paolo fuori le Mura, built in the fourth century and rebuilt after the
fire of 1823 (reconsecrated 1854); San Lorenzo fuori le Mura (fourth
to sixth century); San Giovanni in Laterano (fourth century, but much
restored); Santa Maria Maggiore (fourth–fifth century); Sant'Agnese
fuori le Mura (fourth–seventh century); Santa Sabina; Santa Maria in
Trastevere. The great five-naved basilica of St. Peter, Rome, built by
Constantine, was destroyed during the Renaissance, and is known to us
only from old illustrations.

NEW PLASTIC CONCEPTIONS

The plastics of Triumphal art is the same as that of the final period of
ancient art. The spirit of classical sculpture remained until the fourth
and fifth centuries in the *sarcophagi*, great works in marble, in which

145. Head of Christ. Sarcophagus of Junius Bassus, who died in 359. Marble. *Rome, St. Peter's.*

from the second century onward the pagans had themselves buried when the influence of oriental religions including Christianity replaced cremation by interment. The Roman sarchophagi were decorated with Christian scenes, vigorously carved in the round but gradually declining under Oriental influence, which was to triumph in the sixth century. The face of Christ was most often taken from the Greek adolescent type (pl. 145).

The real innovation of Triumphal art was the figured mosaic. Used in Hellenistic art in the form of pictures for adorning pavements, the mosaic, now set upon walls, showed a host of figures spread over a large surface. The oldest mosaics, vault of the circular aisle of Santa Constanza (after A.D. 337), were marble renderings of the symbolic ornamentation of the catacombs. Those in Santa Maria Maggiore (pls. 130 and 137) form the oldest cycle of evangelical and biblical pictures. They still have traces of the ancient aesthetic—figures shown in three-dimensional space, landscape backgrounds, Greek or Roman dress. But the perspective is already altered: the golden background had not appeared here any more than at Santa Pudenziana (fourth century) which is dominated by a bearded Christ based on the Jupiter type. The mosaics of the Mausoleum of Galla Placidia at Ravenna (fifth century) are still close to the spirit of antiquity and contrast sharply with those of Sant'Apollinare Nuovo and San Vitale, built in the sixth century at the moment when Ravenna was part of the Byzantine Empire and in the grip of the Oriental aesthetic.

BYZANTINE ART

It was in the East, in the great Hellenistic cities of Egypt, Asia Minor and Syria, that the Christian dogma and ritual were shaped before the Church had actually triumphed, as is proved by the abundance of Greek names in the new religion's vocabulary—Christ, Christian, angel, apostle, bishop (*episcopus*), priest, diocese, synod, church (*ecclesia*), baptism, eucharist. It was thus the Eastern empire that rose from the split in 395, which was to be the most active center of Christian art. Whereas the Western empire fell under the onslaughts of the barbarians, the Eastern empire survived until the fifteenth century. Byzantium (Constantinople), which Constantine founded in 327, was to be its center; but in the fourth, fifth and sixth centuries, before the Moorish invasions, Christian art flourished all round the Mediterranean fringe, in Antioch, Syria, Palestine—where splendid basilicas were built on the holy sites— and at Alexandria and Ephesus. Generally speaking, the coastal cities remained faithful the longest to the Hellenistic aesthetic, while under monkish influence the hinterland developed a more Oriental and primitive art which gradually affected the first type. This was the case in Syria and above all in upper Egypt, where the monks decorated their monasteries (Baouit) with frescoes and sculptures full of a primitive vigor already suggestive of Romanesque art (Coptic art, pl. 146).

146. Low-relief, sandstone. Coptic art from Egypt.
Probably 4th century. *Washington, Dumbarton Oaks.*

The period showing the widest extension of the Byzantine empire and its art was the sixth century, when Justinian retook Africa from the Berbers—setting up many basilicas there—and, in Italy, the Exarchate of Ravenna (rotunda of San Vitale, basilica of Sant'Apollinare Nuovo). In Byzantium itself Justinian built the churches of the Holy Apostles, Saints Sergius and Bacchus, and Santa Sophia.

After the conquest of part of the Mediterranean by the Arabs, Byzantine art had a phase which is called the iconoclastic crisis. A gust of puritanism, not unlike that of protestantism later, taxed the excessive image cult which was widespread in the fifth and sixth centuries with being idolatrous. In the seventh and eighth centuries perhaps under the aniconic (anti-image) influence of Islam, Byzantine art was reduced to the level of ornamental background. It was reborn in all its splendor from the ninth to eleventh century, with the Macedonian Dynasty. The finest monuments were in Greece (Daphne; St. Luke's, Phocis); but Byzantium reached into the West, toward Venice (St. Mark's, Venice; churches at Torcello) and, in the twelfth century, to Sicily (mosaics of Palermo, Cefalù, Monreale), and into the East as far as Russia (Santa Sophia at Kiev). In Armenia a prosperous Christian community continued building admirable churches in dressed stone; and monks from Cappadocia evolved a popular art, full of pathos, very different from official Byzantine. In the thirteenth and fourteenth centuries Byzantine art spread into Serbia and Bulgaria; its figurative designs were more economically carried out in paint. The finest specimens are in Greece, at Mistra (Peloponnesus), at Mount Athos and in the territory governed by the Serbian Tsars, in Macedonia and Serbia (Oratchanitsa, Studenitsa, Nagoricino; Sopoćani, pl. 151). Byzantine art endured until our own time in the icons of Russia, and in Crete and on Mount Athos.

ARCHITECTURE

Eastern Christian art in its early stages followed the basilical system, in the Greek churches (St. Demetrios, Salonica), Palestine (Bethlehem), as well as in Syria, Asia Minor (Anatolia), the region round Ravenna, and Africa (Tunisia). The churches there were all roofed with timber as were the Roman churches, though one or two in Anatolia had tunnel vaults. But the real creation of Byzantine architecture was the vaulted church, centrally planned. The central plan often consisted of a simple

147. Interior view of Sta. Sophia, Constantinople.

cupola set on a ring of archways and surrounded by an ambulatory (SS. Sergius and Bacchus at Constantinople, pl. 138; San Vitale at Ravenna, pl. 139; St. George of Izra', in Syria). Then, developing the principle of Sassanian buildings, the Byzantines elaborated complex plans in which the domes and tiered tunnel vaults buttressed each other and took the strain of a lofty central cupola. The centered plan was combined with the basilical plan of Santa Sophia at Constantinople, constructed between 532 and 537 by order of Justinian (pls. 147, 148). The architects were the Anatolians Anthemius of Tralles and Isidorus of Miletus.

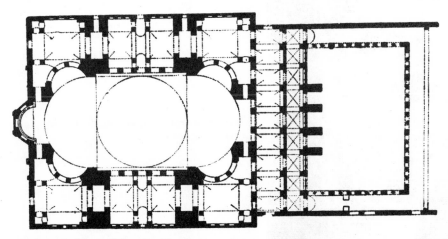

148. Plan of Sta. Sophia, Constantinople (532–537). *After Diehl.*

Ten thousand men worked on the building which is the most grandiose structure of Byzantine art: every province of the Empire sent its most precious materials for its decoration. A high cupola (reconstructed after collapsing, between 558 and 562) by Isidorus the Younger (nephew of Isidorus of Miletus) is 170 feet 6 inches high against a diameter of 100 feet. Its four pendentives rest on four great arches set on enormous pillars: at the north and south it is held by two tunnel vaults and is buttressed at the east and west by two huge semi-cupolas which in their turn rest on retaining recesses or niches. The building is contained in a rectangle of 250 feet by 233 feet. It has two galleries. These vast dimensions reflect a taste for the colossal, at once Roman and Asiatic, in keeping with Justinian's enormous empire. The Greek spirit predominates in the buildings of the Macedonian period, when, using moderate dimensions, architects sought harmony through a pleasing exactness of proportions. They then achieved the perfect central plan in the form of a Greek cross (that is, with all four limbs of equal length) in which four vaults (either barrel, semi-domes or cupolas) counterbalance the central dome (Santa Sophia at Kiev; St. Luke of Stiris at Phocis; various churches in Constantinople; St. Mark's, Venice; the Holy Apostles at Ani, Armenia). Sometimes the cupolas were set on a high drum or circular wall.

Except in Asia Minor and Armenia, where they built with ashlar or freestone, the Byzantine structure was made of enormous solid masses of brick carrying light domes of the same material. The use of

149. Byzantine capital in S. Vitale, Ravenna. 6th century.

freestone led Anatolia and above all Armenia, like later Romanesque art, to the idea of external decoration related to structural meaning, with niches, close buttresses, plain brick clamping against rough-cast walls; the Macedonian architects also gave thought to external plastic effects. But in the fifth and sixth centuries the Byzantine building showed only a naked structure from the outside. All the decoration was reserved for inside, where it was not built-in but applied on the walls by way of adornment in the form of marble facings and mosaics. The worshiper found himself plunged into a supernatural atmosphere by the vastness and lightness of the domes, which hardly seemed to touch their pendentives; and the luxury of the setting, the wealth of color effects, the glinting of the mosaics were all calculated to transport the worshiper into another world.

THE FIGURATIVE ARTS

From the sixth century onward sculpture shows the rapid reabsorption of a technique which had been the chief concern and the main experimental field of Greek art. Sculpture in the round disappeared entirely, and only a few capitals, marble balustrades and, at Ravenna, one or two sarcophagi were treated with the hand drill or bore, but no longer with the chisel. At the same time these features were only decorated with ornamental motifs, not worked in relief but laid on in imitation of the colored effects of mosaic. Deriving from the ancient composite column, the Byzantine capital evolved quickly until by the sixth century it was no more than a down-turned pyramid covered with open tracery (pl. 149). However, the art of relief survived in small articles made out of precious materials such as ivory and gold. Ivory craftsmanship in the fifth and sixth centuries shows a progressive flattening of Greek contours, the immobilizing of attitudes, the schematization of modeling, a tendency seen completely evolved in the *Throne of Archbishop Maximian* at Ravenna (sixth century), which came from Alexandria or Constantinople (pl. 150). In the Macedonian period a tentative renaissance of the plastic sense showed itself in ivories.

In the domain of figurative representation, the mosaic was the great art of the Byzantine period. By the unreality of its gold backgrounds and its glittering colors the mosaic gave the Byzantine artist an ideal medium for his desire to rid the spectator of every naturalistic illusion and suggest the very presence of the supernatural.

150. Detail of the ivory episcopal throne of Archbishop Maximian.
Christian art, Oriental type. 6th century.
Ravenna, Archbishop's Palace.

The great creations of San Vitale and Sant'Apollinare of Ravenna
in their totality show the full achievement of the new aesthetic. A spirit
of monarchical hieraticism inspires the mosaics of Justinian and Theodora
at San Vitale. As in the old Eastern monarchies the *basileus*, whose person is consubstantial with God, has his secular power by divine right,
and appears to his subjects surrounded by the superhuman attributes
of royal pomp. The heavenly court in Sant'Apollinare Nuovo shows
itself to the faithful in all the ceremonial trappings of the monarch's
own court. In the Ravenna mosaics the Oriental aesthetic had overcome the Grecian: the unmodeled forms are flattened into the abstract
surface of the gold background; the manifold gestures of life are frozen
into a few solemn attitudes, nothing remains of the natural figures but
a few stylized outlines; the three-quarter view is replaced exclusively
by frontal and profile positions; while the deliberate repetition of
gestures and attitudes, the frieze arrangements recalling the enameled
ceramic friezes of the Achaemenians (pls. 132, 133) and the taste for
rigorously symmetrical compositions suggest in the spectator's mind a
return of all the forms in the creation to some eternal unity (pl. 136).
The landscape disappears and a few small accessories serve to suggest
the location of whatever scene is represented. When the art of mosaic
revived in the ninth century, the apologetic spirit following the iconoclastic crisis imposed a strict iconographic order on the distribution of
images on church walls. The major works at Kiev (eleventh century),

151. The Dormition of the Virgin. 13th-century fresco
in Sopoćani Monastery, Yugoslavia.

in Greece (Daphne, St. Luke of Stiris, Phocis, end of eleventh century),
Italy (St. Mark's, Venice, end of eleventh century), Sicily (Palermo,
Cefalù, Monreale, twelfth century) show biblical scenes arranged
according to the liturgy and surmounted by the colossal, awesome
figure of the *Pantocrator* (Almighty) who is set in the central dome
at, so to speak, the umbilical point of the church, and with something
of the ancient gods in the gravity of his brow (pl. 136). The Oriental
conception of superhuman divinity has triumphed here over that of the
Greek god, represented on a human scale, which survived in Triumphal
art (pl. 145). The gospel and biblical scenes are emptied of historical
content and have only a symbolic and liturgical meaning. In the
Passion, Christ is always portrayed indifferent to pain and insult. The
modeling, drawing and arabesque tend to a formal perfection that was
to be recaptured by Cimabue in the Trecento (pl. 175).

The more popular art of the fresco—a cheap substitute for the
mosaic—shows different characteristics. The monks who decorated the
cave churches of Cappadocia (Asia Minor) from the ninth to the thirteenth century were the first to try to express the human pathos of the
gospel. This they did with a naïve violence. Strengthened by Western
influences this outlook spread to the Greek painting of Mistra in the
fourteenth century as well as to churches in Serbia, Rumania and Bulgaria. The best school of fresco painters was in Yugoslavia (Sopoćani
frescoes, thirteenth century, pl. 151).

152. Crucifixion. Miniature from the Third Gospel
by the monk Rabula. Syriac illuminated manuscript, about 586.
Florence, Laurentian Library.
153. King David. Miniature from the Paris Psalter. 9th century.
Paris, Bibliothèque Nationale.

The various tendencies to be found in Byzantine art are also reflected in the miniature, the art of book illustration which began in Egypt in the Hellenistic period. The Alexandrian taste for the picturesque persisted there for a long time, thanks to the system of copying prototypes (*Homer* and *Virgil* of the Vatican, fourth century; the *Vienna Genesis*, fifth century; *Joshua's Scroll*, sixth century). It took on a new lease of life in the Macedonian period, in the *Theriaca* (a treatise of medicine) of Nicander (eleventh century, Bibliothèque Nationale) and the *Paris Psalter* (ninth century, same library, pl. 153), which astonish us with images that would appear to be contemporary with the frescoes of Pompeii. Side by side with this aristocratic group, a monastic group shows a more religious and more Oriental spirit: this tradition originated in Syriac monasteries in the sixth and seventh centuries, heralding the pathos of the Cappadocian frescoes (*Rabula Gospels*, Florence, pl. 152).

THE MINOR ARTS

The Oriental taste for luxury appeared in Byzantium in works of handicraft made all over the empire for both local use and export; for the peoples of the West, not yet skilled as craftsmen, readily gave high prices for them. Thus the treasuries of the Western churches have preserved large numbers of ivories, textiles, carved gems and goldsmiths' work. In the sixth century Syria specialized in the production of large, embossed (repoussé) silverware of ancient derivation, while Byzantium exploited the process of cloisonné enameling. The finest ensemble of Byzantine craftsmanship in gold is the *Pala d'Oro*, the altar of St. Mark's in Venice (pl. 154) which is lavishly worked with gold, gems, pearls and enamels. The fabrics woven in Coptic Egypt and in Syria, then in Constantinople after the Arab conquest, often took their inspiration from old Persian and Sassanian patterns and served as a means for making Oriental designs known in the West.

WESTERN ART IN THE EARLY MIDDLE AGES
PRE-CAROLINGIAN

The artistic tradition of the Barbarians who settled in the West in the fourth and fifth centuries had given them little preparation for the complex works of a permanent civilization. Having been accustomed for thousands of years to the few tasks compatible with their nomadic existence (fabrics, articles of finery and equipment) they were now faced with architectural and iconographical needs for which they had to invent everything themselves.

Tribes of the Goths, the most gifted of the barbarian peoples, founded states in Spain (Visigoths) and in Italy (Ostrogoths). They learned all they could from Rome and Byzantium. The Franks, who

154. Pantocrator. Detail of the Pala d'Oro. End of 11th and beginning of 12th century. *Venice, St. Mark's.*

Celtic coins before Caesar had an ornamental tendency.
The Roman invasion introduced a figurative plastic sense.

155. Coin of the Tectosage Volcae (Gaul). Silver. *Paris, Bibliothèque Nationale.*
156. Elusate (from Eauze, France) silver coin. *Paris, Bibliothèque Nationale.*

settled in Gaul, and the Lombards in northern Italy, imbibed Oriental traditions through the Greek monks and the Syrian and Jewish merchants who brought them Byzantine and Sassanian merchandise which delighted their luxurious tastes. The influx of these Asiatic peoples revived the ornamental and abstract tendencies which had found expression in Celtic art before being discouraged by the Roman conquest.

Any study of early Western art should begin with the minor arts, whose aesthetic dominated even architecture to such a degree that sometimes the coursing of walls imitated the patterns of the weaver

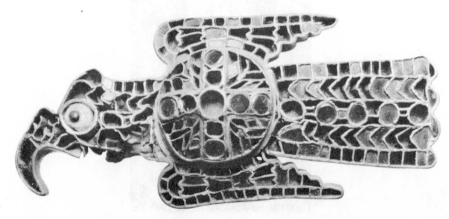

157. Buckle of gold and garnets, in the form of an eagle.
From Cesena, Italy. 6th century. *Paris, Private Collection.*

or the silversmith (pl. 158). The Goths and Franks were to maintain
that technique of cloisonné work in gold which was their specialty
(pl. 157), both in lay works (*crowns of the Visigoth kings*, found at
Guarrazar near Toledo) and by adapting it to religious needs (shrines
and reliquaries). We know from descriptions written at the time that
churches were richly decorated with costly works of this kind.

A supremely monastic art, *illumination,* was brought to Gaul by
monks from Egypt. The monks used it for embellishing holy books
(such as missals and gospels) with a pure decorative impulse which
disdained mere realism. The chimerical imagination of the Barbarians
suggested fantastic forms to them, which they intermingled in a sort
of indecipherable ornamental pattern that we call tracery. It was in
the work of Irish and English monks in the seventh and eighth centuries that this ornamental medium took the most remarkable forms,
in which Celtic, Saxon and Mediterranean influences came together.
The oldest of these works, the *Book of Durrow* (second half of
seventh century, Trinity College, Dublin, pl. 650), has an obvious
relationship to the magnificent trinkets found in the graves of Anglo-
Saxon chiefs (treasure-trove of Sutton Hoo, about 650, pl. 55). Mediterranean influence is seen in the *Book of Lindisfarne* (between 698 and
721, British Museum), while the admirable *Book of Kells* (eighth
or ninth century, pl. 159) shows—at least in the miniatures using the
human figure—the influence of such Byzantine works as the *Rabula
Gospels* (pl. 152) or *Etchmiadzin Gospels.* The *Lichfield Gospel*
(eighth century, Lichfield Cathedral) is in a similar style to the *Book*

158. Decorative coursing. Church at Selommes. 10th century.

159. Page from the Book of Kells. Anglo-Irish art,
8th or 9th century. *Dublin, Trinity College.*

of Kells. The *St. Gall Gospel* (between 750 and 760, Stiftsbibliothek,
St. Gall, Switzerland) is considered to be a purely Irish example of a
style in which the human figure itself became no more than a part of
a rhythmic pattern.

Fourth century Gaul had a period of building activity which
resulted in basilicas of the Roman type, decorated with rich mosaics.
The mosaics gave way to frescoes after the barbarian invasions of the
fifth century. An offshoot of Roman Triumphal art, this form still
flourished in the fifth century, to judge from the rotunda-style *bap-
tisteries* which were used for baptism by immersion, and of which a
number of specimens survive in Provence (Marseille, Fréjus, Aix, Riez,
Mélas, Valence). At Ravenna in Italy, Amalasonte built a domed
rotunda (after 530) on the tomb of his father Theodoric, king of the
Ostrogoths. This cupola is a monolith, 35 feet 9 inches in diameter and
weighing 300 tons, the last example in the West of that taste for materials of colossal dimensions which we noted in the most primitive civilizations. The Visigoth art of Spain, whose capital was then Toledo, has
left few remains (San Miguel de Tarrasa), but some characteristics of
this art appear to have persisted in the monuments raised by the Christian kings of the Asturias in the ninth century, which also show some

Oriental influence (Santullano, San Miguel de Liño, Santa Cristina de Lena, Santa María de Naranço).

The narrative sarcophagi of Arles, imitated from the Roman in the fourth century, show the last traces of ancient plastic traditions in Gaul, but in a profoundly debased form. Figurative sculpture disappeared in the fifth century. The workshops of the Pyrenees continued to produce columns, capitals, sarcophagi, marble plaques for chancels, but all in an exclusively ornamental style. These products of the Pyrenees quarries were exported to northern Gaul (crypt at Jouarre), especially in the seventh century, when there seems to have been considerable artistic activity; but this industry was killed by the Moslem invasions which ravaged the whole of southern France in the early eighth century. Sculpture in the round tended to disappear all over the barbarian area, being replaced by carved paneling in stone which often imitated the goldsmiths' cloisonné work (Cividale altars in Lombardy, pl. 160).

CAROLINGIAN AND OTTONIAN ART

The Carolingian reformation showed the same characteristics in art as in politics and literature. It tried to react against the anarchy of the Barbarians by a return to the traditions of the Roman Empire. It was

160. Tetramorph. Altar frontal of the Patriarch Sicuald (762–786?).
Stone. Cividale del Friuli, Italy.
After Julius Baum, La sculpture figurale en Europe.

in Classical and Byzantine Italy that Charlemagne sought his models for a revival of figurative and monumental art. The Palatine Chapel at Aix-la-Chapelle (Aachen) was only a simplified edition of San Vitale at Ravenna, but enriched with ancient materials taken from Italy (pl. 140). The Carolingian artists eagerly adopted plans for buildings on the principle of the Greek cross (church of Germigny-des-Prés near Orléans) and they made great use of the double-basilica plan (with two apses and two transepts). The influence of the monks, who were the guardians of the literatures of antiquity and of the principles of civilization, now dominated everything. Monasteries were built all over the Empire, and the "ideal" plan preserved at the St. Gall Abbey in Switzerland shows us, fully formed, the typical medieval layout: monastery buildings set round a cloister flanking a church, complete with agricultural, industrial, hospital and teaching accommodation, all giving a good idea of the part that monks were playing in both material and spiritual civilization.

Carolingian art reacted violently against the formlessness of the Barbarians and introduced representation once more. It was often nearer to ancient than to Byzantine art, as can be seen from the frescoes

161. St. Matthew. Miniature from the Gospels illuminated between 816 and 835 at Hautvillers Abbey for Archbishop Ebbo. *Epernay, Library.*

162. Christ. Miniature from the Gospels illuminated between 781 and 783 for Charlemagne by Godescalc. *Paris, Bibliothèque Nationale.*

163. Detail of the Golden Altar. By the goldsmith Vuolvinio,
late 9th century. *Milan, S. Ambrogio.*

in the crypt of St.-Germain at Auxerre, or those in Santa Maria
Antiqua at Castelseprio, rediscovered in Lombardy in 1944. Monastic
schools of illumination flourished all over the Empire (at Reims,
Tours, Metz, in France; at Reichenau, St. Gall, Fulda, in Germanic
countries). The schools of the East were distinguishable by a romantic,
roughish style heralding German Gothic expressionism (*Utrecht
Psalter; Ebbo Gospel*, pl. 161; both illuminated at Reims), while the
Tours school (*Bible of Charles the Bald*) or the so-called Palace school,
which illuminated gospels for the emperors, sought solemnity of gesture
and composition (*Godescalc's Gospel* illuminated for Charlemagne,
pl. 162; also the *Gospel of St. Médard*, Soissons).

We know from old descriptions that the churches were embellished with magnificent bronze objects (so-called *Chair of Dagobert*),
but little trace has remained of them. Gold craftsmanship is better
represented, these objects sometimes attaining a splendor which was not
to be improved on in the Middle Ages (*Charlemagne's Treasure* at Aix-
la-Chapelle). The Carolingian artists were able to revive the ancient
craft of glyptics, the carving of gems. A renewed feeling for relief
came out in ivory carving (ivory bindings for gospels) and through the
embossed work that was done in gold (*Golden Altar*, Sant'Ambrogio,
Milan, pl. 163).

The Carolingian impulse was checked in Gaul by the anarchy brought about through the Norman invasions in the eleventh century. Meanwhile in Italy and above all in Germany under the prosperous Ottonian Dynasty, Carolingian principles persisted into the eleventh century. The schools at Trier and Reichenau produced splendid painted manuscripts of entirely Imperial inspiration. While France could now produce nothing better than shapeless reliefs, the plastic sense in Germany expressed itself wonderfully in the eleventh century in the medium of embossed and cast metals (*Golden Altar*, Basel, now in Cluny Museum). Bishop Bernward had two pillars, a chandelier and bronze doors of fine quality made for his cathedral at Hildesheim (pl. 164), and a little later, in about 1060, the craftsman who cast the doors of Augsburg Cathedral, with mythological and biblical scenes, gave them an Alexandrian grace.

164. Adam and Eve expelled from Paradise.
Detail of a bronze door of Hildesheim Cathedral.

CHAPTER V

THE RISE OF THE WEST—ROMANESQUE AND GOTHIC ART

IF ANY CENTURY in Western civilization deserves the name Renaissance, then it is the French eleventh century rather than the Italian fifteenth. From the sixth to the tenth century nothing had appeared in the West worth calling a style (we speak of Merovingian or Carolingian *art*, not *style*). Planting themselves as best they could on the remains of the ancient civilization they had destroyed, and asking Byzantium for lessons which they hardly understood, the Barbarians from the sixth to the tenth century never abandoned the tedious ornamental crafts they brought with them from their nomadic past, but failed to fetch from their own darkness that coherent system of constructional methods, architectural, plastic and decorative forms that make a style. But suddenly the veil was torn aside. Architecture in the eleventh century made marvelous strides, a sure sign of a return to building cities. From the basilican church, a building with the unfinished look of a framework covered with temporary roofing, emerged the Romanesque church whose vault, dominating the whole economy of the structure, ensured the unification of all its parts. The monument was no longer a mere inorganic set of walls and roofs providing the necessary closed and covered areas. Like the Greek temple the Romanesque church was an articulated organism, all its parts being unified in their functions and proportions. The bay became the standard measurement for length, the story for height, bringing new basic units to architectural composition to replace the column and entablature in Greek art. Rhythmed by its tall shafts, its groined vaults, and the molding of string courses marking the galleries—the entire movement obeys a harmonious regulation of spaces, volumes and surfaces. Leisurely moving from support to archway and from story to story, the eye impresses on the mind the perfect unity of all the building's constituent parts, which are given, as it were, a musical measure by the alternating downward beats of the built-in parts and the upward beats of the open spaces. This constructional arithmetic, which the Greeks had understood intellectually, empirically, and in another mode, was reinvented by the Romanesque artists, who are to be thanked for imposing this notion of

165. Carved pillar in Ste.-Marie, Souillac. 12th century.

order and number on the taste for the indefinite and boundless which the Barbarians and the East had in common. After a long eclipse the West emerged victorious from an uneasy struggle for logic which had lasted six hundred years.

All the characteristics of Romanesque art stem from this notion of order. The decoration which had been scattered here and there like tapestry on the walls of Byzantine churches was now confined to the major parts of the building, and to emphasize them it was raised into relief, so that a forgotten technique was now revived: that of sculpture in which the ancient world had expressed its faith in the life of the body. Sculpture is the daughter of architecture, arising from its needs and sharing its spirit. By the powerful articulation of its volumes the Romanesque monument was, so to speak, modeled spatially.

Whether it aims at grandeur or harmony—except in the province of Poitou, where it lapsed into the picturesque—Romanesque architecture was always sober and restrained in composition. In the few parts yielded to it by the architecture, sculpture, constrained by its narrow frame, wreathes and writhes with a delirious energy. The seductiveness of Romanesque sculpture is due to an analytic view of nature before it was frozen into canons, fixed expressions and attitudes: it is a surge of forms elbowing each other, merging one into the other on arch moldings, pilasters, spandrels and piers (pl. 165). Everything from the very beginnings of mankind came together to enrich this marvelous language in stone: pagan myths and Christian scenes, fragments of antiquity, barbarous ornament, Byzantine, Sassanian, Assyrian and even Sumerian forms, for the old animal symbolism of the cylinder seals of Sumeria and Elam found its final transformation here (pls. 166, 167). Thus Western man, as he began creating once again after six centuries, began by remembering; but he used all the forms that he remembered from the depths of the past as though they were words, creating a new language with them which he spoke with a wonderful oratorical ease. What we have called monsters, those composite creatures which the artist invents out of bits and pieces taken from all the civilizations of the world and to which man himself indulgently lent his own body, did not need to be explained away by St. Bernard as having little or no intellectual content. Unlike Byzantine art, Romanesque had no very deep religious bearing, and when the glow of inner life shines through the faces on Chartres Cathedral or at Saint-Loup-de-Naud, that is because the Gothic genius was wakening there already. This fabulous bestiary is a sign of an orgiastic desire to create forms, gripping man's imagination when it was unleashed after six hundred years of abstinence. In behaving thus the Romanesque architect was spendthrift of his inheritance: freed from the pressure of centuries and millenniums the Gothic image maker was able to see nature with fresh eyes and a virginal imagination.

"Virginal" is the term we are tempted to apply to Gothic art. For it is pure creativity. Everything here is new, structure and setting,

166, 167. Diagram of an Assyrian seal (*left*), compared with a detail from a capital in the Church of St.-Martin d'Ainay, Lyons. *After Baltrušaïtis, Art sumérien, art roman.*

The Law of the Frame

Portrayed on a lintel, a tympanum, or a capital, the same theme finds a different composition in order to comply with the architectural frame.

168. The Feast at Simon's. Low-relief from a lintel. Neuilly-en-Donjon. 12th century.

169. The Last Supper. Capital. Issoire. 12th century.

170. The Last Supper. Low-relief on a tympanum. Charlieu. 12th century.

decoration, inspiration, plasticity. With Greek art, Gothic is the only example in Western civilization of a complete renewal of formal vocabulary through the complete invention of a style. Rome profited from Greece; Byzantium issued from Rome and from the East; while Romanesque art was a quadroon product of the East, Byzantium, the barbarian and the antique; Renaissance art and that of modern times borrowed from antiquity its entire architectural and decorative morphology and a great part of its idea of beauty. Gothic art on the contrary shook off the burden of well-worn forms which cramped the urge of Romanesque art, and started off from nature. The creative impulse of that admirable twelfth century must have been extraordinarily powerful to inspire such courage in the Gothic artist, filling him with the will to start from scratch at the very moment when all over France Romanesque art was only beginning to flower.

Romanesque art was already a century old and its maturity had hardly lasted thirty years when the will to create that gave us Gothic art began to stir in the Ile-de-France. The first Gothic cathedrals were erected in competition with the finishing or even the beginning of the great Romanesque abbey churches in other provinces, so that critics have jokingly remarked that Gothic art was nothing more than Ile-de-France Romanesque.

The discovery of a new vault, or rather the rational analysis of its properties, allowed Gothic architecture to achieve that Christian dream which the Byzantine artist had only been able to satisfy by a sort of mirage. Overcoming its weight, the edifice was to soar light and airy, triumphing over matter. The Cathedral is a vertical flight, just as the Greek temple and the Romanesque church are horizontal in movement. The Romanesque inertia of the surfaces gave way to the vibration of shafts, fenestration, and stained glass windows which causes an interplay of lights in a variety of modes comparable with the tones of instruments in an orchestra. The Cathedral is the realization in stone of that symphonic utterance which Germany was to express in pure sound seven hundred years later. In this sense it is the first mature manifestation of the lyrical gift of the North; but in order to take shape it needed the awakening of specifically French genius which was heir to the plastic imagination and the rationalism of the Mediterranean. The Cathedral certainly embodies a desire for growth and expansion which causes it to develop organically like a living thing, but it also obeys certain inflect-

*The humanization of the Holy face. In one century the
hieratic expression of the divinity became "The Human God."*

171. Majestic head of Christ. From tympanum of the narthex door.
Church of the Madeleine, Vézelay. About 1130.

172. Head of a Prophet. About 1160. *Senlis (Oise), Museum.*

173. Head of Christ preaching.
From the south porch, Chartres Cathedral. Before 1240.

ing rhythms, and this development was achieved through a reasoning
which, by deduction, exploited a principle to its utmost limits. It was
the first appearance of that French logic which later had a sterilizing
effect when applied to pure speculation: but here it was marvelously
fertile because it was acting on nature itself after having brushed aside
everything that went before—just as Cartesian reasoning was to do later
in philosophy. Reason governs the Gothic like a queen, not merely
creating a system but bringing forth a world; for the Cathedral is a
manifold world like the universe itself, in which a host of images have
their being.

The Western sense of imagery came to life—or to a second life—in
Gothic art. If, as Monsieur Emile Mâle has shown, it is true that the
image still subserved the idea, it refused to be its slave and lent rather
than gave itself. Rejecting the yoke of the Byzantine symbol, the image
was no longer a simplified ideogram, but on the contrary it sought to
embody some concrete form already in nature. Thirteenth century
France restored Mediterranean anthropomorphism and realism to the
West, after it had been temporarily supplanted by Eastern ideomorphism
(pls. 171 to 173). This wonderful evolution, which in its progress
takes us from the majestic portals of Chartres to that of Reims, went

through the same phases as Greek sculpture from the sixth to the fifth century B.C. Moreover, from the twelfth century to Claus Sluter, Gothic plastic art followed the same lines as Greek art, from the *korai* of the Acropolis to the Laocoön: there could be no better proof of the constants that are to be found in the life of forms as well as in the progress of the Western mind (pls. 637 to 647).

The architectural and plastic formulas invented by the Ile-de-France were quickly recognized everywhere, for the logical always imposes itself as obvious. So Europe spoke Gothic as the Mediterranean had spoken Greek. But not all Europe: for Italy refused to absorb the Gothic. After 1250 Italy was working out her own renaissance without heeding the example of France, and in a different way—not through a revolution but through a renewal of traditions, an involution. Nicola Pisano and Giotto went direct to antiquity for the new inspiration which led them to a sense of nature and of man. At Siena even Byzantine art,

Cimabue, in Italy, was not only an innovator; he was also the last representative of Byzantine formalism in all its perfection.

174. Byzantine art. Second half of 9th century. Head of Christ. Detail of mosaic from the narthex of Sta. Sophia, Constantinople.

175. Cimabue. Head of Christ. Detail of a panel. *Washington, National Gallery of Art.*

with Duccio, was to have its austerity melted into feeling and tenderness. But the overwhelming tyranny of Gothic art came to check this impulse. For a hundred years Italian art was oppressed as though by a foreign occupation. We can understand why the angry men of the Renaissance, in the fourteenth century, denounced that art as "Teutonic," a name which was to stick. The Gothic principle acted on the Italian mind like a virus, and when Florence at last shook free at the beginning of the fifteenth century, Italian artists had to start from where they had left off in the thirteenth: Donatello's direct precursor was Nicola Pisano; while the innovator Masaccio had, so to speak, to stir the ashes of Giotto.

ROMANESQUE ART

Romanesque art was born in France in the second quarter of the eleventh century. Its name was given to it in 1823 by de Gerville, by analogy with the Romance languages. By 1100 it had emerged from the experimental stage, having already created great buildings, and in the twelfth century it went through a striking development which was reflected in many local variations. It gradually died out as it was ousted by the Gothic style toward the end of the twelfth century. It affected all the countries that had not come under Byzantine influence; but France, Spain and England produced its most characteristic forms. In Italy,

176. The Keep at Loches (Indre-et-Loire). 12th century.

where apart from some French influence it was little more than a continuation of primitive Christian art, it was known as "Neo-Latin," while in Germany the Rhenish school was the outcome of Carolingian and Ottonian art.

FRANCE

ARCHITECTURE

In the eleventh century the demand for works of architecture became heavy, reflecting the changes that were going on in politics and trade. The few civic buildings in stone that have survived are municipal monuments and castles. The latter consist mainly of a large tower or keep, raised on a mound serving as a redoubt or for living in, and surrounded by a wall or *enceinte* (pl. 176). The finest churches were those of the monasteries, for the Romanesque period was the golden age of monasticism. The monastic communities of Cluny and Cîteaux, both in Burgundy, played a fundamental part in the politics and society of the age—a part which quickly became international.

Although it did not entirely ignore the central plan, Romanesque art gave all its energy to developing the basilican plan. In order to meet the new needs of the faith, the church was considerably extended at the east end: to the rounded apse they added a straight part (the choir or chancel, pl. 177) and stepped-up chapels (as in the Benedictine plan, pl. 178) or chapels lined along the transept (Cistercian plan). In some of the largest and most beautiful constructions, Romanesque art laid down the definitive form for Western churches, by prolonging the side aisle of the choir all round the apse (ambulatory) and by radiating the chapels (apsidial chapels) round this ambulatory (pl. 179). The Western church in the Middle Ages was thus a harmonious combination of the basilican plan with the radiating plan.

Like the Byzantine church, the Romanesque church had its sections vaulted over. All its characteristics spring from this form of covering. Domes were sometimes used at the crossing of the transept and otherwise only on the naves, in a group of southwestern churches (school of Aquitaine: St.-Front, Périgueux, pl. 180); groined vaults are usually found only on the side aisles (pl. 181). The longitudinal plan led to the natural use of the barrel or tunnel vault (pl. 188); and as this exerts a continuous pressure all along the shafts, in order to take their

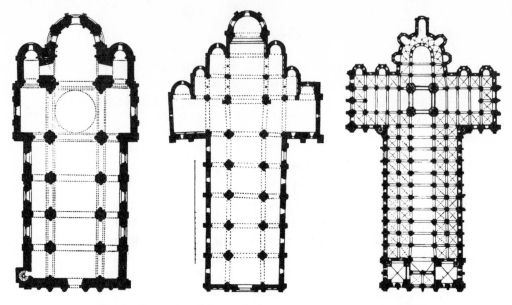

In the Romanesque period, the basilican plan was developed at
the choir *or chancel to allow the insertion of numerous chapels.*

177. Ground plan of the church of the abbey at Cellefrouin.
12th century. *After Lasteyrie.*

178. Ground plan of the church of the abbey at Châteaumeillant. 12th century.
"Benedictine" type of plan, with stepped-up chapels. *After G. Darcy.*

179. Ground plan, with ambulatory, of the abbey church of St.-Sernin,
Toulouse. 12th century. *After Baum.*

180. Interior of the Cathedral of St.-Front, Périgueux (Dordogne). 12th century.
181. Side aisle of the Church of the Madeleine, Vézelay (Yonne). 12th century.

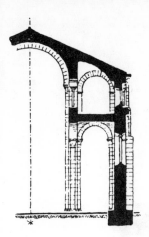

182. Vertical section, St.-Paul, Issoire (Puy-de-Dôme).
12th century. *After Hartmann, Die Baukunst.*
183. Archivolt of porch of church at Audrieu (Calvados). 12th century.

thrust the architect had to use massive piers, and thick walls pierced with narrow windows. The strain of the vault in the high nave, in the best-planned buildings, was taken by raising the side aisle vaults almost to the same height as the central nave, thus blinding it as in the Poitou churches. Sometimes when the nave was very high this burden was borne by galleries over the aisles (Auvergne school, so-called Pilgrimage churches). The purpose of these gallery vaults was perfectly served by basing them on the quadrant (pl. 182). The arches and vaults were generally semicircular, though some schools used the pointed arch.

Byzantine architecture sought broad stretches of surface: in the basilican church the arcades made an unbroken series and nothing intervened to disturb the mural surfaces either inside or outside. The Romanesque church on the contrary, like the Greek temple, tended to knit independent elements which, taken together, result in the total edifice. These elements are the bay on the horizontal plane and the story on the vertical. The bays were separated by the use of shafts which, applied externally to the pillars, rise up into the vault and are usually prolonged under or along the vault surface as far as the opposite bay by thinner supporting arches called arch bands. The columns allow the eye to measure the edifice longitudinally, whereas molded string courses mark the story divisions in the elevation, constituting main horizontal lines which create a perspective effect (pl. 188).

On Roman, basilican or Byzantine monuments, the decoration was no more than an adornment stuck on the walls with no relation to the structure. The Romanesque architect, always after logic, achieved a

184. Apsidal view, Paray-le-Monial (Saône-et-Loire). 12th century.

close co-ordination of decoration with structure, to which end he rein-
troduced molding (pl. 183)—a kind of geometrical sculpture that had
become stunted in Byzantine art but which Greek art had recognized as
useful—in order to stress the main parts of the building. The Romanesque builders liked effects of strength as well as harmony, but occasionally they were tempted by the picturesque, as at Poitou and Sain-
tonge, where they overburdened their façades with carvings. They had
an admirable feeling for the composition of monumental masses by the
forward movement of the naves inside, the radiating rhythm of apses
at the east end (pl. 184), the tier arrangement of façades on the west;
while a new element, the belfry or bell tower, often topped with a
pyramidal roof, added a further upward movement.

The great variety of these schools of architecture is a sign of feudal
separatism. When we reflect that in the twelfth century Gothic art
was arising concurrently with the triumph of Romanesque, we must
agree with the German historians Dehio and Bezold: "French architecture in the eleventh and twelfth centuries, with its divergent styles
flowering simultaneously, is a phenomenon unparalleled in the whole
history of architecture."

The Norman school was the oldest. Between 1025 and 1070 it was
already capable of erecting great structures such as the nave of Mont-
Saint-Michel at Bernay, and l'Abbaye-aux-Hommes and l'Abbaye-aux-

Dames at Caen. It used galleries, but still timbered the high naves to which the thirteenth century would have given ogival vaults. The Normans sought very sober, over-all architectural effects and avoided figurative decoration.

The Burgundian school benefited from being the home of the two great congregations of Cluny and Cîteaux. The Cluniac order built great churches, lavishly decorated with sculptures. In reaction the Cistercians built very stark edifices (Fontenay Abbey). Cluny Monastery church (1088–1120), no longer standing, was then the largest church in Christendom, being 643 feet 6 inches in length. The Burgundian church had a very daring structure (the high nave of Cluny being 96 feet 6 inches tall), while in decoration the Burgundians were influenced by classical architecture (cathedrals of Autun and Langres).

The Provençal school went in for small buildings but gave them very harmonious proportions (St.-Trophime, Arles; Montmajour Abbey). Of all the schools this one owed most to the classical (porch of St.-Gilles-du-Gard).

The Auvergne churches were powerfully buttressed by means of quadrant-shaped galleries which darkened the naves, but they have a harsh grandeur about them (Issoire; Notre-Dame-du-Port at Clermont).

The southwest region (Poitou-Saintonge) made churches with narrow aisles almost as tall as the nave, whose façades were covered with profuse decoration (Notre-Dame-la-Grande at Poitiers).

A group of churches without aisles in Languedoc and in the southwest have series of domes (Cahors; St.-Front, Périgueux, pl. 180). The biggest Romanesque buildings belong to an interregional type found along the highways used by pilgrims to Compostela (St.-Sernin, Toulouse, pl. 179; Figeac; Ste.-Foy, Conques; Santiago de Compostela, pl. 188). These churches have double side aisles and an ambulatory suitable for the crowds of pilgrims and already anticipating the Gothic cathedral.

SCULPTURE

It was at the end of the eleventh century, after six centuries of insecurity, that monumental sculpture came to life again. Languedoc and Spain show the oldest specimens. The low-relief figures at St.-Sernin, Toulouse (Christ, apostles and angels), and the Moissac cloister (apostles) show a still hesitant modeling imitated from Byzantine ivories. Built

185. Porch of abbey church of St.-Pierre, Moissac
(Tarn-et-Garonne). About 1120.

about 1120, the main portal of St.-Pierre at Moissac is evidence of a
school fully versed in its medium (pl. 185), with its tympanum depicting
the Apocalyptic vision of St. John (Christ shown between four beasts,
the Evangelist's symbols which were to appear frequently in Romanesque art).

It was with a generous and lively touch that Romanesque art rein-
troduced figures into sculpture, which until then had been inhibited by
the abstract mentality of the Barbarians: yet sculpturing was not yet
practiced for its own sake, but waved and twisted in order to fit its
frame, lending itself to purely ornamental rhythms (pls. 168 to 170).
The Romanesque artists proved to have unlimited imagination in inventing all kinds of ornamental patterns, in which the human figure was
reconciled to elements taken from the vegetable and animal worlds as
well as from the fabulous code of the East, for the creation of monsters.
A frantic vitality enlivens these figures, in their demonic agitation. One
of the most beautiful decorative features of the Romanesque is the
capital. Its layout devolves from the composite form of the ancients,
which certain schools (Provençal school) carefully imitated: but generally the capitals depict biblical scenes in the form of monstrous shapes
which, set onto the capital, cleverly underline its structure (pl. 186).
The finest series of capitals is in the nave of Vézelay in Burgundy and
is the most fertile in picturesque inventiveness.

The great variety of the Romanesque schools of sculpture, reflecting the different architectural schools, may be classified into two main groups. Some of them show a rule of very elongated proportions, a flat and calligraphic modeling of draperies, a hint of convulsion in the movement: it has been suggested that schools of this type were influenced by the art of illumination. An example is the Languedoc school, the most developed of all, which excelled in tympanums with large, grouped compositions (Souillac; Moissac, pl. 185). In the same spirit the Burgundian school (tympanums at Autun and Vézelay) made rather more confused compositions, more dryly stylized. The Poitou school liked lavish decoration, spread on the façades and especially around the portals. Other schools preferred a system of squat proportions and had a stronger sense of relief. The influence of gold altar fronts inspired several segmented tympana in central France (Ste.-Foy at Conques; Carennac). The full proportions of the Auvergne school probably owe something to the survival of an aesthetic dating from Gallic low-reliefs: Auvergne is the only Romanesque school to attempt carving in the round, in wooden statues of the Virgin which were often overlaid with metal foil. The Provence school (St.-Gilles-du-Gard, St.-Trophime at Arles) showed a powerful feeling for relief in its imitation of antique sculpture and Christian sarcophagi, which were preserved in large numbers at Arles.

186. Capital with monstrous figures.
Abbey church, St.-Benoît-sur-Loire (Loiret). About 1160.

PAINTING AND THE MINOR ARTS

Romanesque art still had the taste of the preceding centuries for luxurious objects in gold. The two main centers of production were in the districts of the Rhine and the Meuse, on the one hand, and Limousin on the other. The Meuse school, influenced by Germanic art, still kept up the Byzantine tradition of cloisonné enameling in delicate colors, sometimes derived from Alexandrian coloring (sea-green, lake, azure). The Limousin school practiced the craft of chasing metals, which consists of running the enamel paste into grooves cut in a bronze plaque: the colorings, much heavier in this case (garnet-red, dark blue), originated from the smithwork of the Barbarians.

The same differences in colorings are to be found in the fairly numerous murals which survive in French churches. The Burgundian school (Berzé-la-Ville) tried to imitate the polychromatic brilliance of the Byzantine mosaic, while the Poitou school (St.-Savin) used a palette reduced to red and yellow ochers reminiscent of Oriental hues. In the course of the twelfth century a new contribution was made to the arts of color in the stained glass leaded window, an outcome of cloisonné (partitioned) metalwork. This developed strikingly in the thirteenth century, though the finest windows date back to the infancy of this art.

ROMANESQUE ART OUTSIDE FRANCE

Romanesque art took a deep hold all over Europe. The closest national school to the French was the English school, which in a sense was the twin of the Norman school, largely on account of the political union between England and Normandy. Thus English Romanesque is known as the Norman style. The great Norman churches (Ely, pl. 187, Peterborough, Durham, Fountains Abbey, Southwell) have the same characteristics as those of Normandy. They are enormous structures, having galleries with thick walls and massive pillars, very tall naves which are generally timbered over—ribbed vaulting usually being reserved for side aisles—and an imposing lantern tower over the transept. Certain specifically English features appeared at that time and lasted into the Gothic period, such as the lengthening of the nave, the decorative arcading, sometimes of intersecting arches on the façades, ornamental arching across the clerestory, draping the high windows. As with the Norman school, the decoration is almost entirely geometrical, but figures

187. Nave of Ely Cathedral. Completed in 1180.
From Hürlimann and Meyer, English Cathedrals.

are more frequent than in Normandy. The finest example of this Norman style is the cathedral of Durham. Durham Cathedral shows a very early use of rib vaulting, though this does not affect the structure or Romanesque appearance of the building. Rib vaults were given to the chancel aisles in 1096 and to the high vault in 1104, the latter being replaced in 1235. The finest development of the art of illumination came in the tenth and eleventh centuries, when the Winchester school's lavish color and daring draughtsmanship had an almost baroque quality (*Benedictional of St. Aethelwold*, British Museum, about 975–980; formerly in Devonshire Collection, Chatsworth).

The Spanish school was related to that of Languedoc. It contributed to the revival of sculpture, and from the end of the eleventh century the workshops at León and Compostela showed a precocious tendency toward sculpturing in the round. The portal of Silo in Castille, the cloister at Ripoll in Catalonia, on the other hand, recall Languedoc carving. The cathedral of Santiago de Compostela in Galicia, the seat of the most famous pilgrimage in the West, belongs to the lineage of the great Cluniac churches (Pilgrimage churches), St.-Sernin at Toulouse, Conques. It has the finest sculptures in Spain, on the Goldsmiths' Portal (which have been dated pre-1117) and on the Gloria Portal, finished in 1188 by the Master Matthew, who introduced an already Gothic conception of statuary into Spain. Catalonia had a fine school of

Romanesque painting, characterized by a taste for lively glittering colors, particularly red and yellow (manuscripts of the Apocalypse; frescoes in the Pyrenean churches, pl. 190).

Italy persisted in its use of the basilican plan during the entire Romanesque period (pl. 189). In its timbered naves it often used alternating strong and weak piers, practically ignored the ambulatory and for preference placed the bell towers on either side of the chancel. On bays with alternating strong and weak piers, Lombardy shows some precocious examples of ogival cross vaulting which do not affect the Romanesque appearance (Sant'Ambrogio, Milan). The finest buildings are in Tuscany (Pisa Cathedral), in Lombardy (Sant'Abbondio at Como, San Michele at Pavia, Modena Cathedral), or in southern Italy (cathedrals of Trani, Bari, Salerno and Ravello). In Sicily the Lombard influence mingled with Norman, Moslem and Byzantine influences (cathedral of Cefalù; abbey of Monreale). As for sculpture, Italy proved hostile to the Romanesque love of metamorphosis and dynamism and remained stubbornly attached to the sculptural outlook of antiquity. The principal works of Romanesque sculpture in Italy are in the Emilia province (Benedetto Antelami, *ambo* of the basilican church or Duomo of Parma, 1178). Italy continued using bronzework for its cathedral

188. Nave, Cathedral of Santiago de Compostela. 12th century.

189. Nave of the (basilican) Cathedral, Fiesole. 11th–13th century.

190. Christ of the Apocalypse. Fresco from S. Clemente at Tahull.
12th century. *Barcelona, Museum of Catalan art.*

doors. It created monumental liturgic furnishings (pulpits, ambos, chandeliers, choir screens) in white marble incrusted with colored marble mosaics. One family, the Cosmati (a name suggestive of Greek origins), became famous for this art from the early twelfth century onward. The art, imported from abroad, enjoyed great popularity in Rome, and was facilitated by the great stocks of marble to be found in the city's ancient ruins. In painting Italy remained an apprentice to Byzantium. The fresco now began to develop. In the thirteenth century the Tuscans began painting on panels, taking Byzantine models as a point of departure. The mosaics in Sicily were imbued with the Greek spirit.

Romanesque buildings in Germany are set along the Rhine and the Danube, the most civilized regions of the Germanic countries at that time. The Rhenish school, related to the Lombard, shows the most affinity with the earlier Carolingian art. It made free use of the double-basilican plan and the system of alternating strong and weak piers, and liked to group the bell towers round the chancel (cathedrals of Worms, Speyer; church at Maria Laach, pl. 191). The block or cushion capitals were only mediocrely decorated, the Germans having little sense of the monumental in sculpture; but to make up for this the relief work inclines to statuary, and the tradition brilliantly inaugurated in the

191. Church of the Abbey of Laach at Maria Laach, Rhineland. 11th–13th century.

Ottonian period found its fulfillment in the Prophets carved round the east choir screen of Bamberg Cathedral, one of the strongest assertions of that feeling for pathos which is essentially German (pl. 192).

The Low Countries were attracted by both the Norman and Rhenish influences, most noticeable in Tournai Cathedral.

The Meuse and Rhenish regions show Germanic skill in the metal crafts. Precious objects in brass and bronze, sometimes embellished with enamels, were made at Cologne and round Liége (pl. 193). Between

192. Statue of the prophet Jonah. Bamberg Cathedral. After 1220.

193. Chased enamel plaque. Mosan (Meuse) art, 12th century. *Paris, Louvre.*

1107 and 1118 Renier de Huy made the bronze fonts for St.-Barthélemy de Liége, a tradition which was passed on to Godefroy de Huy and Nicolas de Verdun, whose work was influenced by German expressionism (reredos of Klosterneuberg, Austria, 1181), while the monk Hugo d'Oignies in the early thirteenth century remained more traditional. On the Rhine and the Meuse there was a faster stylistic evolution than in southern Germany: toward 1200 the shrine of the Magi at Cologne and the stucco-relief choir screen at the Church of the Holy Virgin at Halberstadt show a far more advanced plastic skill than was seen at Bamberg in 1220.

GOTHIC ART

The term "Gothic" is the French equivalent of the expression "tedesco," or Teuton, used by the Italians of the Renaissance to decry medieval art. The term has led to regrettable misunderstandings because in reality the Gothic style was a French creation. It appeared in the Ile-de-France toward 1125 (St.-Denis and Sens) and flourished first in that province, while other regions were still following the Romanesque. Gothic art reached its maturity in the thirteenth century; it quickly spread to England and found its way all over Europe in the thirteenth and fourteenth centuries. Italy was only superficially affected and was the first to give it up when Florence led the way in the early

194. Lateral elevation of the nave, Notre-Dame, Laon (formerly a cathedral). Begun about 1150.

fifteenth century in developing the Renaissance aesthetic. In its belated Flamboyant phase, Gothic art had a strong hold in northern Europe in the fifteenth century. It persisted in France till about 1530 in religious buildings, and in both England and Germany continued in a somewhat debased state until the seventeenth century.

THE CREATION OF GOTHIC ART IN FRANCE

The thirteenth century was the great age of Gothic art. The century of St. Louis, comparable with the Greek fifth century, saw the first creation in the Middle Ages of a coherent political and social system. Religious dogma and philosophical thought were crystallized in great works of which the most important was Thomas Aquinas' *Summa Theologica*. The true dogmatic and intellectual center of Christendom was no longer Rome but the University of Paris, where the Italian St. Thomas was teaching. The cathedral was the monumental expression of that demand for order which dominated the fields of fact and thought: it also marks the awakening of the people and a certain secularization of the faith. The intellectual centers now moved from the monasteries to the universities, while the artistic initiative passed from the abbots to the bishops, who were encouraged by a burst of popular enthusiasm. Like the ancient temple, the cathedral was the city's monument, and

 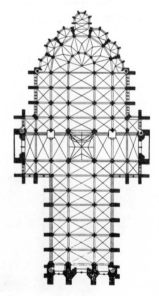

195. Choir vault, Soissons Cathedral. Consecrated in 1212.
196. Ground plan of Amiens Cathedral. 1220. *After Lasteyrie.*

197. Vertical section of the choir, Beauvais Cathedral. 1247. *After Corroyer, L'Art gothique.*

of all the great monumental forms created by civilizations it best expressed the common effort of a whole society. The gradual expansion of the Gothic style throughout France coincided with that cohesive force which tended to weld the whole territory of ancient Gaul into a strong state centered in the power of the throne.

ARCHITECTURE

The decisive elements in the new architectural style were the ogival or pointed cross vault with ribs and the flying buttress.

First invented by the English and the Lombards, but first exploited under its potentialities by the Ile-de-France architects, the pointed ribbed vault is derived from the groined vault, whose essential property is the concentration of stresses at four supporting points, whereas the Romanesque barred vault thrust down all along the length of the supporting wall (pls. 188 and 195). The use of this vault thus eliminated the carrying function of the walls, which in the thirteenth century were replaced by "glass screens." The arches and vaults were profiled in pointed arches, more slender than the semicircular.

The flying buttress is a kind of bridge applied to the resting points of the high ogival vaults. They often pass over the side aisles and transmit the thrust of the central structure to a buttress situated outside the church itself (pl. 197). The flying buttress is in effect a slice cut out of the quadrant vault which stayed the high naves of certain Roman-

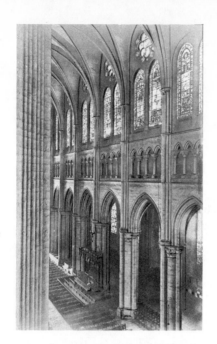

198. Lateral elevation of the nave, Chartres Cathedral. Begun 1194.
199. South tower, Chartres Cathedral.
Begun about 1145.

esque churches (pl. 182). The equilibrium of the Romanesque church was obtained by the resistance of continuous walls; but instead of being surrounded by a rampart of walls the Gothic cathedral, leaning on its light piers and held laterally by its buttresses, could flood the interior with light through its spacious bays (pls. 203 and 217).

This result was only achieved in the thirteenth century. The Gothic cathedrals of the twelfth century (Senlis, Laon, Notre-Dame de Paris) had no flying buttresses, those which are now to be seen on Notre-Dame being added in the thirteenth; the supporting of the central vaults was still ensured by the use of galleries. The internal elevation was in four stories: archways or arcades; the tribune (gallery); triforium or blind gallery (small-arched circulating gallery); clerestory with its windows (pl. 194).

The first great cathedral to be built with flying buttresses and without a gallery was undoubtedly Chartres, the nave begun in 1194 (pl. 198). It inaugurated the thirteenth century type of elevation with three stories (with triforium) which was to be followed at once by Reims (1211) and Amiens (1220).

Gothic art developed extremely rapidly as though with some vital urge to growth. Its development took the form of increasing sparsity of walling, increased elevation, the stressing of the verticality of the naves, the proliferation of images.

In 1240 Pierre de Montereau, who was the architect of the nave of St.-Denis, eliminated walling by placing windowed bays behind the triforium, which was henceforth to be closely associated with the fenestration: the windows were multiplied to fill the free space left between pillars, and were filled with stained or painted glass. The layout of these networks of windows and rose windows has earned Gothic art of the period 1250–1400 the name *gothique rayonnant* (radiating Gothic, pl. 203).

A few figures give ample evidence of the increasing size of vaults: Laon (1150), 78 feet; Paris (1163), 114 feet; Chartres (1194), 119 feet; Reims (1211), 123 feet 6 inches; Amiens (1220), 136 feet 6 inches; Beauvais (1247), 156 feet 9 inches. Beauvais Cathedral shows the end of this craving for height: badly supported by its too isolated framework the high vault, which was finished in 1272, collapsed in 1284, and the structure had to be reinforced by doubling the piers.

The vertical trend followed the growth of vaults, resulting in larger and larger arcades (32 feet 6 inches at Paris, 68 feet 3 inches at Beauvais): the effect of this was further marked by the heightening of the vertical lines, for finer and finer subsidiary shafts, attached to the piers, rose from the floor to the vault, while the clerestory-window mullions prolonged those of the triforium. From 1250 onward sharp pediments over porches and windows (gables) contributed further to this impression of upward movement (pl. 203).

While the nave was raised and cut away, the forms clothing its structure were multiplied, every one tending to gain its independence and to produce secondary forms. This instinct for growth can be noticed particularly in the increased complexity of moldings, sills and window tracery. Still kept in a strict hierarchy by the disciplined mentality of the thirteenth century, these forms ended by covering the whole edifice with an unruly vegetation in the Flamboyant style of the fifteenth century.

The Gothic builders perfected moldings, which were empirically invented by Romanesque art. They created a coherent system of molding, obeying strict laws. On capitals and decorative string courses, the fanciful ornamentation of the Romanesque artists now gave way

200. Capital with crockets. North porch, Chartres Cathedral. About 1230.

201. Château de Coucy (before its destruction in 1918). 13th century.

to supple and living forms based on plant life (pl. 200). The same instinct for growth animates these floral decorations. On foliage capitals (the final metamorphosis of the classical composite style) the buds of the twelfth century burst into leaf in about 1220, and after 1250 became branches.

In the thirteenth century the basic Romanesque castle, influenced by the Crusades, became a scientific and formidable structure (Château de Coucy, pl. 201). The plan usually adopted consisted of a rectangular enclosure flanked with towers at each corner, with the keep in the center (Philippe-Auguste's plan, Louvre).

The best-preserved of these castles are in the Holy Land, where the Krak of the Knights still stands almost intact with its double stone shell. In the fourteenth century a more advanced civilization thought the fortresses of the preceding age much too bleak, and the castle was transformed into a palace (Château de Pierrefonds). The fifteenth century developed the *hôtel* or villa, an urban residence suiting the needs of a new social class, the bourgeoisie (Hôtel Jacques Coeur at Bourges). The Gothic period introduced many new forms of building corresponding with all the activities of a developed society, in the shape of bridges, infirmaries, convents and monasteries, town halls and municipal buildings, law courts, markets and the like.

Gothic art was poorer in provincial variants than the Romanesque. However, in the thirteenth century the different provinces adopted the forms created in Ile-de-France, giving them some local flavor. The Champagne school (Reims Cathedral) was nearest to Ile-de-France classicism. Thanks to a remarkably durable material (Tonnerre stone) the Burgundian school built structures in which elimination of walls was pushed to its farthest limits (Auxerre Cathedral, Notre-Dame at Dijon, St.-Urbain at Troyes). The Norman school made wonderful cathedrals surrounded by fine spires (Bayeux; Coutances, pl. 202; Rouen; Lisieux) and the Mont-St.-Michel Abbey, which, perched above a rocky island off the north coast, is one of the most lyrical utterances of the Middle Ages. The Normans showed an exceptional lack of aptitude for figure sculpture. Anjou gave its attention to the decorative possibilities of multi-ribbed vaults (St.-Serge, Angers). Gothic art came to the south of France (Midi) as a Nordic import, a whole group of cathedrals designed by Jean Deschamps marking this infiltration (Clermont, Limoges, Narbonne, Toulouse, Rodez). However, by reaction

 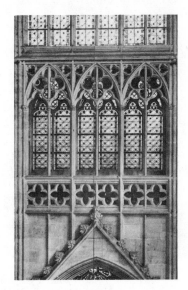

202. Apse of Coutances Cathedral (Manche). 13th century.

203. Clerestory triforium window, Sées Cathedral (Orne). End of 13th century.

the native outlook created at the same time a type of church with a single nave of very large dimensions (Albi Cathedral) which was to be imitated in Spain. Gothic regionalism disappeared in the fourteenth century when architecture was checked by pedantic formulas (St.-Ouen at Rouen); but it revived again in the fifteenth century. The Rouen school was the most outstanding in the Flamboyant manner, which sprang up there under English influence.

SCULPTURE

The birth of Gothic sculpture in the Ile-de-France was not much later than that of Romanesque sculpture, since the Royal Porch at Chartres was started after 1140 (pl. 524). Following what was still a Romanesque convention, the figures on piers and piedroits were raised or flattened to follow the shape of the column (columnar statuary). Relief as such was almost nonexistent and the modeling of folds mainly calligraphic; but the robing was taken from contemporary clothing, and from those stone sheaths sprang heads that were full of personality and life, genuine portraits. The feverishness that twisted the figures at Moissac and Autun was soothed, giving way to calm postures and

204. Tympanum. Porch of the Virgin,
Notre-Dame de Paris. West façade. About 1210–1220.
205. The month of March: Work in the Vineyard.
Amiens Cathedral. About 1225.

206. The Visitation. West front, Reims Cathedral. About 1260–1270.
207. Head of St. Modesta. North porch, Chartres Cathedral. About 1230.

serene expressions. Sometimes a fleeting smile lit up their faces, and while all over France the Romanesque workshops were making wonderful ornamental fancies, the Ile-de-France sculptures sought a methodical observation of nature and the achievement of harmony. The porches at Senlis (pl. 172), Sens, Laon, and the Ste.-Anne porch at Notre-Dame de Paris (about 1170) are major stages in this growing grasp of relief and truthfulness which recalls, astonishingly, the transition from the sixth to the fifth century B.C. in Greek sculpture. This rapid advance resulted in the thirteenth century in the almost classical poise of the Porch of the Virgin at Notre-Dame (1210–1220, pl. 204), north and south porches at Chartres (1224–1240, pls. 173 and 638), or the west portal at Amiens (1225–1236, pl. 205). The search for expression is tempered in them by a monumental balance and an idealism which seems to halo the faces with a sympathetic but austere saintliness. If some of these works recall the serene pediments of Olympia, the cathedral of Reims (west porch about 1225–1270) is the Parthenon of Gothic sculpture. Its statues are the most perfect works of Gothic plastic art, yet are so close to the supple ease of ancient Greece that critics have even suggested that there was some imitation (Visitation group, pl. 206). Facial expressions become more human, optimism was smilingly revealed, but the face lost the lofty spirituality of the previous epoch: worldliness was being introduced into art through the influence of courtly poetry, *la poésie courtoise* (pl. 207). There is no better demonstration of the progress of humanism than the rapid evolution

161

208. Head of the memorial statue to Philip III (the Bold),
end of 13th century. *Paris, St.-Denis.*

209. Page from the Belleville Breviary,
illuminated by Jean Pucelle, before 1343. *Paris, Bibliothèque Nationale.*

of the types of Christ and the Virgin. Purely a theological concept in
the twelfth century, by the end of the thirteenth the Virgin was a tender
maternal figure playing with her child. The formidable Christ of the
Romanesque tympanums was brought down to the piers to welcome
the faithful with an evangelical smile at the church door: under the
influence of St. Bernard, God was no longer worshiped as the supreme
Judge, but the devotion of the faithful was transferred to the New
Testament Christ, God become Man.

All these works were harmonized with each other, according to
the principles of an iconographical program that required a scholar's
knowledge. Byzantine symbolism was a religious symbolism, but that
of the thirteenth century had an encyclopedic character, for it reflected
the scholastic philosophy, intent on imposing the logic of thought upon
the universe. The cathedral is an immense book which tells the history
of the world. Chartres contains no less than 8000 painted or sculptured
images.

At the end of the thirteenth century the portrait began to appear
in *recumbents*, or funerary statues, which are lit up by a smile, a typically French expression (pl. 208).

162

In sculpture as in architecture the fourteenth century was an academic period. Sculpture became detached from the portals and approached carving in the round; but the human expression became empty, the modeling conventional and dry, the artists' impotence betraying itself in nervous hesitant poses with the hips unnaturally set (pl. 640). At the end of the century some health was restored to an anemic art by the vigorous contribution of the Flemish temperament, thanks to Claus Sluter.

THE ARTS OF COLOR – THE MINOR ARTS

If the French school of painting was very inferior to the Italian, this is because painting was not the only form of color expression in France, as it was across the Alps. Stained glass windows, illuminated manuscripts and tapestries, which were hardly known in Italy, filled cathedrals and princely houses with a fairyland of colored images. The stained glass window spread considerably in the thirteenth century in response to the enormous demand from cathedral building yards. Chartres and Bourges have the most complete sets of thirteenth century windows. This art decayed in the fourteenth century through imitating sculpture, then in the fifteenth under the influence of painting, to achieve only a short lease of life again in the early sixteenth century.

210. Shrine of St.-Taurin. 13th century. *Evreux, St.-Taurin.*

Illumination continued to develop in Paris, which its famous University made the center of book production. The liturgical works of the preceding period were now succeeded by psalters, breviaries, books of hours, all richly adorned for the benefit of the higher social order, and always executed on vellum. Thirteenth century illumination was inspired by stained glass (*St. Louis Psalter, Blanche of Castille Psalter*) while architectural forms also intruded (*St. Louis Psalter*). The most elegant works in this art were made in the early fourteenth century in the studio of Jean Pucelle (*Belleville Breviary*, pl. 209). Under Charles V it declined but was to gain fresh vitality from the Flemish contribution at the end of the fourteenth century.

The workshops in which they made both high-warp and low-warp tapestries appeared or are mentioned as being in Paris toward the end of the fourteenth century: the oldest preserved tapestry is the Angers Apocalypse (end of fourteenth century). The Hundred Years' War broke up the Parisian workshops, some being moved to Arras, where they specialized in tapestries with historical or mythological themes, dense compositions with large numbers of characters. The Touraine workshops, until the early sixteenth century, expressed the poetry of nature in tapestries with a green background.

Painting was less vigorous than in Italy: it remained for a long time overshadowed by tapestries, illumination or stained glass, and broke free only in the second half of the fourteenth century. The Parisian style then produced some exquisite works, of which only few have been preserved. On the other hand, before Italy, France appears to have developed a lay art which provided the abodes of princes with hunting and fishing scenes, painted in fresco. An example survives in the Wardrobe Tower at the Papal Palace in Avignon (about 1345). The art of portraiture was in the same vein, and seems to have appeared first in France (*Portrait of Jean le Bon*, Louvre).

The minor arts in the Gothic period were under the tyranny of architecture, which imposed its forms on furniture as on gold- and silverwork (pl. 210). Sculpture in ivory was very much in favor, and was also inspired by monumental modeling.

THE EXPANSION OF GOTHIC ART

The finest Gothic monuments, after the French, are to be found in England. The English were quick to discover this new style—to whose development they contributed by their very early use of ogival vaulting in Durham Cathedral (1096)—and were the only builders to evolve a native form of it in the thirteenth century. The Gothic style was encouraged in England, as in Italy and Germany, by the spread of the Cistercian order. Nothing is more characteristically Gothic than the chancel of Canterbury Cathedral, which was built between 1175 and 1184 by the French architect Guillaume de Sens, who took as his model Sens Cathedral. With the exception of Westminster Abbey, which was influenced by the Ile-de-France and Champagne style and has an apse (*chevet*) with an ambulatory and radiating chapels, the first phase of English Gothic, known as Early English (Lincoln, pl. 211; Salisbury; Lichfield; York; Wells), is parallel with that of thirteenth century Norman Gothic; but whereas the Norman school increasingly shed its native characteristics as it evolved, the English school stressed its own local features. English architects had a liking for straight apses with an elevation resembling that of the façade, as in Durham: long naves, double transepts, slender forms (such as sharp lancet bays and extremely tall and detached columns and shafts). Salisbury Cathedral (pl. 212), which was begun in 1220 and consecrated in 1258, is perhaps the purest and most elegant example of the first phase.

211. Lincoln Cathedral. 12th–14th century.

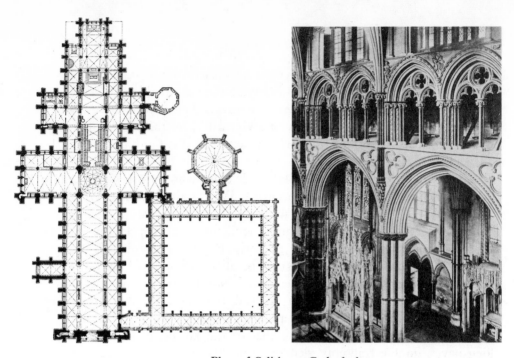

212. Plan of Salisbury Cathedral.
213. Lincoln Cathedral. The "Angel Choir." About 1282.
Both from Hürlimann and Meyer, English Cathedrals.

Toward 1260 there came a sharp division between the development of the Norman and English schools. The Norman school lost its personality and became absorbed into French classicism. While French Gothic architecture suddenly came to a standstill in the fourteenth century, England boldly followed its own internal evolution and toward 1280 began creating the Curvilinear or Decorated style, which both anticipated and begot French Flamboyant. This style, so fully achieved in the choirs of Lincoln Cathedral (about 1282, pl. 213), Exeter Cathedral (about 1280) and the nave of York Minster (1290), is distinguished by a lavish ornamentation spreading even into the vaults, overlaid as they are with intermediate ribs and carvings and with a structure that tends away from ogival vaulting. The taste for curves and flourishes was further developed in the fourteenth century (Lady Chapel, Ely Cathedral, 1321–1349), while the chapter houses, built on a polygonal plan with a central pillar, are remarkably elegant (pl. 214). At a time when all fifteenth century Europe was indulging in elaborate curves, England rejected them to create its Perpendicular style with all the stress on verticalism.

214. Wells Cathedral. Vault
of Chapter House. 1293–1319.

During those three hundred years, parish churches for the most part remained faithful to the simple design inherited from the Saxon period, in which the central tower serves as a massive nucleus for four unequal arms. These churches were often roofed with timber.

In the representational arts, English Gothic is notable—in the same way as in architecture—for its leaning toward elegance. In sculpture this meant the lengthening of forms and a slightly mannered gracefulness (Wells, Winchester, Salisbury, Lichfield; Lincoln, pl. 213). The craftsmen of Derbyshire, Yorkshire and Nottinghamshire carved portable sculptures in alabaster during the fourteenth and fifteenth centuries which they exported all over northern Europe and France. During the thirteenth and fourteenth centuries the miniature achieved great subtlety of line, and the painting of the period derived from it: the *Wilton Diptych* (National Gallery, London, pl. 216), painted toward 1395, portraying Richard II being presented to the Christ Child, is one of

215. William Torel. Effigy for
the tomb of Eleanor of
Castille, wife of Edward I, in
Westminster Abbey. Bronze.
Detail. 1291. *From Tanner,
Westminster Abbey.*

216. The Wilton Diptych (wood).
Richard II of England being
presented to the Christ Child by
his patron saints. About 1395.
London, National Gallery.

the most refined works of the Middle Ages. Historians have attributed
it successively to the French, English and Czech schools, but all that is
certain is that it was executed at the English court. Toward 1400 the
miniature began to return to the international style (*Beaufort Book of
Hours*, 1401–1410).

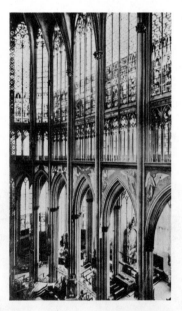

217. Cologne Cathedral, choir elevation. 1248–1322.

218. Freiburg Cathedral. West tower.
Tower 13th century, spire 14th.

Gothic art in Germany was, on the contrary, an imported art. The first Gothic monuments (Limburg-an-der-Lahn, Maulbronn, Bamberg, Naumburg, Magdeburg, Notre Dame at Trier) appeared in the first half of the thirteenth century in a region that was still Romanesque. Cologne Cathedral (choir begun in 1248) was the first really Gothic building in Germany (pl. 217), but it was inspired by Amiens and Beauvais, while the nave of Strasbourg (1250–1270) was a replica of that of St.-Denis. The German churches of the fourteenth century were more original. By their profuse decoration they heralded the Flamboyant without having yet conceived its forms. The buildings were entirely clothed in a sort of vibrating tracery (façades of Strasbourg and Cologne Cathedrals, Cologne's façade plans not carried out until the nineteenth century; openwork spire of Freiburg, Breisgau, pl. 218). In the thirteenth century Westphalia produced a type of church with three equal naves (Hallenkirche, Minden, Münster, Osnabrück, Paderborn) which was to spread in the fourteenth century to the Baltic, where brick construction was the rule.

The workshops of Reims were the source of German Gothic sculpture. About 1235 at Bamberg (Franconia) Gothic sculpture replaced the Romanesque without any transitional stage, after the Romanesque

219. Bamberg Cathedral. Head of "Horseman" statue. After 1230.

220. Naumburg Cathedral. Head of the statue of the Margrave Dietrich in the west choir. Between 1260 and 1273.

had just expressed itself in the fine *Apostles and Prophets* of the east choir (pl. 192). Artists who were no doubt trained at the Reims workshops took inspiration from its elegant forms and gave them a specifically German intensity (*Visitation Group; Church and Synagogue; "Horseman" statue*, pl. 219). The statues of the Church and the Synagogue in Strasbourg Cathedral add a touch of Germanic unreality to the elegance of Reims. At the end of the thirteenth century and the early fourteenth, the Wise Virgins and Foolish Virgins in the same cathedral have a rich local touch which saves them from the academicism that is noticeable in the neighboring porch.

In Spain, the slight artistic traditions of Castille gave a ready welcome to Gothic architecture from the thirteenth century onward. The cathedrals of Burgos and Toledo were inspired by the Bourges and Coutances types, while León Cathedral reflects the forms of Reims and Amiens. Catalonia, where there had been a prosperous Romanesque school, proved more cautious and hesitated between the northern French type with side aisles and ambulatory, and the Languedoc type with side chapels instead of aisles (Gerona Cathedral). The sculptors' shops at Burgos and León give further evidence of the wide influence of Reims.

1. Façade, Orvieto Cathedral (Umbria), begun by Lorenzo Maitani. Early 14th century.
222. Palazzo Vecchio (Piazza della Signoria), Florence.
Begun in 1298 and attributed to Arnolfo di Cambio.

THE RESISTANCE TO GOTHIC ART – ITALY
ARCHITECTURE

Italy was the country most hostile to Gothic art. It never made more than a superficial impression, under its meridional form (Lower Church, Assisi, 1229–1236), which was imported by mendicant monks who also imitated Cistercian architecture. In the late thirteenth and in the fourteenth century a more personal style was developed but which proved to be absolutely opposed to the Gothic spirit, in which the decoration is expressive of the structure: embellishments of polychrome marbles, in the Byzantine manner, covered both the outside and inside of brick-built cathedrals (cathedrals of Siena, Florence, Orvieto, pl. 221). The severe "public palaces" (Florence, pl. 222, and Siena) have a Romanesque character beneath their roughness. The Flamboyant style penetrated the north of Italy as well as the kingdom of Naples. In Lombardy it produced Milan Cathedral, a cosmopolitan work by Italian, French and German architects, which shows an awkward adaptation of Flamboyant sinuosity to the stiffness of its marbles. In Venice the Flamboyant style was mixed with Moorish influence to create a composite art something like the Spanish Mudejar, resulting in some pleasant constructions (Doge's Palace; Cà d'Oro).

SCULPTURE

On the other hand, Italy made a plastic revolution in the thirteenth century in both painting and sculpture, thanks entirely to her own creative efforts. She first broke free from Byzantine influence in sculpture, a technique in which Byzantine art produced little. It was in classical sculptures as well as Christian sarcophagi that Nicola Pisano (spoken

223. Nicola Pisano. Adoration of the Magi. Marble bas-relief on the pulpit. 1260. *Pisa, Baptistery.*

of from 1220 to 1278) found his new conception of sculptural density and his heroic sense of man. (Principal works: *Baptistery pulpit* at Pisa, 1260, pl. 223, Siena *pulpit*, 1266.) This classical tradition came from southern Italy. Nicola Pisano came from Apulia, a region in which in the early thirteenth century there had been an episodic but genuine revival of the classical spirit under the direction of the Emperor Frederick II, a philosopher-prince imbued with skepticism. He admired Arab culture and held a cosmopolitan court at Palermo (Triumphal Arch, Capua, about 1240).

One of Nicola's apprentices, the Florentine Arnolfo di Cambio (1232?–1302), both architect and sculptor, made plans for the Duomo (Santa Maria del Fiore) of Florence and perhaps also for the Palazzo Vecchio (pl. 222). In his sculptured works (*Tomb of the Cardinal de Braye* at San Domenico, Orvieto, about 1282), he tried to recapture Roman grandeur, though with a somewhat stiff dignity.

The plastic tradition established by Nicola Pisano was continued in Pisa and Florence during the fourteenth century, somewhat modified and diluted by increasing Gothic influence which was harmful to native expression. Already Nicola's son Giovanni Pisano (about 1245 to after 1320) was more inspired by the flexible style of Gothic ivories than by the imposing Roman sarcophagi (pl. 224). Still more apparent in Andrea di Ugolino, also called Pisano (d. 1348), French influence diminished in Andrea Orcagna (d. 1368), a painter and sculptor in the Giotto tradition; but it revived with Nino Pisano (d. 1368),

224. Giovanni Pisano. Adoration of the Magi. Marble bas-relief on the pulpit. 1298–1301. *Pistoia, S. Andrea.*

225. Bonaventura Berlinghieri. St. Francis. Detail. 1235. *Pescia, S. Francesco.*
226. Duccio di Buoninsegna. The Stations to Calvary.
Panel from the Maestà. About 1310. *Siena, Cathedral Museum.*

whose Annunciations derive from the rather sickly elegance of the French, but with an entirely Tuscan preciousness.

In short, the genuine Italian Renaissance, based on a revival of the classical tradition, was strongly marked in the second half of the thirteenth century, but was held up by the Gothic invasion of the fourteenth century, which amounted to a foreign occupation. In the early fifteenth century the Renaissance had to begin all over again, by first of all driving out the Gothic infection.

PAINTING

Meanwhile Italy gave the world a new mode of expression in its painting. A national school broke away from Byzantinism toward 1250, under the influence of the new naturalistic and humanistic outlook introduced by St. Francis of Assisi. The first tokens of this were at Pisa and Lucca (school of the Berlinghieri, pl. 225). At the end of the century, Florence and Siena took the lead. The sources of Florentine realism are to be found in certain baptistery mosaics, rather than in Cimabue (recorded between 1272 and 1302) who paid tribute to the theological spirit of Byzantium in some dignified icons (pl. 175). Through Duccio of Siena (recorded from 1285 to 1311) the antique Alexandrian grace preserved by Byzantium began to show some touch of tenderness in his madonnas and saints, but his Passion scenes express a growing sense of pathos in the *Maestà* (Virgin in majesty) of the Siena Duomo (pl. 226).

The future of painting lay in another direction. The true Renaissance was openly affirmed in Rome by Pietro Cavallini (mentioned 1273–1316), who rediscovered classical dignity (mosaics in Santa Maria in Trastevere, frescoes at Santa Cecilia in Trastevere). The Florentine Giotto (about 1266–1337) carried on the efforts of Cavallini and Nicola Pisano, giving Italian painting its main impetus. His principal works are the frescoes of the *Life of St. Francis* in the Upper Church at Assisi (about 1300, pl. 227); those of the *Life of Christ* in the Scrovegni Chapel at Padua (1305, pl. 228); those of the *Legend of St. John and St. Francis* at Santa Croce in Florence (1311–1317). First and foremost a monumental painter and frescoist, Giotto sought the truth of natural forms, while never losing the Byzantine longing for clarity which subjects the composition of the work to some central idea. But this idea, which in Byzantium was spiritual, became both dramatic and plastic in Giotto. His concise art is a work of intellect; he sacrificed the accidental to the greatest expressive concentration. He also brought with him that heroic sense of human life and taste for virile strength which were to inspire Florentine art until the sixteenth century.

The creative effort of Giotto excited such lively admiration in his contemporaries that it resulted in the academic Giottesque style. How-

227. Giotto. Miracle of the Spring. Fresco
from The Life of St. Francis of Assisi. *Assisi, S. Francesco, Upper Church.*

228. Giotto. The Kiss of Judas. Detail of fresco, The Taking of Christ.
1305. *Padua, Scrovegni Chapel.*

229. Simone Martini. The Annunciation. 1333. *Florence, Uffizi.*

ever, his successors were to temper his greatness with the influence of
Sienese tenderness. Such was the case with Bernardo Daddi (mentioned
1317–1349).

The history of Italian painting in the second half of the fourteenth
century shows an eclecticism striving to blend Giottesque precision
with the narrative spirit of the Sienese school and the angular style of
the Gothic. Taddeo Gaddi (d. 1368), who was a direct pupil of Giotto,
remained nearest to his sobriety. Andrea Orcagna was also a sculptor,
and this can be felt in his work. In the third quarter of the century,
Sienese influences took such a hold in Florence that it sometimes becomes
difficult to distinguish Sienese from Florentine works.

At Florence, Giotto imposed on nature a dramatic and aesthetic
order dictated by his intelligence: Sienese art on the contrary is all sensibility, seeking in reality only what makes the quickest appeal. Under
Gothic influence Simone Martini (1283–1344) opposed the supple grace
of his Madonnas to the robustness of Giotto: he achieved intense pathos
not by a concentration of means but by accumulating tragic effects
(*Story of St. Martin*, frescoes in the Lower Church at Assisi; *Annunciation*, at the Uffizi, 1333, pl. 229).

In the second quarter of the century Siena itself came under
Florentine influence. The brothers Pietro and Ambrogio Lorenzetti
assimilated the robust Giottesque plastic outlook while also developing
the feeling for the picturesque which was typically Sienese (*Allegory
of Good and Bad Government*, Siena, Palazzo Pubblico, 1337).

Wearied by this sterile struggle between contrary elements, the
fourteenth century ended in Italy, both in painting and sculpture, in
a decadence which gave no inkling of the wonderful example of creative
energy that Florence was yet to give the world.

CHAPTER VI

ISLAM

ISLAM, which is too often only mentioned casually in histories, or else used as an introduction to the arts of the Far East, is a civilization of the western Mediterranean. Springing from the same monotheistic source as Christian civilization, Islam developed in rivalry with the first forms of Christian art in Byzantium and in the West. Profiting from the rich cultural traditions of the Syrian, Egyptian and Iranian countries on which it was grafted, Moslem civilization flourished far sooner than that of the West, which stagnated in a state of barbarism until the twelfth century and was surpassed three hundred years earlier by the Arabs. The Caliph of Córdoba is said to have owned some several thousand books in the ninth century; almost five hundred years later Charles V of France, who was very proud of his library, had only nine hundred. In every domain of civilization Islam was the first to define the values which were to become those of the Middle Ages: chivalry, courtesy and that noble conduct which Joinville called "prudhommie" (integrity) were moral rules already practiced in the East in the ninth century. It was by trusting to the speculations of Arab theologians and philosophers that Christian thought achieved what it did in the twelfth and thirteenth centuries. Thomas Aquinas knew Aristotle only through the commentaries of Averroës of Córdoba. We also owe our commercial techniques to Moslem civilization (such words as *cheque*, *douane* and *tariff* being Arab), as well as arithmetic, algebra, the first rudiments of medicine, mechanics, chemistry, geography and astronomy. The awakening West was to take all it could from this magnificent source of art and science, by way of Spain, Sicily and the great Italian ports.

The earliest artistic works of Islam were not so unlike those of the West as they might appear. The decorative spirit of the Moslems is nearer that of the early West than was the sacred imagery of Byzantium. Our understanding of Moslem art has been distorted by the accusation that, in obedience to some bar laid down in the Koran, it excluded any image of living things. Nothing of the sort is to be found in the Koran, and only in later texts was the artist warned against the *realistic* reproduction of living things. But if the Moslems created an ornamental

230. Tympanum from a house at Koubatchi (Caucasus).
12th–13th century. *Washington, Freer Gallery.*

system of geometrical devices which perhaps shows their taste for the
abstract speculations of mathematics, in everyday decoration they made
lavish use of animal, vegetable, floral and even human forms. However,
these forms were never "represented" for their own sake as in the
aesthetic which prevailed in the West from the Gothic onward: they
were freely interpreted so as to make a plastic language of infinite
wealth, whose terms all strengthen and enhance each other in a system
of exchanges at which the Oriental imagination excels. This style of
metaphor gives Moslem literature that dreamlike quality which is its
peculiar charm (the poets compare animals with flowers, flowers with
stones and stars; the wound of a gazelle becomes a "pied flower" and
so on). Indeed this art is closest to Romanesque formalism (pl. 230).
The Romanesque and primitive Moslem imageries both sought their
forms in the same Oriental sources—Chaldeo-Assyrian, Sassanian and
Persian—which had been enriched by the peoples of the steppes and
the ornamental instincts of the Barbarians. This stock of imagery,
further enlarged by observing nature, resulted in a system of infinitely
adaptable metamorphoses which allowed the Islamic aesthetic to last
almost to our own time, whereas in the West our equivalent tradition
was interrupted by the rise of realism in the thirteenth century.

The profound difference between Romanesque art and that of
Islam lies in one particular means of plastic expression: for Romanesque
art, originating in sculpture, tended toward carving in the round,

231. Córdoba Mosque, view of the interior.
This part was built by Abd-er-Rahman I in 785.

whereas Islam reduced every form to a surface and expressed itself in polychromy. For the realistic West, sculpture was the fundamental art, while for Islam this was perhaps weaving. Whether it be in stucco, plaster, stone, or openwork marble as in India, Moslem monuments are covered in "tapestries" of forms which drape them like flowing robes (pl. 232).

Starting from myth, Romanesque art seeks the real. During its long life Islamic art never lost the anti-realist instinct of the early civilizations. This instinct rested on a philosophy which denies the very existence of a world in which the whole chain of causality is in the hands of God. Arab thinkers were the first—in the Mediterranean world at least—to formulate the idea of Nothingness. This nonreality of things permits every imaginative fancy to both poet and artist: being embroideries of thought upon appearances they imply no consequences, they are no more than fables and tales. The art of Islam is thus a mirage, a phantasmagoria of images woven on the web of nothingness. The forms so abundantly borrowed from nature are never evoked as anything more than the graceful phantoms of a dream. The scarceness of sculpture in the round perfectly illustrates this aloofness from the real. We are told that a thirteenth century theologian forbade in his home any "images that cast a shade." Three-dimensional sculpture asserts the reality of the space in which it is set: it was to be the chief

232. The Alhambra, Granada. The Lion Court,
built by Mohammed V, 1353-1391.

art in the West, and, when painting came to life, its object was to deceive
the eye, by creating an illusion of three-dimensional space on a plane
surface.

When the Crusaders reached the East they found a decaying
society. The decline of Moslem sciences coincided with a revival of
puritan orthodoxy leading to intolerance. Free thought arose in reaction
to this, and the skeptical philosophers, twelfth century Voltaires, saw
religion as a mere drug, an opium used for secular ends to ensure public
order. Western Islam—the Maghreb—was aware of its decadence: the
refined monuments of Seville and Granada are the decadent forms of
an art which in its maturity had produced the Great Mosque of Córdoba.
However, the Eastern Moslem region was yet to have its true Renaissance, thanks to the new ethnic contribution brought by the Turkish
and Mongol invasions. The eagerness of these barbarians for culture
led to a brilliant renaissance in the arts and letters; they gave fresh youth
to the aging Moslem art by bringing from the refined China of the Sung
Dynasty those elements which, acting like a ferment on the ancient
layers of culture in Iran, produced the exquisite flowering of the Persian
miniature. The miniature is a perfect reflection of Moslem literature
during those Turkish and Mongol periods when, as is to be expected in
an advanced civilization, thought was expressed not so much in the
sciences or metaphysics as in literature, history, lyric and epic poems.

179

233. Córdoba Mosque, Villaviciosa Chapel. Ribbed dome with mosaics, the part constructed by Abd-er-Rahman III. 10th century.

234. Stalactite motif in decoration. Hall of the Two Sisters in the Alhambra, built by Mohammed V. 1353–1391.

235. Coronation cape of the Romano-Germanic Emperors. Silk; woven by an Arab workshop at Palermo for King Roger II of Sicily in 1133. *Vienna, Kunsthistorisches Museum.*

The human figure now predominated; but in the midst of gardens perfumed with flowers and peopled with graceful creatures, it was as intangible as a form seen in a dream. In the same period, in the first half of the fifteenth century, the miniaturists and certain painters of the West such as Pisanello were evoking the fleeting images of the declining Middle Ages in their fairylike, nostalgic creations.

The Turkish and Mongol conquerors had a monumental sense of architecture which raised some imposing works. But perhaps for Moslem art, whose typical form was essentially "minor," this was a symptom of decadence. In the West, there is a decline as soon as architecture becomes ornament; but the opposite was the case in Islam. Delicate decorative effects, traceries in marble, china, tile facings are no longer in scale with the vast spaces and mighty masses of the Safavian or Hindo-Mongol buildings. On the contrary, in the Córdoba Mosque the arabesques hewn in the stonework are symphonically related to the space, which is so cunningly divided by innumerable columns and festooned by the multifoil arches with their interlinking curves.

The art of Islam ended in an extraordinary capitulation to the Byzantine civilization it had overthrown. In Asia Minor, then European Turkey, and very soon throughout their empire, the Ottomans seemed intent on multiplying large and small replicas of Santa Sophia. Islam had been as a spiritual ferment capable of restoring life to the old civilizations it overran, to the peoples of every race that it annexed and whose beliefs it respected in its liberal golden age. Marvelous creations arose from those contacts. But from the sixteenth to the eighteenth century Islam was weary and stopped inventing: it copied itself over and over, imitating what only yesterday it had conquered.

EVOLUTION OF MOSLEM ART
PRIMITIVE PERIOD

The first artistic manifestations of Islam appeared in Syria under the Caliphate of the Omayyads (665–750), whose seat was at Damascus. Transformed Christian churches (El-Aksa Mosque at Jerusalem; the Great Mosque at Damascus) owe most of their features to Hellenistic

236. Low-relief from the castle of Mchatta (Syria). 6th century. Pre-Islamic or proto-Islamic art. *Berlin, Vorderasiatisches Museum.*

and Byzantine art, but the Damascus Mosque already shows the typical
layout of the Moslem sanctuary (pl. 241). The few castles of that period
remaining in Transjordan (Qasr Amra, Mchatta)[1] show the same Hellenistic traits. In 750 the ousting of the Omayyads by the Abbasids
(750–1000) resulted in the transfer of the Caliphate to Baghdad and
enabled Islam to profit from the Iranian tradition (ruins of Samarra).
Islam became more original: under the Caliphate of the Abbasids, which
soon became only nominal, an Iranian and Turkish feudality developed.
Architects turned to brick construction, with great tunnel vaults, or
cupolas, and with applied decorations in stucco or plaster. The encouragement given to all the arts of furnishing by the Abbasids earned
Baghdad a reputation for splendor which was to spread into the West.
Official workshops produced *tiraz* tissues (as the textiles made in state
factories were called); copper and bronze objects which often had
zoomorphic features, inspired by the old animal art of the Sassanians;
pottery which at Samarra, Rakka, Rhagae, Gurgan, revived the Old
Persian art of enameled terra cotta, now enriched by the Arabs with
the process of lead glazing. In Egypt the Tulunids, vassals of the
Abbasids, built large monuments at Fostat which were inspired by those

---

[1] These castles in the Syrian desert used to be attributed to Arab princes before
Islam, vassals of the Sassanians. The present tendency is to consider them as having
been built by the Omayyads; but some doubt remains.

237. Marble pilaster, palace of Medina-az-Zahra, built near Córdoba
by Abd-er-Rahman III in 936. *New York, Metropolitan Museum.*

238. Leaf of a wooden door, from Egypt. Detail. Mameluke art,
13th–14th century. *New York, Metropolitan Museum.*

of Mesopotamia (mosque of Ibn-Tulun, 879), and developed crafts there in the form of textiles, ceramics, woodwork and bookbinding. The Abbasids extended their influence as far as Ifriqiya (Tunisia), where the Aghlabids in the ninth century undertook some great architectural works (mosques at Kairouan in 836, Tunis, Susa: municipal works, fortifications). At the same time, in Spain, a dynasty descended from the Omayyads of Damascus set up its Caliphate in 929 and maintained an art closer to its Hellenistic origins, the masterpiece of which is the Córdoba Mosque (pl. 231), built in 785 and enlarged in 848, 961 and 987. The ruins of Medina-az-Zahra (Medina-Sidonia), 936, contain a palace of that dynasty (pl. 237).

MEDIEVAL PERIOD

The art of Islam was superimposed on the old civilizations of the Mediterranean and Asia. From the eleventh century onward, new elements brought from the interior of Asia by the Turkish and Mongol invasions were to effect some profound changes. The Seljuk Turks who took Baghdad in 1055 remained there until 1250, bringing with them a feeling for grandeur which showed itself in new monumental conceptions of which the vital principle was the vault. They created a type of grandiose mosque with four *liwan* (porticoes) giving onto the central courtyard; then a sort of mosque school (*medersa*, a kind of theological university designed to combat the Shiïte heresy); and finally the domed mausoleum (*turbeh* and *qoubba*) which was a manifestation of warlike pride. Prospering in Mesopotamia (Mosul, Isfahan) the art of the Seljuks extended into Asia Minor (Aleppo, Konya) and the eastern frontiers of Iran (Afghanistan, Khurasan). The Mongol invasion, following on that of the Seljuks (1250–1500), enriched Iranian art with influences from the Far East and quickened the tendency toward splendor. With the Timurids (1370–1500) eastern Khurasan was to produce the finest monuments. The capitals were at Herat and Samarkand, where stands the *Gor-Emir*, the tomb of Tamerlane, built in 1405. Architecture was covered in revetments of enameled faïence: decorative art became somewhat mechanical, but the Persian miniature was now reaching its perfection.

The impact of the Asiatic invasions, accentuating the split in Islamic unity, resulted in a sharper differentiation between the schools. In Egypt and Syria a Caliphate rivaling that of Baghdad, founded in

239. Funerary Mosque of Kait Bey,
at Cairo. 1472.

Cairo by the Fatima Dynasty originating from Ifriqiya (970–1169)
developed an art which hesitated between the various traditions from
Iran. The art of the Ayyubids (1169–1250) and of the Mameluke
Sultans of Cairo (1250–1520) shows Persian, Seljuk and Mongol influences to have predominated in decorative art. The finest monuments
of Moslem art were built at that time in Syria and Egypt, showing a
sound architectural sense (use of stone in two shades, sobriety of decoration, pl. 239). The type of mosque associated with the dynastic
founder's tomb produced very harmonious works at Cairo under the
Mamelukes. To the extreme west of Islam, in the Maghrab (Spain then
included), there developed a style whose unity was favored at the
outset by the common dynasties (Almoravides, 1055–1147; Almohades,
1130–1269), and survived after the empire was dismembered.
This has been called "Hispano-Moorish" art: its principal monuments
are at Marrakesh, Fez, Tlemcen, Rabat, Tunis, Seville (the Giralda, a
twelfth century minaret). At first austere and somewhat archaic, this
style, which was but slightly affected by Iranian influences, ended
in an orgy of ornamentation (The Alhambra of Granada, pl. 232).
In the early period of the conquest Moslem art persisted in Christian
Spain either in its pure state (Alcazar at Seville, fourteenth–sixteenth
century) or in a hybrid Gothico-Moslem form called Mudejar (Ducal
Palace of the Infantado at Guadalajara, 1480–1492).

184

240. The Taj Mahal at Agra. Tomb of Mumtaz-i-Mahal, wife of Shah Jehan.
Built 1630–1648.

THE MODERN PERIOD

In Persia, art reached a brilliant level under the Iranian dynasty of the
Safavids (1514–1720) which succeeded the Mongols. This was a
court art, not very inventive, but which cleverly exploited the heritage of Moslem forms. Shah Abbas I (1587–1628) assuming all the
responsibilities of a modern ruler, rebuilt Isfahan according to an ambitious scheme of town-planning, enriching it with mosques and palaces.
Following the Iranian type with four liwans, the Royal Great Mosque
(1612–1640) is entirely covered with faïence decoration both inside
and out. The royal workshops produced textiles, carpets, ceramics
which were much sought after in the West. Decoration lost its geometrical stiffness and used naturalistic features such as flowers and trees.
The Chinese taste for porcelain began to influence pottery. Tabriz, in
Azerbaijan, became the center for the official school of miniaturists, who
cultivated the Timur (Tamerlane) style.

India under its Mongol Dynasty (1520–1800) enjoyed a great
expansion in architecture (mosques, palaces, tombs at Delhi, Agra and
Lahore). Moslem India proved to have a monumental sense comparable
to that of the West (Taj Mahal, built by Shah Jehan as a tomb for
his favorite wife, pl. 240). The innate naturalism of the Hindu soul
reappeared in the miniature, which they informed with all the poetry
of love and pride. The empire of the Ottoman Turks (1300), which

185

was established at the expense of the Byzantine empire, apparently hoped
to prolong the greatness of Constantinople, after its destruction. After
the downfall of Constantinople, now renamed Istanbul, the church of
Santa Sophia greatly influenced the form of mosques, the tendency now
being toward the central plan (Mosque of Bayazid by Viheir-ed-Din,
1481–1512; Mosque of Suleiman by Sinan, 1550, who built a large
number of monuments, including the Shah Zadeh and Sultan Ahmed
Mosques). Decorative art (textiles, carpets, ceramics) increasingly
took naturalistic themes from flowers and other forms (tulip, marigold,
pomegranate, hyacinth, rose, vine). The art of the Osmanlis (Ottomans)
spread throughout their empire to Syria, Egpyt, Tunisia and Algeria,
to decline entirely in the eighteenth century under Western influence
when it was ruined by rococo features.

ARCHITECTURE

Despite its wide radiation in both time and place, Moslem architecture
owed its remarkable unity to a religious faith and an unchanging way
of life. Concurrently with the West and Byzantium but over a much
greater area, Islam spread vault construction all over the world after it
had been devised by Mesopotamia and Iran. Although construction
with stone materials was almost as much favored as building in rubble
and brick, it was the latter, brickwork, which dominated all Moslem
architecture, resulting in an aesthetic of applied decoration for ornamental effect, rather than a monumental plastic code.

From the very beginning, Islam created a type of sanctuary—the
mosque—adapted to a religion without ritual, but of which the essential
activity was communal prayer. In order to shelter the congregation,
Islam imitated the vast colonnades in the naves of Christian churches,
multiplying them to give the impression of infinite numbers, but placing
them crosswise and not down the length of the building (pls. 231 and
241). The classic mosque was composed of four porticoes or *liwans*
framing a courtyard or *sahn* in the center of which stood a fountain
for ablutions (*midha*). The liwan standing in the far end of the
courtyard and serving as a prayer chamber (*haram*) consisted of
several naves, while the far wall or *qibla* was perpendicular to the
direction of Mecca and marked by an archway or niche, the *mihrab;*
a *mimbar* made of wood served as a pulpit. Sometimes a large, deep nave

led to the mihrab, which was topped with a dome (pl. 233). One or several minarets or belfries were used by the *muezzin* for the call to prayer. These minarets took many different shapes. At first they were strong square towers; then in Mesopotamia they took on the helix form of the Assyrian ziggurats. Persia, from the ninth century, created the definitive type of very slight tower, elongated and slim like a candle, with a balcony at the top. Seljuk Persia in the twelfth century invented a second type of mosque on a cruciform plan, no doubt suggested by the old Sassanian palaces: these had four perpendicular liwans in the central court, opening their high wide vaults upon it. Finally the Ottoman Turks in the sixteenth century gave the mosque a basilican form with a central cupola, inspired by Santa Sophia. The mosque school or medersa grouped four sets of buildings round the central courtyard, corresponding with the four orthodox rites taught there (pl. 242). The Mongols introduced into Persia a circular mausoleum surmounted by a dome, which the Egyptian Mamelukes combined with the mosque. The design of palaces still followed that of the Assyrian palace divided into two parts, each of them grouped round a courtyard: the *selamlik* for public activities, the harem for private life. The audience—or throne—room (*diwan*) opened on to one of the sides of the selamlik. The dwelling showed nothing but blank walls from the outside, the few openings being sealed by wooden grills called *moucharabies*. The interior was veneered with decorations in stucco

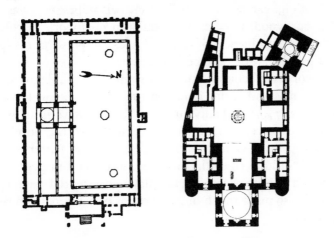

241. Ground plan of the Great Mosque at Damascus, 705.
After G. Marçais, L'Art de l'Islam.

242. Ground plan of the tomb-mosque of Sultan Hasan, Cairo, 1356.
After Woermann, Geschichte der Kunst.

or porcelain, while often fountains played here and there for coolness. Long before the Christians, the Moslems, who love flowers, knew that refinement in the art of living, the culture of gardens (gardens of the Generalife, Granada). The finest palaces still standing today are to be found in Spain and India.

The Moslems were very skillful in throwing light arches over wide spans, sometimes also using the sectional method of construction tested by the Sassanians. From the tenth century onward in Mesopotamia and Spain they discovered how to divide vaults by means of ribbing, two hundred years before the builders of the West (pl. 233). They also had astute carpenters who designed complex ceilings with lavish decorations. The Moslem architects, except in a few early Islamic edifices, used the arch in preference to the lintel. Encouraged by their instinct for ornament they gave their archways and vaults all kinds of profiles, both pointed and round—the stilted arch, the horseshoe, the multifoil, the cusped, the ogee, and the four-centered arch. They sometimes even intercrossed tiered arches (Córdoba Mosque, pl. 231).

The structure prepared by the architect had to take a facing of applied decorations which tended to cover all its surface. The constructional elements themselves rapidly became ornamental motifs such as the corner squinch, used for the transition from the square to the cupola: fragmented and multiplied this feature was transformed into *mukarnas* or stalactites which ended by being grafted everywhere on arches, pendentives, capitals, ceilings, friezes, lintels, etc. (pl. 234). The revetment decoration, carried out exclusively in arabesque, was done in plaster, stucco, wood, mosaic, or in India in openwork marble, and in Persia under the influence of the Safavids in polychrome porcelain which clothed the whole edifice like a robe.

The decorative themes found their source in the foliated scrollwork alive with animals and fruits, common to Hellenistic and Byzantine art (pls. 236 and 237). Gradually in both Mesopotamia and Egypt these scrolls lost all their relief, their design thinned into the purely abstract type of pattern since called *arabesque*. Arabesque patterns throw up against a dark ground their flat braiding, interlaced in geometrical designs in which the starred polygon plays an essential part (pl. 238). The Moslems also made much of inscriptions of extracts from the Koran in Kufic script.

THE MINOR ARTS

While the peoples of the West were still leading a crude barbarian existence the Moslem princes succeeded in bringing all the refinements of intellectual culture and material luxury to the art of living. They attached great importance to the beauty of everyday things and to the decoration of their houses, and set up workshops in their palaces as well as seeking far and wide for objets d'art and skilled artists. Commercial exchanges became so active between the Moslem countries that the exact origin of old pieces is often hard to trace.

The repugnance shown by the Moslems for representation of living figures hindered sculpture, but in the lay crafts there were none of the limitations that restricted decoration in religious buildings, where the geometrical style alone was allowed. The art of Islam, in a word, maintained into modern times the ancient zoomorphic and phytomorphic[2] decorative style of the East, which it took at first hand from Iran and Mesopotamia, where it was still flourishing in the Sassanian civilization at the time of the conquest. Thus living forms were suggested only obliquely, through a decorative stylization which stripped them of all reality or representational value. Perhaps the Shiïte heresy, which at various times took hold of Iran, the crucible of Islamic art, had some indulgence toward this decorative imagery, being at all events less puritanical than was the Sunnite orthodoxy. Varying on both geometrical speculation and the fluid stylization of living forms, the Moslems had thus an inexhaustible stock which they exploited to the full. Under Mongol rule from the thirteenth century onward, Persia showed a bent for human representation which emerged in the highly developed miniature. In its final phase Moslem art was energized once more by the introduction of naturalistic floral themes which gave a springlike youthfulness to their ceramics and tapestries (pl. 243).

Moslem decoration is essentially polychromatic. No doubt weaving was considered as the highest art in Islam. The best tissues in cotton and silk used in the oldest Sassanian decorations are no longer known to us save in fragments so far as the earliest periods are concerned, being mostly treasured in the Western churches which imported them at great cost for wrapping and preserving holy relics. This art also prospered in the West, especially at Palermo in workshops which

---

[2] Decoration based on plant forms.

243. Persian carpet. Detail. 16th century.
Paris, Musée des Arts Décoratifs.

the Norman kings of Sicily maintained on a royal scale (pl. 235). The art of rug-making which flourished in Persia and in Asia Minor gave rise to a brisk trade with the West in the Middle Ages. The oldest specimens remaining date only from the sixteenth century, but earlier Eastern carpets can be studied thanks to the frequency with which they were shown in Western paintings from the fourteenth century on. Carpets woven since the end of the sixteenth century in Asia Minor or in the Armenian mountains (Shirvan; Kuba, Azerbaijan) are designed on a geometric or stylized floral principle. The same is true of Turkestan (Bukhara) carpets. In accordance with their temperament the Persians often enlivened their carpets with hunting scenes, animal combats, trees and flowers portrayed in a naturalistic manner (pl. 243). They kept alive all the spirit of the Hellenistic scroll. Their carpets are often very close to contemporary miniatures (Isfahan, Teheran, Shushagan, Khurasan, Shiraz, Tabriz). Indian carpets imitated the Persian, while those called Hispano-Moorish, of which few preconquest specimens remain, were on geometrical lines. The Eastern Moslem carpets were imitated in China, in the Balkans, and with extraordinary success in Poland.

Pieces of pottery have fortunately been recovered in large quantities by digging, or were found concealed in the walls of buildings. The workshops of Mesopotamia (Samarra, Iraq) or Persia (Susa, Rhagae) soon restored to its high place the art of enameled faïence which had reached such a fine perfection under the Achaemenians. It was they who invented lustered decoration with metallic or mottled sheens, varying from golden yellow to a coppery red, or from brown to green. The best specimens came from the workshops at Rhagae, Sultanabad, Gurgan, Rakka in the eleventh, twelfth and thirteenth centuries. Animal and floral decorative imagery they treated with an exquisite fantasy, and they gave little scope to the geometrical style (pl. 244). In the eighteenth century Chinese influence began to filter into Persia, while Asia Minor was to renew its repertory by adding naturalistic floral decoration with a rich range of color. Lustered decoration spread throughout Islam and in the West resulted in Hispano-Moorish faïence (Malaga, Valencia) which was to survive after the Moslems left Spain (thirteenth to sixteenth century). The working of glass which the Syrians and Egyptians mastered was related to that of faïence and was enriched with enamels, for example in the lamps for mosques.

Moslem metalwork began in Mesopotamia, where copper mines provided the necessary raw material. From the tenth and eleventh centuries the region of Mosul produced bowls, caldrons and ewers in incised copper or brass. A little later, in the twelfth century, they began to make brass objects chased with threads of silver, gold or red copper, a technique known as damaskeening (pl. 246). This art subsequently spread to Syria and Egypt. Its patterns are the same as those of pottery.

244. Faïence with lustered decoration from Rhagae, Persia.
12th–13th century. *Paris, Louvre.*

245. Zoomorphic perfume brazier. Persian art from the excavations in Gurgan. Early 13th century. *Teheran, Museum.*

246. Alms bowl from the Baptistery of St. Louis. Mongol period of Mesopotamian art. Middle of the 13th century. *Paris, Louvre.*

Mixed with pewter, the copper of Mesopotamia gave some fine articles in bronze (fountains, ewers, braziers, mirrors, mosque lamps, door panels), the oldest of which are of Mesopotamian origin (animal-shaped ewers) going back to the ninth century and prolonging the zoomorphic art of the Sassanians. The Fatimids of Egypt and the Omayyads of Spain also had bronze foundries. The objects just mentioned are the only examples of sculpture in the round in Moslem art. The treatment of ivory (caskets) was an offshoot of Byzantine technique, and was a

247. Sailing on the Euphrates. Miniature from the Makamat of Hariri,
About 1220. *Paris, Bibliothèque Nationale.*

specialty of Córdoba (tenth and eleventh centuries) and in thirteenth
century Sicily. Cairo craftsmen excelled in wood-carving, a technique
already well developed by the Copts in the Hellenistic period.

PERSIAN AND HINDU MINIATURES

The oldest examples of Iranian painting have been discovered in "outer
Iran" in the sanctuaries of Turkestan which were decorated between 760
and 840 by the Uigur Turks, Manichees of Persian origin. Their mural
paintings and manuscripts, showing affinities with the oldest Sassanian
paintings of Bamiyan (third to sixth century) and even more so with
those of later Mongolian Persia, prove the continuity of an Iranian
tradition. However, the first great school of miniaturists in Persia of
which we have examples, the Abbasid school of Mesopotamia (twelfth,
thirteenth centuries) is of Arab inspiration. It shows strongly accentuated Semitic types, a tendency toward dramatic composition, a dry
style, a limited range of color and a sweeping execution which leads
us to suppose that they knew the art of the fresco (*Pharmacopoeia of
Dioscorides*, early thirteenth century; *Makamat of Hariri*, Leningrad
and Paris, Bibliothèque Nationale, about 1220, pl. 247; *Fables of
Bidpai*, Bibliothèque Nationale, about 1230).

193

Under the Mongol princes the miniature developed rapidly on a level worthy of the literary, poetic, historical and scientific achievement of Islam. This art was cultivated in the Transoxiana region (eastern Iran), then, after the Mongol conquest, in Mesopotamia. The Mongols brought with them a powerful Chinese influence. Their types, costumes and landscapes are Sino-Mongol in character (*Chronicle of Rachid-ed-Din*, Bibliothèque Nationale, about 1310). In the Timurid period (1370–1500) this element blended harmoniously with the old Iranian manner and Arabo-Abbasid art. Springing from such fertile sources the miniature soon showed an admirable versatility of method and a very rich stock of forms. The lyricism of nature (animals, flowers, fields) and social life, together with a bent for romance, gave the sixteenth century Persian miniature some affinity with the cosmopolitan art which prevailed in Europe between 1380 and 1430 (French miniatures; the work of Pisanello in Italy). The center of that art was then at Herat in Transoxiana (now Afghanistan) (*Apocalypse of Mahomet*, 1436, Bibliothèque Nationale). The famous Bihzad lived toward the end of the Timurid Dynasty, working at Herat from 1469 to 1506 in the service of the last of these kings. Then, after the fall of the dynasty, he moved to the court of the first Safavid at Tabriz, where he died in 1529 leaving a whole school of artists (Sultan Mohammed, Ustad Mohammed) known as the Safavian school. This group was remarkable for a certain decadent mannerism (lengthening of forms, twisting of bodies) and an increasing tendency to worldliness and amorous lyricism. The miniature was no longer confined to books and began to be treated as an independent picture. The portrait, introduced by Bihzad, became very popular. This school persisted into the seventeenth century, gradually losing its better qualities, thanks to a slackness of style as well as naturalism (Agha-Riza, Riza-Abbasi, Shafi-Abbasi).

Under the Mongol emperors in India (sixteenth, seventeenth centuries) a very fertile school of miniature developed which turned to Persia for its material, the Mongol princes ordering artists to copy Persian works. But the school was fundamentally different, owing to the traditional Indian taste for naturalism, which was strengthened by the European influences introduced by the Jesuits. European perspectivism ousted the Persian panoramic vision; the miniature was usually independent of books; and the portrait became a character study. Painters sought effects of atmosphere which they suggested in a natural-

istic way, varying the light according to the time of day and so on.
The sensual eroticism to be found here was as old as the Indian soul
itself (pl. 248).

Persian and Hindu miniatures were executed on paper, which the
Moslems learned from the Chinese how to make. Books were dressed
in sumptuous bindings (bookbinding being probably an Egyptian invention dating from the Hellenistic epoch). The Egyptians illuminated
luxurious Korans with purely geometrical designs.

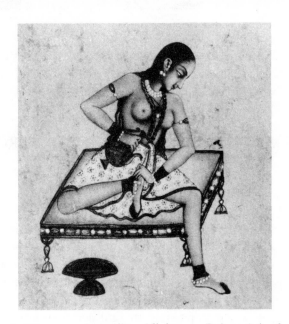

248. Woman at her toilet. **Miniature.** Rajput School,
18th–19th century. *Paris, Musée Guimet.*

MYSTIC NATURALISM

249. Hubert and Jan Van Eyck (Flemish School). Group of Virgin Martyrs. Detail of the Ghent Altarpiece. *Ghent, St.-Bavon.*

CHAPTER VII

THE ARTISTIC CIVILIZATION OF EUROPE IN THE FIFTEENTH CENTURY

AFTER THE UNITY achieved in fourteenth century Europe through the imposition of Gothic by France, the fifteenth century was one of remarkable confusion. There were two warring principles: the Flamboyant style, which was the final phase of Gothic, and the Renaissance style. France was weakened by the Hundred Years' War, and the two creative regions of Europe were now Italy and Flanders, the latter now making its triumphant entry into European civilization.

However, it is not impossible to find some underlying principle in such a rich century, in spite of the many local and national variations and the apparently marked differences of forms. After being a handmaid of a religious faith which tolerated only what could further its own ideals, art broke its bondage to theology and became a means of knowing the external world. The *mirror* is a common symbol of this new art, which reflected nature, and despite stylistic differences, at least in painting, the same phenomena affected the two parent schools in Italy and Flanders.

The veil of symbolism was torn, but the world as the artist saw it with fresh eyes dazzled him like a marvelous vision. Still deeply imbued with mysticism, he responded to the beauty of the universe as the image but no longer the symbol of Paradise: for Fra Angelico, Gentile da Fabriano, Pisanello, as for Hubert Van Eyck and the Rhenish painters, virgins, angels and holy hermits walked in the enchanted meadows of spring; at the dawn of an era of positivism the "dream of love" of the mystic of Assisi yielded its finest flowers.

However, on the intellectual plane the world was soon to be regarded as an object of knowledge and no longer as the subject of sentimental and imaginative outpourings.

The central problem which then worried artists was the conquest of depth and spatial values. A passion for the three-dimensional set sculpture above the other arts: this was the unifying principle of the century all over Europe, and through it Conrad Witz, Paolo Uccello, Rogier Van der Weyden were at one. Certainly their methods differed, for the Flemish artists advanced hesitantly into space, letting intuition take the lead, while the Florentines pursued this quest for spatial values rationally and, like surveyors, caught space in a net of geometry. Dirk Bouts in Flanders was perhaps aware of the power of linear perspective, but that was not what the Flemish were after. It was by the sensual expression of atmospheric values that Jan Van Eyck was able to suggest immense depths in a few square centimeters.

From now on the artist, with the eye of a reporter, discovered an immense field to be explored, the infinite variety of the forms of the world of man and nature. This inquiry was pursued unsystematically

MYSTIC NATURALISM

250. Stefano da Zevio (Verona School). Madonna in the Rose Garden. Detail. *Verona, Civic Museum.*

251. Master of the Upper Rhine.
The Little Garden of Paradise.
About 1420.
*Formerly in Frankfurt,
Städel Art Institute.*

by the northern artists, who built up gradually a vocabulary of gestures and expressions, facial types and natural forms. But for Italy it was an exact science, and Leonardo, the most significant figure in the Quattrocento, dreamed of making painting the crowning glory of human knowledge, since representing the forms of creation implied for him a scientific study of the world.

Retarded for almost a century by the Gothic invasion that like the rest of Europe she had no choice but to accept, it was in the early fifteenth century that Italy achieved that upsurge of artistic civilization for which the peninsula is famous and which has been called the Renaissance. The Swiss historian Jakob Burckhardt in 1860 defined the Renaissance as an affirmation of the individual, who now emerged from the anonymous crowd of the Middle Ages. From now on the work of art was strongly marked by its author's imprint, and the creative activity of the intellect in the field of the arts was to be considered as one of the finest in the history of man. The artist was promoted from the status of artisan to become an aristocrat of the mind. Yet the time had not come when great isolated workers, commissioned by the society of their time, were to leave their ivory towers to overwhelm mankind with their messages. Setting a distance between itself and the masses, the art of the Renaissance was exalted by the enthusiasm of an aristocratic class of patrons and intellectuals. It became a princely activity, and now, more than in earlier periods when it had been swept along by the collective urge of society, it came to depend on patronage. Freed from all spiritual or temporal usefulness, the work of art as it became an "objet d'art" was to be an end in itself. It was made for a pure act of contemplation to which only an enlightened élite could aspire. The fertility and variety of Italian art of the Quattrocento benefited from the political division of the peninsula into rival principalities which resulted in great competition in all cultural matters. The Medici at Florence, the Aragons at Naples, the Sforzas at Milan, the Estes at Ferrara, the Gonzagas at Mantua, and the Montefeltros of Urbino outbid each other for artists of repute. Works of art, valuable evidence of the greatness of man, were now collected by princes as priceless treasures: the idea of the Museum, a temple reserved for the cult of Beauty, belongs to the Renaissance.

The art of the Quattrocento was the most heroic attempt that had been made to bring the world down to the human scale. Whatever in the world cannot be grasped by the senses or the human intelligence, all the infinitude of nature and the yearnings of the soul toward the beyond, whatever can be perceived only by mystical intuition and escapes the pure lucidity of consciousness, all this was rejected from a world ruled by the arts of architecture and sculpture whose logic is based on the idea of limitation. The Quattrocento went farther along this humanistic road than the antiquity it thought it was reviving: the

THE OBSESSION WITH RELIEF

252. Conrad Witz. Sabothay and Benaiah. Detail from the reredos of the Mirror of Salvation. About 1435. *Basel, Kunstmuseum.*
253. Andrea del Castagno. Portrait of Pippo Spano.
Florence, Cenacolo di Sta. Apollonia.

notion of "man the measure of all things" must have been powerfully rooted in the make-up of Mediterranean man, to have been capable of asserting itself so strongly after fourteen hundred years of Christianity in which man had lived bowed under the yoke of God. Faith, the need to accept values which the mind considers as supreme, now gave way to that instinct toward Knowledge which drives man to accept only such ideas as can be proved true by reasoning. Rationalism was the true

THE PAINTERS OF "HARMONY"

254. Hans Memling. The Virgin with Apple. Wing of the Diptych of Martin Van Nieuwenhoven. 1487. *Bruges, St. John's Hospital.*

255. Perugino. The Holy Family. Detail. *Paris, Louvre.*

256. Master of Moulins. The Virgin and Child. Detail of central panel of the Moulins Triptych. About 1498. *Moulins, Cathedral.*

principle of the Italian Renaissance; it dictates its every step in the field of thought and art. Dedicated to the understanding of nature, art became a rational pursuit of the appearances of the external world, but this conquest of the visible found itself checked by a speculative inquiry no less logically pursued—into the abstract "laws" of beauty. This contradiction caused a tension resulting in a host of creations of genius, such as mankind had never seen before. Even Greek art never had such a wealth of talent—though it is true that classical humanism expressed itself in philosophical speculations which Italy had nothing to equal. It was in creations in the plastic field that Renaissance humanism found its most powerful expression, its works of pure thought being over-shadowed by the revival of ancient philosophy. Quattrocento Italy is perhaps the most remarkable instance of a civilization developed mainly in plastic terms.

Their sharp minds and eagerness for knowledge fitted the Floren-tines for the task of presiding over the new civilization. The Medici family, and especially Cosimo who first established its power, has a title to the glory of the early Renaissance, which for a century brought such fame to Florence. The first half of the Quattrocento witnessed the final flowering of the Gothic aesthetic in the northern and central provinces of Lombardy and the Marches. Toward the 1460's in Venetia (Padua and Venice) a new center began to develop values which were alien to the intellectualist aesthetic of the Florentines. Sixteenth century art sprang from the union of Florence and Venice.

The other European countries did not ignore the Italians' brilliant example, but they first had to soothe their nostalgia for a vanishing enchanted world, and that is why fifteenth century North Europe pro-duced one of the deepest expressions of the Middle Ages. It was not without some anguish that Knowledge began to challenge Faith in men's minds. The art of the fifteenth century which gave such prominence to expressing the pangs of death is evidence of that tragic debate: it is as though the more Italy exalted man's greatness, the more desperately Northern civilization clung to Christianity and sought to diminish man. Italy itself was not entirely untouched by these passionate debates, as can be seen from the tragic and victorious offensive of the Germanic Flamboyant style against the Ferrara school. The Renaissance spirit slowly advanced against such trials as these. France remained less aloof from it than any other country, and the keen-minded Jean Fouquet is a lay brother of Fra Angelico. However, the situation looked desperate and there seemed little hope of the North emerging from its tangled forest of belated Gothic when, in about 1480–1490, the cloud suddenly broke. As though the word had been passed round, artists of every nationality shook free of the torments of expressionism, and Italy herself threw off the harshness of a style which was intent on Truth alone. At Venice, Bellini; in Umbria, Perugino; in Florence, Ghirlandaio; in Flanders, Memling and Gerard David; in Germany, Holbein the Elder and Tilman Riemenschneider; in France, Michel Colombe and the Master of Moulins devoted themselves to a calm vision of harmonious forms. Resistance was overcome, and through the broken dykes Italy was to overflow into the North in an invasion which produced a crisis that was to have enduring aftereffects in the artistic development of all Europe.

THE RENAISSANCE IN ITALY
ARCHITECTURE

The great Florentine artists' innovation early in the century was to deliberately cast aside Gothic principles in an attempt to return to the architectural forms which had been developed in classical antiquity. Since they had never understood the inner form of Gothic architecture they had no qualms in giving up what for them had never been more than a setting for something else. The architect Brunelleschi and the sculptors Donatello and Ghiberti early in the century began studying the remains of Ancient Rome, which at that time were still almost intact, and became the leaders in the new Reform.

In the field of architectural forms, the Renaissance left behind the complex designs and intricate planes of the Gothic, returning to simple compositions with clearly defined volumes and sharp surfaces, of which many an example was still to be found in Roman art. The great idea of that time was the central-plan building arranged round a main dome, the masterpiece of this type being Bramante's plan for St. Peter's, Rome. Brunelleschi (1377–1446) brought to completion a work begun in the fourteenth century, crowning with a mighty dome (344 feet 6 inches elevation to the lantern light) his crossing of Santa Maria del Fiore (Florence) which was inspired by the Pantheon in Rome. At San Lorenzo (pl. 260) and Santo Spirito he left medieval forms behind and gave his churches all the bright harmony of basilicas. The dome of

257. Duomo, Florence. Campanile begun by Giotto in 1343; dome (1420–1434) by Brunelleschi.

Santa Maria del Fiore was competed for in 1417 and built between 1420 and 1434 (pl. 257). San Lorenzo, the Medici family's church, was begun in 1416 and swiftly completed. In this building as in the Pazzi Chapel of Santa Croce (after 1430) Brunelleschi returned to the classical decorative grammar, with Corinthian columns, entablatures, pediments, fluted pilasters, rose windows, scalloping, garlands, cornices, ovolos, denticulation, semicircular arches.

It remained for Michelozzo (1391–1472), who was a pupil of Brunelleschi and Donatello, to create the typical Florentine palace (Medici-Riccardi Palace), a strong stone cube enlivened with classical decorations and topped with a monumental cornice. Closed off from the outside world in the manner of the Greek or Roman villa, its interior contains a charming pillared courtyard or *cortile*.

Leon Battista Alberti (1404–1472) had the most speculative mind of his time. His researches resulted in the art of Bramante, and he wrote the first treatise on architecture (*De re aedificatoria*); but he contented himself with intellectual pursuits and most of his designs were carried out by others.

In the Rucellai Palace (1446–1451) Alberti was the first to reintroduce the idea of superimposed orders (Doric, Ionic and Corinthian) followed by the Romans, which he did in the applied decorations of his façade (pl. 258). The basilican church of Sant'Andrea, Mantua, which was built after his design at the end of the century is a single-naved building which later inspired Vignola's Il Gesù in Rome. In the Tempio Malatestiano (San Francesco) at Rimini (about 1446) his façade is based on the classical triumphal arch.

One of the finest achievements of the Quattrocento is the great castle built at Urbino in the Marches, by Duke Federigo da Montefeltro. It was begun in about 1455 and finished about 1480, the work being carried out from 1466/67 by the Dalmatian Luciano Laurana and later the Sienese Francesco di Giorgio. Decorative sculpture has rarely reached greater delicacy than here. The ducal apartments have several chambers fraught with humanistic meaning: a twin chapel with a Temple of the Muses, a *studiolo* or study decorated with portraits of great men and inlaid work with symbolic patterns.

The architectural creations of the second half of the century in Florence had not the same genial inventiveness as this. Bernardo Rossellino (1409–1464), Benedetto da Maiano, who in 1489 built the finest of Florentine palaces in the Palazzo Strozzi, Giuliano da Maiano (1432–1490) and above all Giuliano da Sangallo (1445–1516) all prepared the way for the masterpieces of the great builders of the sixteenth

258. Rucellai Palace, Florence. Built after the plans of
Leon Battista Alberti, 1446–1451.
259. Façade window of the Certosa di Pavia. Façade begun in 1473 by
the Mantegazzas and continued by G. A. Amadeo.

260. San Lorenzo, Florence. By Brunelleschi. Nave, begun in 1419.

century by their patient researches in matters of detail. At the end of the century the new style developed in Florence spread all over Italy. Lombardy, which had felt the Gothic influence more strongly than any other Italian province, applied it in a diluted form, largely picturesque, in the Certosa di Pavia (pl. 259). Founded in 1396 but not completed until much later (begun by Giovanni Solari, continued by the two Mantegazzas, Giovanni Antonio Amadeo, 1447–1522, and others), the Charterhouse is the most famous example of this new style, and it is a pity that the Italian Renaissance was to be known to Europe by this, rather than by Florentine examples. Pure Gothic lingered on in Naples, which was under the patronage of the Aragon family. Venice passed rather late from the Gothic—which like Milan it had known in the Flamboyant mode—to the Renaissance style, which Antonio Rizzo (d. 1498) transformed into a flowery, cheerful style in the tradition of Laguna (Adriatic) art. Florentine influence came to the fore with Pietro Lombardo (d. 1515), a sculptor and architect who, with a sense of perfection tending to Byzantinism, both built and decorated the marble gem, Santa Maria dei Miracoli. In lively contrast with the cold straight masses of the Florentine palace—which derives from the fortress—the spirit of fenestrated architecture which had held sway in the Laguna in the Middle Ages appeared once more in the Renaissance Venetian palace, whose first completely developed expression is the Palazzo Vendramin-Calergi on the Grand Canal, a work designed no doubt by Mauro Coducci (d. 1504).

261. Ghiberti. The Creation of Adam and Eve. Bronze.
Panel of the Door of Paradise, east door of the Baptistery, Florence.

262. Donatello. The Annunciation. Marble. About 1435.
Florence, Sta. Croce.

In the first half of the fifteenth century the ferment of the Renaissance is thus seen to have wrought its work in Florence alone, in an Italy which was otherwise overrun by Flamboyant Gothic.

SCULPTURE

In the portrayal of figures sculpture was now the major art, for sculptors were twenty-five years ahead of painters in the discovery of the new style, the painters always keeping their eye on the sculptors' experiments. The statue was the ideal of the period. No doubt sculpture owed its prominence to the fact that it was an essentially physical art in a period whose main aim was to give their due to the beauty and strength of the human body. It is also privileged by being situated in real space, and all the arts of the Quattrocento were dominated by an urge to master the three dimensions of space either in reality (through sculpture) or in appearance (through painting). Side by side with the shaping of marble the Italians developed bronze statuary, which incidentally they had never allowed to fall into neglect.

Of all the great masters who gave their share to the new plastic outlook, only one was not a Florentine. This was Jacopo della Quercia (1374–1438), who was from Siena. With a minimum of modeling he attained from the very start that vigorous sense of the human body which was to haunt the whole century until it was caught again by Michelangelo. The Florentines Lorenzo Ghiberti (1378–1455) and Donatello (1382?–1466) were slower in breaking with the Gothic spirit. Ghiberti kept something of the Gothic sense of the picturesque, its naturalistic spatial lyricism and its canon of elongated proportions, but he was able to give spatial depth to his low-reliefs by the *schiacciato* process of flattened modeling, which he invented and which consists of giving an impression of great depth even with a very thin base of material, whether marble or bronze, by means of a heavy foreshortening in the modeling.

Ghiberti was the laureate of the famous competition for the second bronze door of the Florence Baptistery (1401) with which the great sculptural ventures of the century began: he took the prize against Quercia and Brunelleschi, who were also competing. From 1403 to 1423 he made this door in a style close to the Gothic, inspired by the first door, which had been sculpted by Andrea Pisano in the fourteenth century. The third door (carried out between 1425 and 1452), called the *Paradise Door* (because of its subject and its beauty), shows his personal art at its very height: exploiting the metal's thickness, with tremendous virtuosity he managed to suggest depth effects such as are found in painting (pl. 261).

The genius of Ghiberti, like Fra Angelico's, drew him toward the expression of harmony: Donatello on the contrary was carried along by a dramatic tenseness and a longing for grandeur. Italian art has always hesitated between these two paths, the first of which led to Raphael, and the second to Michelangelo. Nanni di Banco (1384–1421) sought his inspiration in classical statuary even more deliberately than Ghiberti had done, but Donatello was the first to use themes taken from paganism. Unlike Ghiberti he was blind to the beauties of nature and all his art was dedicated to the praise of the human form, whose inner structure he studied with an analytic keenness which sometimes led him to stress muscles and tendons so that they stood out as if the model were flayed. He freed the statue from architecture to which it had been subservient since the Middle Ages, and made it into a detached form, valid from every angle, conceived as a volume in the three dimensions of space. He created the sculptured portrait bust (*Niccolò da Uzzano*). A soul tormented by his passionate vision of the human drama, he was a direct forerunner of Michelangelo.

His first works, at the Florence Duomo (*St. John*, 1411?), Or San Michele (*St. George*, 1416?) or on the campanile of the Duomo (*Prophets*, 1416–1435), were still closely connected with their architectural setting. It was in the course of a visit to Rome in 1432–1433, when he was much impressed by classical works, that Donatello was freed from his dramatic expressionism. He then began to express the beauty of the human body in the flower of its youth (*Love; David; St. John the Baptist; Annunciation* of Santa Croce, pl. 262; *Dancing Loves* [putti] of the Prato pulpit and on the Cantoria of the Florence Duomo); yet the bronze bas-reliefs of the Santo at Padua (1444–1448) show a return of his dramatic instinct and a wish to imitate the fluidness of painting. In 1453 he set up in Padua his equestrian statue of the *Condottiere Gattamelata*, the image of self-assured power, for which Donatello took his inspiration from Imperial Roman statues. This rider is one of the loftiest expressions of humanistic pride of the Quattrocento, a symbol of the triumph of intelligence over brute force (pl. 263).

In the second half of the century sculpture in Florence showed the same phenomenon of relaxed tension as can be seen in painting and architecture. The art of Donatello gave the lead to the whole of the next generation. Luca della Robbia alone (1400–1483) proved unwilling to follow him: in polychromatic ceramics (pl. 265) he created a religious

263. Donatello. Statue of Gattamelata, at Padua.
Bronze. About 1447–1453.
264. Andrea del Verrocchio. David. 1476.
Florence, Bargello.

265. Luca della Robbia. Virgin and Child. Enameled terra cotta.
Florence, Bargello.

266. Agostino di Duccio. Angels, making music. Marble. 1460.
Perugia, Oratory of S. Bernardino.

imagery whose devoutness and fluid style recall Fra Angelico; but he learned more from the harmony of classical drapery than any of his contemporaries. Mino da Fiesole (1431–1484), Desiderio da Settignano (1428–1464), Antonio Rossellino (1417 to about 1478), Benedetto da Maiano (1442–1497), who all worked in marble, were decorators who did their best to recapture Donatello's gracefulness, but made it somewhat insipid. The Sienese Agostino di Duccio (1418 to about 1481) on the other hand expressed it with a mannerist incisiveness (pl. 266). The bronze workers found in Donatello a terser sense of analysis which they sometimes mannerized; this was the case with Bertoldo (d. 1491), who popularized his master's art in small statuettes, and with the goldsmith Antonio Pollaiuolo (1431–1498). The nearest to genius was Andrea del Verrocchio (1435–1488), who left a young *David* of steellike intensity (pl. 264) and above all an equestrian statue, the *Colleone* (Venice, 1485), which was a reply to Donatello's Gattamelata in which the Quattrocento's instinct for power and pride is asserted to the point of bombast.

In the other Italian provinces the Donatellesque manner took root in the second half of the century. There, sculpture turned more readily to decoration and was secondary to the architecture, as in the case of

Matteo Civitali (1435–1501) of Lucca, and Lorenzo Vecchietta of Siena (1412–1480). The Triumphal Arch of Aragon which was set up between 1451 and 1453 in the Castel Nuovo was the first sign of the Renaissance in Naples: this great sculptural opus was at one time attributed to Francesco Laurano, an artist of Dalmatian origin (active between 1458 and 1502) who was helped in his work by a number of other artists. It was Antonio Rizzo (d. 1498) who brought the style of Donatello to Venice. Lombardy alone, faithful to its Gothic traditions, remained immune, and the declamatory art of Niccolò del Arca (d. 1494) and Guido Mazzoni (1450–1518) shows strong traces of Germanic influence.

PAINTING

It was in the North, at the turn of the fourteenth century in Lombardy, the old Italic province of "long-haired Gaul," that the craze for naturalism first showed itself in the portrayal of animal and floral forms, in the work of such delightful draughtsmen and illuminators as Giovanni de' Grassi. In that central province of northern Italy, which was still deeply imbued with feudal civilization, the old ideals of chivalry and courtly love which had seduced the medieval imagination flowered once more in the first half of the fifteenth century, when nature became the servant of fantasy. At Verona, Stefano da Zevio (1375 to 1438 or after,

267. Pisanello. The Vision of St. Eustace. *London, National Gallery.*

pl. 250) and above all Antonio Pisano, called Pisanello (1397–1455), uttered the last echoes of the Middle Ages, although Pisanello showed all the feverish curiosity of the Quattrocento in his studies of animals. Pisanello grasped all the living arabesque of animals, the texture of plumage and coat, while paying little attention to anatomical structure, which guided the Florentines in their studies of the human body (pl. 267).

Pisanello's paintings, which are very scarce, consist of little more than a few pictures and the Verona frescoes of the *Annunciation* at San Fermo Maggiore, and the scene of *St. George Rescuing the Princess* which is treated in legendary fashion, at Sant'Anastasia (1431). This artist also modeled and cast medallions (pl. 281), and this experience led him to create the profile portrait (*Princess of Este*, in the Louvre).

This representational lyricism spread through central Italy of the Marches and Umbria, where it met another important stream, the old Sienese style, to produce that exquisite painter Gentile da Fabriano (1360–1440) whose masterpiece is the *Adoration of the Magi* in the Uffizi in Florence (1423). This princely procession is imbued with all the charm and fantasy of the medieval mind (pl. 268).

Pisanello and Gentile are the Italian exponents of what we might call "naturalistic mysticism," a feeling of adoration for the marvels of nature, which in the Middle Ages they called *mirabilia*. It remained for Florence to introduce a more scientific naturalism.

268. Gentile da Fabriano. The Adoration of the Magi.
Detail. 1423. *Florence, Uffizi.*

269. Masolino da Panicale. The Story of Herod. Detail. Fresco. About 1420.
Castiglione d'Olona, Baptistery.

It was only toward 1425 that the Florentine school of painting, which lagged behind sculpture, managed to break its enslavement to a senile Giottism which had been only slightly rejuvenated by the sincerity of the Camaldolite monk Don Lorenzo Monaco (about 1370–1425?). The founders of the Florentine school were Masolino (1383–1447, pl. 269), Fra Angelico and Masaccio. Though Fra Angelico was a Christian painter and Masaccio founded pagan humanism, both of them belong to the Renaissance in their plastic outlook. Fra Angelico was a meeting point of styles and ideas emerging from the past but seeking the future, and if he glimpsed a heavenly beatitude he was none the less carried along on the wave of discovery that gripped his generation. With Paolo Uccello he created perspective, and with Masaccio he mastered modeling, expounding the laws of a harmonious composition in his invention of the layout of the *Sacra Conversazione* in which he set the saints in a semicircle round the Virgin, or in attendance at her coronation (pl. 270). The serene abstractness of his style makes him an early classical master, halfway between Giotto and Raphael.

A latecomer to painting, Giovanni da Fiesole, called Fra Angelico (1387–1455), gradually broke away from Gothic illumination. Entering the Dominican friary at Fiesole in 1407 he decorated the San Marco friary with frescoes after it was founded in 1436 by Cosimo de' Medici for the Florentine Dominicans. He was called to Rome in 1445

COLOR PLATES

1. SASSETTA. The Journey of the Magi.
   The Metropolitan Museum of Art, New York.
   Bequest of Maitland F. Griggs, 1943.

2. ROGIER VAN DER WEYDEN. The Annunciation.
The Metropolitan Museum of Art, New York.
Gift of J. P. Morgan, 1917.

3. ANDREA DEL CASTAGNO. The Youthful David. About 1450.
National Gallery of Art, Washington, D. C. Widener Collection.

4. El Greco. Laocoön. About 1610. *National Gallery of Art, Washington, D. C. Samuel H. Kress Collection.*

5. REMBRANDT. Man with a Magnifying Glass.
The Metropolitan Museum of Art, New York.
Bequest of Benjamin Altman, 1913.

6. VERMEER. Officer and Laughing Girl.
Copyright The Frick Collection, New York.

7. HIROSHIGE. Suwara or Travelers Sheltering in a Teahouse. From the series "Sixty-nine Posting Stations of the Kisokaido."
The Metropolitan Museum of Art, New York. Bequest of Henry L. Phillips, 1940.

270. Fra Angelico. The Coronation of the Virgin.
Florence, Uffizi.

by Eugene IV, where in 1449–1450 he painted frescoes showing the
Stories of St. Stephen and St. Lawrence in the Chapel of Nicholas V
in the Vatican. He had a large output and made great use of his
apprentices.

In Fra Angelico's work the human creature is still that fragile
being who draws all his strength from God alone. Masaccio (1401–
1428) was the first in painting to define the plastic and humanistic ideal
of the Renaissance without the slightest hesitation. He died at the age
of twenty-seven and left little more than the frescoes of the *Life of
St. Peter* in the Brancacci Chapel in the Carmine in Florence, but this
chapel became a sanctuary for the training of a long line of Italian artists
until Raphael and Michelangelo (pl. 271). Masaccio was a forerunner of
genius who at one stroke found the target which the Italian school as
a whole was to reach only fifty years later. Renewing Giotto's ideal of
concentrated strength, he heralded the sixteenth century by his monumental sense of composition that points the way to Raphael, and his
broad and powerful notion of the human body, his heroic and dramatic
intensity which only Michelangelo could rival. But his contemporaries
went no further than the experimental stage. They were still trying to
find the laws of painting, which for them was a problem in itself: they
were after a definition of spatial laws, that is to say, how to represent
the three dimensions of real space on the flat canvas. They found the

271. Masaccio. The Payment of the Tribute Money. Detail. Fresco.
About 1427–1428. *Florence, Sta. Maria del Carmine.*

as yet unformulated rules of linear perspective and, by foreshortening their modeling, took a lesson from sculpture, whose effects they tried to reproduce by the device of illusionism or *trompe-l'oeil*, or through the cameo. Paolo Uccello (about 1400–1475) brought a naïve passion to these semi-scientific researches and remained sensitive to the charms of nature. On the contrary the sharp and metallic art of Andrea del Castagno (1390?–1457?) ignored landscape and his world seems to have been one of bronze or marble (pl. 253). He saw everything from the point of view of volume. He reduced nature to a pure geometry of his own creation.

The main works of Paolo Uccello are battle scenes (Paris; London, pl. 272; Florence) and the poorly preserved frescoes in the Chiostro Verde of Santa Maria Novella, Florence, showing the Deluge.

Andrea del Castagno painted frescoes in a sculptural style for the Sant'Apollonia Convent in Florence (pl. 253).

Meanwhile the Florentines who followed this generation of pioneers were not on the lookout for new territory to conquer. Painters, sculptors and goldsmiths, Andrea del Verrocchio (1435–1488) or the brothers Piero (1443–1496) and Antonio (1432–1498) Pollaiuolo, still remained obsessed by form in relief. Most of these artists were content with exploiting new discoveries without adding to them. Fra Filippo Lippi (1406–1469), who was an unfrocked monk and a lay rival of

214

272. Paolo Uccello. The Rout of S. Romano. Detail.
About 1450–1460. *London, National Gallery.*

Fra Angelico, expressed a romantic anguish which anticipates Botticelli.
Ghirlandaio (1449–1494) fell into a bourgeois optimism, while Benozzo
Gozzoli (1449–1497) undertook a facile second version of the "poetry"
of Gentile da Fabriano. Only Alessio Baldovinetti (1425–1499), thanks
to his researches into harmonic composition which were all pursued
round a main theme, that of the Virgin and Child, shows early signs of
that intellectual view of perfection which, "scientifically" arrived at,
could do nothing more than repeat itself—I mean that of Leonardo da
Vinci.

With the Pollaiuolo brothers, Piero di Cosimo (1462–1521) and
Sandro Botticelli (1444–1510), the end of the century led to the harshness, oddness and morbidities of mannerism, that "sickness of styles"
which mannerism always suffers at the end of a creative period. The
case of Botticelli is typical of the intellectualist frenzy which was then
widespread in Florence. This mystic soul, torn between Christianity
and paganism, but possessed by the demon of intellect, was condemned
to a restless existence. The languishing sadness of his Madonnas, the
nostalgia of his portraits, his nervous and troubled style which gives all
his compositions a spasmodic rhythm and quickens the edge of his line
and the impetuousness of his figures betray the deep torment of an art
that has reached its limits and can only react against its own impotence
in a final spasm of genius.

215

273. Sandro Botticelli. The Birth of Venus. *Florence, Uffizi.*

Botticelli was at first a goldsmith, then a pupil of Antonio Pollaiuolo and Filippo Lippi, and became a religious painter (*Madonna of the Magnificat;* Sistine frescoes); then toward 1485 he began painting themes inspired from Antiquity (*Primavera; Birth of Venus,* pl. 273); Savonarola's preaching brought him back to Christianity and he returned eagerly to religious painting.

274. Sassetta. The Marriage of St. Francis and Poverty.
Detail of the Three Virtues. 1443. *Chantilly, Musée Condé.*

275. Piero della Francesca. The Resurrection. Detail. Head of Christ.
Sansepolcro, Palazzo Communale.

Siena, in its isolated mountain position, remained a medieval town into the fifteenth century. Sassetta (1392–1450, pl. 274) and his follower Sano di Pietro (1406–1481) had all the candidness and wonderment of the primitives. Matteo di Giovanni (1435–1495), Neroccio (1447–1500), Giovanni di Paolo (1403–1482) and others finished by adapting the learned art of Florence to the outmoded "cantilena" of Siena.

It is outside Florence and in schools to which she had taught independence that we must seek further signs of the great movement of discovery which animated the Quattrocento. Piero della Francesca (about 1416/1420, died 1492) inherited something of the keenness for perspective of Paolo Uccello and Castagno, as well as Masaccio's taste for monumental grandeur. He gave his figures a granite consistency (pl. 275) and no artist more haughtily expressed the pride of Quattrocento man. Piero della Francesca's chief work is a series of frescoes in San Francesco at Arezzo portraying the *Story of the True Cross*. He left also the remarkable portraits of the Duke of Urbino, *Federigo da Montefeltro*, and his wife *Battista Sforza* (both Uffizi).

The Florentine view of art was brought to the painters of the North by the Tuscan sculptors, Donatello among them, who came to work in Padua. The intellectualist turn of mind of the Florentines, as it made itself felt in a region where Germanic influences were still active, gave rise to a school of painters in Ferrara who were fired by a quest for the supernatural and whose tense style and fantastic imagination came as a Flamboyant intrusion into Italian painting.

The liveliest of these painters was Cosimo Tura (1430–1495), who owed something to Piero della Francesca (pl. 276). Francesco del Cossa (about 1435–1477) was the author of a series of frescoes in the Schifanoia Palace at Ferrara. Ercole de' Roberti (d. 1496) and Lorenzo Costa (1460–1535) toned down the pitiless style of Tura and Cossa.

The Florentine school died of anemia through setting all its faith in the intellect and thus failing to appreciate the gifts of the imagination. The intellectualist leaven of Tuscany, however, working on a powerful imagination, produced the greatest painter of the Quattrocento in the Paduan Andrea Mantegna (1431–1506). He added to the spatial values of the Florentines what Berenson has called "tactile values": not content with the visual appearance of things, he tried to give the illusion of material texture. He pushed the mania for antiquities much farther than the Florentines had done, and achieved in paint Alberti's dream of

276. Cosimo Tura. Pietà. *Venice, Civic Museum (Correr)*.
277. Mantegna. St. James Led to Martyrdom. Fresco (destroyed).
About 1454. *Formerly at Padua, Eremitani.*

re-creating a vision of the Latin world. He renewed the traditional garments and introduced Roman costumes into art, observing them with all the exactness of an archaeologist. Being a Northerner he introduced nature into the Florentine abstract world, while submitting natural forms to the decorous laws of architecture and sculpture. His art was a broad synthesis of the many ideals by which Quattrocento man was lured.

Mantegna's work as it came down to us was fairly plentiful, but unfortunately the frescoes of the *Life and Martyrdom of St. James and St. Christopher* in the Eremitani Church of Padua (1449–1454), one of the finest achievements of the Renaissance, were almost completely destroyed by bombardment in 1944 (pl. 277). Of his great decorative works the *Gonzaga Family* still remains in the ducal palace at Mantua, as well as the series the *Triumph of Caesar* (Hampton Court), paintings in distemper which were intended as settings for the theater in the palace at Mantua.

Venice, which was long a theater of Byzantine art, only threw off that influence in the early fifteenth century. Jacopo Bellini (d. 1470), with an inquiring mind typical of his century, was the first to sift in his paintings the mingled influences of Byzantinism, Gothicism and the Florentine "scientific" outlook which were struggling for possession of the Venetian school about 1430. It was then that two streams became

218

apparent at Venice, which were to survive until the dawn of the sixteenth century. Gentile Bellini (1429–1507), son of Jacopo, and Vittore Carpaccio (d. before 1527), contemporary of Giorgione, painted works of a picturesque and other-world quality which prolong the credulity of a Pisanello, filled with wonderment both by the real and the imaginary. Gentile Bellini, who made a journey to Constantinople in 1479, came under the influence of Eastern art. Vittore Carpaccio gave an ear to Gentile's teaching. He had a taste for narrative cycles and spectacular *mises en scène*, which he executed for various Venetian societies and confraternities (*Legend of St. Ursula*, 1490–1498; *Lives of St. Jerome and St. George*, 1502; *Life of the Virgin*, 1504; *Story of St. Stephen*, 1511–1520).

Another group of painters cast their eyes toward the Paduan studios in which Donatello and Mantegna set the plastic inquiries of the new century in opposition to the picturesque spirit of the Gothic. This tradition was carried on by Carlo Crivelli (d. 1493), Antonio (d. 1476) and Bartolommeo (d. 1499) Vivarini, to end in Giovanni Bellini (d. 1516). Giovanni was the younger brother of Gentile, and after beginning with Byzantinism was drawn away from it by Mantegna, who became his brother-in-law in 1453. Taking up the oil-color technique which had been brought to Venice in about 1475 by the painter Antonello da Messina (pl. 278), he softened the harsh sculptural style

278. Antonello da Messina. Portrait of the Condottiere. 1475. *Paris, Louvre.*

279. Giovanni Bellini. The Transfiguration (central part).
About 1480. *Naples, National Museum.*

of Mantegna, insisting much less on the clear outline of his forms than
on the transitions that join them together. By turning away from the
analytic outlook of the Quattrocento and toward a pursuit of harmony
he helped to prepare for the Cinquecento, and Giorgione and Titian
learned a good deal from him (pl. 279).

Meanwhile in a neighboring province, while Florence was still sunk
in its tense struggle to achieve the impossible, the Umbrian Perugino
(1446?–1523) was working on the same lines as Giovanni Bellini toward
those aspects of the harmonic ideal which were to prevail in the sixteenth
century: he was one of the teachers of Raphael. Luca Signorelli (about
1450–1523), also of Umbria, was already haunted by those nightmares
of terror that obsessed Michelangelo, and his work contained some of
the rudiments of the baroque style. Everything was now ready for a
second powerful drive in Italian art.

Of Perugino's work there remain some frescoes (Sistine Chapel,
Rome, and the Cambio at Perugia) and numerous religious paintings
(pl. 255). His art declined and became somewhat slack toward the end
of the century. Luca Signorelli's best-known work is in the frescoes of
the *Last Judgment* in the Orvieto Duomo. Another artist who came from
Perugia, Pinturicchio (1454?–1513) was a follower of the facile and
picturesque art of Benozzo Gozzoli. His most outstanding work was the
decoration of the Borgia Apartments, carried out from 1492 to 1494 by
Alexander VI in the Vatican.

THE MINOR ARTS

The minor arts in Italy during the Quattrocento followed the same principles as the major ones. The Italian decorative sense has always been spoiled by the figurative and monumental emphasis given to everything in imitation of architecture and sculpture. Italian artisans from the fifteenth century onward specialized, in matters of furnishing and jewelry, in pieces composed of many different materials which they put together in the same way as carved or painted objects. Their furniture derives from the classical styles, their tables imitating the Roman *cartibulum* and the coffers or cassoni of the sarcophagi (pl. 280) while their chairs take the X-shape of the chairs used by Roman magistrates. Decorative pottery, which was influenced from the outset by Hispano-Moorish faïence, flourished in centers at Gubbio, Deruta, Urbino and Faenza, but it soon took on a historical or narrative bias. The cult of antiquity also had something to do with the revival of the medallion portrait, of which Pisanello was the greatest exponent (pl. 281). Italy was never outstanding in the art of illumination, except in Lombardy where the French influence was felt. The best Italian achievements in this line were *tarots* or playing cards. As for engraving, it came from Germany, by way of Venice. The clear-cut works of the Florentines and of Mantegna above all are masterpieces of copper engraving.

280. Carved chest. End of the 15th century. *Perugia, Collegio del Cambio.*

281. Pisanello. Bronze medallion of John Palaeologus VII, Emperor of Byzantium. About 1447. *Florence, Bargello.*

LATE GOTHIC AND THE RENAISSANCE IN EUROPE

THE FLAMBOYANT STYLE

While Florence, isolated even from the rest of Italy, was busy throwing off the Middle Ages and developing a monumental art based on classical models, the rest of Europe was plunged in the excesses of the late Gothic style called "Flamboyant" because of its sinuous forms (pl. 282).

This style began in France at the close of the fourteenth century, in the Amiens and Rouen areas. It stemmed from a "biological" evolution of those Gothic principles which, more rapidly in England than elsewhere, had given rise to the English Curvilinear or Decorated style (1280) which inspired the first Continental experiments in the Flamboyant. This evolution was modified by the rationalistic outlook of France. The Flamboyant spread all over Europe, meeting no resistance except in Italy, where none the less it triumphed in Venetia, Lombardy (Milan Cathedral) and the kingdom of Naples, but was checked by the Florentine Renaissance. The most obvious forms of this style were perhaps those to be found in Germany and Spain. England gave up its sinuous style just when the rest of Europe was beginning to adopt it, and toward 1350 invented the Perpendicular style, which is typified by an over-emphasis on stiff vertical lines and fan tracery vaults with intricate ribbings (Gloucester and Winchester Cathedrals, York Minster,

282. Martin Chambiges. Rose window, south transept, of Sens Cathedral. 1490–1497.

283. Divinity School, Oxford. Ceiling, 1470–1483.

Abbey Church at Bath, St. George's Chapel, Windsor, Henry VII Chapel, Westminster, King's College Chapel, Cambridge, the Divinity School, Oxford, pl. 283).

The fifteenth century did nothing to modify the Gothic structure. Buildings were now more solidly constructed in spite of the light appearance given by the openwork carving of their decorations whose lavishness overlaid the main divisions of the edifice. All the members of these structures assumed an independent life, multiplying at each other's expense; their molding with all its complexities became squarish and may be called *prismatic* molding. The vaults, whose structure became farther and farther removed from the original design of ogival vaulting, were now covered over with a dense network of superfluous ribs which took on either a star pattern as in Spain, or a pattern of interlaced branches as in Germany.

The overseers of these works now did their best to surprise the eye by suggesting instability or some feat of skill by means of dropped keystones, pillars with rope molding whose twisted effect suggests that they are giving way beneath their load. The over-all emphasis on curvature, especially noticeable in the tracery of windows, suggests the writhing of flames (by a system of reticulations, pl. 282) which earned the name Flamboyant for a style which, by comparison with the fine, logical clarity of the thirteenth century, gave expression to a tormented and impassioned state of soul. The same anxiety was to take hold of sculpture. This time it was the Netherlander Claus (or Klaas) Sluter who created the typically fifteenth century "pathetic" style (pl. 284).

223

284. Claus Sluter. Statue of Moses.
Detail from the Moses Fountain, 1395–1404.
Former Charterhouse of Champmol, Dijon.

THE FLEMISH GENIUS

Flemish genius appeared as a new artistic force in fifteenth century Europe. If architecture, whose formulas were invented in France, was still alive enough in that country to give birth to a final change of style, yet the Gothic plastic outlook was withering by the end of the fourteenth century, when it had already exhausted all its potentialities. It was the grafting of Flemish genius which was to restore energy to France and enable it to prolong the Middle Ages until about 1500.

The first Flemish artists, who were both painters and sculptors (André Beauneveu, the Limbourg brothers), began by enriching the French school with their talent, for they were attracted by the reputation of Paris. The political fortunes of the Duke of Burgundy, which were now favored by the disasters of the Hundred Years' War, allowed the Flemish genius to find its native expression. At the turn of the fourteenth century the sculptor Claus Sluter, of Haarlem, was already defining at Dijon the principles of a new art of statuary in which everything was to be governed by emotional expression (*Tomb of the Dukes of Burgundy;* porch and Calvary pedestal called the *Moses Fountain* at Champmol charterhouse, pl. 284). Claus Sluter freed the statue

from architecture. In his hands it is no longer merely a figure applied
on a porch or door, but has all the appearance of coming to life under
the stress of some passionate movement that frames its gestures, distorts
the face and makes the draperies swirl (pl. 284). The artist refound the
classical, theatrical sense of drapery which can amplify both gestures
and expressions; he stressed its billows and folds and reliefs, his intense
realistic curiosity turning him into a keen observer of individual types
and facial expressions. Claus Sluter's genius invented a whole dramatic
repertoire of gestures, expressions and models, which was so fraught
with the pathetic sense of expectation obsessing the fifteenth century
that the whole of Europe adopted it. Strangely enough it was in Flanders
that this was to have the least fruitful outcome, and it was from Dijon,
where his work was preserved, that Sluter's style spread across Germany
and France and into Spain.

Flemish painting emerged from a great international movement
which, at the close of the fourteenth century, tended to fuse the
Paris school's linearism and the delicacy of Lombard coloring with the
naturalism that originated in the North. The brothers Jan, Pol and

285. Limbourg brothers. October. Miniature from the Book of Hours
of the Duc de Berry. Between 1411 and 1416. *Chantilly, Musée Condé.*

Hennequin de Limbourg accomplished a revolution by introducing the landscape copied direct from nature into their painting. At the same time, as they worked for a French prince, they kept close to a traditional *genre* and expressed themselves through the medium of the miniature (*Très Riches Heures du Duc de Berry*, painted between 1411 and 1416, pl. 285). The brothers Hubert (d. 1426) and Jan (d. 1441) Van Eyck freed painting from the tyranny of the book and monumental composition, by creating easel painting. Together they painted the great altarpiece, the *Adoration of the Lamb*, at St.-Bavon, Ghent, which was finished in 1432 (pl. 249). After his brother's death, Jan Van Eyck gave himself mainly to portraiture. The brothers Van Eyck showed themselves against the Middle Ages and fully committed to the Renaissance spirit by bringing the principle of integral realism into their art. Casting aside the entire paraphernalia of medieval conventions, they translated the symbols of the great theological composition of St.-Bavon through human characters observed from life and against a background of genuine landscapes. At the other extreme from Byzantine art, this meant a remarkable effort to represent the supernatural world through the most concrete appearances of the external world. In his portraits (pl. 286) Jan Van Eyck knew how to transfer the models who posed for him onto the painted panel with a lifelike exactness that no other painter has surpassed. The Van Eyck brothers discovered spatial depth at the same time as the Italian Quattrocento painters, but suggested it through different means, using a diminishing scale of tones according to distance (color or aerial perspective). Whereas the Italians

286. Jan Van Eyck. Jan Arnolfini and His Wife. 1434. *London, National Gallery.*

287. Rogier Van der Weyden. The Descent from the Cross.
Between 1435 and 1443. *Madrid, Prado.*

made nature fit their geometrical vision, the Van Eycks enveloped everything in a flood of light and atmosphere. They gave such vital truth
to reality that their pictures fill the spectator with an almost hallucinat-
ing sense of immediate presence. In order to express such intense
realism the Van Eycks used the technique of painting in oils, which they
perfected and established. Since it makes it possible for the painter to
set off successive transparent layers or "glazes" of color one against
the other, this process enables him to render the texture and other
qualities of any kind of element or object, whether it be cloth, gold,
flesh, sky, water or light itself.

Jan Van Eyck's was entirely a painter's eye: he saw everything in
terms of its fluid and colored values; he was completely free from the
tyranny of sculpture which gives the brush the edge of a chisel and
which dominated the whole century both in the North and in Italy.
But after his death the incisive style was to invade Flemish painting
immediately. Rogier Van der Weyden, known in France as Roger de
la Pasture (d. at Brussels in 1464), did not turn to Sluter's example for
the principles of his sculptural manner, but found it in the traditions of
the more angular French Gothic which he learned at Tournai, his
birthplace, a city which had a prosperous school of monumental (funerary) stonemasons dating from the fourteenth century. Rogier's masterpiece, the *Descent from the Cross* in the Prado (pl. 287), was
conceived as a painted low-relief, the figures projecting their shadows

227

on a background of gold. By comparison with Jan Van Eyck, Van der Weyden casts back to the medieval outlook, with his sharp-edged linear style, his taste for the ascetic, his lack of interest in landscape, which are all Gothic features. His outlook on life was entirely Christian in its renouncement and mortification, and it was with intense pathos that he portrayed the sufferings of the Passion.

The art of Jan Van Eyck, which was perhaps too far in advance of his time, did not leave a very deep mark on it. Only Petrus Christus (d. 1472/73) tried to carry on his style, while slightly Italianizing it—there being some evidence that he worked in the peninsula where he knew Antonello da Messina. It was therefore Van der Weyden rather than Van Eyck who created the traditional Flemish style. Dirk Bouts (sometimes known as Thierry Bouts), who died at Louvain in 1475, derived pretty closely from Van der Weyden, although he engaged in plastic experiments which are not unlike those of his contemporaries in Italy (see the linear perspectivism of the *Last Supper* at Louvain, pl. 288). The same applies to Hugo Van der Goes (d. 1482), who also seems to have known Italy (*Portinari Altarpiece*, Uffizi). After the Florentine artists, whose style was tensely set in a sort of exasperation

288. Dirk Bouts. The Last Supper. Central panel of the Louvain Triptych. 1465-1468. *Louvain, St.-Pierre.*

of feeling, fifteenth century Flemish painting ended by relaxing in the work of Hans Memling (or Memlinc), a painter of Rhenish origin who settled in Bruges (d. 1494). The symmetry of Memling's compositions, the suavity he gave to facial expressions, his gentle modeling and elegance of line were perfectly fitted to express that ideal of piety and that feeling of bourgeois security which he had in common with Perugino (pl. 254).

GERMANY

Fifteenth century Germany shows a very active though confused artistic production. In keeping with the political division of Germany into minor states and the tendency toward a municipal, provincial outlook, local schools abounded and flourished. These schools were centers on the Rhine and the Danube, spreading into Bavaria, Franconia and Bohemia and as far as the Hanseatic towns and along the Baltic Coast. A land of extremes, Germany tended equally toward mystic unreality and naturalist materialism. The dominant bourgeoisie cared less for the aesthetic quality of a work of art than for its representational values, and expected a work to be didactic, moving and lifelike. Mysticism and materialism met in an expressionist crisis which was to remain acute throughout the century.

German architecture lost no time in adopting the Flamboyant style, in which it found a vehicle for its own lyrical tendencies. Germany delighted in lavish ornament and openwork decoration, encouraging fantastic vaults rich in fan tracery, and pierced spires (Ulm, Vienna, Strasbourg). The "hall church" with aisles the same height as the nave which developed in Westphalia in the thirteenth century spread to southern Germany (Liebfrauenkirche, Munich, 1468) and Austria and Bohemia as well as to the north and along the Baltic as far as Danzig, where there was an outcrop of brick architecture influenced by the English Perpendicular style (town halls of Thorn, Lübeck, Stralsund and Danzig).

Sculpture now made great progress all over Germany, especially in the form of wood-carving which produced huge altarpieces seething with figures and ornamentation. The German plastic principles derived from Sluter, but with more emphasis on expressionism. The enormous output of works was spread over many centers: Nicolas Gerhaert Van Leyden (recorded 1462–1473) at Strasbourg and Trier; Hans Multscher

289. Veit Stoss. Altarpiece of the Virgin. Detail, head of an Apostle.
Wood. 1477–1486. *Cracow, Church of Our Lady*.

(about 1400–1467) at Ulm in Swabia; Michael Pacher (about 1435–1498) in the Tyrol; Bernt Notke (d. 1509) at Lübeck (*St. George*, Stockholm); Veit Stoss at Nuremberg (about 1440–1533). All these workshops, whether in the north or south, showed the same trend toward expressionism (twisting of bodies, convulsive movement of draperies with numerous broken folds), toward a naturalism which led artists to go in search of popular folk types (Hans Multscher) and even physical deformities (*Altarpiece of the Virgin* by Veit Stoss, Cracow, 1477–1486, pl. 289), but sometimes also resulting in a graceful and slightly feminine mannerism (Madonna statues). At the end of the century Italian influence made itself felt through the South and sweetened the harshness of the German style. Adam Krafft (d. 1509) of Nuremberg and Tilman Riemenschneider (d. 1531) of Würzburg mark the transition from the Gothic to the Renaissance manner.

There was considerable activity in the schools of painting, but it was very mixed in its aims because of the many foreign influences which poured into Germany from every side—the French via the Rhine, the Italian through the Tyrol, the influence of the Burgundian (Dijon) school from the west and south, and the Flemish from the north. In the course of the fourteenth century the class of Sienese and French contributions gave rise—though with different proportions

230

of each—to the Gothic schools of painting at Cologne (*Clarissan Altarpiece*) and in Bohemia. The influence of the Franco-Flemish miniaturists subsequently gave Germany a touch of the worldly art of the Limbourg brothers. Early in the fifteenth century Cologne and Westphalia gave themselves over to a mystic ideal which was markedly ethereal yet naïvely inclined toward a poetic, pastoral charm (Conrad von Soest, pl. 290). This form of art reached its height about 1430. Its last exponent was Stefan Lochner (d. 1451) in Cologne, who gave it a hint of bourgeois piety.

However, toward 1450 the sculptural style broke into Germany from the north and south at the same time. In the south, the Burgundian style resulted in the popular dramatic manner of Hans Multscher (pl. 291) in Cologne, and at Basel the lofty art of Conrad Witz (about 1390–1447), whose powerful, statuesque density and geometrical vision (pl. 252) recall Paolo Uccello and Andrea del Castagno. Meanwhile the Flemish sculptural style represented by Rogier Van der Weyden and Dirk Bouts went down the Rhine, met the Burgundian style and penetrated right into Germany with Hans Pleydenwurf at Nuremberg, Friedrich Herlin at Nördlingen. Cologne imitated this with such

290. Conrad von Soest. The Death of the Virgin.
About 1420. *Dortmund, Museum.*

291. Hans Multscher. Christ Carrying the Cross. 1437.
Berlin, Kaiser Friedrich Museum.

success that one might well imagine it as coming in the orbit of Flanders rather than of Germany (Masters of the *Life of the Virgin, Lyversberg Passion* and *St. Severin Passion*); the bonds uniting the Rhineland school and Rogier Van der Weyden are attested by Memling, who brought back to Bruges a breath of mysticism from Cologne. However, in the last decade of the fifteenth century a national German style was developed in the middle-Rhine and in southern Germany (Jan Pollack, Michel Wohlgemut), springing from the mixture of the Burgundian and Flemish styles, which gave to painting something analogous to what the Flemish style gave to architecture; this was mainly achieved by Martin Schongauer at Colmar (d. 1491). Very much influenced by Rogier Van der Weyden, Schongauer's medium was mainly that of engraving, a new technique for reproducing drawings which gratified the craft instinct in German artists, their liking for careful workmanship, their passion for infinitely complex detail (pl. 292). It was only at the very end of the century that Italian influence filtered into the Tyrol, where Michael Pacher was inspired by Mantegna, and reached Augsburg, where the elder Holbein was attracted by the harmonious style of Giovanni Bellini.

FRANCE

Of all the countries of northern Europe, France came closest to the Renaissance. Weakened by the misfortunes of the Hundred Years' War, through which she lost the guiding role she had hitherto played in European civilization, France gave herself without reserve and for a whole century to the excesses of the Flamboyant style in architecture. But the evolution of sculpture shows a progressive detachment from

292. Martin Schongauer. Foliated design. Copperplate engraving.

the hard dramatic style of Sluter which, first affecting Burgundy, then descending the Rhone valley, finally made its way into the Midi (*Prophets and Sybils*, choir screen of Albi Cathedral). The setting up of the Court on the banks of the Loire gave that region a new importance, and brought to the fore that temperate spirit for which it is renowned. Toward 1460 the style of draped forms became less rigid, expressionism became much milder, the individual character of faces was modified, while artists were now attracted by youthfulness, grace and femininity. Following the demands of the national temperament, pathos was now portrayed more restrainedly, rather by suggesting its inward spiritual meaning than through its outward, physical and dramatic effects. At the end of the century, after the war with Italy, the native French leaning toward harmony found itself in agreement with the Italian stream, as is shown in the work of Michel Colombe (about 1430–1512), who made the tomb of Francis II of Brittany and his wife in the cathedral at Nantes.

Taking Europe as a whole, French painting is seen to be, with Italian, the farthest removed from the Gothic outlook. The school of Paris having been dispersed by the Hundred Years' War, the new art centers were in the North, on the Loire, and in Provence. The Valenciennes and Amiens painters followed the Flemish style while slightly toning down its harshness. Avignon, which thanks to its position had already become a great cosmopolitan (French-Italian) art center in the fourteenth century, produced two of the finest works of the period toward 1450, in the *Coronation of the Virgin*, by Enguerrand Quarton (also known as Charonton), and the *Avignon Pietà* (pl. 293). The latter painting, one of the highest expressions of mysticism, brings to-

293. School of Avignon. Avignon Pietà. About 1460. *Paris, Louvre.*

294. Jean Fouquet. Etienne Chevalier and St. Stephen.
Berlin, Kaiser Friedrich Museum.
295. Jean Fouquet. The Beheading of St. James.
Miniature from the Book of Hours of Etienne Chevalier.
After 1450. *Chantilly, Musée Condé.*

gether in an admirable synthesis all the intensity of spiritual passion,
a monumental rhythm of composition, and an abstract beauty of sculptural modeling, worthy of a Florentine painter of the Quattrocento.
The Italian spirit also moved the same unknown master who illuminated after 1460 *Le Cuer d'amours espris*, which was an allegorical
romance by René I (Vienna Library). On the Loire, Jean Fouquet
of Tours (d. between 1477 and 1481)—who traveled to Italy
in 1445—eschewed the Gothic spirit in favor of the plastic outlook
of the Quattrocentists, of which he contrived to give a French version.
He adopted architecture of the classical type, renounced the complicated
curves of Gothic modeling for the fluted draperies of the Florentines,
and like the Italians became interested in problems of spatial foreshortening while managing to combine a geometric perspective with
aerial color perspective in his landscapes. His *Madonna* in the Antwerp
Museum, one of the most perfect works of the fifteenth century, is a
paragon of harmony, to be set beside the Madonnas of Baldovinetti.
His portraits have all the grandeur of Italian works, but with a more
emphatic truth in them (pl. 294). Although he remains a min-
iaturist (*Book of Hours of Etienne Chevalier*, pl. 295; illustrations
for *The Jewish Antiquities* by Josephus), Jean Fouquet showed
France the way to the Renaissance. The tradition of which he was
the founder was to be enriched by a fresh Italian strain in the Master

of Moulins (pl. 256), who, thanks to his harmonious aesthetic and his pious quietism, is a genius related to Giovanni Bellini, Ghirlandaio, Perugino and Memling.

In the minor arts, France brought the art of tapestry to perfection. Retreating before the English occupation, the Parisian workshops moved to Arras and Tours. The craftsmen of Tours produced poetic works with a royal and pastoral tone (pl. 296), while at Arras they wove mainly crowded historical scenes in the Flemish style.

SPAIN AND PORTUGAL

It might be thought that fifteenth century Spain came into the orbit of Italy; but on the contrary she refused to do so and her romantic temperament led her to adopt the Flamboyant style. In both sculpture and painting she was dependent on Flemish and German art, which she was to export even into Italy, through the Neapolitan and Sicilian provinces of the house of Aragon.

The Flamboyant style was introduced by the architects of the North. The fifteenth century saw the creation—probably by the Flemish—of Seville Cathedral, a splendid structure with five naves which was inspired by a regional type for which Barcelona Cathedral set the first example in the fourteenth century; in the sixteenth century the cathedrals of Segovia and Salamanca were to derive from Seville. The architect Hans of Cologne, who was brought to Burgos by a bishop

296. A scene from the tapestries of The Lady with the Unicorn.
About 1500. *Paris, Cluny Museum.*

who had been attending the Council of Basel, built at Burgos Cathedral two pierced spires (1442–1458) imitated from those which were designed for Cologne Cathedral. The Burgos workshop produced the first Flamboyant monuments to be found in Spain (*Constable's Chapel*, 1482, Burgos Cathedral, by Simón de Colonia, son of the Hans already mentioned). Finding a willing soil, thanks to the Moorish traditions which were still deeply rooted in Spain after its liberation, the Flamboyant style now mingled with the Moorish, to create at the time of the Catholic Kings the Mudejar art in which the excess of decoration, taken over from both styles, swarmed over the whole monument. The style of the Catholic Kings, sometimes called the "Isabelline" style, is the first really native expression to be found in Spanish architecture. Enriched with heraldic emblems and Mudejar features, it is a haughty expression of the triumphant monarchy. The son of an emigrant from Lyons, Juan Guas built in that style San Juan de los Reyes at Toledo (1478) and the Infantado Palace at Guadalajara (1480), while Enrique de Egas, the son of an expatriate from Brussels who was now an overseer at Toledo Cathedral, built the Royal Chapel which houses the tombs of the Catholic Kings in Granada Cathedral. One of the finest monuments in this style is the Colegio de San Gregorio at Valladolid (pl. 297), whose author remains unknown; the decoration was made

297. Colegio de S. Gregorio (1488–1496) at Valladolid. Entrance.

298. Gil de Siloé and Diego de la Cruz. Carving on the altarpiece of the Charterhouse church. Gilded wood. 1494–1499. *Miraflores (near Burgos), Church of the Charterhouse.*

299. Pedro Berruguete. Trial by Fire. *Madrid, Prado.*

up of floral and vegetable shapes as in the Manueline art. During the period of the Catholic Kings the layout of the different parts of the church took on an original character which was to last until the eighteenth century: the choir (*coro*) was placed in the end bays of the nave, west of the crossing, and closed in with high walls full of carvings; east of the crossing, the *capilla mayor* ended in a blank wall with a large decorated altarpiece (*altar mayor*) in front of it. Exquisite grilles or screens in ironwork serve to close off the choir, the Capilla Mayor and the chapels.

Spanish sculpture developed in much the same way as architecture, producing enormous decorative backgrounds, liturgical furnishings, gigantic altarpieces alive with figures, stalls (*sillerías*) and choir screens (*trascoros*). A great many artists came from Burgundy, France and Germany to work on these items; the greatest was at Burgos, Gil de Siloé, no doubt a converted Jew from Flanders or Germany who, working as easily in wood (*Altarpiece* of the Charterhouse at Miraflores) as in marble (*Tombs of John II and Isabella*, Miraflores, begun in 1489), introduced a strongly Germanic style, graceful in its mannerism and of a pathetic intensity, which gave a start to the Castilian school of sculpture (pl. 298).

Painting was based on Flemish models. In Catalonia Luis Dalmau,

237

who went to Flanders in 1431, carried out what amounts to a pastiche of Van Eyck in 1445, in the *Counselors' Altarpiece* in Barcelona. Jacomart Baço, Jaume Huguet, Bartolomé Bermejo, Pablo Vergos, Fernando Gallegos, were all in the same way disciples of the Flemish tradition. Under the Catholic Kings, the Castilian artist Pedro Berruguete (d. 1503), who worked for a time in Italy, was to free painting from its Flemish bondage by turning decisively toward the Quattrocento outlook (pl. 299). The Andalusian Alejo Fernández (d. 1543) sweetened Flemish harshness with Italian gracefulness.

Following its great discoveries across the seas, Portugal had a sudden burst of prosperity which in the reign of King Manuel (1495 to 1521) showed itself in the rapid strides that were made in art owing to this ruler's initiative. Portugal then created a style of lyrical exuberance which is unusual in the West, and which reflected the excitement of its great explorers. This is known as the *Manueline* style. As with the art of the Catholic Kings, this style had two phases, the Gothic and the Renaissance. The Manueline style was developed by Boytac at the Setúbal church and the monastery at Batalha (about 1509); Diogo de Arruda at the Convent of the Knights of Christ at Tomar (about 1510, pl. 300); Francisco de Arruda at the Tower of Belém (1516, pl. 301).

300. Diogo de Arruda. Window in Manueline style,
Convent of the Knights of Christ, Tomar, Portugal. About 1510.

301. Francisco de Arruda. Tower of Belém, Lisbon. 1516.

302. Nuno Gonçalves. Triptych of the Infante, altarpiece from the Chapel of St. Vincent. Detail, the Benefactors. About 1460. *Lisbon, National Museum.*

All these men built the most poetical works in this form of architecture, a kind of naturalistic symphony in stone.

The Spaniard Juan de Castillo was to dry up this creative vein by transposing it into a flat (plateresque) decorative technique (Hieronymite monastery at Belém, 1517).

Portuguese painting, like the Spanish, was a derivative of Flemish. It produced several artists with a sharp eye for realism as well as one of the highlights in fifteenth century art, namely the *St. Vincent Altarpiece* (Lisbon Museum). This painting is a portrait composition of an intense realism suggestive of Jan Van Eyck (who visited Portugal in 1428): it was commissioned from Nuno Gonçalves (pl. 302) about the year 1460.

303. Leonardo da Vinci. The Last Supper,
showing the dominant principle of the composition.
Milan, Sta. Maria delle Grazie.

CHAPTER VIII

THE RENAISSANCE IN EUROPE IN THE
SIXTEENTH CENTURY

UNTIL the sixteenth century the different artistic civilizations of the West followed smoothly one upon the other, each begetting the next. Even in the fifteenth century the Gothic and Renaissance styles could live peacefully side by side: the Milan Cathedral was near completion when the one in Florence was begun. But after the sixteenth century Western art was split by the warring forces of ideologies that were mutually exclusive and even by national rivalries. The maturing of new nations—each of which had its contribution to make, which had to vie with the longer-established modes of culture—was to multiply the West's wealth of expression and give rise to three hundred years of creative tension in Europe.

Two personalities represent the hostile ideologies: Erasmus and Luther, the humanist and the prophet, the peacemaker and the revolutionist. Erasmus, whose dream was to introduce the heroes of a Pantheon into Paradise, and who could only see what things have in common between them, did his utmost to rescue the spiritual unity of Europe; for him there were no differences that reason could fail to reconcile; he considered Faith itself as an established truth which like the wisdom

240

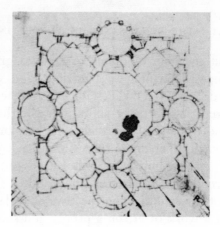

THE CENTRAL PLAN

304. Plan of the Holy Apostles Church, Ani. Before 1031.
After J. Strzygowski, Die Baukunst der Armenier und Europa.
305. Plan of a centrally planned church. Drawing by Leonardo da Vinci.
Paris, Bibliothèque de l'Institut.

of the Ancients had already become part of the human heritage; and it might be said that he was not far from confusing revelation with inspiration. As for Luther, the "God-intoxicated man," against this rule of reason he uttered the protest of the mysticism which he thought humanism had flouted. Faced with this conscious ideal of man turning his life into a cunning balance of the faculties under the guidance of reason alone, and giving the divine, like the human, no more than the share to which it was entitled, Luther brought from the depths of the Middle Ages an image of man in his feebleness incapable of Good with-

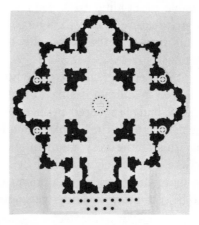

306. Bramante. Plan for the Basilica of St. Peter, Rome.
307. Michelangelo. Plan for the Basilica of St. Peter, Rome.

out the help of divine grace, and groaning beneath the sinner's fate imposed on him by a terrible God whom he now revived from the rediscovered Old Testament. At the moment when the Church was preparing to make allowances for the dreams of Christian humanism, and while the Papacy in Rome was bringing paganism to the baptismal font, Luther drove the Church back into its mysteries.

Even Italy now found itself torn between these two forces. On grounds of intellect in Rome and of sensibility in Venice, Raphael and Titian were defining the laws of a classicism which bases the economy of a work of art on a proper and successful balancing of its parts one against the other, thus demanding the minimum of individual features, and the sacrifice of any marked expression to the serene impersonality of an ideal Beauty. At the same time, Bramante, heir to the long experiments of the Quattrocento, gave his Roman works the exact proportions of ancient classical architecture. It was he who brought the *central plan* to its perfection, as a symbol of harmony, after it had long haunted the Quattrocento (pls. 304 to 307). However, this classical idealism was to be immediately compromised by Michelangelo, for if he glorified man's power to the point of making him a Superman, it was the better to reveal man's ridiculous weakness when compared with the Almighty; the heroes of the Sistine Chapel are heavy with a strength which they know will never avail them in their struggle with the Infinite. This unbalance gives rise to a despair which torments their bodies and darkens their faces. If Michelangelo was able to keep these extremes of expression in the bounds of his canon of Beauty, that was a miracle within his own competence and no other's, but after him there was nothing capable of holding back such violence. Michelangelo gave "muscles" to architecture as he had done to the human body; he turned his monuments into athletes, before his successors made circus strong men of them.

At Venice, Tintoretto, who was obsessed by Michelangelo, was involved in another drama. The weakness that the painter of the Sistine Chapel had discovered in man by comparison with God was seen by the decorator of the Scuola di San Rocco on the cosmic scale. Tintoretto saw this at the very moment when Copernicus was proving that this little earth, which men had believed to be the center of things, was no more than a speck in a universe whose bounds were suddenly found to be infinitely remote—yet another sixteenth century principle of contradiction which threw man back into his puniness just when he was priding himself on his self-mastery: Bruegel (sometimes spelled Breughel) in Flanders was to settle this conflict by his idea of the "sovereign peace" of nature. Tintoretto's humanity seems to be at grips with vastness—torrents of darkness, floods of light, whirlpools of space carry the forms twisting and turning in their wake, losing all their density, torn into shreds by the teeth of shadow and sunshine, gnawed by the Infinite.

The search for effects at the expense of' harmonious proportions; violence of expression; the breakdown of equilibrium by showing a trancelike movement instead of a state of repose; the quest for the boundless that interferes with the integrity of shapes which are devoured by shadow, light or space—these are only a few features of a new aesthetic which historians have called the "Baroque."

It was from an obscure interaction between classicism and baroque that the crisis called "Mannerism" emerged in Italy in the second half of the century. Except for the Venetian school, which kept all its

The clear-cut draftsmanship of the 15th century seeks precision of structure; whereas the 16th century painter smooths out all the outlines of his modeling by gentle transitions. Raphael sacrifices expression to harmony, while Michelangelo achieves a synthesis of conflicting elements.

308. Carlo Crivelli. Madonna della Candeletta. Detail. 1488(?). *Milan, Brera.*

309. Raphael. Madonna del Granduca. Detail. About 1505. *Florence, Pitti Palace.*

310. Michelangelo. The Delphic Sibyl. Fresco. Detail. 1508–1512. *Rome, Sistine Chapel.*

vitality, perhaps because it was the last comer, all the Italian schools were to suffer from this sickness of styles—a sort of neurosis, a symptom of their inability to define themselves which led the second-rank artists, overwhelmed by the authority of the Great Masters, into an extravagance of gesture and expression, an overlengthening of proportions, and unnaturally twisted attitudes in the portrayal of figures.

This nervous unbalance was passed from Italy to the rest of Europe. The contact between the Renaissance and Gothic Europe was at first a kind of rapture. Without in the least changing their structure, the schools of the different nations were content to take from abroad an ornamental vocabulary which they used as another embellishment in the Flamboyant manner. Failing to grasp the implications of the pure works being made in Florence, they sought models for their Renaissance style in the notorious Certosa of Pavia, which, tattooed as it is with arabesques, overlaid with balustrades and candelabra and cupids and insets of every kind, was still not enough to shock men who were quite used to the lacework of their own cathedrals. Such were the sources of the Spanish plateresque style, as of the Loire castles and the German Renaissance.

At all events, when toward 1530 Rome's prestige imposed its examples of the full Renaissance style, Europe found itself unequal to it, and instead of following the awe-inspiring models of Leonardo, Raphael or Michelangelo took to the eccentricities of Italian art, that is to say Mannerism, whose contortions followed naturally on the Flamboyant. The crisis resulting from such an upheaval in values could only favor the spread of Mannerism, which thrived at Amsterdam, Leiden, Antwerp, Fontainebleau, Basel, along the Danube and down into Spain and Portugal.

When we consider what a nightmare the Italian Renaissance must have been for a Europe lost for centuries in the maze of Gothic, it is surprising that the chaos was not even worse. But the Gothic style had exhausted all its possibilities and the fertilizing influence of Italianism all over Europe brought fresh sap into its withering veins. One country after another found renewed creative strength and became confident of being able to express its native genius. Taking to itself the expatriate Cretan, El Greco, Spain exploited the Mannerist "trance" to convey the rapture of ecstasy. At the other extreme Bruegel made a Flemish contribution to humanism by giving a pantheistic definition of

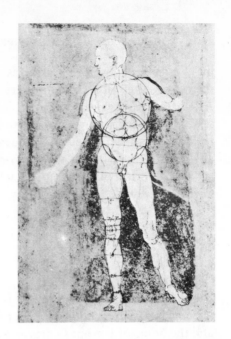

311. Dürer. Proportions of the
human body. Drawing.
Vienna, Albertina.

man's relationship to the universe. At Nuremberg, Dürer's pessimistic philosophy summed up the German soul's inability to bring the infinite complexity of the world down to the scale of man; outside Italy he was perhaps the greatest artist in Europe and the one who was most lucidly aware of the limitations of the Renaissance. But the most surprising event in sixteenth century Europe was the startling and sudden conversion of France. The resourcefulness of that part of Europe, fortuitously placed between the North and the Mediterranean, is nowhere better shown than in the ability of a country that had created Gothic civilization—so well adapted to its own genius—to give it up so readily and so completely as to absorb the new aesthetic to the point of becoming the guardian of a classicism which Italy herself rejected.

Europe had scarcely assimilated the Renaissance when she found herself faced by another movement from beyond the Alps in the shape of the Counter Reformation aesthetic. In the widespread revision of values that was taking place, Europe was to find its real maturity, which, after a new but brief period of growth, was to allow the wonderful achievement of the seventeenth century, which was to be the finest period known to Europe.

But the Counter Reformation, tending toward a new Christian humanism, belongs properly to the sixteenth century. Between 1560 and 1580, rules were laid down for architecture as for the other arts, whether by Vignola or by the Carraccis; Caravaggio, who revolted against them, was after all a contemporary of Agostino and Annibale Carracci. All these artists who together founded the aesthetic from which the seventeenth century was to draw its principles will be studied in the following chapter; they are evidence of the fertility of that remarkable century in which a whole world of ideas came into being, a whole world of forms and feelings, in which the austerity of Reason was to come into conflict with the most vehement passions.

ITALY

In the sixteenth century all Italy's strength was absorbed by Rome. The Eternal City was awakening from its medieval sleep and, thanks to the activity of the great Popes Julius II, Leo X and Paul III, it was to become both the recognized center of the spiritual power of the Church, and the home of European arts and letters as well as the mother country of the Humanists. After 1540 all the artists of Europe met in Rome. The other Italian schools, weakened by these demands, became her satellites. Between 1480 and 1510 the old Florentine school still acted as the workshop in which Italian artists went through their apprenticeship, but it was very soon frustrated by the loss of its most promising members and became an easy prey for Mannerism. Venice alone was deaf to the call from Rome and went her own way, gathering round her an important section of northern Italy.

ARCHITECTURE

Quattrocento architecture was an interplay of lines and surfaces, while that of the Cinquecento exploited masses and volumes and sharply articulated the monument into bays and stories. Imitation of the antique was no longer confined to decoration, and architects were now inspired by the very *structure* of ancient buildings. Originating in Florence, the art of building tended toward gracefulness and elegance in the fifteenth century, but sixteenth century architecture, since it developed in the city of the Emperors and Popes, undertook colossal programs and sought above all to convey an impression of strength.

Donato Bramante (about 1444–1514) carried out the transition between the two centuries. After a period in Milan when his work suffered from the poor taste of the Lombards, he went to Rome in 1499

312. Bramante. The Tempietto, S. Pietro in Montorio, Rome. 1502.

and completely changed his art at a rather late stage in his life after seeing some classical monuments. In making the graceful Tempietto of San Pietro in Montorio (1502, pl. 312) he firmly applied the principles of the Doric order as defined by the classical architect Vitruvius. At the request of Julius II, he worked out plans for a grandiose pontifical city at the Vatican. He removed the old basilica of Constantine and planned an immense dome for St. Peter's, to be set upon four cradle vaults and flanked by four secondary cupolas (pl. 306). The central plan had been adopted several times for buildings of a universal or imperial significance (Pantheon in Rome, Santa Sophia in Constantinople, Palatine Chapel at Aix-la-Chapelle). Here it asserted the radiation of Catholicism, and it fascinated the men of the Renaissance, to whom no other plan seemed so perfect, being based as it was on the circle, that complete geometrical figure which has neither beginning nor end. Bramante renewed the Vatican Palace close to St. Peter's. He did this by joining the palace of Nicholas V with Innocent VIII's *palazzetto* by means of two long galleries. Basing his over-all plan on the Roman *stadium* he centered the whole perspective on a huge open-air semi-dome, suggested by the classical *exedra*—the *Belvedere Niche*.

Michelangelo (1475–1564) stressed the members of the building by using the "colossal" order linking two stories (Laurentian Library, Florence; Piazza del Campidoglio [Capitol], Rome). Fifteenth century architecture was composed of hollowed surfaces and bays, whereas that of the sixteenth had its skeletal structure thrown into relief by vertical supports and horizontal entablatures. Michelangelo

313. Farnese Palace, Rome. Courtyard. The two lower floors, built from 1530 to 1546 after the plans of Antonio da Sangallo the Younger; the upper story, about 1547–1550, by Michelangelo.

314. Dome of St. Peter's, Rome. Designed by Michelangelo in 1546, it was erected as far as the drum at the time of his death in 1564. It was completed in 1581 by Vignola, Giacomo della Porta, and Domenico Fontana.

315. Giulio Romano. Palazzo del Te, Mantua. 1525–1535. Detail.

executed the finest palace of the Renaissance in that spirit, the Farnese Palace in Rome (pl. 313) which was begun by Antonio da Sangallo— also known as San Gallo (1455–1534). In 1546 Pope Paul III entrusted Michelangelo with the work that was now being resumed on St. Peter's after a lapse following Bramante's death. Rejecting the Latin-cross form suggested by Raphael and Baldassare Peruzzi, he chose Bramante's central plan but gave greater emphasis to its inner structure (pl. 307). A cupola 387 feet high and 136 feet 6 inches in diameter is set on four piers 86 feet wide; the width of the building, 447 feet. The framework of the building is marked by huge Corinthian pilasters running up three stories, the dome itself marked by sixteen powerful ribs to which there correspond double columns on the sustaining drum (pl. 314). Michelangelo's version of St. Peter's was to be finished after his death by Giacomo Barozzi, called Vignola (1507–1573). Michelangelo's most faithful disciple introduced into architecture a severeness in keeping with the taste of the Counter Reformation. In the Gesù church (Jesuit) in Rome, projected in 1567 and begun in 1568, he built a church which was to serve as a model for the seventeenth century (pl. 378).

Inclining to the picturesque, the architectural works conceived by Raphael (1483–1520) had something to do with the development of Mannerism. His pupil Giulio Romano (1492–1546), who was also a painter, was even more than Vignola the representative of Mannerism in architecture. The Palazzo del Te at Mantua, which he built from 1525 to 1535 (pl. 315), was decorated throughout with his frescoes, and heralds baroque architecture.

316. Palladio. Façade of the
Redentore church, Venice.
1577–1592.

In its rivalry with Rome, Venice adopted the new style invented by the Eternal City, but overlaid it with lavish decoration. At the Libreria Vecchia di San Marco, Sansovino (1486–1570) multiplied the pilasters, columns, entablatures, balustrades, statues, in order to contrive a richness of effect nearer to the spirit of painting than to architecture. Andrea Palladio of Vicenza (1508–1580) showed the same taste for splendor in the Basilica (1573) and the Teatro Olimpico in Vicenza, the latter being finished by his pupil Scamozzi; but in the most original part of his work (villas built in Venetia; Church of the Redentore in Venice, pl. 316), on the other hand, he renounced all lyricism in the decorations and sought after a greater classical purity. Of all the artists of the Renaissance he came nearest to the canons of Greek architecture.

In the sixteenth century in Italy, architecture tended to become a theoretical science. Numerous editions of Vitruvius' treatise, enriched with engravings, together with illustrations of Roman monuments, and the treatises of Serlio (1537), Vignola (1562) and Palladio (1570) guaranteed the spreading of the classical manner in architecture throughout Europe.

After the model of the Roman villa, Renaissance Italy created many princely residences in the country. The house or *casino* stands above a set of terraces embellished with yew trees, flower beds, pools and fountains, statues and "rustic" buildings. The most famous of these, the Villa d'Este (1549), was designed by Pirro Ligorio (d. about 1580) for the Cardinal Ippolito d'Este (pl. 317).

317. Villa d'Este at Tivoli, begun in 1549 by Pirro Ligorio.

PAINTING AND SCULPTURE

The aesthetic of the High Renaissance was worked out in the first third of the century by a few great artists. The oldest of them, Leonardo da Vinci, born in 1452, still belongs to the Quattrocento by virtue of his inquiring mind and scientific genius. Born within a few years of each other, Raphael, Michelangelo, Giorgione and Titian were all of the same generation, but Giorgione and Raphael died relatively young and the careers of Michelangelo and Titian stretched late into the century. Born in 1494 Correggio belongs to the following generation, but had already given his full measure before his death in 1534; and by his genius for innovation he must be considered as one of the leaders of the Cinquecento. Within their lifetimes these great masters founded schools of their own, which prolonged their art, even while degrading it, until the last quarter of the century, when the art of the Counter Reformation began to appear.

Leonardo da Vinci (1452–1519) served his apprenticeship in Florence, in Verrocchio's studio; he then worked in Florence and Milan. Called to France in 1516 by Francis I he died there, near Amboise. Leonardo painted very few works, which unfortunately have badly deteriorated because of his technical researches into the chemistry of colors. The best-known of his paintings are: *Madonna of the Rocks* (1483?), Louvre; the *Last Supper* (1495–1497), Santa Maria delle Grazie, Milan (pl. 303); *Virgin and Child with St. Anne* (about 1508/10?, pl. 318) and the *Gioconda*, or *Mona Lisa* (about 1503), both in the

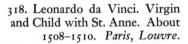

318. Leonardo da Vinci. Virgin and Child with St. Anne. About 1508–1510. *Paris, Louvre.*

Louvre. He completed the researches of the fifteenth century into the human body, but he was intent on adding to it his discoveries in the realm of psychology. The *Last Supper* is a systematic study of shades of expression which are inflected according to the individual, while in the *Gioconda* he tried to convey the mystery of the inner life. Abandoning the sharp outlines of the sculptor-painters of the Quattrocento—still noticeable in the *Madonna of the Rocks*—he rendered the luminous, fluid vibrations of atmosphere and the softness of flesh by veiling the modeling through a chiaroscuro technique called *sfumato*. He corresponded to the Renaissance conception of the "Universal Man." His scientific treatises, which remained unpublished during his lifetime, his host of drawings, all show a thirst for knowledge in all its fields—astronomy, the physical and natural sciences, biology, mechanics, hydraulics, aviation, chemistry and the like. However, he made painting, which is a reflection of nature, into the supreme creative art, and indeed the very end of both the sciences and the arts.

Raffaello Sanzio (1483–1520), or Raphael, gave a definitive form to the ideal of harmony toward which Italian art had been moving for two hundred years. Born at Urbino, he was a pupil of Perugino, under whose guidance he painted his earliest works (*Marriage of the Virgin*, or *Sposalizio*, at Milan, 1504). It was Florence, where he spent the years 1504–1508, that brought him intellectual freedom. There he developed his type of Madonna with the pure oval face, impersonal and idealized as the faces of classical statues (pls. 309, 320). From 1508 to 1511 he was painting for Pope Julius II, undertaking a series of frescoes in the Stanze (chambers), particularly the Stanza della Segnatura, of the Vatican (*School of Athens*, or *Philosophy*, pl. 319; *Parnassus*, or *Poetry*; *Glorification of the Holy Sacrament*, or *Religion*, known as the *Disputà*; and three scenes together representing the *Law*). Enlivened by intellectual inspiration, Raphael's idealism here achieved an admirable monumental fullness; the happy combination of an artistic temperament with the thought of his age produced in the Stanza della Segnatura one of those major works in which form is the more sublime because of the idea it contains. His portraits (*Baldassare Castiglione*, Louvre; *La Donna Velata*, Pitti Palace) express the humanistic ideal of a calm existence, certainty and self-possession. He was less successful in his religious works, for a systematic idealizing of figures results in a kind of devotional art which is banal, cold and insipid and was unfor-

319. Raphael. The School of Athens. Fresco in the
Stanza della Segnatura. 1510–1511. *Rome, Vatican.*

tunately to be favored by the lords of the church for three hundred
years (*Sistine Madonna*, Dresden; *Madonna di Foligno* and the *Transfiguration*, both in the Vatican; the *Holy Family*, Louvre). In the
other frescoes he painted in the Vatican Stanze (*Fire in the Borgo*,
the *Miracle of Bolsena*, *Heliodorus Driven from the Temple*, 1511–
1514) Raphael, who was easily influenced, showed himself to be somewhat disturbed by the power of Michelangelo and by Venetian coloring. His last monumental work, partly carried out by his pupils, was

320. Raphael. Study for a
Madonna. Drawing.
Vienna, Albertina.

the *Story of Cupid and Psyche* in the Villa Farnesina, in which he invented the mythological models of the modern age. The Vatican Loggie, on which work was begun under Raphael's direction, were finished by his pupils. There the biblical scenes are set in a background by Giovanni da Udine (1494–1561), suggested by ancient ornaments recently unearthed in the Baths (*grottae*) of Titus and which for this reason were known as *grottesche* (pl. 321). This arabesque form of ornamentation was to be copied all over Europe. We also owe to Raphael the cartoons for the tapestry series of the *Acts of the Apostles* which was woven at Brussels.

Michelangelo Buonarroti (1475–1564), born at Caprese in Tuscany, was the most Florentine in spirit of all the artists of the sixteenth century. His plastic outlook was that of the sculptor-painters of the Quattrocento who were concerned only with relief, and even his painting is a transposition of volumes onto a surface; he carried to the point of frenzy that lust for strength which had obsessed the painters of the preceding age; but, being profoundly Christian, he opposed to human strength the power of God which thwarts it and makes it of no avail. This painful strife, man's struggle against an evil destiny, the fury of a Prometheus against the chains he can never unloose, gives his art a dramatic intensity which is in violent contrast with the humanistic ideal of harmony embodied in Raphael. The gigantic and uneasy *David* in marble, 16 feet 3 inches in height (Florence, Academy), which he carved in 1502–1504, and his earliest paintings (the *Holy Family* in the

321. Giovanni da Udine. After Raphael. Decorative painting *alla grottesca* in the Loggie of Raphael. *Rome, Vatican.*

322. Michelangelo. The Creation of Man. Fresco. 1508–1512. *Rome, Sistine Chapel.*

Uffizi) are still faithful to the Quattrocento principles he imbibed in the studio of Bertoldo, a pupil of Donatello's, while he was learning the art of painting from Ghirlandaio. Called to Rome, he revealed his genius to an amazed world in the frescoes he did for the Sistine Chapel between 1508 and 1512, where he painted scenes from the Old Testament (pl. 322), prophets and sibyls in an architectural setting on which he posed sham "statues" of adolescents, the *ignudi*. His herculean idea of the human body derived from ancient statuary of the Hellenistic period then newly unearthed in Rome (the *Laocoön; Belvedere Torso*). Almost all the sculptures he conceived in colossal terms remain unfinished. The *Tomb of Julius II* was not completed by Michelangelo, but three of his statues for it are *in situ:* the overpowering *Moses* (pl. 324) and two *Sibyls.* Other sculptures originally planned for the tomb are the two unfinished *Captives* (Paris, pl. 323) and four unfinished *Slaves* (Florence). He worked from 1523 to 1534 on the *Tombs of Giuliano and Lorenzo de' Medici* at San Lorenzo in Florence; there his desperate soul is reflected in the allegorical figures on the tombs (*Day, Night, Dawn, Twilight*) and the *Virgin* in the Medici Chapel. His most violent work is the fresco of the *Last Judgment* in the Sistine Chapel (1535 to 1541), where a gigantic Christ is shown striking down mankind—a gesture which, in the mind of a great republican and Christian artist who was a follower of Savonarola, was perhaps aimed at the Papacy. In this work the balance which Michelangelo had so far maintained in the Sistine Chapel between beauty and expressionism was upset in favor of the dramatic, and it is already a baroque work.

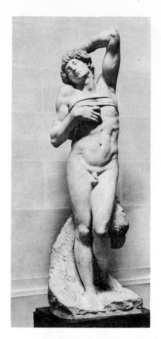

323. Michelangelo. Dying Captive, intended for the tomb of Julius II.
Marble. *Paris, Louvre.*

324. Michelangelo. Statue of Moses, on the tomb of Julius II.
Marble. *Rome, S. Pietro in Vincoli.*

Being by nature more given to enjoyment than to knowledge,
unlike Florence, Venice created an art more expressive of sensibility
than of intellect. The Venetian artists therefore addressed the senses
rather than the spirit, and their magic color suggests the material presence of the world. Three artists worked out, in Bellini's studio, the
Venetian art of the Seicento. They were Giorgione, Titian and Palma
Vecchio.

Giorgio da Castelfranco, called Giorgione (1477–1511), plunged
man into the very heart of nature; he gave the Florence-trained artists
no more than the elements of a setting thrown into the distance like a
backcloth. The Venetian picture was to be essentially based on landscape (pl. 325), and even if its distinct forms were not represented, the
natural was always in evidence in the warm light playing subtly on
faces, flesh and draperies, and in the atmosphere enwrapping everything. Giorgione founded the principles of modern painting—so-called
symphonic painting in which the colors, like orchestral sounds, acted
each on the other and were no longer flatly applied inside the outlines

256

of the drawing according to the principles of "local tone" which Raphael so scrupulously observed.

Tiziano Vecelli, called Titian (1477?–1576), had an exceptionally long life. In Venice he became a sort of regent over the arts. He worked for Alfonso d'Este, Duke of Ferrara (*Bacchanals* of the Prado and the Louvre, *Venus of Urbino* in the Uffizi, pl. 326); for the Marquis of Mantua (*Entombment*, in the Louvre), and for Pope Paul III, who summoned him to Rome in 1545. His genius earned him the patronage of the Emperor Charles V, who made him a count palatine and called him to Augsburg several times, notably in 1548, when he painted *Charles V at the Battle of Mühlberg* (in the Prado). After the Emperor's death, Philip II continued patronage and for him the artist made several pictures, among them *Jupiter and Antiope* (Louvre).

Titian was the expression, in the sensuous Venetian mode, of the ideal of harmony and certainty of which Raphael's art was the intellectual form. He interpreted the epicurean temperament of Venice, but with a fullness of health which completely purified it, and had a poetry, by turns pathetic and meditative, which makes him one of the most profound painters of the soul. His work is a vast encyclopedia

325. Giorgione (?). The Adoration of the Shepherds. Detail.
Washington, National Gallery of Art.

326. Titian. The Venus of Urbino. About 1538. *Florence, Uffizi.*

of human feelings in which the pagan dream of the Golden Age, the Christian mysteries, the delights of love, the ritual of death, the splendors of light and all the beauty of nature come together. He is the first of the "universal" painters whose works are a microcosm of the world.

Palma Vecchio (1480 to about 1528) is related to Titian, but has more sensual overtones (pl. 327).

327. Palma Vecchio. Portrait of an Unknown Lady. *Milan, Poldi-Pezzoli Museum.*

In the Venetian orbit a painter from Cremona, Giovanni Antonio Licinio, called Pordenone (1483–1539), a talented forerunner who was creating the baroque at the moment when Titian was developing his serene classicism. He foreshadowed the art of Tintoretto, even of Caravaggio, and prepared the way for Parmigianino (frescoes for the cathedrals of Cremona, 1520–1523, and Spilimbergo, 1524).

At Parma, Antonio Allegri, called Correggio (1494?–1534), brought into being an art of sentimental voluptuousness which owed something to Florentine scientific draughtsmanship, as well as to Leonardo's delicacy and the sensuality of the Venetian school. His mannered feminine type (*Mystic Marriage of St. Catherine*, Louvre, 1519), his fluid compositions (*Madonna with St. Jerome*, Parma, about 1528), his expressions of rapture and ecstasy, his decorations of cupolas in sharply receding upward perspective—the first known to painting (San Giovanni at Parma, pl. 328; Cathedral at Parma, 1530)—make him, with Michelangelo, one of the founders of baroque art.

The example given by these great innovators had a paralyzing effect on their contemporaries and successors, which showed itself in their retreat into a lackadaisical conformity or else that irritable style known as Mannerism. Every great master left behind him a trail of imitators grouped into a "school." At Milan, Ambrogio de Predis (1430?–1520),

328. Correggio. Vision of St. John. Fresco in cupola. 1520. *Parma, S. Giovanni Evangelista.*

Marco d'Oggiono (about 1470–1530), Cesare da Sesto (1477–1523), Giovanni Boltraffio (1467–1516), Bernardino Luini (about 1480–1532) all vulgarized and diluted the art of Leonardo; Sodoma (1477–1549), who worked at Siena, added a disquieting sensuality to Leonardo's charm; the art of Fra Bartolommeo (1475–1517) and Mariotto Albertinelli (1474–1515) was an empty parallel with that of Raphael; the cold exactness of Andrea del Sarto (1486–1531) makes him perhaps the most abstract of them all.

Deriving from Michelangelo, Correggio, and Andrea del Sarto, a number of painters working at Florence and Parma who are often called Mannerists represent the first baroque generation. They are all typified by a deliberate cult of distortion by which they tried to give the fullest expression to their figures. Their portraits, with posed attitudes and staring eyes, have a strangeness about them which in Bronzino (Florence 1502–1572) reaches an almost hypnotic tension (pl. 329). At Parma, Parmigianino (1504–1540) refined on Correggio's feminine type, lengthening limbs and body to make it more gracefully fluid (pl. 330). Primaticcio (1504–1570) was to introduce this type

329. Bronzino. Portrait of Lucrezia Panciatichi. About 1540.
Florence, Uffizi.
330. Parmigianino. The Madonna of the Long Neck. 1532.
Florence, Uffizi.

into France (pl. 334). In Florence, Andrea del Sarto's pupils proved into what decay the oldest Italian school had fallen: Pontormo (1494–1555) lengthened his forms beyond all reason and painted strange compositions in which the classicism of this school was oddly abused; Il Rosso (1494–1540), who was called to France in 1531, accentuated the pathos of Michelangelo by dramatic gesture. In Rome and Mantua, Giulio Romano (1492–1546), who was a kind of studio overseer for Raphael, tried to continue his master's art by adding a touch of Michelangelesque overemphasis. His style had an enormous influence all over Europe. Sebastiano del Piombo (1485–1547), who came from Venice to Rome about 1509, was also led away by this grandiose but dangerous example.

Were it not for Michelangelo, it might be said that the sixteenth century saw the decadence of Italian sculpture, which had been so rich in the Quattrocento. In Padua, the bronzeworker Andrea Riccio (1470–1532) carried on the tradition of Donatello; in Venice the emigrant Florentine Jacopo Sansovino imitated ancient statues to the point of pastiche. Michelangelo's example overwhelmed such artists as Baccio Bandinelli (1493–1560), Guglielmo della Porta (about 1510–1577) and Bartolommeo Ammanati (1511–1592). Other artists of the Florentine school such as the Frenchman Jean de Boulogne (known as Giambologna, 1524–1608, pl. 331) and the bronze- and goldworker Benvenuto Cellini (1500–1571, pl. 365) brought the Mannerist style into sculpture.

The Venetian school, the latest comer in the history of painting, was the only school in Italy to ignore the Mannerist crisis. With its energy still unspoiled it produced some great masters in the second half of the century. Paolo Cagliari, known as Veronese (1528–1588), came originally from Verona and was a talented decorator. He painted immense canvases, which he arranged as dazzling stage settings in the midst of splendid works of architecture (*Marriage at Cana*, Louvre; ceilings of the Doge's Palace, Venice, pl. 332). His gay coloring, silvery and musical, expresses all the generosity of the senses and the taste for material luxury for which Venice is noted. Jacopo Robusti, known as Tintoretto (1512?–1594), was one of the creators of baroque art. A pupil of Titian, his eyes were opened by Michelangelo's works in Rome. His tormented genius and creative frenzy poured themselves out on a vast scale in his huge compositions (*Last Judgment* at Santa Maria dell'Orto; *Old and New Testament* scenes, Scuola di San Rocco; decorations in the Doge's Palace, where he painted the biggest painting in

331. Giambologna. Venus. *Florence, Villa della Petráia.*

332. Veronese. The Republic of Venice. Ceiling. After 1577.
Venice, Doge's Palace.

333. Tintoretto. The Last Supper. Detail. *Venice, S. Giorgio Maggiore.*

the world, the *Paradise*, which is 2153 square feet in area). Tintoretto toned down Venetian coloring in order to render subtler shades of pathos; he was haunted by the notion of space and showed man swept away in a sort of cosmic drama (pl. 333). In the town of Bassano, Venetia, the Bassani school have a rustic feeling close to the Flemish style, not often found in Italy.

Several northern Italian towns came directly under the influence of Venice. At Bergamo, Lorenzo Lotto (1480–1556) was one of the few Mannerists of the North. Giovanni Battista Moroni (1525–1578) was a remarkable portrait artist who was as strictly objective as Holbein. At Brescia, Moretto (1498–1554) and Savoldo (about 1480–after 1548), both influenced by Giorgione's chiaroscuro, herald some of the experiments to be made in the seventeenth century. Dosso Dossi (about 1479–1542) at Ferrara gave further evidence in his work of that taste for the unusual which is common to Ferrarese painting; this he did in a manner deriving from Giorgione.

THE SPREAD OF THE RENAISSANCE IN EUROPE

FRANCE

The early French Renaissance, on which Italian influence was not very deep, developed mainly in the region of the Loire. Decorative features taken from Milanese art—arabesques, *putti*, candelabra, medallions and lusters—were superadded to Gothic elements in the castles built for Louis XII or his ministers at Blois, Amboise, Chaumont, Gaillon (near Rouen). In the châteaux dating from the first half of Francis I's reign (Blois, Chambord, Azay-le-Rideau, Chenonceau) an Italianate decoration was still often superficially applied on buildings planned and constructed on traditional French lines. This composite style died out toward 1530, a time when a complete assimilation was achieved, particularly in the region of Paris. In 1528 Francis I decided to make Fontainebleau a center of Italianism. When it came to decorating the rooms and galleries of his new palace, he invited artists from abroad—Primaticcio, Il Rosso and Niccolò dell'Abbate—to do the work. There he amassed his first items for a collection of antiques, and masterpieces of the great Italian artists; this was the beginning of the Louvre museum. The rather awkward external architecture of the palace was designed by Gilles le Breton, and was very much in the spirit of the preceding gen-

334. Primaticcio. Stucco in the Old Room of the Duchesse d'Etampes,
Palace of Fontainebleau.

eration; but Il Rosso and Primaticcio (pl. 334) gave the interior a stucco
and painted decoration rich in figures; this style, as yet unknown to
Italy, was the first instance of baroque decorations and had great influence all over Europe (1533–1544). It was not to appear in Italy until
about 1550 (Palazzo Spada, Rome).

However, the arrival of two Italian architects, Vignola and Serlio,
who were invited to France in 1541, must have helped the French to
throw off their outmoded traditions. In Henry II's reign the ancient
classical style was elegantly applied by three great artists, Pierre Lescot,
Philibert Delorme and Jean Goujon. Pierre Lescot (about 1510–1578)
superimposed the three Greek orders in his reconstruction of the Louvre
(1547, pl. 335). Philibert Delorme (about 1510–1570), almost all of
whose works have been destroyed (the Tuileries) or interfered with
(Château d'Anet), further stressed the French trend toward classical
purity by way of reaction against the decorative style introduced by
the Italians (pl. 336); but overlavish decoration was to return to favor
during the reign of Henry IV. As for church architecture, it was only
toward 1530 that it accepted Italianate decoration, applied to entirely
Gothic structures. This state of affairs continued into the seventeenth
century (St.-Eustache, Paris).

Meanwhile the builder's craft was beginning to free itself from the empirical approach of the medieval master mason, to become the architect's science. Following the Italian example, the French now published treatises on architecture. In 1547 Jean Goujon prefaced a French translation from Vitruvius, issued by Jean Martin, with what was no less than a manifesto in favor of the creative architect. Philibert Delorme, who published a dissertation on architecture in 1567 as well as various technical works, wanted the architect to become a Universal Man, versed in all kinds of learning and philosophy. Jean Bullant also published a treatise in 1564. Very soon French classical monuments themselves began to be quoted as examples and models, and Jacques Androuet du Cerceau issued his *Plus Excellens Bastimens de France* between 1576 and 1579.

In the first half of the century, sculpture followed the restful style of the preceding century, tinged with Italian influence. The tomb of Francis II, Duke of Brittany, at Nantes, sculptured by Michel Colombe after the design of Jean Perréal, and that of Louis XII, which was finished at St.-Denis, Paris, by the Italian Giovanni Giusti in 1531, were in the traditional manner, but the tomb of Francis I, which was finished by Philibert Delorme in 1558 at St.-Denis and embellished with sculp-

335. Façade of the Louvre Palace courtyard, begun in 1547 after plans by Pierre Lescot, decorations by Jean Goujon.

336. Philibert Delorme. Tomb of Francis I and Claude of France.
Finished in 1558. *Paris, St.-Denis*.

337. Jean Goujon. Nymphs. Low-relief from the Fontaine des Innocents.
About 1546. *Paris, Louvre*.

tures by Pierre Bontemps, was a triumphal arch (pl. 336). Equally
classical was the tomb of Henry II executed by Primaticcio between
1564 and 1570. Jean Goujon (low-reliefs for the rood screen of St.-
Germain-l'Auxerrois, Paris, now in the Louvre, 1544; bas-reliefs in the
Palais du Louvre, 1549–1562; *Fontaine des Innocents*, 1546, pl. 337)
imposed a classical discipline on Rosso's art and created a fluidly elegant
style unmatched in Italy. Germain Pilon (1534–1590) added a realistic
touch to it, while Ligier Richier (d. 1567), a Lorraine artist, pursued
the dramatic Gothic strain with a certain bombast (*Entombment* in
St.-Etienne at St.-Mihiel).

The art of Jean Bourdichon (d. about 1521), who worked under
Louis XII, is neither illumination nor exactly painting, and is evidence
of the Gothic decline. France had to turn to foreign artists, but these
were all deeply influenced by French society. In the many ensembles
they painted, notably at Fontainebleau, both Il Rosso (who came in
1531) and Primaticcio (from 1532 onward) developed an art Italianate
in style but in which the mythological amorous themes, the lyricism
of the huntsman and the forest, the feminine atmosphere, all express

266

certain characteristics that were to endure in French art over the centuries. Their contact with French life helped these artists to cast off the restlessness of Italian Mannerism and replace it with a calm and temperate style, fluid and supple, a style known as that of the "Fontainebleau school" which was to be imitated, sometimes most awkwardly, by anonymous native artists, as it was by Jean Cousin and his son of the same name.

France evolved its own idea of portraiture, the psychological portrait centered on the face itself, in which the features which best reveal the dominant qualities of character are most fully brought out. Here again France had to call in foreign artists, to wit Jean Clouet, a native of Antwerp (settled in Tours in 1521, died in 1540) whose art was carried on by his son François Clouet, who was born in France (d. 1572), and Corneille de Lyon, a native of The Hague. The Clouets showed a preference for portraits drawn in chalks of only three colors: black, white, red. Jean Clouet's art consists of a deep psychological penetration; his drawings, which were swiftly executed sketches with irritable strokes running across them, show something of his creative impatience (pl. 338). The art of François Clouet, steeped in Italianism and less acute in its vision, is more suave; he was at his best in female portraiture (pl. 339). A number of artists carried this tradition of drawn portraits

338. Jean Clouet. Drawing for the Unknown Man with a Volume of Petrarch. About 1535. *Chantilly, Musée Condé.*

339. François Clouet. Diana Bathing. *Richmond (England), Private Collection.*

into the seventeenth century, among them Pierre Quesnel and his two sons (François, who died in 1619, and Nicolas), the Dumonstier family (Pierre, Étienne and Daniel, the latter dying in 1646), and Pierre Lagneau.

The religious civil wars resulted in a decadence which Henry IV tried to arrest. The second Fontainebleau school, with Ambroise Dubois of Antwerp (1543–1614), Toussaint Dubreuil (about 1561 to 1603) and Martin Freminet (1567–1619), introduced Romanism into France, but in the form of the Antwerp Mannerism.

THE LOW COUNTRIES

Italianism filtered into the Low Countries by way of the early Renaissance French style (Palais de Justice, Malines; Palais des Princes Evêques at Liége, 1526–1533; Greffe du Franc at Bruges, 1535). More direct importation took place after 1550, particularly under the influence of Cornelis Floris (Hôtel de Ville, Antwerp, pl. 340; rood screen of Tournai Cathedral, 1572; Hôtel Plantin at Antwerp, 1576). The Antwerp publisher Pieter Coek Van Aelst published treatises on architecture by Serlio, Vignola, Palladio and Vitruvius. In the second half of the century architecture tended toward an ornamental style and the pic-

340. Cornelis Floris. Hôtel de Ville, Antwerp. 1561–1565.

341. Quentin Matsys. Altarpiece for the Confraternity of St. Anne. 1509.
Brussels, Musée des Beaux-Arts.

turesque. Hans Vredeman de Vries (1527–1604) engraved and published several works on ornamentation and a treatise of architecture in French after Vitruvius, works which became sources of European baroque art.

Flemish sculpture passed even more directly from the Flamboyant to the baroque style than did architecture, and missed out the classical transitional stage in which France after Italy remained arrested. The fusing of the two styles had already occurred in the architectural and sculptural ensemble built at Brou in France by Margaret of Austria in 1522–1532. In the second half of the century Cornelis Floris at Antwerp and Jacques du Broeucq in Wallonia learned much from the Mannerists as well as from Michelangelo.

Painting remained the major art in the Low Countries, as in the earlier period. Italian influence was soon apparent in the admiration for Leonardo which affected Jacob Cornelisz (about 1470–1533) at Amsterdam; Joos Van Cleve at Antwerp (about 1485–1540/41) and Quentin Matsys of the same town (about 1466–1530) whose *Relations of the Holy Family* of 1509 was already marked by the gracefulness of Leonardo (pl. 341). Jan Gossaert, called Mabuse (about 1470–1533), of Maubeuge, had a sculptural vision of the world deriving from Mantegna

342. Hieronymus Bosch. The Burning Church.
Detail from The Temptation of St. Anthony. *Lisbon, National Museum.*

though corrected by Michelangelo. The imaginary world of Hieronymus Bosch (about 1460–1516), haunted by all the medieval terrors of hell, was untouched by Italian influence but his very modern sense and treatment of color foreshadowed Venetian painting (pl. 342). Lucas Van Leyden (1494–1533) was influenced by Germany and shows early signs of Mannerist anxiety. In the second half of the century Antwerp in Flanders and Utrecht and Haarlem in Holland tended to become the chief centers of artistic activity. Neo-Roman influence brought with it the Mannerism which from now on was to throw Northern painting off its balance. The Flemish school quickly degenerated with Frans Floris (1516–1570), with his unconvincing imitations of Michelangelo, and Bernard Van Orley (about 1492–1542), who hid his lack of inspiration under a hotchpotch of Raphael, Giulio Romano, Michelangelo, Mabuse and Dürer. Dutch Mannerism was more original in its agitation. Jan Van Scorel (1495–1562), the unbridled Martin Van Heemskerck (1498–1574, pl. 343) were the Northern painters who followed Rome most closely. Anthonis Mor (1517–1576/77) of Utrecht made energetic and concentrated portraits which recall those of Bronzino (pl. 344).

However, in the second half of the century one great artist stood immune from the Mannerist crisis and rediscovered the true tradition of Northern painting; that is to say the lyrical portrayal of nature. The

343. Martin Van Heemskerck. Christ Crowned with Thorns. 1532.
Ghent, Musée des Beaux-Arts.
344. Anthonis Mor. Cardinal Granvelle's Dwarf.
Paris, Louvre.

longing for universality which had already moved Joachim de Patinir
(about 1480–1524) led Pieter Bruegel the Elder (about 1525–1569)
toward an admirable cosmic synthesis in those panoramic landscapes in
which we feel the throbbing of the great manifold creation (pl. 345),
but he associated human existence with that organic life. To the painter
of social manners that Bruegel fundamentally was, human existence
seemed to be governed by the primary instincts, which are closely

345. Pieter Bruegel. The Census at Bethlehem. Detail.
Brussels, Musée des Beaux-Arts.

related to the forces of nature. Although he traveled south of the Alps in 1552–1553, Bruegel took no more than his intellectual discipline from Italy, and his style, stemming from that of Bosch, is one of the most original native expressions of the Nordic genius.

GERMANY

The elements of the Renaissance style did not reach German architecture before the second half of the sixteenth century. Southern Germany (Augsburg and Nuremberg) drew its Italian influences at first hand, whereas the whole North and the central Rhine depended on the Renaissance style as developed in Flanders. This Flemish influence spread right along the Baltic which was still following its tradition of building in brick and stone, and Danzig itself was built by Flemish architects. The group of buildings composing Heidelberg Castle (from 1556 to 1609) owed much to the rich fund of decorative features created in Antwerp and popularized by engravers (pl. 346). The items taken from the new style were treated as additions only, applied in the manner of Flamboyant Gothic on a fenestrated structure which was entirely medieval in spirit. This style, more Baroque than Renaissance, was to survive right through the seventeenth century.

346. Heidelberg Castle. The Frederick Wing. 1601–1604.

347. Peter Vischer. Statue of St. Paul, on the Shrine of St. Sebald. Bronze. 1507–1519. *Nuremberg, St. Sebald.*

348. Lucas Cranach. Venus. *Formerly in Frankfurt, Städel Art Institute.*

There are two names which sum up the two stages of the Renaissance in German sculpture. Tilman Riemenschneider (1460?–1531) of Würzburg was the last of a long line of sculptors of Gothic altarpieces, whose expressionist style became calmer toward 1520. Peter Vischer of Nuremberg (d. 1529), who revived the technique of casting in bronze, was much earlier in welcoming the Italian plastic outlook which he probably knew through the works of the Venetian sculptor Sansovino (*St. Sebald's Shrine* at Nuremberg, 1519, pl. 347; figures on *Maximilian's Tomb* at Innsbruck). Vischer's style was carried on by his descendants at Nuremberg.

But it was mainly in the arts of drawing, painting and engraving that the German temperament was most spontaneously expressed. The history of German painting, which had its Golden Age in the sixteenth century, was cut across by a clash between Italianism and the native bent for expressionism which however had but slight difficulty in overcoming the Southern invasion. The aesthetic of Bellini's school was 1524) and Hans Burgkmair (1472–1553) but at the same moment the adopted at Augsburg by Hans Holbein the Elder (about 1460/70 to Danube school witnessed a flowering of German expressionism and the involved forms of the belated Gothic infused with Mannerism in Lucas Cranach (1472–1553), Luther's friend who introduced mythological nudes into German art (pl. 348), and more especially Albrecht

273

349. Albrecht Altdorfer. The Battle of Alexander.
Detail. 1529. *Munich, Pinakothek.*

Altdorfer (about 1480–1538) who in his lively landscapes (*Battle of Alexander*, 1529) gave his answer of grandiose, cosmic expression to the appeal for universality which a little later was to haunt Bruegel (pl. 349). Matthias Grünewald (about 1470/80 to about 1528), who worked in the middle Rhine and Alsace, was the most remote of all these artists from the Renaissance outlook. In one of the most tormented styles known to painting, he interpreted the anguished ecstasies and visionary sufferings of the Rhenish mystics of the Middle Ages (*Isenheim Altarpiece* at Colmar, 1510–1519, pl. 350). He was the greatest German colorist. In Alsace, Hans Baldung Grien (1484/85 to 1545) imitated his style but made it more complacent. In Switzerland, the struggle between the Gothic and the Renaissance resulted in a Mannerist crisis which is betrayed in the extravagance and fantasy of Hans Leu (about 1490–1531), Nicolas Manuel Deutsch (1488–1530) and Urs Graf (about 1485–1527/28, pl. 351), who painted soldiers.

However, two great painters in Germany were to throw themselves fully into the Renaissance aesthetic: Albrecht Dürer and Hans Holbein the Younger. Albrecht Dürer (1471–1528) was the son of a goldsmith in the city of Nuremberg, one of the shrines of Germanism, which was to remain the center of his activities, although in his eagerness to know more about European art he visited a number of foreign countries. In the course of one of these educational trips across Germany

350. Matthias Grünewald. The Isenheim Altarpiece. 1510–1519.
The Crucifixion. *Colmar, Museum.*

in 1490–1494 he came across the Germano-Flemish tradition of Schongauer at Colmar and studied the technique of copper engraving. A
voyage to Italy in 1494–1495 revealed the art of Mantegna and Bellini
to him, and he returned there in 1505–1507. In 1520–1521 he traveled
in the Low Countries, where he studied Flemish painting and met
Erasmus. Like Leonardo he was insatiably curious about every aspect
of the world and wrote several aesthetic and technical treatises, in par-

351. Urs Graf. German Footsoldier.
Pencil drawing. 1523.
Basel, Kunstmuseum.

ticular on the proportions of the human body (pl. 311). The *Paum-gartner Altarpiece* (about 1500) was still Gothic in spirit, but the influence of the Bellini manner goes deep in his *Festival of the Rose Garlands* (Prague, 1506), *Adoration of the Trinity* (Vienna, 1511) and above all the *Four Apostles* at Munich (1526), which is his masterpiece (pl. 352). Wood or copper engraving and drawing were the mediums in which Dürer wrestled most with the German temper. In his hundreds of engraved plates and drawings he poured all his genius into an analytical enthusiasm for the forms of nature which was unrivaled outside Leonardo da Vinci. Freed from the restrictions of harmony that he set himself in his paintings, he returned spontaneously to the tortured, graphic technique of the late Gothic which he had inherited from Schongauer. Out of the conflict between Germanic pantheism and Renaissance idealism, this great mind seems to have shaped a pessimistic philosophy which found an outlet in several of his engravings: *Nemesis* (1503), *The Knight, Death and the Devil* (1513), and *Melancholy* (1514, pl. 353), a symbol of the vanity of the science and works of mankind.

A son of Holbein the Elder, Hans Holbein the Younger (1497–1543) left Augsburg for Basel in 1515. He traveled into Lombardy and crossed France, then, driven out of Basel by the Reformation troubles,

352. Dürer. St. John with St. Peter. 1526.
Munich, Pinakothek.

353. Dürer. Melancholy.
Copperplate engraving. 1514.

354. Hans Holbein. Portrait of Sir John Godsalve.
Wash drawing about 1532. *Windsor Castle.*

he sought refuge in England, which he reached by way of Flanders. Once in England, he became court portraitist under Henry VIII. A friend of Erasmus, Holbein lost little time in devoting himself entirely to portraiture, and is the most fully European of Renaissance painters. He made a synthesis of all the influences that impinged on him in the course of his wanderings—the Italian sense of harmony and unity, the Flemish painters' objectivity, the Germans' sharp sense of analysis (pl. 354). Perhaps he gave us the most moving images of the Humanists and princes of northern Europe. Like the Clouets, this psychologist liked the drawn portrait; his engraved works are less spontaneous.

SPAIN

The Renaissance was introduced into Spain at the end of the reign of the Catholic Kings, by rather piecemeal importations into a land given over to the excesses of the "Isabelline" style. The powerful Mendoza family seems to have played an important part in this new fashion, for it is to be noted that its name is associated with the first monuments in which the new style made its appearance (Colegio de la Santa Cruz, Valladolid, by Lorenzo Vasquez, 1489; Duke of Medinaceli's Palace, Cogolludo (before 1501); Santa Cruz Hospital, Toledo; Infantado Palace, Guadalajara). Enrique de Egas (d. 1532), who also worked in the Gothic style, built the Renaissance style Royal Hospital at

Compostela (1501) and Santa Cruz Hospital at Toledo (before 1514). In these buildings the Milanese ornamental features were applied on the monument regardless of any architectonic or decorative rhythm, entirely as facings, in keeping with the traditional outlook of the Peninsula which had been imbibed through Moorish art; this art has earned the epithet *plateresque* on account of its resemblance to gold plate (*platería*). In creating new decorative patterns based on the arabesque and on chimeras brought from Italy, the plateresque artists showed an inexhaustible fund of formal inventiveness which can be compared with that of Romanesque art; the Spanish artists' natural gift for sculpture was now unleashed, but was completely undisciplined and hampered architecture. Castille was the purest center of the plateresque which followed naturally on the Flamboyant; Salamanca, the seat of the great Spanish university, was decked all over with monuments in this style; the anonymous façade of the university (1516–1529), in the form of an altarpiece, is in the same spirit as, though a different style from, that of the Colegio de San Gregorio at Valladolid.

Andalusia, with no Gothic tradition and with an orderly landscape suggestive of decorum, was the center of the purest reaction against the anarchy of the plateresque; this was due to Diego de Siloé, the son of the Gothic sculptor Gil de Siloé, who built Granada Cathedral (planned in 1528) in a Corinthian style but with an uneasiness of

355. Juan de Herrera. Façade of the Escorial. 1561–1584.

spirit which shows an incomplete assimilation: the cathedral of Granada
was to be the origin of other Andalusian cathedrals at Malaga, Baeza and
Jaén. The cathedral of Jaén (planned in 1533) by Vandaelvira, with
its quadrangular plan without an ambulatory and its pleasing proportions, shows a marked progress toward understanding classical architecture. In Andalusia the plateresque decoration instinctively tends
toward statuary (pl. 356).

The Hapsburg dynasty gave its support to this influx of classicism
against the trends of the native tradition. In 1526 Charles V invited
Pedro Machuca to draw up plans for the Alhambra at Granada which
was to be an immense palace in pure Roman style but which remained unfinished after a century's labor. Even more radical was
Philip II's initiative, for he associated himself with the Counter Reformation, reacting against the medieval imagination and preaching austere
rationalism to the Christian world. To counteract the ornamental wild-
ness of the plateresque, Philip II, who had set up his court at Madrid,
between 1561 and 1584 built a combined palace and monastery on the
Escorial: this was designed in a classical unadorned style (*estilo desorna-
mentado*) which has been called the *Herreran style* after the name of
its architect. In a rectangle 715 by 520 feet, fourteen courtyards were
laid out symmetrically round a cupola; the pointed roofs, an unusual
feature for the Spanish climate, recalled the Flemish style in the same
way as the Alcazar at Toledo. At once a monastery, palace, seminary,

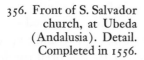

356. Front of S. Salvador
church, at Ubeda
(Andalusia). Detail.
Completed in 1556.

hospital, university, library, museum and tomb, this monument—which is a sort of lay Imperial Vatican—is one of the most ambitious expressions of monarchism, typical of the Hapsburg belief in the Divine Right of Kings (pls. 355 and 373).

Herrera also planned an imposing structure which unfortunately remained unfinished, the cathedral of Valladolid, in the same unadorned style as the Escorial. The Jesuit Bartolomé Bustamente in 1565 set up the Hospital of San Juan de Afuera, Toledo, in the style of Bramante. The Herreran style prevailed in Spain for the first half of the seventeenth century, being increasingly opposed by the baroque invasion.

Spanish sculpture in the sixteenth century produced some great works which derive from the belated influence of Donatello and the contemporary influence of Michelangelo, both of which were brought into Spain by such Italian artists as Domenico Fancelli, Jacobo Fiorentino called Indaco, or Pietro Torrigiano (d. 1528), a fellow pupil of Michelangelo who came to Seville in 1528 after working in England. Spaniards educated in Italy also brought back the new style, for instance Alonso Berruguete of Valladolid (1486/90–1561), son of the painter of that name, who was a pupil of Michelangelo (*Altarpiece* for San Benito, in Valladolid Museum, 1526–1532; alabaster sculptures on the choir stalls of Toledo Cathedral, 1539). The Castilian tradition for pathos, mingled with Michelangelo's torment, made Berruguete one of the earliest representatives of European Mannerism. His style, anticipating El Greco's by fifty years, may be compared with the latter's by its impassioned restlessness, the writhing attitudes and lengthened proportions of his figures, the feverish agitation of bodies, whose souls seem to be bursting from them as though thrust out of the flesh by some ungovernable tension (pl. 357). The French artist Juan de Juni (d. 1577) seems to have been trained in the school of the Milanese sculptors Guido Mazzoni and Niccolò dell'Arca; he added a pathetic realism and a violent expressionism to Berruguete's frenzy, both of which are alien to the native tradition of his country of origin (pl. 646). Reacting against this romanticism, in 1579 Philip II called Pompeo Leoni from Milan, a bronze sculptor who had a haughty and impressive style inspired by Donatello in which he cast for the Escorial the fifteen statues of the Capilla Mayor (1582–1590), the five figures for the *Tomb of Charles V* (1597) and yet another five for the *Tomb of Philip II* (1598).

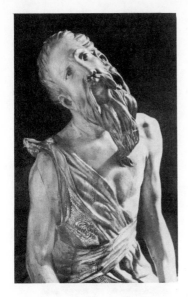

357. Alonso Berruguete. Statue of Abraham. Detail.
Wood. Altarpiece of S. Benito. 1526–1532. *Valladolid, Museum.*

358. El Greco. The Burial of the Count of Orgaz. 1586. Detail.
Toledo, S. Tomé.

Spanish painting in the sixteenth century was still almost entirely in the hands of foreigners. Ferdinand Sturm of Zeeland (at Seville in 1539), Peeter de Campeneer of Brussels (at Seville in 1537) brought Flemish Mannerism with them; Luis de Morales (d. 1586) shows the influence of Quentin Matsys in his religious images; the Fleming Anthonis Mor, whose name was styled in Spanish form Antonio Moro, became the official court portraitist and founded a tradition which was taken up by the Spaniard Sanchez Coello (1531/32–1588) and the Spaniard Pantoja de la Cruz (1551–1610). Scorning the Spanish painters, Philip II brought from Italy the Genoese Luca Cambiaso in 1583, the Florentine Federico Zuccaro, 1586, and the Bolognese Pelligrino Tibaldi (1588) to work on the Escorial decorations. Another great painter was to become the very incarnation of the deep Spanish soul: Domenico Theotocopulo, known as El Greco (1541–1614), was born on the isle of Crete: he was trained at Venice under Tintoretto and the Bassani and in 1577 we find him established in Toledo which was then the shrine of the mystery and chivalry of old Spain. It was there that he painted his masterpiece, *Burial of the Count of Orgaz* (pl. 358). Greco's aesthetic, with its exaggerated lengthening of figures,

281

359. El Greco. The Resurrection. About 1598. *Madrid, Prado*.
360. El Greco. The Descent of the Holy Ghost. *Madrid, Prado*.

convulsive attitudes, dark and sulphurous tones, is a striking aspect of the Mannerist frenzy which was spreading all over Europe at the end of the sixteenth century (pls. 359 and 360); but this antinaturalistic formalism became, in his work, a sublime means of expressing the crises of ecstasy and torments of ascesis which at the same date St. John of the Cross and St. Theresa of Avila were also experiencing in Castille. El Greco was the founder of native Spanish painting for which nothing counts but the inner life. And yet his manner was to have but slight influence on the plastic development of the school. His studio followers were to continue his pious imagery for a while. Luis Tristan (1586–1640) was the only pupil of his who managed to keep something of his master's outlook in the new realistic style adopted in the seventeenth century under the influence of Caravaggio.

In Portugal, the Spanish architect Juan de Castillo dried up the creative vein of the Manueline style by giving it an Italianate setting (Hieronymite monastery, Belém, 1517). This Milanese vocabulary was perhaps introduced by French sculptors originating in Rouen, Nicolas Chantereine, whose mind had also a Burgundian cast, and more especially Jean de Rouen. The cloister of the Convent Palace of the Knights of Christ was begun in 1558 at Tomar by Diogo de Torralva, in a style derived from Serlio. Earlier than Spain and perhaps more spontaneously, Portugal, which had been hostile to Gothic, readily imbibed the classical experiment and was less close to Lombard art than to that of the Florentine High Renaissance and the severity of Bramante (centrally planned buildings of Dom Jesus de Valverde at Mitra, near Evora; chapel of the Conceição, Tomar; palace church of Salvatorre de Magos). Toward 1440–1450 and thus before Herrera, Diogo de Torralva planned the austere *Capela Mor* of the Hieronymite monastery, Belém. Alfonso Alvares in the cathedrals of Leiria (1550) and Portalegre (1556) and perhaps the Jesuit Church at Evora (1567) carried on that classical spirit which was further strengthened by the arrival in Lisbon of the Italian Filippo Terzi (São Vicente de Fora, planned in 1582).

ENGLAND

England was the final country into which the Renaissance style penetrated, and there it met with the greatest opposition. A timid Italian influence at first resulted in no more than a slight modification of the Perpendicular Gothic style into the new Tudor style, typified by the use of flattened, four-centered arches. Following on the Reformation, there was great activity all over England in the sixteenth century, in the erection of public buildings, castles, university colleges, country houses and halls with superb carved woodwork. The interior decoration was sometimes more Italianate than the façades (Hampton Court). In the Elizabethan period the mingled influences of Italy, Germany, Flanders and France, brought in mainly by printed books, gave rise to a new style or rather a new composite approach to decoration. The decorated part of the building often took the form of a large porchway with the orders superimposed (pl. 361). This style survived into the seventeenth century. Sculpture showed the same eclecticism, borrowing features from neighboring countries. Henry VIII employed such Italians as Guido Mazzoni and Pietro Torrigiano. Torrigiano made the tombs of Henry VII and Elizabeth of York in Westminster Abbey (1512–1518). Painting, almost entirely confined to portraiture, owed much to foreign masters attracted to England by the glamour of the court, such as the German Holbein and the Fleming Anthonis Mor (Antonio Moro). The Elizabethan period saw the beginning of a native style in portraiture, represented by anonymous masters and miniaturists like Nicholas Hillyarde (recorded 1560 to death, 1619) or Isaac Oliver, of French origin (about

361. Kirby Hall, Northamptonshire. Porchway. 1572. *From Lloyd, A History of the English House.*

362. Nicholas Hillyarde. A Youth Leaning against a Tree among Roses. Portrait Miniature. About 1590. *London, Victoria and Albert Museum.*

1565/67–1617). The Fleming Hans Eworth (d. 1574), who came to England toward 1545, subjected Holbein's realism to the contemporary international Mannerism.

THE MINOR ARTS

The minor arts in the Renaissance period increasingly imitated the forms of the major arts of architecture, sculpture and painting. The chief item of furniture invented in Italy in the late fifteenth century was the cabinet, usually a piece made in two tiers and used for holding manuscripts and valuables. This article of furniture was made all over

Europe in the second half of the sixteenth century. It was generally decorated with sculptural features, caryatids, terminals, garnished columns, carved studs and panels—taken from printed works showing the devices used by Italian and Flemish ornamental sculptors. The fronts of these cabinets were often treated in the same way as the façades of buildings, with blind windows, pediments, piers and columns (pl. 363). The Italians specialized in cabinets with colored inlay in wood, the inside often containing perspectives recalling theatrical settings. In northern Europe, after the Milanese-style decoration with its flat-relief and candelabra, medallions and *putti*, in the second half of the century they introduced decorations in the round. Northern Europe created other items of furniture such as the two-paneled wardrobe, the two-storied sideboard which replaced the medieval dresser. Walnut, which is of a closer grain than oak, was now preferred to oak which had pride of place in the Middle Ages; in France the most refined work was produced in the Ile-de-France region, but that of Dijon and Lyons had more life in it.

Ornamental ceramics flourished in such centers as Faenza, Caffagiolo, Gubbio (pl. 364) and above all Urbino, which came to the fore in 1500; all Europe hastened to imitate Italian faïence and in France Bernard Palissy (d. 1590) went farther by making ceramics with naturalistic reliefs. Florence produced luxurious jewelry, mounted pieces set

363. French cabinet. Second half of 16th century.
Paris, Musée des Arts Décoratifs.

364. Maestro Giorgio. Gubbio faïence. 1528. *Private Collection.*

365. Cellini. Earth and Sea (Amphitrite and Neptune).
Golden salt cellar. About 1540–1543.
Vienna, Kunsthistoriches Museum.

with enamels and precious stones on which Mannerist ill-taste imposed its finicking network of shapes: Benvenuto Cellini was the most famous artist in this genre (pl. 365). The Venetian workshops showed great virtuosity in glasswork, embellishing it with filigree, reliefs, gold bases, crackles and the like.

Stained glass and enameling, which had been the glory of medieval France, now succumbed to painting. The technique of monumental leaded glass which the Le Prince family of Beauvais handled so brilliantly under Francis I was carried on with less originality till the end of the century; but under Henry II the stained glass window tended to become a painting on glass (Ste.-Chapelle, Vincennes), merely another form of picture. Jean Cousin and Robert Pinaigrier designed cartoons of this type. Germany and Switzerland excelled in making miniature medallion pictures which were fitted into the windows of private houses and imitated enamels. Enamelwork, indeed, also abandoned the *champlevé* technique (chasing) and was handled as no more than straightforward pictures painted on copper with colors that could be fired; the main centers of production were still at Limoges (workshops of Léonard Limousin and the Pénicaud family, pl. 366). As for their compositions, the craftsmen in glass, enamel and wood tended to make

no more than unadorned copies of the numerous German engravings
which were circulating in Europe, particularly those of Dürer.

The tapestry workshops in Brussels were now outstripping those
of France; their tapestries lost their essential character to become no
more than a direct reflection of paintings: the two most famous sets
woven at Brussels were the series of *Acts of the Apostles*, carried out
between 1515 and 1519 after cartoons commissioned from Raphael by
Leo X, and those of *Maximilian Hunting*, after cartoons by Bernard
Van Orley. Between 1530 and 1535 Francis I ordered Primaticcio to
set up a factory at Fontainebleau, where more respect was shown for
the decorative nature of tapestry.

366. Jean II Pénicaud. Cavalry Battle. Enamel. *Paris, Louvre.*

ROYALTY

*Van Dyck (center) delights in the aristocratic elegance of
the "first gentleman of the kingdom"; Rigaud (right) paints
the King decked in full regalia; for democratic Holland
(left) a king is only a bourgeois in a staid doublet.*

367. Hendrijk Pot. Charles I of England.
Detail. Painted in 1632. *Paris, Louvre.*

368. Anthony Van Dyck. Charles I of England.
Detail. 1635. *Paris, Louvre.*

369. Hyacinthe Rigaud. Portrait of Louis XIV. Detail.
Painted in 1701 for the Madrid court. *Paris, Louvre.*

CHAPTER IX

THE BAROQUE PERIOD

RIGHTLY OR WRONGLY, two words are always associated with the seventeenth and eighteenth centuries: Baroque and Rococo. Whether it comes
from the Spanish *barrueco* (Portuguese *barroco*), a term from gem-
mology meaning an irregular pearl, or from *baroco*, a scholastic syl-
logism, or, what is less likely, from an Indian word, the term "baroque"
was synonymous with extravagance and bad taste for the neo-classical
critics who used it early in the nineteenth century. The epithet "rococo"
has the advantage of being older, but its reputation is no better; it was
used by the engraver Cochin in 1755 to mock the fanciful forms of the

Louis XV style. The two terms have now lost their former pejorative meaning. Baroque is even praised by contemporary aestheticians, who have extended it to cover an artistic attitude which they oppose to classicism, and of which seventeenth century art is only one aspect. As for the rococo, we can now find some pleasure in it, since we are no longer under the dogmatic tyranny of neo-classicism.

No doubt in their strict sense these expressions are worth no more than most historical labels. "Renaissance" is no more apt, while "Gothic" is absurd. If we are to grasp the general implication of a form of art which gave Europe its specific character, we might say that, coming after the instinct for free inquiry that marked the sixteenth century, it was essentially a *formalism*. It matters little whether this formalism was classical or baroque. The seventeenth century had, so to speak, two liturgies, one of them classical in tendency and the other baroque. But whether they insisted on a curved line or a straight one, the dogmas are similar in that they both tended to give a *representation* of existence as seen by the intellect; for seventeenth century man saw everything, and his own life first and foremost, as a kind of show. An awareness of human dignity gave rise to that philosophy of "eminence" which makes the whole universe a stage, sumptuously set for the King, the lord of creation. Louis XIV thought himself the royal incarnation of this hero. Antwerp in the seventeenth century shows us another, more modest model of this, but one no less significant. Something of an aristocrat, an artist of genius, a good Christian, but with an epicurean delight in the fleshly and spiritual joys of existence, Rubens is one of the highest expressions of the humanism which inherited from the Renaissance all the indulgence toward human nature so eagerly preached by the Jesuits.

The opera, which was the essential creation of these two centuries covering 1600–1800, is difficult for us to judge today. But those fairy-like displays, operas fixed forever in stone and paint, stucco, marble and gold, are still there before our eyes. Two stage settings were provided for God and the King—the two rulers most honored by the Grand Siècle: these were the church and the palace—one might say God's palace and the King's temple.

In order to understand the poetry of the baroque one must have seen Mass being celebrated at St. Peter's or any Jesuit church in Europe. Thanks to the grace of the liturgy, in the perfumed mist of incense and organ music one sees no longer a mere world of marble and paint, a

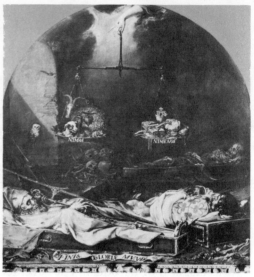

DEATH

Many paintings reflect the anguish of death which haunted the 17th century. Spain, obsessed by the void, deplored the misery of the human lot in the face of God. The French painters saw and represented death in terms of a philosophical meditation.

370. Georges de La Tour. The Magdalen with a Lamp.
Paris, Louvre.

371. Valdés Leal. Finis gloriae mundi. About 1671.
Seville, Charity Hospital.

human world, but a great composition in which the movements of the painted figures and the ritual of the priests combine in a grand symphony. The solemn cadence of the incense bearers vibrates from column to column, and the preacher's eloquence replies from the pulpit to the urgent apologetics of the Apostles and Martyrs whose effigies adorn the columns. In the depths of the chancel some apparition seems to be stirring in the lights of the high altar, while clouds of incense, rising into the vaults, mingle with pale clouds of marble in which groups of angels spread their wings. And instead of the drab uniform we wear today, we must imagine the rich medley of colors from the theatrical costumes men wore in those times. The Catholic Church, which from time immemorial has known how to stimulate fervor in the faithful by appealing to their senses, offered the Christian of the Counter Reformation an accessible image of the beyond—an operatic spectacle.

Differences of ritual gave rise to different emphases in the churches of the baroque period and style. In spite of its underlying exuberance, the Italian baroque always observed the norms of architecture, for the architecture lent itself to this *rinforzando*, this *crescendo*, those thousand modulations and mimicries that are needed in order to contrive a spectacular effect. The Spanish Churrigueresque (after the Churriguerra family) smothered architecture in adornment, so that Spain returned to the woeful excess of ornament she had long imbibed from Moorish influences: in no other country was the thirst for images to be taken so far; no stage set was ever more thoroughly worked out than a Capilla Mayor. The Austrian rococo, like the Swabian and Bavarian, was like frozen music with its thousands of chords and deep reverberations; those palace halls and monastery churches gave birth to the

DEATH AND GLORY

This work was inspired by the funeral rites of the baroque period. Confident of the survival guaranteed to him by his Glory, the hero advances firmly toward the grave which is held open by Death, whom "mourning France" tries to restrain; the flags are symbolic of victories, the animals, of conquered enemies, while Hercules represents military power.

372. Jean-Baptiste Pigalle. Tomb of the Maréchal de Saxe. 1756–1777. *Strasbourg, St. Thomas.*

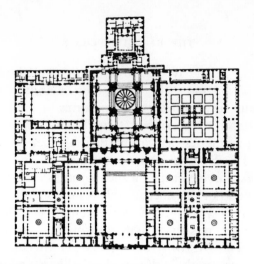

*The plan of the Escorial, with its buildings set round
a church, was adopted all over Europe. The church
became the axis, the generative cell of the whole construction. At Versailles the King's bedchamber was to
hold that position, the chapel being thrust to one side.*

373. Plan of the palace-monastery of the Escorial.
By Juan Bautista of Toledo (1561) and Juan de Herrera.

harmonies of Mozart. Flemish baroque flowed into painting: Rubens
gave southern Formalism the rich life blood of color that he inherited
from Van Eyck.

Just as there were several religious liturgies, so there were different
modes of courtly ritual. The Escorial and Versailles rivaled each other
in pride and dignity. In the solitude of Guadarrama, Philip II made
himself an immense structure in naked stone so that no worldly appear-

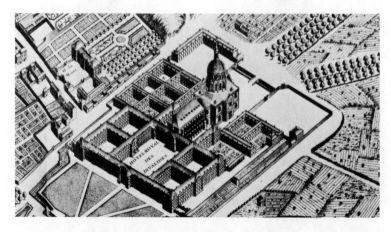

374. Plan of the Hôtel des Invalides, Paris. By Libéral Bruant (1671)
and Jules Hardouin-Mansart (1677). *After the "Turgot Map" of Paris.*

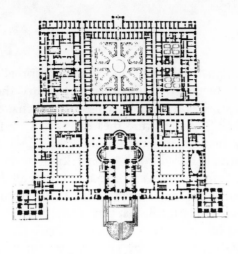

375. Plan of the palace-monastery of Mafra, Portugal.
By Ludovice. 1713.

ance could intrude on the sublime intimacy between God and his
earthly representative, who was king by Divine Right. More profane,
a hundred years later, Louis XIV called on Olympus and not Heaven
to celebrate his glory. And the grand opera of Versailles laid on a permanent show of a kind of allegorical sun worship. Here all external appearances were invited to take part in the display—water, sky, trees,
marble and gold, real and imitation nature. Philip II found only one imi-
tator, João V, who in the eighteenth century built the palace-monastery
of Mafra in Portugal: all eighteenth century Europe copied Versailles at
a time when French taste was reacting away from it. The French were
tired of display, and if they left the court it was in favor of the city.

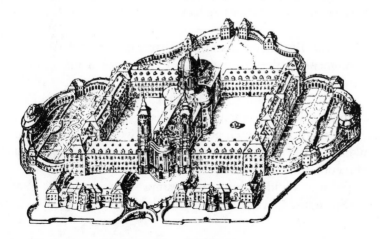

376. Plan for the monastery at Weingarten in Northern Bavaria.
Bird's-eye view. Woodcut. 1723.

Then private life came to the fore, and a domestic ritual came into being to replace that of the court. All eighteenth century thought expressed itself in the confidential tones of drawing-room exchanges, the drawing room and salon being its miniature theater. When "sentiment" became fashionable, they made a melodrama out of it. Last of all came the love of nature which called forth a new kind of show, that of the "natural." Rocks and cornflowers, streams and windmills, cottages and marble temples filled the stage. Every day, Marie Antoinette came and played her walking-on part, till such time as the theater was temporarily closed, threatened by the invasion of real drama.

Yet again Italy gave Europe an aesthetic on which it lived for two hundred years. For Italy, the baroque was not a point of departure, but on the contrary the supreme effort of a school weakened by a long period of fertility, and now trying to recuperate by gathering its forces into a doctrine, and reaping the harvest of its past in the most rational manner possible. By draining the essentials off the wealth of Italian art the Carracci brothers toned down features which were too exclusively local, and by giving their cunning mixture the impersonality of a logical system, they enabled the gains of the sixteenth century to be passed on to other schools. As for Caravaggio, he came just at the right time to give new life to painting, by infusing some naturalism into it after it had been sapped by Renaissance idealism. This great figure made the way for Zurbarán, Georges de La Tour, the Le Nain brothers, Velázquez, Rembrandt and even Vermeer—in short, all those who refused to yield to the passing fashions of the century and probed deeper into the mystery of human nature. In the face of so many actors and light-weights, these few individuals rediscovered the greatness of authentic man.

Despite the Protestant dissidence, baroque art was the most harmonious moment in the "concert" of Europe. In a great upsurge of enthusiasm, all the peoples who had by now reached their full maturity brought their contribution to a common task. They exchanged their doctrines and talents; French and Italian specialists swarmed over Europe, Flemings and Dutchmen came to work in Paris, while the whole world met in Rome, where the two greatest French painters of the seventeenth century became Romans by adoption.

Europe was divided into two camps as regards the dominant aesthetic. Spain, the Germanic countries, and Flanders eagerly embraced an aesthetic which so thoroughly suited their native instinct. Behind this showy curtain Germany, deeply afflicted by the Thirty Years' War, contrived to hide its real decline, to revive again in the eighteenth century. Spain, where only the Church had any rights to speak of, found a marvelous means of governing souls, in this apologetic imagery. Rubens quickened the baroque orchestration by giving it that vital energy which enables forms to reproduce each other in an unbroken rhythm. He created a new pictorial technique, and in the eighteenth century both the French and English schools were to be enriched by it.

It was natural for the Protestant countries to reject this "glorifying" art. Holland, which had no external worship to offer God or King, turned toward man and nature; in the seventeenth century it was the only country to see reality as something more than a spectacle or show. England created a great school of architecture, her restraint in expression, fundamental to her insular temper, leading her from 1630 onward to adopt those principles which were to lead all Europe a hundred years later toward neo-classicism. As for France, her attitude was most complex. It cannot be said that she completely refused the baroque, since Europe owes her the whole setting of royal ceremonial as well as the civilized background of an "art of living." But the true vocation of French art was to provide, in both painting and architecture, the most perfect definition of that classicism whose rules had been laid down by Raphael, Titian and Bramante and which had been stifled by the overgrowth of baroque. France's decorators brought her share to European baroque art, while her architects and her greatest painters continued and completed the work of the Renaissance. Watteau perhaps owed Rubens less than has been suggested; he profited from Rubens' technique but his poetic expression is related to Titian's and above all Giorgione's.

The unity of the European movement is demonstrated in the great international drive which in about 1760 led all the schools toward a second classical revival, this time based on Etruscan and Greek sources. Antiquaries from every country shared in the excavation of pre-Roman art, the great archaeological centers being at Florence, Naples and Rome. France sent the Comte de Caylus; Germany its famous Winckelmann who in 1764 wrote the first *History of Ancient Art*. The Frenchman Clérisseau and the Englishman Robert Adam worked side by side on the ruins of Diocletian's palace at Spalato. If it is true that France, thanks to an internal revolution, reached the principles of the so-called Louis XVI style at the same time as England, nobody can deny England the first place in the conception of a certain architectural purism—in her "Palladianism," amounting to a neo-classicism—that was not to affect French art until the last years of the Ancien Régime.

This style contains the germs of the "Spartan" art of the Revolution and the Empire period, which was to put an end to the ostentation and preciousness of the Ancien Régime. Involved in his own tragedy, man no longer set himself up as a stage show for his own amusement.

THE SPREAD OF BAROQUE
ITALY
ARCHITECTURE AND SCULPTURE

Deriving from Michelangelo, Italian baroque architecture sought to astonish by the powerful and magnificent effects obtained by emphasized volumes and heavy decoration; but however much it was overladen, architecture never allowed itself to become throttled by ornament as was the case in Spain, and the relationship of mass to mass was always energetically asserted. The original creation of this style was a new type of church. The prototype was the one which was carried out according to Vignola's plans from 1568 to 1577, the Gesù or Church

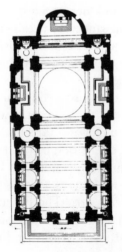 

377. Vignola. Ground plan of the Gesù church, Rome. 1567.

378. Vignola and Giacomo della Porta.
Façade of the Gesù church. 1568–1577.

of Jesus in Rome. Inspired by the Languedoc Gothic church style, which had found its way into Spain, whence the Jesuits brought it to Rome, this structure shows the final triumph of the simple basilican plan, without an ambulatory and with a single nave, fringed with small chapels instead of aisles, and with its crossing crowned by a cupola (pl. 377). The barrel vault over the nave, pierced with lunettes (round windows), rests on enormous piers without the help of buttresses; the series of bays is boldly marked by great Corinthian pillars and piers which rise from the floor into the vaults; designed by Giacomo della Porta, a pedimented façade whose upper part is linked to the lower by projecting scrolls closes the nave (pl. 378). This type of church was built at first in a sober style for from 1580 to about 1625 Counter Reformation art, influenced by Protestantism, showed something of the Church's concern for austerity. Examples of this are now hard to find, since these churches were overlaid with rich decorations in the following period, but we might quote Montepulciano Cathedral by Ammanati (1570), Santa Maria degli Angeli, Assisi, by Alessi (pl. 379). In the same spirit Carlo Maderna (1556–1629) added a nave to Michelangelo's St. Peter's and gave it a façade (1606–1626). But Urban VIII's pontificate (1623–1644) was the point of departure for a fashionable splendor, and for the second time Rome saw the revival of a Triumphal art, a symbol of the Church's victory. It was in 1629 that Pope Urban VIII gave Bernini

The two aspects of the Counter Reformation: Asceticism (16th century) and the Triumphal style (17th century).
379. Basilica of Sta. Maria degli Angeli at Assisi.
Begun in 1569 after plans by Galeazzo Alessi.
380. S. Ignazio, Rome. Begun 1626. By Fr. Orazio Grassi.
After the drawings by Domenichino.

(1598–1680) the task of furnishing and decorating St. Peter's, an undertaking which was continued under Popes Innocent X (1644–1655) and Alexander VII (1655–1667). This artist buried the purity of Michelangelo's and Maderna's work under a coating of marble facings, bronzes, stucco and gilt (1647–1653), filling the church with outsize statues and colossal furniture (*Baldacchino*, 1624–1633; *Chair of St. Peter*, 1656–1665). At the same time he built a great circular piazza surrounded by a double colonnade (1656–1673). The Roman churches already built were now covered with a similar garb; others were built in this style in Rome (pl. 380) and all over Italy (pl. 381) to a great variety of plans—central, elliptical, or in the form of a Latin cross; their vaults opened on celestial visions, apparitions in stucco or painting whose upward perspective was stressed by cunning foreshortening (vault of the Gesù and St. Ignazio). The pompous palaces built by the Roman nobility were larded with similar adornments; in the Roman Campagna (Frascati), the nobles and prelates built villas in the midst of geometrically laid-out gardens in which fountains played. Apart from Bernini, to whom we also owe the church of Sant'Andrea del Quirinale (1678), the principal architects in Rome were: Girolamo Rainaldi (1570–1653); Pietro da Cortona (1596–1669), author of the pure cupola of San Carlo al Corso and of Santa Maria della Pace (1655), and above all Francesco

381. Baldassare Longhena. Santa Maria della Salute, Venice. 1631–1656.

382. Francesco Borromini. S. Carlo alle Quattro Fontane (S. Carlino).
Rome. Begun 1634. Façade finished 1667.

Borromini (1599–1667), author of San Carlo alle Quattro Fontane
(pl. 382) and of Sant'Agnese in Agone which herald the rococo in
use of waving curves. In Venice, Baldassare Longhena (1604–1682)
raised the fine cupola of the Salute (1631–1656, pl. 381) as well as the
Pesaro and Rezzonico Palaces (1679 and 1680) which have all the
traditional Venetian splendor. At Genoa, Naples, Milan and in the
south (Lecce), architecture became baroque very early with the increasingly daring use of curves, a tendency which appeared in Rome with
Borromini and was accentuated at Turin with Guarini (1624–1683) in
his Carignano Palace (1680). Eighteenth century Rome was rarely to
fall into the excesses of rococo in architecture (Palazzo del Grillo),
but remained faithful to the imposing effects of the baroque style
(Luigi Vanvitelli, 1700–1773). Certain artists such as Filippo Iuvara
(1685–1735) showed an early tendency toward neo-classicism (at Turin:
Palazzo Madama, 1718; Basilica at Superga, 1706–1720). At the end
of the century the archaeological trend advocated by Winckelmann led
to a pastiche of ancient Roman architecture (*Museo Pio-Clementino*
built at the Vatican by Simonetti). Meanwhile rococo invaded internal
decoration and furnishing in Genoa, Naples and above all Venice.
Naples felt the influence of the Spanish Churrigueresque.

Italian sculpture in the seventeenth century was entirely over-
shadowed by Bernini who, under Urban VIII and Alexander VII, found

himself entrusted with the dictatorship over the arts that Michelangelo had exercised in the century before. All Bernini's plastic outlook was governed by a quest for movement and expression. The violence of the passions and of human ecstasy was rendered by the physical disorder it provokes; the swooning attitudes of the saints (*St. Theresa*, 1646, pl. 383; *Blessed Lodovica Albertoni; Santa Bibiana*) are a theatrical expression of the sensual but devout mysticism which was to take hold of the faithful in the seventeenth century and result in excesses which were condemned by the Church. Bernini also created a type of tomb (*Tomb of Urban VIII*, 1642; *Tomb of Alexander VII*, 1672) which is like a stage setting for Death, symbolized by a skeleton. By dint of exaggerating the inflections of his modeling, by the use of colored marbles, and through the fluidity of his figures' attitudes, the sculptor sought to vie with painting—a tendency which was further emphasized in the seventeenth century, when the Neapolitans (Conradini, Sammartino, Queirolo) were to outdo each other in a virtuosity which was in the worst of taste.

PAINTING

Weakened by three hundred years of creativity unparalleled in history, Italian painting by the end of the sixteenth century, after the Mannerist crisis, had reached a state of decline of which perhaps the Florentine school shows the most lamentable examples with Vasari, Salviati, Zuccaro, Allori. Reacting against this decadence, three painters of the Carracci family (two brothers, Annibale and Luigi, with their cousin

383. Bernini. The Ecstasy of St. Theresa. 1646. *Rome, Sta. Maria della Vittoria.*

384. Annibale Carracci. Diana and Endymion. Fresco,
ceiling of the Gallery. 1594. *Rome, Farnese Palace.*

Agostino), founded an Academy in 1595. This amounted to a school of
Fine Arts which aimed at a return to the traditional rules of art by
teaching the methods of the great masters, taking from Raphael, Titian,
Michelangelo and Correggio those qualities in which each of them
excelled. The Carraccis thus created a kind of plastic "rhetoric" which
they applied as freely to devotional painting as to mythological subjects.
The ceiling of the Farnese Palace (1594), inspired by both Michelangelo and Raphael, was to have an enormous influence all over Europe
(pl. 384). A host of pupils of that school filled the churches and
palaces of Rome with enormous displays, both pious and pagan: Guido
Reni (1575–1642); Francesco Albani (1578–1660); Carlo Dolci (1616–
1686); Giovanni Lanfranco (1582–1647); Andrea Pozzo (1642–1709),
who specialized in ceiling decoration. Guercino (1590–1666) was the
only painter of this school with any imagination and who understood
that the truth was to be found elsewhere, in Caravaggio (pl. 385).

While the Carraccis, by a clever but unoriginal reform, were con-
solidating the failing Italian school and guaranteeing it an almost official
role in Europe, a painter of genius was carrying out a revolution which
contained the germ of almost everything of any stature in seventeenth-
century painting. Understanding that the Italian school was worn out
by three hundred years of intellectualism, Michelangelo Merisi da
Caravaggio (about 1565–1610) forced Italian and the whole of European art to take a dose of naturalism. In a country where nothing was

301

385. Guercino. The entombment of Sta. Petronilla. 1621.
Rome, Capitoline Museum.
386. Caravaggio. Descent from the Cross. 1602–1604. *Rome, Vatican Pinacoteca.*

being painted but Venuses and Madonnas, he took the humblest types
of Roman men and women as his models for saints and heroes (*The
Calling of St. Matthew*, and other paintings in San Luigi dei Francesi
and Santa Maria del Popolo; the *Death of the Virgin*, Louvre, and the
Descent from the Cross, Vatican, pl. 386). By the impressive simplicity
of his composition, the violent contrast of lights and shadows which he
obtained from oblique lighting, he brought back a powerful frankness
of volumes to Italian painting, and led the whole school back to its
plastic traditions which since Giotto had always implied a sculptural
conception of form.

All that was really worthwhile in Italy owed something, however
little, to Caravaggio. In Rome a whole cosmopolitan school exploited
his chiaroscuro effects and his popular lyricism. Besides Orazio Gen-
tileschi (1563–1646) we find a French painter, Valentin de Boulogne
(1591–1634), and Dutchmen from Utrecht, Theodor Van Baburen
(d. 1623); Ter Brugghen (d. 1629); Gerard Honthorst (d. 1656) whose
nocturnal paintings earned him the nickname "Gherado delle Notte";
we also know from the German Sandrart (1606–1688) that there was a
German colony at the same time. These foreigners were to spread
Caravaggio's style all over Europe.

The Italian provinces, which had been the least touched by academicism, were particularly warm in hailing "Caravaggism." Caravaggio

387. Bernardo Strozzi. The Three Fates. *Milan, Private Collection.*
388. Alessandro Magnasco. The Synagogue. Detail.
Seitenstetten Abbey, Austria.

found a spiritual disciple in Naples, in Caracciolo (1570?–1637), while
the Spaniard Jusepe Ribera ("Il Spagnoletto") took his reforms back
with him to Spain. In Milan, Daniele Crespi (1592–1630) had his own
romantic manner which he drew from various sources; while at Bergamo
Evaristo Baschenis (1617–1677) composed still lifes with musical instruments, which he painted in chiaroscuro. The most eclectic school of
all was at Genoa, which profited from Rubens and Van Dyck, who
both spent a time there. Bernardo Strozzi (1581–1644) heralds Goya,
through his violent satirical style and daring technique (pl. 387).

In the eighteenth century the Italian school as a whole stood aside
from the European movement, and the French school took the lead.
Except for Venice, the schools were producing only sound but not
outstanding painters: Naples had Solimena, and Luca Giordano; Milan,
Giuseppe Maria Crespi (1665–1747). However in Rome, Pannini
(1691–1764) invented a *genre* which enjoyed a spectacular success—
the painting of ruins. In Genoa the genre painting of Alessandro
Magnasco (1681–1747) heralded Goya's romanticism (pl. 388). Meanwhile the Venetian school, the youngest of all, was still lively enough
to provide the swan song of Italian painting, which it did in a great
apotheosis of light, color and splendor. Its painters all portrayed the
beauties of Venice and the decadent and sensual charm of its civilization.
Venice had portraitists, Vittore Ghislandi (1666–1743) and Alessandro

Longhi (1733–1813); the genre painter Pietro Longhi (1702–1785); land-scape painters, Canaletto (1697–1768), Francesco Guardi (1712–1793, pl. 389), who exalted the beauty of its light, its palaces and canals; great decorators such as Piazzetta (1682–1754) and above all Giambattista Tiepolo (1693–1770), who rivaled Veronese and was the most versatile of Italian ceiling painters, skilled in the art of setting angels and gods in the radiant glow of limitless spaces, whether on the curves of a cupola or the flat surfaces of walls (pl. 390). His art had a strong influence in central Europe and Germany, where he was invited to paint (Residenz, Würzburg).

FLANDERS

Flanders adopted baroque architecture with the same eagerness as she had welcomed Flamboyant Gothic in the fifteenth century. The transi-tion from Flamboyant to baroque was made smoothly and gradually thanks to the activities of the ornamental decorators of Antwerp, through whom it came. Without understanding its architectural import, the Flemings saw the baroque only in terms of ornament, and they applied baroque decoration on the Gothic framework of their buildings, just as previously they had applied Flamboyant patterns. Their houses thus remained, as in the Middle Ages, façades pierced all over with windows, just as, despite the Jesuit Fathers' efforts to introduce new forms, the type of three-naved church lingered on, while sometimes even medieval elevations were favored. The extraordinarily lavish

389. Francesco Guardi. Sketch. *Paris, Louvre.*

390. Tiepolo. Cleopatra Leaving Her Barge. Fresco. About 1750. *Venice, Palazzo Labia.*

391. Houses on the Grand' Place, Brussels. From left to right: The Fox, 1694; The Horn, 1696; The She-Wolf, 1696; The Sack, 1697.

decoration, which was often gilded to give it relief, even on the outside of the building, was hung on the wall like a picture, without being built into the structure; the baroque curves on the gables of houses, ousting those of the Flamboyant style, introduced many new ornamental patterns. The churches were now filled with heavy, symbolical wooden furnishings (pulpits and confessionals, etc.). Sculpture was mediocre (Duquesnoy; Lucas Faidherbe; Jean Delcour), which is not surprising since the Flemish genius all flows into painting. The Grand' Place in Brussels, built before 1700 (pl. 391), and the St. Charles Borromeus church at Antwerp (1615-1621) and Rubens' house at Antwerp are masterpieces of Flemish baroque architecture.

305

392. Rubens. The Descent from the Cross. 1611–1614.
Antwerp, Cathedral.

Flemish painting did not escape the crisis of depression which
upset all Europe at the end of the sixteenth century. After the waves
of Italianism, which in its various forms—Lombard, Roman, Mannerist
—had seemed like a series of nightmares, the Antwerp school seemed
to have worked itself out. However, at the very close of the century
several artists, Abraham Jansens (1575–1632), Adam Van Noort (1562–
1641) and Otto Veenius or Van Veen (1556–1629), at last managed to
make the Italian plastic code their own and made Rubens' development
possible. After he left the studios of Van Noort and Van Veen, Peter
Paul Rubens (1577–1640) completed his training in Italy from 1600–
1608, where he absorbed the lessons of the Venetians, of Michelangelo,
the Bologna school and Caravaggio. On his return he painted his first
two masterpieces, the *Elevation of the Cross* (about 1610) and the
Descent from the Cross (1611–1614, pl. 392), for Antwerp Cathedral.
He soon made Antwerp one of the main centers of European art and
commissions came from every side: his output, organized on workshop
lines with the use of assistants, was the most fertile in the history of
painting. Between 1621 and 1625 he carried out his greatest monumental
work, the *Life of Marie de' Medici*, now in the Louvre. After being

306

four years a widower he married, in 1630, Helena Fourment, a sixteen-year-old girl, and then his art had a gentler and more intimate note. He then retired into the country, and in smaller canvases in which landscape held an increasingly important place, he expressed his spiritual vision of universal life. Rubens' work is the greatest world of forms ever created by a painter. The energy of life pervades every shape and gives dynamic quality to gesture and expression: any picture by Rubens is a series of interrelated movements, spiraling or passing obliquely through space (pls. 393 and 634) and the impetus seems to pass beyond the limits of the frame; it is the archetype of baroque or "fleeting," open composition which gives a brief glimpse of the perpetual motion of the life of the universe. All his forms are bathed in a mellow fluid medium, thanks to the wonderful means of expression he created in his transparent handling of paint, which allows the laying of glaze upon glaze, a technique taken over from Van Eyck which was lost after Rubens.

The Flemish school in the seventeenth century gives a remarkable example of solidarity and singleness of purpose. In the sixteenth century the Flemish painters had aimed at investigating the forms of nature, and

393. Rubens. The Rape of the Leucippides.
Toward 1618. *Munich, Pinakothek.*

artists had specialized in historical canvases, landscape, or still lifes, or genre or anecdotal paintings. This division of labor gave them great skill in their special line, until in the seventeenth century they began to come to each other's help, so that Rubens' workshop was the most outstanding example of artistic co-operation.

The apparent complexity of the Flemish school may be reduced to two main streams which actually meet in Rubens. One of them derives from the heroic and statuesque vision of the Italians and tends to bring its monumental forms into the foreground and middle ground, thus reducing the architectural framework or the landscape to no more than a setting or decoration. This is properly speaking the "modern" stream. Started by Van Noort and Van Veen, Rubens became its focal point. Jordaens and Van Dyck derive from it, as well as the host of artists who came under Rubens' influence; the bevy of historical painters, Erasmus Quellin, Gaspard de Crayer, Van Thulden, Van Diepenbeeck, Cornelis de Vos; the *animaliers* or animal painters, Snyders (pl. 394), Fyt and Paul de Vos. In landscape, this trend is seen in a decorative view of nature, scenes being laid out in broad masses harmoniusly balanced one against the other; this style, deriving from Paul Bril, is represented by Jacques D'Arthois, Lucas Van Uden, Wildens and later Huysmans. Jacob Jordaens (1593–1678), who was more deeply influenced by Caravaggio and Bolognese formalism, further stressed the plebeian expression of Rubens; his heavy, brownish coloring

394. Frans Snyders. Still Life. *Brussels, Musée des Beaux-Arts.*

unfortunately owes nothing to the Antwerp master. The same cannot be said of Anthony Van Dyck (1599–1641), a pupil of Rubens and for some years one of his closest collaborators (pl. 368); he worked in Genoa and Rome, where he was profoundly influenced by Titian. He ended by specializing in portraiture; after emigrating to London in 1632 he became Charles I's favorite painter and, taking the English gentry as his models, he was able to satisfy his tastes for aristocratic postures and refined, decadent expressions.

The second stream of Flemish painting is a direct continuation of the "microcosmic" vision of the sixteenth century, in which the human or animal figure is reduced in scale against a vast universal setting. The first stream we mentioned sprang from heroic humanism in the Italian manner, but the second continued the satirical vein of the sixteenth century: Jan ("Velvet") Bruegel (1568–1625), who inherited it from his father, is the center of this group (pl. 395). David Teniers (1610–1690) belongs to the same tradition, with Sebastian Vrancx, Snayers, David Vinckeboons, Gonzales Coques, Van Der Meulen. Adriaen Brouwer's (1605/06–1638) experience in Frans Hals's studio at Haarlem helped him to find a freer and less literal manner than that of Teniers (pl. 396). The composite landscape, seen from a height, which began with Patinir and Pieter Bruegel the Elder, found lively exponents in Valkenborch, Jan Bruegel, Joos de Momper and others. Roelandt

396. Adriaen Brouwer. Drinking Scene. *Amsterdam, Private Collection.*

Savery and Tobias Verhaecht carried on the fanciful type of landscape. Flemish painting is so rich that these two main streams left a number of isolated streams untouched. Painters in Bruges and Brussels, within easy reach of Antwerp, paid no heed to Rubens and sprang more directly from the Roman school. In landscape Jan Siberechts of Antwerp (1625–1703) had close affinities with the rustic realism of Le Nain. This marvelous movement lasted for three quarters of a century, but after 1680 the school collapsed and nothing remained but a few provincial artists.

SPAIN

ARCHITECTURE

In the course of the seventeenth century Spain showed a slow recovery of the native temper as against the stark architectural style invented by Juan de Herrera (d. 1597) in the Escorial which eventually led to the cold and narrow work of Nuestra Señora del Pilar at Saragossa, begun in 1681 by Juan Herrera el Mozo. At the same time the Jesuits' policy of power and pomp could not remain satisfied for long with such severe externals. They built, on the Roman plan of the Gesù, vast churches in which the classical canon can be seen debased in a grandiloquent setting: Clerecía de Salamanca, begun in 1617 after plans by Juan Gómez de Mora; San Isidro el Real in Madrid, begun in 1622 by two lay brothers of the Jesuit order, Brother Sanchez and Brother Juan Bautista; San Juan Bautista in Toledo, by the latter brother, Juan Bautista. In the second half of the century the baroque

style developed in the great painted or gilded altarpieces, laden with
pictures and sculptures, which became the objects of heavy ornamentation; for the most part the ornament was borrowed from the provi-
sional settings used in theaters or festivals, while the capitals were
carried on enormous columns decked with imitation vines (a eucharistic
symbol), a form of decoration imitated from that of the classical column,
to be found also at St. Peter's in Rome, which was then thought to
have originated in Solomon's temple, hence the name Solomon pillar
given to such supports. This kind of decoration, which also spread to
Portugal (pl. 408), finished by passing from wood to stone and thus
became architectural. It was at the close of the seventeenth century
that Spain invented its personal version of the baroque, which is rather
abusively called the Churrigueresque style after a family of artists
founded by José Churriguera (1655–1725). This style amounted to a
disintegration of the architecture which was devoured by ornamentation
—garlands, fruits, flowers, festoons, moldings, cartouches, medallions,
Solomon pillars, imitation draperies, and, to crown it all, a maze of
scrollwork twisting this way and that like a tapestry over the façades
or covering the reredos, much as the arabesque forms of the plateresque
had done formerly. In 1693 José Churriguera designed the colossal
high altar of San Esteban at Salamanca, the town where he and his
brothers, cousins and sons worked together (towers of La Clerecía,
Plaza Mayor). In Madrid, Pedro Ribera (1722–1790) began replan-
ning the city and decorated it with costly monuments (Hospicio
Provincial). The most extraordinary work of Spanish baroque is the
Transparente (stained glass window) in Toledo Cathedral, by Narciso
Tomé; this vast composition of marble, painting, gold and light, inspired
by the operatic scenario, so completely suited the national temperament
that in 1732 its dedication was greeted with splendid festivals and its
praises were sung in a poem in Latin. Eastern Spain and Andalusia gave
themselves up to the greatest excesses of baroque, in which architecture
became swamped in ornament: sacristy of the Charterhouse of Granada
(1727–1764), palace of the Marqués dos Aguas, Valencia (pl. 397); choir
of Córdoba Cathedral (1748–1757) by Pedro Duque Cornejo. At
Compostela, on the contrary, ornament was held in check by the great
rhythms of the architecture; the old Romanesque cathedral, piously
preserved, is as though sunk in a setting of wrought stone. After 1680
Domingo Antonio de Andrade built the imposing Clock Tower;

397. Ignacio Vergara. Ornamental gateway, palace of the
Marqués dos Aguas, Valencia. 1740–1744.
398. Fernando de Casas y Novoa. The "Obradoiro" façade.
Built from 1738 to 1750. Cathedral at Santiago de Compostela.

Fernando de Casas y Novoa designed the west façade, the Obradoiro
(1738–1750, pl. 398), a lofty, resplendent monstrance in stone, whose
heavenward movement recalls that of Gothic façades.

Just as the Hapsburgs had led the onslaught on the national
plateresque art, so another foreign dynasty, the Bourbons, was to
revolt against the Churrigueresque. The royal houses, Aranjuez (1715–
1752), la Granja (1721–1725), the Royal Palace in Madrid (1738–1764),
were all built on the model of Versailles by Italian or French architects.
In the reign of Charles III, the San Fernando Academy founded in 1752,
which was given the power of judging and condemning new buildings,
very soon appeared intent on putting an end to the Churrigueresque;
the expulsion of the Jesuits in 1767 was a further step toward the neo-
classical purge. Religious architecture, completely sterilized, lost its
poetry; Ventura Rodríguez, following the precepts of Vitruvius, rebuilt
San Francisco el Grande in Madrid in an academic style inspired by
St. Peter's, Rome. At the end of the century Juan de Villanueva
(1739–1811) introduced a new, more graceful style in the neo-
Palladian spirit.

SCULPTURE

Spanish sculpture in the seventeenth and eighteenth centuries, which was entirely given over to religious images, pushed the art of *trompe-l'oeil* realism farther than any other school has done. Wooden statues were painted in lifelike colors, and were sometimes jointed dummies covered with luxurious clothes and jewels (so-called *vestir* statues); sometimes they had eyes of enamel or agate set in the sockets, and they had real hair, eyelashes and eyebrows; certain statues, grouped in tableaux, were borne in procession on Good Friday (*los pasos*). In the seventeenth century, the output was in the hands of two schools, those of Valladolid and Seville. At Valladolid Gregorio Hernández (1576–1636) was responsible for the transition from Mannerism to the baroque, by changing the feverishness of Berruguete and Juan de Juni into a formalism full of pathos; the attitudes were always violent, both in the pangs of suffering (pl. 399) and the raptures of ecstasy. The art of Martínez Montañés (1568–1649) at Seville was graver and more inward, and his works are one of the highest expressions of religious feeling in the seventeenth century (*high altar* at Santiponce, 1609, pl. 400). At Granada, Pedro de Mena (1628–1688) sculptured classical types of devotional imagery, while Alonso Cano (1601–1667) developed that austere art toward the rendering of womanly gracefulness which was

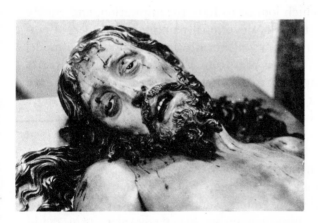

399. Gregorio Hernández. The Dead Christ. Detail. Wood. *Valladolid, National Sculpture Museum.*

400. Martínez Montañés. St. John the Baptist. Detail of high altar. *Santiponce (near Seville), S. Isidoro del Campo.*

401. Ribera. The Martyrdom of St. Bartholomew. 1630 or 1639. *Madrid, Prado.*

to become the tradition in Granada in the eighteenth century (José Risueno, d. 1721). When it was dying out, the art of colored sculpture was stimulated for the last time at the hands of the Salzillo family, who brought to Murcia the mannered and affected art of the Neapolitan carvers of cribs, with their large groups of characters.

PAINTING

In a country where the Inquisition was all powerful, painting was practically a church monopoly. Court paintings were just tolerated, but mythological painting hardly existed, and landscape not at all. It was in the South and East, which looked to Italy for inspiration, and chiefly at Valencia and Seville, that the devotional painting developed. Francisco Ribalta (1551/55–1628), a Valencian painter, brought the model for this form from Italy. It was also from Valencia that Jusepe Ribera (1588–1656) left for Naples in 1616, where he made his career. Indeed he was Caravaggio's most ardent disciple, using his chiaroscuro still more violently; but his Spanish harshness of temperament led him to seek his models in the dregs of society, and in his scenes of martyrdom he seemed to delight in painting the human body under torture (pl. 401). The two facets of the Spanish Christian soul were expressed in Seville by two famous painters, Zurbarán and Murillo. Francisco Zurbarán (1598–1662), who has been called the "monk painter," was a mystic who lived his daily life on a supernatural plane; but like medieval man he could think of the supernatural only in terms of the concrete (pl. 402). Of all artists he was perhaps the one who best portrayed that Spanish

402. Zurburán. St. Hugh Visiting the Carthusian Refectory.
Seville, Provincial Museum.

403. Murillo. St. Anne Teaching the Virgin as a Child.
Detail. After 1674. *Madrid, Prado.*

humanism for which the truth is only to be found by confronting the self with God, and which allows the external world no reality whatever; his sculptural forms, so aggressively carved, and as it were hewn out of darkness, seem to rise out of the void under the eye of the God to whom they owe their existence. On the other hand it was the homely, sensual piety of Andalusia which inspired Bartolomé Esteban Murillo (1617–1682), the painter of the Virgin, and the only Spanish artist besides Velázquez who seems to have been touched by feminine charm (pl. 403). His sweet and somewhat suave art goes back to Raphael and Correggio. Another Sevillese, Juan de Valdés Leal (1630–1691), showed a taste for theatrical settings which led him away from the native bent for realism, and this gives him affinities rather with the visionary tradition of El Greco: he was a kind of belated Mannerist (pl. 371). Diego Velázquez (1590–1660) was trained in Seville and the first phase of his work had the harsh realism of that school; he painted still lifes with kitchen themes (*bodegones*), and devotional pictures; he never lost the Christian view of the blemish in human nature, and this led him to take idiots and weaklings as his models; he had also a satirical approach to mythology which he mocked in trivial forms such as *Los Borrachos* and *Vulcan's Forge*. He was appointed chief painter to the royal family in 1623, and in the following year he went to Italy where he

315

came in contact with Venetian painting, which helped him to put off his early Caravaggian manner. He made a second voyage to Italy in 1649. Abandoning the sharp sculptural modeling of that school, he no longer tried to show the individuality of forms by means of clear outline, and painted in bright patches of *impasto* which show delicate tinges of light flowing across flesh and materials. As the official court painter, he occasionally painted groups in movement such as *The Surrender of Breda*, or *The Maids of Honor* (pls. 404, 405), or *The Weavers*. His single portraits, in which the models are shown almost without accessories, are in the tradition of Sanchez Coello and Pantoja de la Cruz (pl. 406). The figure is like a vision emerging from a haze, and sometimes the ground beneath his feet is indistinguishable from the background. No painter ever went farther toward expressing the hopeless mystery of human solitude with regard to the world in which he lives that has always tormented the Spanish mind.

Juan Bautista del Mazo (about 1612?–1667) and Juan Carreño de Miranda (1614–1685) brought Velázquez's art down to a popular level. After him, the Spanish school had no life left in it. In the eighteenth century, the Spanish princes had to call in French and Italian painters. However, the school had a final flash of genius in Francisco José de

404. Velázquez. The Maids of Honor. Detail. 1656.
405. Velázquez. The Maids of Honor. Detail.
Madrid, Prado.

406. Velázquez. Portrait of Pablo de
Valladolid. Between 1624 and 1633.
Madrid, Prado.

Goya y Lucientes (1746–1828), whose visionary art is a desperate satire
of human nature as well as of Spanish society; he outlived the baroque
period and anticipated the French romantic movement by a generation
(pl. 407).

407. Goya. The Maja Unclothed. About 1797–1798.
Madrid, Prado.

PORTUGAL

Less gifted than Spain in both painting and sculpture, Portugal in the seventeenth and eighteenth centuries achieved its best work in architecture. Unlike what might be expected, the latter owed little to the neighboring example of Spain. Portugal developed a type of church of its own, with a compact layout, tending to be contained in one quadrangle, having no dome, and with all the annexes, sacristies and consistories harmoniously fitting into the whole, giving a pleasing impression of unity. The same classical simplicity was shown in public buildings, in which ornaments were harmoniously, even harmonically spread over the naked walls, in such a way as to avoid any impression of overloading.

The seventeenth century saw the erection of fine religious buildings in a Doric style and with a monastic simplicity, which carry on the austerity of the Counter Reformation: the Jesuit church at Coimbra (1598); Jesuit church of São Lourenço dos Grilos, Oporto (1614); São Bento da Vitoria, Oporto (1614); Santa Clara Nova, Coimbra, by João Turriano (1648). The baroque spirit appeared in the North under Spanish influence in about 1680 (churches at Braga). In the eighteenth century, on the king's initiative a renewed Italian influence brought fresh life into the Portuguese school and helped it to find its original vein. King João V (1706–1750), whose fortunes were improved by gold brought from Brazil, had an architect of German origin, Ludovice, build the enormous palace-monastery at Mafra (1713–1735, pl. 375). The plan was based on the Escorial but was baroque in its architectural excesses. The art of Lisbon and of the South (*Alentejo*) remained nearest to the Neo-Roman spirit of Mafra. Another foreign contribution, thanks to the Sienese artist Nicolo Nasoni, was to strengthen the North's natural taste for the baroque by creating a decorator's style at Oporto which was full of energy and splendor (São Pedro dos Clerigos, begun in 1732; bell tower, 1748). On the basis of these elements which were further enriched by Chinese influences, Minho Douro (archbishopric of Braga) during the reign of Dom José (1750–1777) developed a baroque art with a dynamic power and naturalistic verve that recalled Manueline art; this movement was arrested toward 1780 by the neo-classicism of Cruz Amarante, favored by English influence. Meanwhile Lisbon was preparing a harmonious fusion of the various regional tendencies in Portugal which led to an elegant

408. "Solomon" type of column from the main reredos of S. Bento at Oporto.
Detail. About 1705.
409. Church of S. Francisco at Oporto.
A Gothic structure covered in a decoration of gilded wood.
17th and 18th centuries.

art in which the baroque decoration was governed by the structure of the building: Queluz Castle (1758–1790); basilican church of the Estrela at Lisbon (1779–1790), by Mateus Vicente.

However lavish the decoration in Portugal, and even in the most lyrical works of Minho Douro, its distribution always followed rhythmic principles which recall monuments that were being erected in the same period in Austria and Bavaria, whereas Spanish architecture was more intent on astonishing than pleasing by its deliberate disproportions. The same is true of the internal decoration, consisting of gilded woodwork which sometimes covered the whole elevation up to the vaults themselves. Unlike the Spanish churches, in which altarpieces were devised to show off sculptures, the Portuguese ensembles obey a purely decorative rhythm that reduces the host of ornaments into a pattern. The finest examples of this art of *entalhadores* are to be found at Oporto: São Bento (pl. 408) and São Francisco (pl. 409).

Portugal gave a great impetus to the art of enameled faïence which it learned from the Mudejar workshops in the sixteenth century. At first polychromatic, these ceramics tend to be made in a blue tone only, whence the name *azulejos*. The patterns were entirely decorative in the seventeenth century (*azulejos de tapete*) and became representational in the eighteenth, when they were influenced by Delft china. Whole cycles of pious or profane images were painted in this way, many of them being copies of engravings from the Antwerp school.

LATIN AMERICA

From the sixteenth century onward an immense field of expansion was opened to Western art as a result of the conquest of America by the Spanish and Portuguese. The conversion of the natives gave an unlimited scope to religious art. The Jesuits marked the stages of their missionary zeal with huge monumental buildings, while the different religious orders vied with each other in their plans for new undertakings, and the last generation of cathedrals rose on American soil. The Cathedral of Mexico (1573–1656), one of the biggest structures in Christendom, derives from the classical plan of the Andalusian cathedral of Jaén; the same plan was to be followed in the cathedrals of Puebla, Mérida, Guadalajara, Oaxaca, in Mexico, and of Cuzco and Lima in Peru, and Bogotá in Colombia. Transplanted to New Spain, the Churrigueresque style gave rise in that tropical climate to a wild profusion of forms not unlike that of Hindu architecture in the Middle Ages (pl. 410). In Mexico and Bolivia especially, Indian labor gave

410. The Sagrario Metropolitano, adjacent to the Cathedral, Mexico City. 18th century.

411. Aleijadinho. The Prophet Isaiah. Detail.
1800. *Congonhas, Brazil, Church of the Good Jesus.*

the imported style a plastic flavor reminiscent of the early pre-Columbian arts. Mexico had a school of painters who were successful in
imitating Sevillese painting; everywhere else both painting and sculpture show a spontaneous revival of artistic conventions that reach back
to the primitives.

The awakening came later in Brazil, where it only began toward
the end of the sixteenth century. In those still uncivilized parts the
lack of any native artistic tradition encouraged the planting and growth
of an art which was able to continue that of the metropolis in an original manner. However, by the eighteenth century the colony's level
of civilization now allowed it to set up its own artistic schools, capable
of inventing their own forms, especially in a region which was thriving
since the discovery of gold there, and where the town of Ouro Prêto
was built; there, at the end of the eighteenth century, the son of a
Portuguese architect and a black slave, Antonio Francisco Lisboa (1730–
1814), styled Aleijadinho (the little invalid), produced one of the most
remarkable expressions of baroque style. Does the presence of Negro
craftsmen explain entirely that aptitude for sculptural form which
reached a higher level in Brazil than in the Metropolis itself? At all
events that tendency resulted in the genius of Aleijadinho's work,
which brought a great lyrical breath and a primitive energy into the
baroque, which by then was languishing in Europe as a result of formalism and virtuosity (*Prophets*, at Congonhas do Campo, 1800; pl. 411).

CENTRAL EUROPE

While Western Europe was resisting the southern baroque aesthetic, the style was finding favorable soil in central Europe and spreading into the Slavic and Scandinavian countries.

In the Germanic countries the sharp succession of the baroque and the belated Renaissance styles at the end of the seventeenth century was encouraged by the break in their traditions which was caused by the Thirty Years' War (1618–1648). While the Renaissance style for them had meant no more than applying modern ornament on a Gothic structure, the German artists, educated first by the Italians, then the French, were very quick in absorbing the Mediterranean baroque outlook which sees a monument as a powerfully modeled composition of volumes. The projection of masses was energetically stressed, while all the items of secondary modeling—cornices, pediments, capitals, vertical divisions—were brought into strong relief thanks to a variety of ornaments which were closer to statuary itself than to low-relief; the column and the telamon played a fundamental part, while the bell towers ended in a bulbous crown which no doubt derived from Russian art. After about 1730 the baroque style evolved into rococo: overlaying and *rocaille* increased; the ornamentation became asymmetrical and all the features merged into a symphony in space, thanks to the rhythmical movement of curves and countercurves. Two great streams met in this melting pot of the baroque: the first Italian stream triumphed in the religious architecture which saw a wonderful revival in Austria, Bavaria, Franconia and Poland. Introduced early by the Jesuits, the "Triumphal" style was welcomed with enthusiasm. Round Vienna, in Bavaria and Swabia, great convents and monasteries were built more or less on the Escorial plan (centered on a church, pl. 373) but with a frenzy of ornamentation in the two main centers of display, the library and the church. Coming from the West after about 1720, the French influence brought the charm of French taste and the example of Versailles, which was regarded by great and small German princes as the supreme model of court art. But no sooner was the French style brought into Germany than it had to join the Italian baroque and became rococo. French influence remained the stronger—though it was profoundly changed by German lyricism—in the decoration of private and civic buildings. The general layout of palaces and gardens was based on French models (Versailles, Trianon, Marly); but the decora-

412. Matthäus Daniel Poeppelmann. The Zwinger Pavilion, Dresden.
1711–1722. Badly damaged in World War II.

tion was specifically German in its *rocaille* and telamones. While
Austria remained closer to the Italian baroque, the rococo triumphed
in Saxony, Prussia, Franconia and in the Rhineland. Austria was very
early initiated by the Italians and produced some great architects: J. B.
Fischer von Erlach (1656–1723), author of Prince Eugene's palace
(1703), also the St. Charles Borromeus church in Vienna (1717) and
the design for the Schönbrunn Palace (1694); Lukas von Hildebrandt
(1668–1745), who built the Belvedere Palace in Vienna, together with
its gardens (1693–1724); and Jakob Prandtauer (1660–1726), who
made one of the finest baroque pieces in Europe, the monastery at Melk
on the Danube.

In Saxony from 1711 to 1722 Poeppelmann (1662–1736), who had
visited Versailles and Rome, built the most baroque monument in all
Germany, the Zwinger in Dresden; this building, damaged in the
Second World War, was like an immense open-air theater (pl. 412). In
Bavaria and Swabia the brothers Asam, the Thumb and Beer brothers,
the brothers Zimmermann, and Johann Michael Fischer built monasteries inspired by Austrian art, while at the court at Munich where the
Frenchman Cuvilliès (1695–1768) was working they followed Parisian
models or that of Versailles. The finest and most princely residence
in Germany was the Residenz at Würzburg, in Franconia, built
between 1719 and 1744 by Johann Balthazar Neumann (1687–1753),
in which Tiepolo painted his masterpiece on the huge staircase ceiling
between 1750 and 1753. Magnificent staircases were a specialty with this

413. Pulpit in the pilgrim church of Wies, Upper Bavaria.
Built between 1745 and 1754.

414. Egid Quirin Asam. The Assumption of the Virgin. Sculptures in chancel.
About 1717–1722. *Rohr Church (near Regensburg).*

architect, who also built one of the finest churches in Germany, the Vierzehnheiligen in Franconia, as well as Brühl Castle in the Rhineland. At Berlin, the Royal Palace (inspired by the Palazzo Madama in Rome), several of the buildings of which were erected by Andreas Schlüter (1664–1714) from 1698 onward, is the only great monument in the Italianate manner. Near Berlin, at Potsdam, Frederick the Great emulated Louis XIV in building a royal city. The eclectic Knöbelsdorff (1699–1753) remodeled the Potsdam castle in a very sober neo-Palladian style (1744) and designed Sans-Souci and its gardens (1744), a fine example of Dresden rococo.

In the Germanic countries, sculpture remained entirely decorative; it was the most tormented in Europe and had something of the broken style of belated Gothic. The religious sculptors went in for what amounted to theatrical settings with their sculptured groups (Egid Quirin Asam, 1692–1750), while the stuccoists of southern Germany showed great virtuosity (pls. 413 and 414). Meanwhile French influence helped Andreas Schlüter to make the statue of the *Grand Elector of Brandenburg*, inspired by Girardon's *Louis XIV*. Decorative painting shows signs of Tiepolo's teaching in the work of Maulpertsch at Vienna (1724–1796) and Cosmas Damian Asam at Munich (1689–

1739). The French artist Antoine Pesne (1683–1757) introduced
Berlin to the court portrait in the French manner, which was taken up
by Daniel Chodowiecki (1748–1801).

The neo-classical reformation was late in reaching German architecture (F. W. von Ermannsdorf, 1736–1800; Simon Louis du Ry,
1726–1799). In 1790 K. Gotthard Langhans (1732–1808) brought in
the archaeological style with the *Brandenburg Gate* at Berlin, inspired
by the Propylaea in Athens. Germany made an early contribution to
the international colony of Roman antiquaries, notably the theorist
Winckelmann (1717–1768), who arrived in Rome in 1755 and published his *Reflections on the Imitation of Greek Works* in the same
year, then his *History of Ancient Art* in 1764, in which he advocated
a slavish copying of classical art, an aesthetic outlook applied in painting
by his countryman Anton Raphael Mengs (1728–1779, pl. 415).

RUSSIA

The most remote center of Western architecture was in Russia, a country which held aloof from Europe until the seventeenth century. Its
architecture, which was entirely religious, had been a derivative or
province of Byzantine art until the twelfth century (Kiev region).
Then the example of native building in timber, together with some
Asiatic influence, helped Russia to find its most original style, which
at the end of the sixteenth century was followed mainly in the region

415. Anton Raphael Mengs. Parnassus. Frescoed ceiling. 1761.
Rome, Villa Albani.

416. St. Basil's Church, Moscow. 1555–1560.

417. Rastrelli. Winter Palace, Leningrad. Detail. 1754–1762.

of Moscow (pl. 416). Features of Italianate decoration, simply applied on the native structure, were introduced in the sixteenth century. However, Peter the Great overthrew all his country's traditions, scornfully discouraged the promise of Muscovite architecture, and in 1703 set a team of foreign artists to building the city of St. Petersburg (Leningrad) on the banks of the Neva, intending it to be European in style. It was the Empress Elizabeth (1741–1762) who in fact turned the Tsar's project into a reality. The Italian architect Rastrelli (1700–1770) used a baroque style, with a strong element of German rococo, in the Winter Palace (1754–1762, pl. 417); the Grand Palace of Tsarskoe Selo; the cathedral and convent of Smolny (1748–1755). But Catherine II (1762–1796) preferred the French manner; she therefore condemned the Rastrelli style and gave support to the classical reform which was furthered by her Academy of Fine Arts. This neo-classical style was followed by the French artist Vallin de la Mothe (Fine Arts Academy, 1765–1772); the Italian Rinaldi (Marble Palace; Gatchina Palace, 1766–1781). The Scotsman Cameron (minor apartments and colonnade of Tsarskoe Selo, Pavlovsk Palace, 1782–1785) and the Italian Quarenghi (Alexander Palace at Tsarskoe Selo, English Palace at Peterhof) introduced a Pompeiian decoration and a Palladian elegance which were readily absorbed by the Russian Starov (Tauride Palace, Leningrad, 1783–1788, pl. 418).

418. Starov. Hall in the Tauride Palace, Leningrad. 1783.

419. The Mauritshuis at The Hague. Built in 1643–1644 after plans by Jacob Van Campen.

THE RESISTANCE TO BAROQUE
HOLLAND

After the political truce in 1609, the seven northern provinces of the Low Countries (to which one of them, Holland, had given its name) found themselves cut off from the twelve provinces of the South. To a Europe which was monarchical, Catholic and theocratic, the United Provinces were to give a precocious example of a lay democracy based on a bourgeois society almost free of class distinctions. This completely upset the conditions on which artistic production depended all over Europe and resulted in fewer civil and religious undertakings on any large scale, the slowing down of religious inspiration, the almost complete suppression of mythological images which had no interest for the Amsterdam and Haarlem merchant. Reduced to circumstances which had so little encouragement to offer the artist, that small country which held out against all the large European states, one after the other, contrived for over sixty years to produce an admirable art, by making the best of the one resource left to it, which was Realism.

Dutch architecture has never been given the place it deserves in the history of art. Almost entirely confined to domestic needs, it produced only small buildings, but in exquisite taste (pl. 419). From the beginning of the seventeenth century Holland was the only country to reject baroque rhetoric, and by 1650 it discovered a very pure architecture based on good proportions which, after being interpreted by the English, helped to form the neo-classical style. Dutch construction in brick was relieved only by a few stone moldings to underline doorways, windows or cornices; occasionally on more important houses broad flat pilasters were set right up the wall. The few religious buildings of the period were also of simple design. Sculpture was so little practiced that foreign artists were called in for the few modeled works (tombs) of any importance.

Painting was therefore the supreme form of artistic expression in Holland. The fluid and mellow quality of the light, which is one of the beauties of the great sea-girt plain, gave the Dutch—like the Venetians—a discerning eye for pure tonality and color. The bourgeois, positivistic society must have encouraged an art of acute observation which tended to become a faithful mirror of its own existence. Paintings were small, of a size intended for the private house. In order to go about their great naturalistic inquiry the Dutch artists—even more than the Flemings—became specialists of one kind or another: painters of still lifes or animals, painters of domestic scenes, church architecture or landscape, the latter being of several subsidiary kinds—marine painting, pastorals, urban scenes, animated landscapes with figures, and ruins.

The wealth of talents that thrived almost as an industry in Holland makes it difficult to classify them satisfactorily. The local schools were not strongly marked and there were constant exchanges going on between them, while distinction according to subjects, which is often used, is too superficial. But perhaps in the same way as with Flanders we may follow two main streams, of which the first was thoroughly Nordic; while the second shows the Northern analytical temperament blending with the synthetic outlook brought from Italy.

For the most part Dutch painting springs from the analytical vision discovered by Van Eyck, which makes, so to speak, a careful check of objects, accounting for them one after the other in a select and deliberately limited field of observation; the painter's task is confined to a faithful visual record with little or no interpretation. Other painters, thanks to their inspiration, their experiments in composition and the life-size scale of their figures, are related more to the main current of European art, and particularly by the link with "Romanism." The two streams mentioned above may be distinguished in all the genres.

Thus the still-life painters of the Utrecht school, R. Savery, Abraham Boschaert, M. Simons, A. Mignon, J. Davidsz de Heem (1601–1683), continued the analytical, monographic vision of the North, painting each object as though it made the whole picture. Others, Pieter Claesz (1591–1661, pl. 420), Willem Heda (1594–1680/82), Willem Kalff (1622–1693), arranged objects into subtle compositions in such a way as to contrive a picture out of them; they preferred the pictorial quality of things to a strictly impersonal representation of them. The compositions of such an animal painter as Paul Potter (1624–1642) sometimes aspired to the monumental, while certain paintings by Melchior d'Hondecoeter are purely analytical. The monographic vision was particularly the field of the minor masters of genre painting, which in its wide range of subjects covered the whole social life of Holland (popular realism of Jan Steen, Adriaen and Isaac Van Ostade, Brekelenkam, Judith Leyster, Jacob Duck and others; genteel realism of Gerard Ter Borch (1617–1681, pl. 421), Metsu, Gerard Dou, Pieter de Hooch). This indoor-painting admirably suited the patient enumeration of forms and objects. The portraitists differ according to the degree of skill with which they set figures in a given space or framework; most of the painters of group portraits (for confraternities, councils and guilds), a type of picture very common in the Dutch school, often had trouble in grouping all their worthies into one composition. A Jan de Bray or a Van der Helst found it hard to show a number of people round a table in a natural, lifelike manner; while

420. Pieter Claesz. Still Life. *The Hague, Mauritshuis.*
421. Gerard Ter Borch. The Gallant Cavalier. *Paris, Louvre.*

422. Hals. Feast of the Guild of
Arquebusiers of St. George. 1616.
Haarlem, Frans Hals Museum.

423. Jacob Van Ruisdael. Windmill
of Wijk bij Duurstede. *Amsterdam,
Rijksmuseum.*

Frans Hals or Rembrandt solved the same problem with ease (pl. 422).
The greatest of the landscape painters, Salomon Van Ruisdael (1600–
1670) and Jacob Van Ruisdael (1628/29–1682, pl. 423), Van Goyen,
De Koninck, owe their superiority to the art with which they composed their pictures with unified designs and well-balanced values,
whereas Hobbema merely accumulated observed details one on the
other. The Italianate painters (Asselijn, Poelenburgh, Van Berchem)
followed without any thought of variation the types of landscape composition they had brought back with them from Rome. Others specialized in town scenes (Berckheyde, Van der Heyden). Of those who
painted only churches, Saenredam (1597–1665) had a fine sense of
light (pl. 424).

424. Pieter Saenredam. Church interior. *Boston, Museum of Fine Arts.*
425. Hals. Malle Babbe, the Witch of Haarlem. Detail. About 1628.
Berlin, Kaiser Friedrich Museum.

Holland did not remain cut off from European art. Italianism was brought in by the Romanist painters who lived in Rome and who almost all belonged to the Utrecht school. These were Pieter Lastman, Abraham Bloemaert, Gerard Honthorst, Hendrick ter Brugghen (1588–1629), Theodor Van Baburen. They kept the Caravaggian method of showing volumes by oblique lighting, the art of making compositions with a number of figures, and a taste for rather vulgar realism in scenes from low life such as drinkers, card players, cabaret musicians, gambling dens and guard rooms. Frans Hals and Rembrandt were produced by this movement. Frans Hals took from it his taste for shady and "tough" haunts, while Rembrandt gained a sense of historical painting and of monumental composition. They both broke up the "monographic" and objective composition of Dutch painting and their handling of paint was untraditional. Frans Hals (1580–1666), both as a portraitist and as the recorder of Haarlem society, handled his paint with bravura; his brush—the movements of which can be seen on the canvas—seems to obey an eager improvisation, and the artist gives more attention to the pigments' effects than to a lifelike imitation of the model (pl. 425).

Rembrandt Van Rijn (1606–1669) is the greatest Dutch painter; his considerable body of work contains a world of its own like that of Titian and Rubens. Rembrandt came to Amsterdam in 1631, where he spent the rest of his life. Beginning with an art which still respected

331

426. Rembrandt. Wash drawing. *London, British Museum.*
427. Rembrandt. Portrait of the Burgomaster Jan Six. About 1654.
Amsterdam, Six Collection.

all the bourgeois conventions of his age, he achieved wealth and success, but as the circumstances of his life impelled him more and more to obey some inner compulsion instead of trying to please the public, his popularity declined until in 1656 a court order made him sell all his belongings. He passed his last years in poverty and in a state of extraordinary spiritual tension. He then gave himself increasingly to painting works inspired by the Bible, through which he expressed the radiant love and peace within him (pl. 428). Three pictures serve to sum up his career as a painter. *Professor Tulp's Anatomy Lesson* (1632) was still a collection of "lifelike" portraits, painted with a painstaking and objective brush. In the *Night Watch* (1642) the artist treated his models—to their dissatisfaction, as events proved—as no more than accessory figures in the scenario of a great spectacle, of which the latent theme is an impassioned struggle between light and darkness: he neglected external reality for the poetry of his subject and beauty of effect. In the *Syndics of the Cloth Hall* (1661) the characters' physical reality was dimmed, and the eloquent intensity of their souls makes the members of the Syndicate more like a group of philosophers. Rembrandt's brush, ever more urgent and inspired, makes no more than passing references to the external meaning of things, and on great smears of darkness the artist handles oozes of color that catch the highlights in sudden stretches of impasto (pl. 427). His drawings, also, convey the overflowing of a creative imagination (pl. 426). Rembrandt's psychological and pictorial development is nowhere better seen than in the extraordinary collection of over sixty self-portraits—feverish probings into his own soul, toward the end of his life they became moving revelations of human suffering.

Jan Vermeer of Delft (1632–1675) combined the two great traditions of Dutch painting in his work. This "intimist," for whom the whole universe could be contained in a bare room animated by one or two figures, belongs to the Van Eyck line by virtue of his intense objectivity which gives a kind of magical presence to reality (pl. 429). But it was from the Italians that he inherited his strict science of composition whose hidden geometry can be detected in his apparently "natural" scenes only after careful analysis; it was to the remote but widespread influence of Caravaggio that he owed the art of rounding his volumes by the device of lateral lighting. He was very Dutch in use of that poetry of light giving things their shapes, colors and very existence. He belonged fully to that "philosophical" century in which a few painters, notably Rembrandt, Velázquez, Zurbarán, Georges de La Tour and himself, saw human beings as the transcendental presence of a soul.

The Dutch school declined at the end of the seventeenth century as a result of the fashionable French and English influences which

428. Rembrandt. The Pilgrims of Emmaus. 1648. *Paris, Louvre.*

429. Vermeer. Lady Standing at the Virginals. About 1658.
London, National Gallery.

thwarted the native realistic tradition. The portraitists Gaspar Netscher (1639–1684), Frans Van Mieris (1636–1681) were influenced by court portraits; still life began to imitate the French floral painters; in the eighteenth century Cornelis Troost (1697–1750) imitated the society art of the Regency and Louis XV and showed English influence. The school of Gerard Dou was prolonged by several painters after 1750.

BRITAIN

ARCHITECTURE

Passing without a well-defined transitional style from the Gothic to the classical, England scarcely felt—and then only very late—the indecisions of the Mannerist crisis which marked the Renaissance in other Nordic countries. Scarcely had a few "antique" decorations been used in Elizabethan mansions, when at the beginning of the seventeenth century the architect Inigo Jones (1573–1652) brought back his passion for Palladio, after a journey in Italy. He designed the Banqueting House in Whitehall (1619–1622) in a very pure style, and urged the utmost simplicity in the fronts of ordinary dwelling houses. After the Restoration (1660) Sir Christopher Wren was asked to plan the rebuilding of London after its destruction in the Great Fire of 1666. He rebuilt St. Paul's Cathedral in a Roman style imitated from St. Peter's, Rome, with a dome deriving from the design Bramante had intended for St. Peter's; this building was to have great influence in France and America in the eighteenth century (pl. 430). A large number of churches were built in London after Wren's designs. Dutch influences affected domestic architecture, which was very plain, brick-built with very simply molded sash windows, the only ornament being a doorway of elegantly classical style. Several instances of restrained baroque were created by two architects who had worked with Wren, Nicholas Hawksmoor (1661–1736) and John Vanbrugh (1664–1726), who built two colossal mansions, Blenheim Palace (Woodstock, 1705–1724) and Castle Howard (1699–1712). In the Georgian period (1714–1760) renewed speculation about architecture led to a revival of Inigo Jones's Palladian style; a de luxe edition of Palladio's treatise, annotated by Jones, was published in 1715. Such was the vogue of architecture that even the aristocracy turned its hand to it. "Palladianism" was to become the national style in Great Britain. William Kent (1684–1748) was the moving spirit in the period; he introduced the Anglo-Chinese garden

430. Wren. St. Paul's
Cathedral, London.
1675–1710.

about 1720, with an irregular layout, and here and there a Palladian,
Gothic or Chinese pavilion. Palladian structures and Anglo-Chinese
gardens were not long in crossing the channel and became popular in
France. Bath, the fashionable spa, built by John Wood and his son of
the same name, became a sort of English Vicenza. A new phase began
in 1758, when Robert Adam (1728–1792) returned from a voyage to
Pompeii and Spalato to introduce features of a Neo-Hellenic style,
exquisitely elegant, which influenced both façades (pl. 431) and internal
decoration (pl. 471) in which the artist introduced arabesques, and
which was to be imitated in the French Directoire style. English architecture shows a remarkable continuity in its pursuit of a very pure
classical manner, in which ornament is used only to bring out the proportions. It is not the smallest of English paradoxes that in spite of that

431. Robert Adam. Osterley
Park. Portico. 1761.

evolution, the Gothic style should have persisted in the eighteenth century in university buildings (Christ Church College, Oxford, seventeenth century), in Fonthill Abbey (1795) or even country houses (Strawberry Hill, Twickenham, 1748).

PAINTING

Modern English painting derived from the Flemish school; it was founded by Anthony Van Dyck, who came to London in 1632, and by his best disciple, Sir Peter Lely (1618–1680), who was of Dutch origin. To this far-reaching source further Dutch influences were added in the course of the century, and above all some desire to emulate the "gallant," refined art of Watteau whose manner was revealed to London by Philippe Mercier and the engraver Gravelot. Gravelot in particular helped Hogarth to find his own style, and guided Gainsborough in his early period. William Hogarth (1697–1764) perhaps owed something of his verve and broadness of style to Sir James Thornhill (1676–1734), his employer, whose daughter Hogarth married and who was the only native-born painter of baroque decorations in England. Influenced by the theater, Hogarth painted series of paintings which follow one another like the chapters of a novel, and with a moralizing tendency: *The Rake's Progress* (1735); *The Harlot's Progress* (1738); *Marriage à la Mode* (1745, pl. 432). He found more freedom in the magnificent figures which he brought out boldly with a rich and lively brush (*The Shrimp Girl; Garrick*). In the Georgian period, painting was mostly devoted to portraiture. Sir Joshua Reynolds (1723–1791), first president of the Royal Academy in 1768, fixed the characteristics of the English portrait: sulky feminine portraits with a touch of sentimentality (*Nelly O'Brien*, pl. 433; *Kitty Fisher; Countess Spencer*); masculine portraits which, in spite of an affected casualness bring out fully British personal pride and character (*Colonel Saint Leger, Lord Heathfield, Earl of Eglinton*). Very much of a theorist and the author of *Discourses on Painting*, Reynolds tried to wrest their secrets from the great masters, Raphael, Correggio, Rubens, Rembrandt, Titian. The art of his rival Thomas Gainsborough (1727–1788) was more spontaneous. Gainsborough took to painting with a taste for landscape, but when he came into fashion as a portrait painter he still kept that sense of naturalness which he had gained in his contact with the countryside. His art, which is sentimental, like Watteau's by which it was

432. Hogarth. After the Wedding. Second picture of the series
"Marriage à la Mode," completed in 1745. *London, Tate Gallery.*
433. Reynolds. Nelly O'Brien, 1763. *London, Wallace Collection,
reproduced by permission of the Trustees.*

influenced, is a poetic expression of aristocratic elegance (*The Blue
Boy; The Morning Walk; Mr. and Mrs. Robert Andrews*) and of the
melancholy, dreamy feminine soul (*Perdita; Mrs. Sheridan; Miss Margaret Gainsborough,* pl. 434). He turned the portrait into a mood
attuned to some evocation of nature. Allan Ramsay (1713–1784), of
Scottish origin, influenced by Quentin de La Tour, Perroneau and
Nattier, painted portraits of great natural delicacy. Sir Henry Raeburn
(1756–1823) remained in Edinburgh, where he confined himself to
painting the robust health, military swagger and red cheeks of Scottish
society (pl. 435). John Hoppner (1759–1810), of German origin, and
George Romney (1734–1802), who spent two years in Italy, both
introduced a neo-classical coldness into the portrait, a manner which
Sir Thomas Lawrence (1769–1830), who painted for all the courts in
Europe, brought to icy perfection. The Anglo-Saxons were also
responsible for neo-classicism in historical painting; it was in Rome,
under the influence of the archaeologist Winckelmann, and then in
London, that between 1763 and 1775 Gavin Hamilton (1730–1797)
and the American-born Benjamin West (1738–1830) re-created the
historical genre, more than a decade before the French painter David,
who did not forget their example. Here again, as in architecture, England gave the lead to France.

Though they lacked the prestige of portraiture, which brings fame

337

434. Gainsborough. Miss Margaret Gainsborough. Detail.
London, National Gallery.

435. Raeburn. Colonel Alastair Macdonell of Glengarry.
Edinburgh, Museum.

and fortune to its exponents, the other types of painting were also practiced by the English school. Gainsborough's landscapes, which were inspired by the Dutch, Rubens and Watteau, would be enough to make his reputation. The refined Richard Wilson (1714–1782), who was in Italy from about 1750 to 1756, where he met Joseph Vernet, interpreted the mountains of his native Wales through the honeyed light of Claude Lorrain, whom he greatly admired, as did many of his contemporaries (pl. 436). George Stubbs (1724–1806), painted conversation pieces, portraits, horse portraits, animals and rural scenes with a cool, clear honesty (pl. 437). Born in Regensburg, the cosmopolitan Johann Zoffany (1733–1810), an anecdotal painter neo-classical in style, is often classed with the English school because of the long periods he spent in London. Imported from Holland, the caricature developed in England in the eighteenth century; casually introduced by Hogarth, it was practiced with great wit and as a genre of its own by Thomas Rowlandson (1756–1827). The miniature portrait, which had reached such a high level in the Elizabethan period, had further success in the eighteenth century with Richard Cosway (1742–1821). Water color was practiced as an independent genre by such landscape painters as A. Cozens (about 1717–1786), J. R. Cozens (1752–1797), Thomas Girtin (1775–1802), and the caricaturist Rowlandson.

338

436. Richard Wilson.
An arch at Kew.
1761–1762. *Collection
of Brinsley Ford, Esq.*

UNITED STATES
ARCHITECTURE

The architecture of the British Colonies in North America, generally referred to as Colonial, had its beginnings in the austere wooden buildings of New England in the late seventeenth and early eighteenth centuries. It was an architecture of necessity rather than luxury, replacing the first dwellings of the settlers, which were hardly more than rude shelters. The earliest frame houses in Massachusetts with their overhanging second stories and combination adobe and clapboard construction are derived from the middle class urban architecture of medieval England (pl. 438).

The Georgian architecture of the later Colonial period (1720–1790) was a style that admirably expressed the new prosperity and

437. George Stubbs.
Lord and
Lady Melbourne, with
Sir Ralph Milbanke
and
Mr. John Milbanke.
1770.
Private Collection.

438. The Paul Revere House, Boston, Massachusetts. *The Greater Boston Chamber of Commerce.*

security of the Colonists. Typical of the American imitations of the Georgian Palladian style in England are the Longfellow House in Cambridge, Massachusetts (1759), and "Westover" in Virginia. These are only two of the distinguished examples of this American baroque style which was followed in all the Colonies. In ecclesiastical architecture the Wren style found its way to America in such buildings as Christ Church, Philadelphia (1766), and King's Chapel in Boston (1749). To this same style belong such famous buildings as Independence Hall in Philadelphia and Faneuil Hall in Boston.

The establishment of the Republic necessitated a monumental architecture to serve as a symbol of the new democracy and to house its multiple branches of government. One of the leading sponsors of architecture in the Federal period (1790–1820) was Thomas Jefferson

439. Thomas Jefferson. The Virginia State Capitol. *Virginia Chamber of Commerce.*

(1743–1826), whose espousal of the forms of Roman architecture inaugurated the neo-classic revival in the United States. The principal monuments to Jefferson and his theories are the capitol at Richmond (pl. 439; the first temple building, inspired by the Maison Carrée at Nîmes), and the University of Virginia, a series of temple pavilions disposed on the plan of a village green, an arrangement anticipated in Joseph J. Ramée's design for Union College in Schenectady. In the first of these enterprises Jefferson was assisted by C. L. Clérisseau, the teacher of Robert Adam. The style of the Adam brothers was the inspiration for Samuel McIntyre (1757–1811) of Salem, Massachusetts.

PAINTING

As late as 1800, owing to the limited economy of the Colonies as well as the Puritans' prejudice against idolatry and their regard for art as luxury, portraiture was the only accepted form of expression in painting. Like the architecture of the Colonial period, the portraits of the seventeenth and eighteenth centuries were reflections of various European manners ranging from a provincial prolongation of the work of Tudor limners to American imitations of the formulas of Lely and Van Dyke. John Smibert (1688–1751) purveyed a wooden version of the seventeenth century Continental manner with an emphasis on likeness rather than grace. A certain elegance, with more flattering portraiture and attention to the richness of textures, made its appearance in the work of Robert Feke (1705–1750). His portraits, as well as those of Joseph Blackburn (1700–1765), reveal the same expression

440. John Singleton Copley. Mrs. Thomas Boylston. *Courtesy of Harvard University.*

of luxury and refinement evident in the Georgian houses of the Tory aristocracy. The culmination of the Colonial style is found in the painting of John Singleton Copley (1737–1815, pl. 440). With what little training he was able to acquire from men like Blackburn, Copley devised a manner notable not only for the striking candor and conviction of characterization, but also for the magic realism in the precise delineation of textures that gives his portraits something of the precise, crystalline definition of still-life paintings. In their completely straightforward, objective recording of the sitter's appearance, Copley's portraits are among the most American pictures ever painted. Benjamin West (1738–1820), often called the Father of American Painting, spent most of his mature career in London, where, thanks to his early indoctrination by Raphael Mengs and Joshua Reynolds, he became one of the originators of neo-classicism in historical painting. His importance resides more in his teaching of generations of American artists who for more than fifty years flocked to his London studio. Among West's pupils were John Trumbull (1756–1843), portraitist and painter of scenes of the Revolution, Charles Willson Peale (1741–1827), inventor, painter, and founder of the Pennsylvania Academy of Fine Arts, and Gilbert Stuart (1755–1828). Stuart, no less incisive than Copley in his ability to catch a telling likeness, brought to American art of the post-Revolutionary period his own version of the facile grace and ideality and the magnificent technical bravura of the best of the English eighteenth century portraitists.

FRANCE

ARCHITECTURE

Religious activity (Oratorians, Jesuits, and Order of the Visitation); the nobility's desire for display; the rise of a new parliamentary and administrative middle class; private and royal initiative, and town-planning schemes all resulted in an enormous demand for new architecture in the seventeenth century. At the dawn of the century the Jesuits introduced their new type of church and Etienne Martellange (1569–1641) built many structures in this style (Le Puy, 1605; La Flèche, 1607; Avignon, 1617; St.-Paul-St.-Louis, Paris, 1627). This was the predominantly used plan (Val-de-Grâce; Church of the Sorbonne) but did not completely replace the Gothic type with side aisles and ambulatory (St.-Sulpice, Paris). The plain decoration in all these churches was strictly functional; marble facings were confined to certain parts of the church, and until the eighteenth century these buildings reflected the sober outlook of the first Roman style of the Counter Reformation. There was a heavy demand for lay buildings, châteaux, country houses, and for "hôtels" or town houses. The château, which followed the medieval closed-in design until about 1640, tended after that date to open onto the countryside and to cluster round a central building. The Louis XIV period found a pleasing design for town houses, the "hôtel" type built between a courtyard and a garden; the façade did not give aggressively onto the street as in Italy, but had a surrounding wall pierced by a large gateway. In the eighteenth century, when the refinement of social life and taste for privacy led to rooms each having a specific function, architects found various elegant solutions for the problem of how to lay out and relate the different parts or wings. In the seventeenth century, pride of place in both castle and town house was given to the *galerie* or hall (used for banquets, receptions, balls), a long room containing all the finest decorations and furnishings in the building; this was changed under Louis XV. The organic grouping of the main elements of a township round a central square, together with the regulation of traffic by building arterial thoroughfares; the siting of public buildings; in a word everything we now mean by town-planning, all this began in the early seventeenth century when Henry IV created the first "royal square," or *place*, laid out as a kind of royal monument, in the Place des Vosges and Place Dauphine. This feature persisted in Paris under Louis XIV (Place Vendôme, Place des Victoires) and under Louis XV (Place de la Concorde), after which it was imitated all over France and spread into other countries.

Baroque decoration, derived from the ornamental Fontainebleau style which tended to stifle classicism in Henry IV's reign, sat heavily on many civic buildings in Louis XIII's reign (Hôtel Sully, Paris; Hôtel de Ville, Lyons). Architecture was purified and decoration handled more rationally after 1640 thanks to the classical outlook of Jacques le Mercier (1585–1654), who was responsible for the present Sorbonne; and François Mansart (1598–1666), the author of the church of the Val-de-Grâce in Paris and the Château de Maisons-Laffitte; and Louis Le Vau (1612–1670), who designed for Fouquet, then Superintendent of Finance, the Château de Vaux, the forerunner of Versailles. André Le Nôtre (1613–1700) planned its gardens.

With the more personal rule of Louis XIV, activities tended to center on the King. A superintendent or minister of works (the first of whom was Colbert) now supervised public enterprises, for which an official architect (Jules Hardouin-Mansart) and a "first painter" (Le Brun) produced designs. The founding of the Academy of Painting and Sculpture in 1648, the French Academy in Rome in 1666, the Academy of Architecture in 1671, the setting up of the Gobelins factory for furniture and tapestries in 1662, all tightened official control of the Fine Arts through teaching, the dictatorship of the academies and centralized production.

Louis XIV first turned his attention to the dynastic palace of the Louvre, whose enlargement was taken in hand, Claude Perrault constructing the façade of the Colonnade (pl. 441) to a composite design. This masterpiece of French classicism, the Parthenon of French architecture, amounted to a protest against the baroque style of Bernini, whom Louis XIV had invited to France to submit plans for its completion. But it was the more personal undertaking at Versailles which ended by absorbing the finest efforts of his reign. Versailles was begun in 1668 and finished in 1690, after plans made by Le Vau and subsequently Jules Hardouin-Mansart (1646–1708), the nephew of François Mansart, in a park which had been already laid out by Le Nôtre between 1661 and 1665. With the host of statues of characters from mythology, in the gardens, and its luxurious Galerie des Glaces, 239 feet 6 inches in length, its ceilings painted by Le Brun, its huge imposing apartments faced with marble, Versailles was intended as a kind of Olympian residence, set round the solar symbol of Apollo and

441. Colonnade of the Louvre. Begun in 1665 and completed after the designs of Le Vau, Le Brun and Claude Perrault.

442. Versailles. The Park and Palace, viewed from the air.

designed for the glorification of the King (pls. 442, 467). The park was planned in what we now call the "French Garden" style, in which nature is arranged architecturally. The checkerwork of avenues based on a main vista or perspective enclose stretches of water and *broderie* or trimmed boxwood, little glades or open-air "rooms" for all kinds of entertainment and containing architectural furnishings (pl. 443). Statues stand all over the park; great jets play in the fountains which, in repose, are called "mirrors of water." In the park, a short distance away from the palace, Louis XIV had a charming rest house built by Mansart, the Grand Trianon, in limestone and pink marble.

443. The Open-air Ballroom in the Park of Versailles. Carried out between 1680–1683 after the plans of Le Nôtre and the rock gardener Berthier.

444. Jules Hardouin-Mansart. Church of St. Louis, in the Invalides,
Paris. 1677–1701.

The monuments and gardens of Versailles were imitated all over
Europe in the eighteenth century: in Italy (Caserta; Colorno), in Spain
(Buen Retiro; La Granja; Royal Palace, Madrid), in Sweden and Russia
(around Leningrad), but such imitations were most numerous in Austria
and Germany. As late as the nineteenth century Ludwig II of Bavaria
had a replica of the Galerie des Glaces built into one of his castles.

Jules Hardouin-Mansart was also responsible for the Versailles
Chapelle du Palais (1700–1710) which was finished by his nephew
Robert de Cotte, and above all the Church of St. Louis, or Chapel of
the Invalides in Paris (pl. 444), with the most elegant dome built in
the seventeenth century, in which the vertical movement is well related
to the relative weights of the different stories.

In the eighteenth century external architecture offers an increasingly strong contrast with internal decoration and furnishing. In spite
of one or two digressions toward the rococo (such as the planning of
Nancy by Boffrand and Héré) there was a more rational approach and
the architect J.-F. Blondel, in his famous book *L'Architecture française,*
was justified in boasting of the classicism of the French school. Jacques-
Ange Gabriel (1698–1792) summed up the national classicism in his
works, deriving from Perrault's Louvre Colonnade (Place de la Bourse,
Bordeaux, 1747; Place de la Concorde, Paris, 1754; Petit Trianon,

346

445. Nicolas Ledoux. The Villette Rotunda, Paris.
(One of the Farmer Generals' area headquarters, 1785–1789.)

1762, pl. 447). This trend developed further under Louis XVI, owing to the influence brought from Rome by Soufflot (1713–1780) who was under the spell of St. Peter's (Pantheon, Paris, 1764), while the most important factor was the archaeological tendency which, after the discoveries made in Greece, Tuscany and Herculaneum, led to an emulation of pure Greek as well as Etruscan; the Roman Corinthian was abandoned in favor of the Doric and Ionic of Greece, and the fashion was for severe, ungarnished walls (Brongniart, Chalgrin, Gondouin; Ledoux, Louis, pls. 445, 446). This trend, further encour-

446. Victor Louis. Grand Theater, Bordeaux. The main staircase. 1775–1780.

447. Jacques-Ange Gabriel. The Petit Trianon, Versailles. 1762.

aged by English influence, resulted in "Palladianism." But the "Anglo-mania" also acted in the opposite direction, driving out the classical French garden and substituting the meandering, rustic English garden with its romantic implications.

The interior decoration of rooms, since the sixteenth century, had consisted of wooden panels applied to the walls, except under Louis XIV when a certain amount of marble was used. During the Regency, with the growing fashion for small apartments, the style of decoration was based more on rococo curves, a tendency toward elaborateness which increased under Louis XV and began to take asymmetrical forms. Two interior designers, Oppenordt (1672–1742) and Meissonier (1695–1750), specialized in the *rocaille* style which was supplanted in about 1760 by a return to the straight line: the vogue for Neo-Greek brought in decorations with Pompeian arabesques in stucco or paint; but in spite of its classical origins this type of decoration remained some-what heavy.

SCULPTURE

French sculpture in the seventeenth century is a remarkable instance of French resistance to European baroque. The statues in Versailles Park, which match so well in their classical balance with the antique pieces, are in astonishing contrast with the violent movement of Le Brun's paintings in the Galerie des Glaces. Pierre Puget (1622–1694, pl. 448), who has been described as the French Michelangelo, is the exception proving the rule; for his work is easily explained by his Marseilles origins, his contacts with art circles in Genoa and Rome, his

448. Pierre Puget. Milo of
Crotona. 1671–1682.
Paris, Louvre.

training in ornamental art and as a decorator of the royal galleys. The
sculptors of Louis XIII's reign, Simon Guillain, Jean Warin, Jacques
Sarrazin (1588–1660), Gilles Guérin, the Anguier brothers, have a
slightly rough, realistic honesty in the tradition of Germain Pilon.
The classicism of Coysevox (1640–1720) and Girardon (1628–1715)
and of the Versailles sculptors goes back, rather, to the elegant idealism
of Jean Goujon. In the *Apollo's bath* group (pl. 449), it is remarkable
how Girardon, reaching back across the centuries, rediscovered that
grace and power of gesture which so perfectly suggests the god's
grandeur on the pediment of Olympia. Some of Girardon's statues are

449. Girardon and Renaudin.
Apollo Attended by the
Nymphs. 1665–1677. The
Baths of Apollo in the Park
of Versailles.

the nearest to Phidias that have been made in the West: with him, French sculpture turned back to the ancient Greek plastic outlook at the very height of the Roman baroque. Antoine Coysevox made some admirable portraits of the great men of his time, in busts whose heroic dignity in no way detracts from the sitter's personality (pl. 450). French sculpture in the seventeenth century also produced a fine funerary art whose subdued reserve is in marked contrast with the pompousness of Roman tombs.

Even more remarkable is the continuity of this classical tradition in the eighteenth century, in spite of the steady infiltration of the baroque aesthetic. The brothers Nicolas and Guillaume Coustou (*Horses of Marly*, 1740–1747) and Robert Le Lorrain (1666–1743) were of a distinguished line of Versailles sculptors. In Louis XV's reign J.-B. Lemoyne (1704–1778), the brothers Sloditz and Adam, and later the portraitist J.-J. Caffieri (1725–1791), were attracted by graceful distortions of the rococo, but Edmé Bouchardon (1698–1762) rebuffed it with his deliberate classicism, which is somewhat cold and academic. Jean-Baptiste Pigalle (1714–1785) wavered between the two tendencies (pl. 372), but Jean-Antoine Houdon (1741–1824, pl. 451), the greatest sculptor of the century, who proved himself with his *Diana* to be in

450. Coysevox. Bust of the Great Condé. Bronze. 1688. *Paris, Louvre.*

451. Houdon. Bust of Alexander Brongniart as a Child.
Terra cotta. Dated 1777. *Paris, Louvre.*

the direct line of descent from Jean Goujon, and whose terra cottas are quivering with life, turned resolutely toward classicism. In the Louis XVI period, the neo-classical purge led to an elegant formalism, with a touch of insipidness which was heightened by the Pompeian influence in Falconet (1716–1791), Pajou (1733–1809) and Julien Vassé (1716–1772). Clodion (1738–1814) popularized this form of art in his statuettes.

One of the finest themes of French sculpture in the seventeenth and eighteenth centuries was the royal statue, impressive equestrian images of the King of which all the numerous examples were unfortunately destroyed during the Revolution.

PAINTING

The seventeenth century saw the beginning of a state of things peculiar to French painting, when creative artists were driven into isolation by an "official" art, with decorative and academic tendencies, amounting to a closed "school." The official style was created by Simon Vouet (1590–1647). Returning from a long stay in Rome in 1627, to find French painting still given to Mannerism, Vouet introduced the outsize mythological or religious painting in the Bolognese style. Jacques Blanchard, Laurent de la Hire at once absorbed this style, while François Perrier and Claude Vignon remained faithful to Mannerism. Eustache Le Sueur (1617–1655) went more directly to Raphael and Pietro da Cortona. In the reign of Louis XIV the taste for order and hierarchy made people see painting as an art governed by a set of rules and precepts, as taught by the Academy of Painting and Sculpture, founded in 1648 and officially recognized in 1663. Moreover, architecture now dominated the other arts, so that painting had to be content to play a decorative part. Charles Le Brun (1619–1690) was a pupil of Vouet. After a stay in Rome from 1642 to 1645 he became practically a dictator over the arts during the reign of Louis XIV (pls. 466, 467). With an astonishingly large output, Le Brun took in hand all sorts of projects in architecture, furnishing, tapestry and sculpture; he organized the pompous gala background which Louis XIV wanted as a setting for his glory. His great painted work is the ceiling of the Galerie des Glaces at Versailles, which he began in 1679. His loud, long-winded art is the nearest thing to the rhetoric of the Carraccis to be found in France. A distinguished group of decorators gathered round him.

Pierre Mignard (1612–1695), Le Brun's rival who succeeded him as the official painter, was also a follower of the Bolognese school. At the close of the reign Hyacinthe Rigaud (1659–1743, pl. 369) and Nicolas de Largillière (1656–1746) created a type of ceremonial portrait in keeping with the aesthetic and ethical outlook of the period, for which the example was set by the King himself. Majestically clad in his courtier's uniform, the model is portrayed in all the symbols of his social status, appearing quite satisfied with the transfer of personality thus brought about.

The creative vein of French painting, apart from the "schools," is to be found among artists who for the most part passed their lives in isolation, untouched by official developments. They all belong to the reign of Louis XIII. Two streams stand out in this very fertile class of artists: the classical and the realistic. The two great artists who created the French classical tradition in painting, Poussin and Claude Lorrain, spent their lives in Rome, far from the pomp and circumstance of the court, and equally aloof from the ostentatious style imposed on it by Bernini. They both pursued the mirage of Antiquity, in Rome. Nicolas Poussin (1584–1665) passed beyond Bolognese baroque and was in the direct line of Italian classicism: Titian's generous humanism dominated his first Roman period (*Bacchanal; Kingdom of Flora*, formerly in Dresden); then Raphael gave him a more intellectual conception of art so that his strictly calculated compositions, in which form·· is the servant of the idea, are governed by the meaning of the subject (the *Seven Sacraments* series, *The Israelites Gathering Manna*, Louvre). Just when his art might have been spoiled by an overdose of rationalism, Poussin's love of nature came to his aid. From 1648 onward landscape took an increasingly important place in his work. He defined the ideal of classical landscape, which reduces the infinite complexity of the world to an intellectual unity, and humanized nature by associating it intimately with some moral theme, whether religious (*St. Matthew and the Angel*), historical (*The Burial of Phocion*), philosophical (*Diogenes*), mythological (*Polyphemus*, pl. 452) or poetic (*Orpheus*).

The art of Claude Gelée, called Lorrain (1600–1682), who painted nothing but landscapes, sprang from that of the Northern painters established in Rome, the German Elsheimer and the Fleming Paul Bril who were the first to work out the aesthetic of landscape composition. Claude's keen sensitiveness to nature expressed itself in wash drawings.

452. Poussin. Polyphemus. 1649. *Leningrad, Hermitage.*

But for him nature was a human theme, a source of reverie, just as for Poussin it was a matter for meditation. A native of the misty northern province of Lorraine, Claude was entranced by the diffusion of light in space, but satisfied himself with opening a window onto eternity in his paintings of ports, in which imposing buildings serve as an archway to the sea, which is tinted with the rays of dawn or sunset (pl. 453).

453. Claude Lorrain. Embarkation of St. Paul at Ostia. *Madrid, Prado.*

Other seventeenth century artists revived the native realist tradition, interpreting the world as a source of human emotion. The revolution carried out by Caravaggio helped French art to rediscover its deep interest in the common people that had already been evident in the Middle Ages, seeing them as the vital source of the great elemental powers of the soul. The Lorraine painter Georges de La Tour (1593–1652) took directly from Caravaggio his passion for night pieces and his way of interpreting biblical scenes through peasant characters: he painted ascetic canvases of deep mystical significance (pl. 370). The Le Nain brothers (Antoine, 1588–1648, Louis, 1593–1648 and Mathieu, 1607–1677) portrayed peasant life with a serious and almost priestly simplicity (pl. 454). This lofty sense of human dignity also permeates the work of a painter of Flemish origin, Philippe de Champaigne (1602–1674), who in spite of being a portraitist at Louis XIII's court was unaffected by the official style and left some thoughtful studies of Jansenists (pl. 455).

An important evolution in taste is to be seen at the end of the seventeenth century. People were tiring of cerebral works and of an ideal beauty as defined by the Academy of Painting and Sculpture. This change took shape in the quarrel between the "Poussinists," who favored intellectual painting and the primacy of drawing over color, and the "Rubenists," who defended color and sensual painting. The latter tendency triumphed after Mignard's death, when the lavish, brightly

454. Louis Le Nain. Peasants at Table (known as La Bénédicité).
Paris, Louvre.

455. Philippe de Champaigne. The Ex Voto.
Mother Catherine-Agnes Arnauld and Sister Catherine of St. Susan at prayer.
Paris, Louvre.

colored painting of Largillière—who was brought up in Antwerp—
went straight back to Rubens, in the same way as Rigault's. The Rubens
Medici Gallery in the Luxembourg Palace was to play the part that
hitherto belonged to the Carraccis' Farnese Gallery.

The intellectual work of the seventeenth century was followed,
through Antoine Watteau, a native of Valenciennes (1684–1721), by
an art of sensibility, addressed to the heart, more like sketching than
painting, in which a mood is evoked by a suggestive setting (pls. 456,
457). He began by painting small military scenes in the Dutch manner
(*The Bivouac* in Leningrad). It was undoubtedly Gillot who

456. Watteau. L'Enseigne de Gersaint. *Berlin, Museum.*

457. Watteau. Nude. Sketch in red chalk. *Paris, Louvre.*

gave him his taste for scenes from the Commedia dell'Arte when the Italian players, after Louis XIV's ban, reappeared in Paris in 1716 (the *Mezzetin*, Metropolitan Museum; *Pierrot and Columbine* and *Gilles*, both Louvre). But his fame was made particularly by his *fêtes galantes* or pastorals, pictures with no defined subject, which show lovers idling in a landscape—a sentimental theme which Rubens had seen as a possible genre toward the end of his life.

It becomes more difficult to follow the two streams we have mentioned, in the later eighteenth century, when all painting tended more or less toward decoration. Having lost sight of the intellectual mission entrusted to it in the seventeenth century, painting now had little to aim at but pleasure. Its job was to provide a pleasant background for existence. Two traditions may be seen in decorative painting, the first deriving from Watteau, and the second from Italianism. While Watteau's immediate pupils Jean-Baptiste Pater (1696–1736) and Nicolas Lancret (1690–1745) made *fêtes galantes* with decorative themes, set in the woodwork paneling, the tradition of painting for effects in the Italian manner was carried on by Jean-François de Troy (1679–1752), François Lemoyne (1688–1737), Charles Coypel (1694–1752) and especially François Boucher (1703–1770, pl. 458), but they treated history on a romantic level influenced by opera, and in a style that was overlaid with the mannered flourishes of the rococo. The

458. Boucher. Renaud and Armide. 1734. *Paris, Louvre.*

459. Nicolas de Largillière. Mlle. Duclos, of the Comédie-Française, as Ariadne. *Chantilly, Musée Condé.*

460. Fragonard. Fantasy Portrait. *Paris, Louvre.*
461. Greuze. The Father's Curse (The Prodigal Son). 1778. *Paris, Louvre.*

portrait also indulged in this "gallant" eroticism, with Nicolas de Largillière (pl. 459) and Jean-Marc Nattier (1685–1766), who was the first to travesty themes from mythology for the benefit of his models: Diana and Hebe, the goddess of Youth, were the most frequent vehicles of his flattering symbolism. Jean-Honoré Fragonard (1732–1806) elegantly blended the influence of Tiepolo, Pietro da Cortona, Rubens and Rembrandt. He was the most gifted artist to exploit the "gallant" style and was beyond doubt the painter most characteristic of his century, of which he had all the happy-go-lucky optimism, the frivolous tastes, the erotic sensibility, the spontaneous fancy, the versatility, the variety of gifts, the lack of purpose, the charm, and the innate and refined breeding (pl. 460). Jean-Baptiste Greuze (1725–1805) was a very talented artist led astray by literature: he created an unsatisfactory type of composition which combined the "gallant" erotic outlook with would-be edifying but sentimental intentions which he took from Rousseau and Diderot (pl. 461).

Fortunately the Northern schools infused sincerer feelings into French art. François Desportes (1661–1743) and Jean-Baptiste Oudry (1686–1755) were primarily decorative painters, the inventors of decorative still lifes and hunting scenes, but they showed a refreshing honesty in their portrayal of animals, as well as objects and landscapes (pl. 462). Trained as he was in the Dutch school, Jean-Baptiste

357

462. Oudry. The Wolf Hunt. 1748. *Nantes, Museum.*

Chardin (1699–1779) represents the strongest protest of the native French character against the elegant frivolity of the time. Like the Le Nain brothers, in such homely scenes as *La Bénédicité* (pl. 454) and *La Pourvoyeuse* (Louvre) he sought his inspiration in the rich life of the common people; and in his still lifes he painted common-place things in everyday use, with the same restrained emotion as his scenes from domestic life (pl. 463). His grainy texture, with the paint laid on generously but never with the full brush, makes him one of the

463. Chardin. Pipe and Crockery. *Paris, Louvre.*
464. Maurice Quentin de La Tour. Self-portrait.
Pastel. 1751. *Amiens, Museum.*

most impressive technical masters of painting. The realism of Maurice Quentin de La Tour (1704–1788), a pastel painter, goes back rather through Robert de Nanteuil (1625–1678) to the psychological tradition of Clouet; there is something of Voltaire's critical outlook in his acute analysis (pl. 464). Madame Vigée-Lebrun (1755–1842) was to introduce both naturalness and neo-classical style into portraiture.

Landscape, which was composed like an operatic setting during Louis XV's reign, came closer to a sincere expression of nature under Louis XVI. Hubert Robert (1733–1808) specialized in the painting of ruins, but many of his studies show a gift for observing the picturesque (pl. 465). Louis-Gabriel Moreau (1740–1806) painted park scenes which already had a Romantic flavor about them.

All these artists had a following of imitators and plagiarists— such a plethora of talents being characteristic of any civilization in its last stages.

At the end of the eighteenth century there was a strong reaction in both the moral and plastic sense against the "gallant" academicism that Boucher had imposed. The reviving taste for classical composition, the idealistic conception of the beautiful and works of pure intellect, brought back Bolognese influence as well as Poussin's, resulting in a fresh wave of Greco-Roman influence which was stimulated by the discovery of Herculaneum and Pompeii. This tendency can be seen

465. Hubert Robert. A View of the Park of Méréville.
Paris, Private Collection.

466. Louis XIV visiting the Gobelins factory, October 15, 1667. Tapestry,
The History of the King, woven at Gobelins after cartoons by Charles Le Brun.

in Callet (1741–1823), Vien (1716–1809), Vincent (1746–1816) and
Suvée (1743–1807). It produced David's *Oath of the Horatii*, which
was virtually the manifesto of a new art (pl. 476).

THE MINOR ARTS

The minor arts assumed considerable importance in the seventeenth
and eighteenth centuries, as a result of the refinement of social and
private life which created a demand for furnishings. As France had
shown Europe the way in perfecting the "art of living," it is not
surprising that the types of furnishings created in eighteenth century
France were imitated abroad.

The founding of the Manufacture Royale des Meubles de la
Couronne—the Gobelins—in 1662 was a determining factor in the success of French furnishings (pl. 466). The Manufacture de la Savonnerie,
set up in 1604, specialized in making carpets, while the Beauvais factory,
dating from 1664, made small-scale tapestries (in *petit-point*) which
were often used for covering chairs.

In France the lavish decoration of interiors contrasted with the
simplicity of the architecture. Rooms were covered with painted
paneling and adorned with carvings and gilt. In the Regency period
the large rooms and halls which still prevailed under Louis XIV were

no longer fashionable, and apartments tended to be divided into smaller rooms (*pièces*) each of which was used for some special domestic or social activity. In spite of an increasing simplicity in social ceremony, the decoration of these living apartments was still very rich.

The seventeenth century interior had few items of furniture (chairs, consoles, tables, beds, buhl cabinets), but these were massive and were usually set in a row along the walls. Regency furniture was lighter, and could be arranged anywhere in a room. A great variety of furniture was made and for every possible requirement (flat or roll-top desks, screens, writing tables, book rests, work tables, dressing tables, tables for playing backgammon, chests of drawers, occasional tables, chiffoniers, cabinets; every kind of chair—stools, tall chairs, cabriolet armchairs, study armchairs, *marquises* and *bergères* (easy chairs), "gondola" armchairs, winged armchairs, "duchess" sofas and settees, "duchess" four-posters, and beds of every kind). All these were made with every refinement of craftsmanship and materials (precious woods, lacquers, polishes), the most luxurious being finished in gilt. Tapestries were still produced; but the slavish imitation of painting which had been enforced by J.-B. Oudry, who became director of the Beauvais factory in 1726, led to a rapid decline in this minor art form.

467. Versailles. Galerie des Glaces.
By Le Brun and Jules Hardouin-Mansart. 1679–1684.

468. Dutch wardrobe. 18th century. *Amsterdam, Rijksmuseum.*

The Renaissance style of architectural furniture persisted all over Europe in the seventeenth century, except in France where a new direction was taken under Louis XIV. Only in the eighteenth century did Europe abandon Renaissance in preference to the French styles, interpreting them with a baroque emphasis that resulted—particularly in Venice—in overdecorated furniture. However, Spain, Portugal and Holland kept up their own architectural style until about 1730 (pl. 468). Thanks to its use of jacaranda wood from Brazil, Portugal made furniture of an extraordinary sculptural density. England, in the same period, produced some original developments in its use of mahogany, introduced in 1725. The evolution of English furniture passed from the sinuous forms—some of Chinese origin—of the Chippendale style (so called after the family, of which the most outstanding member, Thomas, published a famous catalogue of models in 1754), to the severe, infinitely light and graceful designs of the Adam period. These two styles had a profound effect on Portugal, which was closely associated with England by the commercial treaty of 1701.

French jewelry became the most famous in the whole of Europe. Hardly any examples are left in France, and the Lisbon Museum has the only complete set of jewelry that has survived from the eighteenth century: it was commissioned in France by Dom José of Portugal. The set of jewelry made for Catherine II of Russia, carefully preserved over a long period, was broken up twenty years ago.

Ceramics owed its enormous development to its increasing use for everyday purposes. The Italian potteries declined in the seventeenth century, but from that time the Delft potteries in Holland flooded Europe with china in blue monochrome and in other colors, many of which are imitations of Chinese porcelain (pl. 474). There was a great output of French porcelain from the various provincial potteries (Rouen, Nevers, Moustiers, Marseilles, Strasbourg). The finest ceramics in England were those of Josiah Wedgwood, who at the Etruria factory set up in Staffordshire in 1768 made pieces in the neo-classical style and even close imitations of the Greek. It was in Saxony in 1709 that it was first discovered how to make hard-paste porcelain in the Chinese manner by using kaolin. The Meissen factory, which was at once set up by the Elector Frederick Augustus I, turned out luxurious tableware and ornamental pieces in the rococo style. Several other factories were founded in Germany, where the new process was exploited. France was able to produce hard porcelain only after 1769, when kaolin was discovered at Saint-Yrieix (Limousin). The Sèvres pottery dates from 1753. Portugal used ceramics for mural decoration: at first it was in polychrome, but in the eighteenth century was confined to blue, as a result of which the tiles became known as *azulejos*.

The styles of the decorative arts in France under the Ancien Régime have been divided according to the various reigns from Louis

469. Cabriolet armchair. Louis XV period.
Paris, Musée des Arts Décoratifs.

470. Venetian armchair. 18th century. By Andrea Brustolon. *Venice, Accademia.*

471. Robert Adam. "Etruscan" decoration. Osterley Park. 1775–1777.

472. Salon. Louis XV period. Hôtel de Soubise, Paris.

XIII to the Revolution, but such a rough-and-ready classification is deceptive. The Regency style goes back to 1700, while the Louis XVI style dates from about 1755, long before the death of Louis XV in 1774. The sober and gloomy Louis XIII furniture reflects the architectural outlook of the sixteenth century. Louis XIV furniture was relieved by a baroque decoration set off with gilding, but never lost its stiff design. The Regency style, which was no more than the second phase of the Louis XIV style, adopted a shell-shaped ornamentation called *rocaille*, and curved outlines. Sinuosity of line and the use of asymmetrical *rocaille* both became more pronounced in the so-called Louis XV style. It produced a chair, the *cabriolet* armchair, which was admirably suited for all the psychological and material uses required of a chair, and it is a masterpiece of refinement and civilization (pl. 469). The period as a whole, of which the tone was set by Madame de Pompadour, was the moment when French decoration most lent itself to the flowing gracefulness of the *rocaille*, a taste strengthened by Chinese influence, which was also responsible for the fashion for lacquered and highly polished furniture.

The reaction against the *rocaille* style began to be felt in 1755, when the carver Cochin, who had been to Italy in 1749, published his *Plea to Jewel Cutters and Wood Carvers* (*Supplication aux orfèvres ciseleurs et sculpteurs sur bois*) in which he exhorted them to give up their "excess of twisted, extravagant patterns" and to return to the

473. Salon. Louis XVI period. Hotel Necker, Geneva.

straight line. The Marquis de Marigny, who was the head of the Beaux-Arts from 1751 to 1773, helped Cochin's ideas to prevail. Furniture, like interior decoration, returned to the straight line, sometimes at the expense of functional logic. Interiors began to take fluted pilasters and pediments from external architecture, and arabesque decorations in imitation of those unearthed at Herculaneum and Pompeii became all the fashion. The return to the straight line, for all that, did not mean a return to simplicity: under Louis XVI both decorations and furniture remained fairly ornamental, and it was the so-called Directoire style, after the Ancien Régime, which brought with it a crisis of puritanism.

474. Delft ware with Chinese patterns.
Paris, Musée des Arts Décoratifs.

475. Leo von Klenze. The Propylaea, Munich. 1848–1860.

CHAPTER X

THE NINETEENTH CENTURY CRISIS

INTENT on the scientific mastery of the forces of nature, the modern world has seen a slackening of that impressive creative tension which, from its early beginnings, had led Western civilization to seek a representation of the world in works of art. However, acting as heir to a Europe which found itself suddenly without a single major talent, France still managed to rear a school of painting which in the course of the century was to produce great masters worthy of those of the past. These men, whom we now grant a foremost place in history, and who for the most part were despised by their contemporaries, help us to forget the horde of mediocrities who were showered with official honors and awards during their short-lived reputation, and in whom an upstart, self-satisfied society found a comforting reflection of its own worthlessness. A handful of geniuses gave our common heritage of art many a significant utterance that can be placed beside the great literary works of the century; but the mediocrities were none the less the true expression of their age. The now forgotten architects, sculptors, painters and decorative artists showed general tendencies which together made a "style," and that style was international. Delacroix, Courbet, Manet, Gauguin had no parallel in the rest of Europe. But Paul Delaroche of Paris, Karl von Piloty of Munich, Louis Galliat of Brussels were "brother geniuses." A common conception of history is to be found in the French Horace Vernet, the German Alfred Rethel, or Nicaise de

366

Keyser of Antwerp, all of whom painted battle scenes. It was such artists as these, bolstered up by society, who together formed a school cutting across all national frontiers: Vernet had his imitators in Belgium, while the Lyons school of religious decorators was inspired by the German "Nazarenes."

This international unity had its source in a common point of departure, the neo-classicism which resulted between 1750 and 1800 from the converging efforts of all the schools in Europe. Western civilization, whenever it passes through a crisis, always looks for salvation toward its mother civilization; that is to say, classical antiquity. That is what happened in the Carolingian period, when the Emperor's initiative sought to put an end to the anarchy of the barbarians; it occurred again in the Quattrocento, when Italy had prepared the way for a new culture which she was about to offer the world in place of the declining Gothic. But Bramante's and Raphael's classicism, which emerged from that effort, was at once thwarted by the unexpected triumph of the baroque aesthetic. This time, it was France and England that were to cling to classicism. In about 1750, the English, French, Germans and Italians, in their wish to avoid the blind alley into which rococo was leading, saw no choice but to appeal to that classical art which is ever the stand-by of the Western aesthetic. The discovery of Etruscan, Campanian and Greek sites revealed far purer models than were to be found in Roman art. England, encouraged by its own Palladian tastes, gave Europe the lead in its intuitional desire for an Attic architecture. The representational arts began to seek their principles in ancient statuary and painting. If it is true that David was anticipated by a few English academicians, he gave these aspirations a dignity of form which at once caught the imagination of the whole of Europe. David, who swept away all the theatrical trappings in which Antiquity had been smothered for two hundred years, replacing them by the genuine costumes and settings of Greece and Rome, holds a place not unlike that of Mantegna, who threw aside the medieval coats of mail used for representing Roman emperors and gave them the *laurica* and the *paludamentum*. David gave a final form to the aesthetic which was to rule over Europe and the official French school throughout the century: the superiority of line and volume over color, and of thought over sensation; the picture, whose arrangement was dictated by intellectual data, by subject, was thought of as a painted bas-relief,

476. Louis David. The Oath of the Horatii. 1784. *Paris, Louvre.*

477. Delacroix. The Death of Sardanapalus. Salon of 1827. *Paris, Louvre.*

THE FOUR PERIODS

while cold tones without any modulation of color scale were used to stress the statuesque effect. Whereas David's art tended to give the illusion of volume, that of his pupil Ingres, inspired by the Grecian vase, flattened its shapes to suggest all the gracefulness of the arabesque. Meanwhile, at the very time that Ingres was creating his linear style, a few German painters in Rome in 1810 grouped themselves together under the name of Nazarenes, in the San Isidoro monastery. They were

REALISM

478. Courbet. The Artist's
Studio. Detail. Salon of 1855.
Paris, Louvre.

IMPRESSIONISM

479. Manet. Le Dejeuner sur
l'Herbe. Salon des Refusés,
1863. *Paris, Louvre.*

OF MODERN PAINTING

after a fresh aesthetic formula which they sought not in the Ancients, but in the early Renaissance. Deceived by the apparent smoothness of Perugino's and Raphael's early work, they were led by mystical enthusiasm to adopt the form and composition of these masters, so as to create —no doubt without realizing it—a new academicism inspired by the platitudes of fresco painting. This movement had repercussions all over Europe: signs of it can still be seen in the Paris churches. Thirty years later a group of English painters renewed this aesthetic, which they called "Pre-Raphaelitism" and injected it with a certain realism.

The neo-classical aesthetic, which resulted from the enthusiasm stirred up by the rediscovery of Greek art, together with the intention of counteracting rococo, unfortunately found itself quite out of key with the general evolution of thought and sensibility which was urging the West to discover a new form of human consciousness in the shape of *Romanticism*. Temperamentally uneasy, the artists of the period found themselves being offered sculpture as their model; while they felt inclined to convey the passions through art, they were offered an idealistic aesthetic; at a moment when they were interested in the Middle Ages, they were asked to shape everything according to classical patterns. A great confusion came out of all these clashes. The first generation of Romantic artists, whom we might call the Pre-Romantics, were armed with a brand-new neo-classical technique and wore themselves out in their efforts to make statues gesticulate or dream: such was William Blake (1757–1827), who was haunted by Dante, Milton and Michelangelo, and his friend the Anglo-Swiss painter Henry Fuseli (1741–1828), whose inspiration was related to Goya's but who was racked in the strait-jacket of neo-classicism from which Goya alone of that generation was able to break loose, creating a romantic technique which, incidentally, had no future. In France, Prud'hon (1758–1823) got round the difficulty by swamping his statues in shade, while Girodet (1767–1824) tried to blend the inspiration of Ossian and Chateaubriand with David's heroic style. In Germany Philipp Otto Runge (1777–1810) tightened his line and modeling and forced his color in his attempts to wring a human note from the frozen style.

A technique at all suitable for the Romantic outlook could only be found by turning to the Venetian school, which had used color for its emotional values; or more especially to Rubens, a painter who was despised by the academies. It was in David's very studio that a man of genius, Gros, rediscovered that forgotten language, which he used side by side with the Davidian principles of bas-relief composition. Two artists who came to the fore in 1820, Géricault and Delacroix, added the English element to the example given by Gros. Géricault still saw his painting with a sculptor's eye, but Delacroix rediscovered the principles of symphonic and spatial painting common to Tintoretto, Veronese and Rubens. This was the true Romantic plastic code, though,

THE PRE-ROMANTICS

480. Goya. "Sleeping Reason gives birth to monsters."
Engraving from the Caprices. 1799.
481. William Blake. The Gate of Hell. Watercolor. *London, Tate Gallery.*

apart from a few minor artists who imitated Delacroix without understanding him, it found no serious following. The development of Romanticism was thwarted at the outset, not by any doctrinal dictatorship, but by the banalities of Realism. Realism pandered to the lazy imagination of the middle class, by making art a means of reproducing the material world, which was all they cared about. Between 1830 and 1850 it contaminated both Neo-Classicism and Romanticism to produce in architecture, painting and all the ornamental crafts a sort of utilitarian art which the French called "Louis-Philippe" and the Germans "Biedermeier"—an art for shopkeepers. Thanks to this impure aesthetic born of the uneasy alliance between Neo-Classicism and Realism, Romantic subjects found favor with the public. This was the art turned out in France by Paul Delaroche, Louis Boulanger, Horace Vernet, Ary Scheffer; in Germany by all the Düsseldorf school; in Belgium by L. Galliat, G. Wappers, N. de Keyser; while in Brussels, Antoine Wiertz, who thought he was a new Michelangelo, merely proved his incapacity for creating a technique at all equal to his pretensions. Meissonier in France and Henri de Brakelaer in Belgium amused the bourgeoisie with a lifelikeness which, when applied to the past, revived genre painting.

371

This paradoxical state of things explains why in France, the sole country where artists had enough genius to rise above the prevailing mediocrity, creative ability could only make itself felt by revolutionary tactics. The repeated failures of the official humbugs of art merely strengthened their resistance, so that Impressionism found it even harder to achieve recognition than Romanticism and Realism had.

Four major movements show the continuity of French genius in the course of the nineteenth century: Neo-Classicism, Romanticism, Realism (which might better be called Naturalism) and Impressionism. Although they sprang from a series of reactions the one against the other, yet seen historically they amount to a continuous evolution, leading from fiction to nature, from the intellectual construction to the record of sensations, from an ideal beauty to the observed fact. Landscape, which invaded painting more and more to the point of becoming its chief end, had not such serious obstacles to face as subject painting. Fortunately, Antiquity could offer no ready-made models for landscape painters to imitate, though to make up for it they were urged to copy Poussin. But while reducing nature to a dictionary of forms, Neo-Poussinism did not forbid its direct study, and this outlet enabled Corot to develop from the neo-classical stem. The landscape painters, freed from the tyranny of bas-relief, were able to find a technique suitable for Romantic expression while taking lessons in craftsmanship from the Dutch school. This line was pursued independently by two contemporaries, the Englishman John Crome (b. 1768) and the Frenchman Georges Michel (b. 1763). In France the 1830 or Barbizon school, following this Neo-Dutch tradition, conveyed the infiniteness of nature in the loneliness of forests, the organic strength of trees, the solidity of the land. The intensive use of water color enabled the English school to discover means of translating light and atmospheric values: John Constable enriched the palette, while Turner wavered between a visionary art in the Romantic manner, and the pure expression of optical sensations—the path Impressionism was to follow in France.

Impressionism inherited all the technical researches of the century, and found in *peinture claire* (painting the dark tones *after* the light and half-tones) the technique that had been so desperately sought after: no more line, no more volume, nothing but the direct message of pure color. Impressionism was a belated victory of painting over bas-relief. Created by Manet and Claude Monet, and enthusiastically taken up by

COLOR PLATES

8. JACQUES LOUIS DAVID. The Death of Socrates. 1787.
The Metropolitan Museum of Art, New York. Wolfe Fund, 1931.

9. RAEBURN. The Drummond Children.
The Metropolitan Museum of Art, New York.
Bequest of Mary Stillman Harkness, 1950.

10. MONET. Vétheuil. 1880.
The Metropolitan Museum of Art, New York.
Bequest of William Church Osborn, 1951.

11. CÉZANNE. Still Life with Apples. 1890–1900.
The Museum of Modern Art, New York.
Lillie P. Bliss Collection.

12. WINSLOW HOMER. Palm Tree, Nassau.
The Metropolitan Museum of Art, New York. Lazarus Fund, 1910.

13. CHARLES BURCHFIELD. Old House by Creek. 1932–1938.
Collection of the Whitney Museum of American Art, New York.

14. PICASSO. Three Musicians. 1921.
The Museum of Modern Art, New York. Mrs. Simon Guggenheim Fund.

many artists who form a genuine group, a school, their technique was to serve the purpose of the different aesthetics which emerged toward the end of the century. While Puvis de Chavannes tried to revive classicism by giving it a symbolic value, the nineteenth century closed in an apotheosis of light and color, blessed·with that profusion of talents which is always a sure sign of the triumph of a genuine mode of expression.

THE ARTS IN FRANCE
ARCHITECTURE AND SCULPTURE

The nineteenth century discovered no form of architecture to call its own. Until 1850 France followed the austere neo-classical manner developed at the end of the eighteenth century by Brongniart, Chalgrin and Ledoux. Percier and Fontaine created the Empire style, which was a majestic version of the Louis XVI style, but the latter showed itself mainly in the decorative and furnishing arts. The shortness of Napoleon's reign and the protracted wars prevented the great schemes that were drawn up for Paris from being completed. All that was carried out were: the Arc de Triomphe de Carrousel, the Bourse, the Colonne Vendôme. The rue de Rivoli, the Madeleine (a copy of the Corinthian temple, at first intended as a "Temple of Glory"), and the Arc de Triomphe de l'Etoile were only finished under the Restoration and the July Monarchy. All these works are marked by a taste for the colossal. During the Restoration and Louis-Philippe's reign, the neo-classical style underlined its native soberness to the point of poverty. Napoleon III gave up Neo-Greek austerity in favor of a pompous style more or less inspired by Versailles, corresponding with the lavish tastes of the Second Empire bourgeoisie. Paris was replanned by Baron Haussmann, who thrust great thoroughfares through the old city and set up public buildings which are unfortunately in the worst of taste. The main undertakings under Napoleon III were the completion of the Louvre, entrusted to Visconti and Lefuel, and the Opéra (1860–1875) by Charles Garnier (1825–1898), a theater glittering with paint, marble and gilt (pl. 482). Toward 1890 the taste for baroque which was making itself felt under all this exaggeration was frankly admitted in the Art Nouveau, a strange but short-lived revival of the "vegetable" ornamentation of Flamboyant Gothic. Under the influence of Viollet-le-Duc

482. Charles Garnier. The Grand Staircase. Paris Opera House. 1860–1875.

(1814–1879), Gothic architecture came into fashion again for church building under the Second Empire. The study of the principles of architecture encouraged the fashion for steel construction, not only in civil engineering but in architecture.

Sculpture suffered throughout the century from its submission to antiquity. The Empire and Restoration sculptors Bosio, Lemot, Cortot were competent decorators. François Rude (1784–1855), whose master-

483. François Rude. The Volunteers of 1792. ("The Marseillaise"). Bas-relief on the Arc de Triomphe, Paris. 1832–1834.

piece was the *Departure of the Volunteers of 1792* on the Arc de Triomphe, Place de l'Etoile, found a heroic and monumental style, corresponding in sculpture to what Gros did for painting, but he did not found a school (pl. 483). David d'Angers (1788–1856) was a portrait sculptor, romantic in intention but not in form. It was by abandoning academic models and studying animals at first hand that Barye (1796–1875) found a fresh vigor yet without breaking the laws of classical modeling. However, it was Carpeaux (1827–1875), preceded by the experiments in modeling made by the painter-lithographer Daumier (1808–1879), who freed sculpture from the static convention and sought effects of fluidity, movement and life directly observed from nature (pl. 484). The century at last found its romantic expressionism in the neo-baroque of Auguste Rodin (1840–1917), whose feverish art, tormented by grandiose conceptions, has left works of rhetoric which are not suitable for monumental expression (pl. 485). Right through the century a host of sculptors, who carried out hundreds of public monuments, followed the neo-classical aesthetic with as little hesitation as they had ability. The least mediocre of them was perhaps Pradier (1790–1852).

484. Jean-Baptiste Carpeaux. Bust of Mlle. Fiocre. Plaster.
Paris, Louvre.

485. Rodin. The Burghers of Calais.
Detail. Plaster. *Paris, Rodin Museum.*

PAINTING

Painting alone escaped the general bankruptcy, partly because it lends itself to individual expression, whereas architecture and sculpture are fundamentally public, social arts. The neo-classical school represented by Ingres, David and their dull but overplentiful following still thought of painting as being subordinate to its decorative function. It submitted all the elements of the picture to a hierarchy dictated by the intellect and produced a still whose coldness of form allowed no freedom of interpretation. The Romantics freed painting from these shackles: and in the hands of a few artists down the century, painting was entrusted with all the secrets of the human heart and became a means of exploring the mysteries of nature.

A convert to Bonapartism, the revolutionary and regicide Louis David (1748–1825) sought in contemporary events (the *Crowning of Napoleon*, 1807, Louvre; the *Distribution of Eagles*, 1810, Versailles) subjects well adapted to the heroic style, based on ancient statuary, which he perfected with the *Oath of the Horatii* (1784, pl. 476) and the *Rape of the Sabines* (1799). His capacity for objectiveness, his noble conception of the human form, make him one of the greatest portraitists of the French school (pl. 486). He developed a sober and sound craftsmanship, painting in pure colors in well-blended *demi-pâtes* which leave no trace of the brush stroke, yet without freezing his colors like his pupils or imitators such as Vincent, Régnault, Girodet, Gérard,

486. Louis David. Portrait of Mme. Sériziat. Salon of 1795. *Paris, Louvre.*

487. Ingres. Recumbent Odalisque. Salon of 1819. *Paris, Louvre.*

Guérin. Pierre-Paul Prud'hon (1758–1823) had a contrast of lights and shades which helped him to link neo-classicism with the elegiac romantic manner of the eighteenth century. In the second quarter of the century the hopes of the *beau idéal* doctrine were pinned on Jean-Dominique Ingres (1780–1867), a pupil of David, who, however, spent a period in Italy from 1806 to 1824 where the influence of Raphael and Greek vases overcame his leaning toward Greek statuary, so that he came to prefer the arabesque to volume. Lacking David's sense of the heroic, Ingres had a very mediocre imagination, so his large compositions are cold and meaningless (*Vow of Louis XIII*, 1824, Montauban; *Apotheosis of Homer*, 1827, Louvre; *Martyrdom of St. Symphorian*, 1834, Autun). With a longing for harmony that was instinctive rather than intellectual, he achieved it empirically by making a laborious selection of the features provided by his model. His best works are his smaller and more limited canvases—his portraits, his nudes (pl. 487) and his admirable drawings (pl. 488). Ingres, who was Director of the French Academy in Rome from 1834 to 1841, had a sterilizing influence on official art. He was responsible for a second-rate line of decorative painters, of whom the most representative was Hippolyte Flandrin (1809–1864) of Lyons. However, officialdom and public taste also favored those painters who sought to hide their meager imagination in an uninspired realism, such as Horace Vernet (1789–1863), who filled the Versailles museum with acres of battle scenes, or the genre painter

377

488. Ingres. Portrait of M. Lesueur, architect.
Drawing. Detail. *Bayonne, Bonnat Museum.*

489. Corot. Marissel Church. Salon of 1867. *Paris, Louvre.*

Meissonier (1815–1890). Paul Delaroche (1797–1856) tried to give classical atmosphere to his historical realism. Thomas Couture (1815–1879) reacted against this decadence by taking some of his stylistic principles from the Bologna school and Veronese, and it was he who set the tone for the Second Empire decorators.

The classical idea of nature as something to be arranged and moralized about like a theatrical setting was maintained till about 1850 by a series of official painters (Bertin, Bidault, for instance). Jean-Baptiste-Camille Corot (1796–1874) followed the system of composing landscapes in the studio, all his life; but he was the only one of the classical school to make anything worthwhile of his outdoor studies. In his wanderings across Italy and France, he painted the abiding essence of the land civilized by man's presence, which can be felt in the slightest idiosyncrasy, every tree or path having a human rather than a haphazard, natural significance. His poetic sensitiveness is seen in the increasing emphasis given to the figures in his landscapes, which became pretexts for reverie and feeling (pl. 489).

The origin of Romantic painting is to be found in Jean-Antoine Gros (1771–1835), a pupil of David, who without in the least toning down their violence, painted battle scenes which David's aesthetic would have condemned according to the strict tenets of the *beau idéal*

490. Gros. The Plague at Jaffa.
Salon of 1804. Detail.
Paris, Louvre.

(*The Plague at Jaffa*, 1804, Louvre, pl. 490; *Battle of Aboukir*, 1805, Versailles; *Battle of Eylau*, 1810, Louvre). Influenced by the bas-relief composition of David, he found a more eloquent use of color in Rubens and the Venetians. The struggle between his Romantic aspirations and the doctrinal tyranny of his school caused Gros such anguish that he ended by committing suicide. Théodore Géricault (1791–1824) belongs to the Empire school by his cult of energy, but he introduced English influence into France. Even more than Gros, whom he so much admired, he was obsessed by suffering and death (*The Raft of the Medusa*, 1819, Louvre). His early death robbed the school of a great painter's maturity (pl. 491).

Eugène Delacroix (1798–1863), a portraitist who excelled equally in historical pieces, still lifes, landscapes and animal painting, aspired to the ranks of those universal geniuses who made painting an encyclopedia of man and nature. He received a classical training from Guérin;

491. Géricault. Horse Being
Halted by Slaves. 1817. *Rouen,
Museum.*

492. Delacroix. Study for "Liberty Guiding the People."
Drawing. *Paris, Louvre.*

but it was in Rubens, the Venetians and Constable that he sought the
principles of expression through all the resources of color, based on the
vibration of shadows. A trip to Morocco gave him a glimpse of Oriental life in 1832. In his youthful works the rotating composition that
runs right across the canvas (pl. 492) follows no laws but those of life
itself, and his dramatic intensity was never afraid of extravagance (the
Massacres of Scio, 1824, Louvre; *Death of Sardanapalus*, 1827, Louvre,
pl. 477). However, in his maturity he tended to integrate Romantic
expressionism into the formal system of the classicists (*Trajan Giving
Judgment*, 1840, Rouen; *Fall of Constantinople*, 1841, Louvre). These
tendencies made him take themes from antiquity for his major decorations in the Senate Library and the Chambre des Députés (1838–1847),
and the Louvre. The Chapelle des Sts.-Anges which he painted in
St.-Sulpice, Paris, between 1853 and 1861 was his artistic and philosophical testament. Théodore Chassériau (1819–1856) tried to reconcile
Ingres' manner with Romanticism.

A fresh eagerness for feeling and knowledge brought man into
contact with a many-sided universe whose infinite variety and depth
had been hidden under an outdated humanism. Georges Michel (1763–
1843) sought some echo of this in the open fields in the northern suburbs
of Paris. It was in the Fontainebleau forest, in the neighborhood of the
little village of Barbizon, that the Romantic landscape painters tried to

493. Rousseau. Village of Becquigny. Salon of 1864.
New York, Frick Collection.

follow the technical example of the Dutch and English. Théodore
Rousseau (1812–1867, pl. 493), Jules Dupré (1811–1889), Narcisse
Diaz (1807–1876) reached closer to the mystery of nature. But apart
from Rousseau, whose objective vision tried to pass beyond appearance
into the inner meaning of things, they all saw nature as something passionate, stormy, uneasy and dramatic like their own souls.

Under the Ancien Régime art was the handmaid of a king or aristocracy, but the nineteenth century restored to it something of the
moral urgency of expression that it had in the Middle Ages. Millet,
Daumier, Courbet, indeed all those who toward 1848 gloried in the title
of Realists, were always chiefly attracted by the human drama, and in
their search for man they explored the masses, the common people in
whom human nature has a timeless, enduring quality. Jean-François
Millet (1814–1875) exalted the dignity of rustic toil, the source of
human life, with a religious and almost ritualistic seriousness that recalls
the treatment of the Months in medieval cathedrals. Honoré Daumier
(1808–1879) recorded with profound compassion the abject poverty
of the new industrial masses in the towns. Like Courbet he was an
ardent socialist and in his lithographs gave a scathing condemnation of
middle-class selfishness. Daumier's impetuous painting, with its violent
impasto, is perhaps the most successfully "romantic" of the century
(pl. 494). Gustave Courbet (1819–1877) gave the bourgeois of his time

494. Daumier. Don Quixote. *Munich, Neue Pinakothek.*

the scandalous picture of a tough, primitive humanity, close to the soil and to nature, and in his paintings he exalted the mud and even the muck of farm and field. Compared with Corot, who represents the pure French tradition for which painting is either an act of mind, or a revelation of the heart, Courbet was a painter of raw sensation and represents a crisis, a turning point for the French school. Throwing away both the patient craftsmanship of the classicists and the ingenious, cunning resources of color discovered by Delacroix, he founded an entirely instinctive manner of painting that consisted of laying one impasto on another by means of the palette knife (pl. 478).

Rejecting fiction and everything they could not see with their own eyes in everyday life, the Realists of 1848 none the less saved something of Romanticism—that is to say, the heroic tone, the tendency to exalt the greatness and anguish of the human situation. Round about 1860 we can see how a transition was made from this romantic and plebeian naturalism to an analytical realism, the refined, urban realism of Manet and the Impressionists.

It was at the Salon des Refusés, 1863, that the painters who founded the Impressionist school first became aware of their common aims. They grouped themselves round Edouard Manet (1833–1883), who caused a scandal in this salon with his *Déjeuner sur l'Herbe*, which shows some art students picnicking with a naked model (pl. 479). Manet showed the way by freeing painting from all irrelevant rational and literary elements; he saw things entirely as pictorial values. After a "black" period, so called because it was inspired by Spanish painting, which lasted until 1870, he deliberately concentrated on scenes from the everyday life of his own time and took to *peinture claire*, putting in darker tones last. Except for Manet, the group of innovators, who were systematically barred from the official Salons, formed themselves into a society for showing their own works. At the first show, which caused an enormous scandal in 1874, a journalist dubbed these artists "Impressionists" after the title of one of Monet's canvases, the *Impression, Soleil Levant* (Musée Marmottan, Paris). Monet (1840–1926, pl. 495) proved to be the real leader of the Impressionist revolution which had been implied also in the work of Boudin, a native of Normandy (1824–1898), and the Dutchman Jongkind (1819–1891), who had settled in France. Monet ended by seeing the world as no more than an interplay of appearances in perpetual movement, and delighted in analyzing the infinite variations of light on the same view (*Argenteuil*, 1872–1875; *Débâcles des Glaces*, 1879–1880; the *Cathedrals*, 1893; *Views of London*, 1902; *Nymphéas* [Water Lilies], 1899–1926). Monet subjected all that usually serves to define shapes—such as contour, modeling, shadow—to an intense light, so that nothing remains on the canvas but patches of

495. Monet. The Houses of Parliament, London. *Private Collection.*

color. Having observed that every tone in nature contains several other colors, and is again modified by the reflection of surrounding tones as well as by the quality of the light that falls on it, Monet broke up the whole tone scale by building up his canvas in touches of pure color. The Englishman Alfred Sisley (1839–1899) was less remote from the traditional vision, in his paintings of skies and rivers of the Ile-de-France region (pl. 496). Camille Pissarro (1830–1903) gave Impressionism the atmosphere of the French village (pl. 497); Berthe Morisot (1841–1895) tried to render the human figure in the *plein-airiste* manner, like her brother-in-law Manet. After his experiments in the visual riots of color of the Impressionist school (*Moulin de la Galette*, 1876, Louvre; *Le Déjeuner des Canotiers*, 1881, Phillips Collection in Washington, pl. 498), Pierre-Auguste Renoir (1841–1919) tried to pass beyond it. After his Impressionist phase he imposed a stricter discipline on himself, in order to regain a sense of form and volume, going so far as to seek his inspiration in Ingres and even a bas-relief by Girardon (*Les Grandes Baigneuses*, 1885, Tyson Collection in Philadelphia). After making sure of his grasp of all the technical resources he needed, he then began to portray mankind in a Golden Age natural setting, reinvigorated by a primitive nakedness which he thought could help man to rediscover a pagan innocence (*Judgment of Paris*,

496. Sisley. The Drinking Trough at Marly in the Snow. 1875.
Paris, Private Collection.

497. Pissarro. A Corner of the Hermitage at Pontoise. 1874. *Winterthur, Switzerland, Oskar Reinhart Foundation.*

498. Renoir. Le Déjeuner des Canotiers. 1881. *Washington, D.C., Phillips Collection.*

1908, Stang Collection, Oslo). While all the nineteenth century artists painted opaquely, he was almost the only one besides Delacroix, one of his masters, to use color in fluid and transparent glazes, which give his painting a sensual depth that had been forgotten since Rubens.

The sunshine of Impressionism drove out the gloomy dreams of the Romantics, and after Courbet's dramatic vision a dazzling sensation of the joy of existence invaded painting. However, Edgar Degas (1834–1917) and Henri de Toulouse-Lautrec (1864–1901) still retained all the disillusion of Romanticism, if not its inspiring energy. Gripped

385

499. Degas. The Absinthe Drinkers. About 1876–1877. *Paris, Louvre.*

by a pitiless lucidity, they set out to destroy deep-seated human illusions, and with all Ingres' acuteness of line they analyzed the manners and vices of their contemporaries with a hard objectivity (pls. 499 and 500).

The French mind, which dislikes excess of any kind, could not remain satisfied for long with the buoyant unrestraint of the Impressionists, or their faith in fleeting aspects of things. Several artists tried to inflict an intellectual order on art again, a trend which between 1884

500. Toulouse-Lautrec. Fernando's Circus. 1888. *Chicago, Art Institute.*

and 1890 crystallized into a deliberate reaction. Paul Cézanne (1839–1906), from Aix-en-Provence, aimed at a classical poise without giving up direct observation: he called this "doing as Poussin did, but after nature." After a first "black" phase of aggressive Romanticism, ending in 1872, he tried Impressionism at Auvers-sur-Oise, but gave it up in about 1880. He now wanted to rediscover some classical sense of form, while desiring to convey volume and space by means of color alone. He carried out this purpose slowly in a series of still lifes, then in landscape, and finally in composition (pl. 502); his finest landscapes were inspired by the view of Ste.-Victoire, a mountain that dominates the Aix-en-Provence countryside (pl. 501). Georges Seurat (1859–1891), the

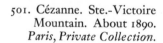

501. Cézanne. Ste.-Victoire Mountain. About 1890. *Paris, Private Collection.*

502. Cézanne. The Card Players. 1890–1892. *Merion, Pennsylvania, Barnes Foundation.*

503. Seurat. Sunday Afternoon on the Island of La Grande Jatte.
Salon des Indépendants, 1886. *Chicago, Art Institute,*
Helen Birch Bartlett Collection.

founder of Neo-Impressionism, wanted to give a systematic, scientific basis, founded on the physicists' theories of light, to the breakdown of the tone scale which Monet had practiced by pure instinct (pl. 503). Seurat invented a methodical process for his painting which has been called "divisionism" or pointillism. This new aesthetic appealed to several artists, including Signac and for a short time Pissarro, after it appeared in 1886. Paul Gauguin (1848–1903) reacted mainly against the naturalistic element in Impressionism. Rejecting visual "lifelikeness," he refused to see painting as representation, but rather as the expression of some inner vision. After some long periods spent at Pont-Aven in Brittany, where he founded a school of painters (1886–1890), he went off to Tahiti in 1890 in search of exotic surroundings more in keeping with his dreams. His art runs parallel with the literary Symbolist movement (pl. 504). The Symbolists also regarded Odilon Redon (1824–1916) as a kindred spirit, for like them he was a painter of dreams, as well as the academic Puvis de Chavannes (1824–1898), a monumental mural painter whose work is the last manifestation of the *beau idéal,* which in his hands became an allegorical interpretation of the world of the psyche. On the other hand, it was in favor of a fervent Expres-

504. Gauguin. "Nafea foa ipoipo" (When will you be married?).
1892. *Basel, Kunstmuseum.*
505. Van Gogh. The Road with Cypresses. May, 1890.
The Hague, Kröller-Müller Museum.

sionism that the Dutch painter Vincent Van Gogh (1853–1890) raised his pathetic protest against Impressionism, though he used their pure-color technique (pl. 505).

It is with these artists, in revolt against the naturalism which had been the driving force in painting since the Romantics, that the nineteenth century ended, an extraordinary century which gave us at least twenty painters of genius, and showed a creative fertility unrivaled since the Italian Renaissance.

WESTERN ART OUTSIDE FRANCE

ARCHITECTURE AND SCULPTURE

The majority of nineteenth century artists, except in France, have a following in their own countries, where they expressed something of the national temperament, but very few have a world-wide appeal or reputation.

All over Europe architecture showed the same developments as in France: it was neo-classical until about 1850, after which it was unable to produce any new form and became "classic," that is to say a hotchpotch of all the styles ever known in the West. The dignified Empire style did not produce its finest example in France, but at St. Petersburg, where Alexander I seems to have set himself the task of fulfilling Napoleon's thwarted dreams. He replanned the city and gave it some imposing monuments worthy of the great river Neva. Inspired by French sources, this style developed from the ideas of Ledoux, Percier and Fontaine and was partly executed by French architects: Thomas de Thomon, who designed the Stock Exchange (1805–1816); Ricard de Montferrand, who based St. Isaac's Cathedral (1817) on Soufflot's Panthéon (Paris), and the Alexandrian Column (1829) on the Colonne Vendôme; the Russian Zakharoff built the Admiralty (1806–1810, pl. 506), and Voronikhine the cathedral of the Virgin of Kazan (1801–1811) which was inspired by St. Peter's (Rome) and its peristyle. The Italian Rossi continued this public style under Nicholas I but with far less purity. Germany fell into a tendency to archaeological pastiche, at first confined to Neo-Hellenism but later imitating Renaissance and Gothic. The two main centers of architecture were Munich and Berlin. In Munich Leo von Klenze (1784–1864) built an imitation of the Propylaea (pl. 475) and built the first museums that were rationally planned (Glyptothek, 1816; Alte Pinakothek); he also set up a replica of the Parthenon in Regensburg (1830), Germanizing it by a dedication to the gods of Valhalla. Under Ludwig I, Munich be-

506. Adrian Zakharoff. Gateway of the Admiralty, Leningrad.
1806–1810. *After I. Grabar, L'Art en Russie.*

507. The Houses of Parliament, London, rebuilt after the fire of 1834.
by Charles Barry and A. W. N. Pugin.

came a sort of architectural museum full of imitations of famous European monuments. In Prussia, Karl Friedrich Schinkel (1781–1841) imitated Soufflot's Panthéon at Potsdam (1830) and built the Guard House in Berlin (1816) in Greek Doric, and the Old Museum (1824) in Ionic; but he also set the fashion for the Gothic revival which was to affect churches and castles. At the end of the century Germany witnessed a curious reappearance of native rococo, which was to have repercussions in France (so-called *Munich style* of the Petit Palais and the Grand Palais, in Paris, built for the Paris Exhibition, 1900). England, which was also at first inclined toward Neo-Greek, found a national form in its revival of the native Gothic style, the laws of which A. W. N. Pugin (1812–1852) was carefully investigating. After the fire in 1834, the Palace of Westminster was rebuilt by Pugin and Charles Barry on an imposing scale and in a Perpendicular Gothic style of striking dignity (pl. 507). At the end of the century, in Barcelona, Antonio Gaudí planned one of the strangest and most fantastic buildings ever put together: a wild mixture of Gothic and Churrigueresque, it is the Spanish equivalent of Art Nouveau (pl. 587).

As for sculpture, few names are worth mentioning. The Italian Canova (1757–1822) was the best interpreter of the neo-classical aesthetic (pl. 508). The Dane Thorwaldsen (1777–1844), had a European reputation but turned the Neo-Greek into something quite cold

391

508. Canova. Pauline Borghese, sister of
Napoleon, as Venus Victrix. 1809.
Detail. *Rome, Villa Borghese.*

and lifeless. Gottfried Schadow (1764–1850) was a German Canova,
though with more strength and less gracefulness.

In the United States Thomas Jefferson's adoption of Roman forms
was only the beginning of a wholesale application of the neo-classic
formulas to every kind of building. This was a type of building in
which the plan of the interior was coerced into the preconceived classic
form of the façade. Charles Bulfinch (1763–1844) added the severity
of classicism to the Georgian style in his capitols at Boston, Massachusetts, and Augusta, Maine. The Greek Revival in America begins as
early as 1798 with Benjamin Latrobe's (1766–1820) Bank of Pennsylvania, which boasted Ionic porticoes derived from the Erechtheum.
Latrobe and Bulfinch were responsible for the general disposition of
the capitol at Washington based on an earlier plan by William Thornton.
Actually, the building with the present dome was not completed until
1865. The plan of the city of Washington had been drawn in 1791
by Major Pierre Charles l'Enfant. The great period of florescence of
the Greek Revival style was in the second quarter of the nineteenth
century, when temple houses and temple banks sprang up around every
village green from Maine to Florida and westward to the frontier. In
its nostalgic evocation of an earlier style this revival was an aspect of
Romanticism. It was not long before these borrowings from the Greco-
Roman past were followed by imitations of Gothic architecture, again
a symbolical rather than a functional adaptation of European originals.

In the United States, although a number of early sculptors like William Rush (1756–1833) were capable of a realism in portraiture similar to the work of the painters, for the most part the carving of the early nineteenth century is the plastic counterpart of the taste for classic forms in architecture. Horatio Greenough (1805–1852) was the designer of a colossal statue of Washington in the attitude of the Phidian Zeus. The Greek Revival in sculpture produced a veritable petrified forest of marbles derived from Canova and Thorwaldsen, manufactured for the American public by sculptors like Hiram Powers (1805–1873). The one original sculptor of the nineteenth century in the United States was William Rimmer (1816–1879), a strange, tortured spirit who executed a number of statues which in their suggestion of inner suffering through physical contortion anticipated the work of Rodin.

PAINTING

Painting had some prosperous schools in Europe, so far as the number of painters was concerned. Generally speaking, with the exception of England, Romanticism failed to find its proper form and the first half century shows a steady decline of Classicism, whereas the second half sank into the most dreary Realism which was hardly redeemed by the imperfect assimilation of Impressionist features at the end of the century. Germany has a strange paradox to offer. Entranced by the apparent serenity of Classicism, Germany willfully turned its back on its own genuine native tradition of Expressionism, which would have enabled German art to find a pictorial medium for its Romantic sensibility. In 1810 a group of artists gathered in Rome at the San Isidoro monastery, calling themselves the Nazarene school, turned Germany away from the neo-classical tradition imposed by Winckelmann, while exalting the work of Perugino and the early Raphael. Overbeck (1789–1869) and Peter Cornelius (1783–1867) applied their new doctrine in a cycle of frescoes showing the story of Joseph, in the Casa Bartoldi in Rome, for which they were commissioned in 1816. They developed a style of frozen pastiche, with flat hues and a hard line, which made itself felt all over Europe (pl. 509). To their Italian sources Overbeck, Peter Cornelius and Schnorr von Carolsfeld soon added archaic elements from fifteenth and sixteenth century German art, whose deep pathos they never grasped. The two best painters of the period in

509. Friedrich Overbeck. Joseph Being Sold by His Brothers.
Berlin, Nationalgalerie.
510. Caspar David Friedrich. Cliffs at Rugen. *Winterthur, Switzerland,*
Oskar Reinhart Foundation.

Germany were two free-lances, the portraitist Philipp Otto Runge
(1777–1810), who came very close to Expressionism, and the exquisite
and intuitive landscape painter Caspar David Friedrich (1774–1840),
sometimes called the German Van Eyck (pl. 510). The school of historical painters at Düsseldorf (Wilhelm von Kaulbach, 1805–1874,
Alfred Rethel, 1816–1859) took up the Nazarene style but gave it a
Realist touch. The French naturalism of 1848 came to Germany through
Franz von Lenbach (1836–1904) and Wilhelm Leibl (1844–1900). Max
Liebermann (1847–1935) was a disciple of the French Impressionists.

In Spain, Francisco José de Goya y Lucientes (1746–1828), the
first half of whose career sets him in the eighteenth century, threw off
his neo-classical training and was a pioneer in his discovery of a technique
more suitable to his romantic leanings. The misfortunes of Spain, which
was torn by civil war, inspired him to paint some of the most dramatic
works of the century, but his meteoric genius found no followers in the
peninsula (pl. 480).

Britain, after making concessions to formalism through the portraitist Sir Thomas Lawrence (1769–1830), who painted all the great
European statesmen, had the privilege of discovering the proper
lines and medium for the Romantic landscape. In this the English
painters were helped by the fashion for water color, which was used
side by side with oils for open-air studies. John Crome (1768–1821)

511. John Crome. Moonrise on the Yare. 1808.
London, National Gallery.

founded the school of landscape painters known as the Norwich school, and turned to the Dutch for his conception of landscape. He had a very thorough craftsmanship, exploiting opacities to the full and drawing his effects from contrasted lights and shades (pl. 511). John Sell Cotman (1782–1842) was a member of the Norwich group: first and foremost a water-colorist, he was passionately concerned for a landscape of flattened, carefully ordered planes. John Constable (1776–1837) developed a rich and varied palette and a bold execution ideally suited for portraying the fluidity of skies, in which he saw the very basis of landscape. His brilliant technique was to have a decisive effect on the development of French Romanticism (pl. 512). In J. M. W.

512. Constable. River scene. *London, Victoria and Albert Museum.*

513. Turner. The Burial at Sea of
Sir David Wilkie. *London,
Tate Gallery.*

Turner (1775–1851), a painter of genius and vision, an imagination
that was given to reverie came into conflict with a gift for penetrating
observation. Obsessed by Claude Lorrain's historical and mythological
scenes, he was a forerunner of the Impressionist "cosmic" landscape,
reduced to a whirl of water, sky or sunlight (pl. 513). Though cut off
by an early death, Delacroix's friend R. P. Bonington (1802–1828)
painted landscape with a brilliant fluency. Samuel Palmer (1805–1881)
based his small intense visionary landscapes, some of the most remarkable in English painting, on the closest observation of nature.

Toward 1850, after having appeared to escape the aberrations that
had befallen other national schools, England adventured into "Pre-
Raphaelitism." Like French Symbolism a little later, this movement
was both literary and artistic. In 1848 a few writers, a sculptor and
three painters, Dante Gabriel Rossetti (1828–1882), William Holman
Hunt (1827–1890) and John Everett Millais (1829–1896, pl. 514)
grouped themselves into a "Brotherhood" in defense of a doctrine
which made painting a visual version of literary material. Rebelling
against the official worship of Raphael, the more fanatic of the group
gave themselves to so strict a realism that they sometimes took years
to complete a single picture. Pre-Raphaelitism also had a moral aim,
directed mainly against the standardization resulting from modern
industry and mechanization. Ruskin defended the movement with
passionate eloquence in his aesthetic writings. Other artists who were
not members of the Brotherhood followed its principles of realism,
including Ford Madox Brown (1821–1893). Naturalism unsoiled by
literary pretension or easy sentiment informs the drawings and few
paintings of Charles Keene (1823–1891).

The ambitious work of the Swiss painter Arnold Böcklin (1827–1901, pl. 515), who enjoyed a great reputation in Germany, is not unrelated to Pre-Raphaelitism in its literary pretensions, but it has also a certain Germanic harshness. In France the Symbolist aims of Gustave Moreau (1828–1898) were not furthered by the garish, pseudo-Romantic tricks he employed. The reliance of painting on literature is a striking example of the crisis through which Europe was passing, in its desperate search for a medium to convey its various aspirations, whether ideological, emotional or naturalistic.

The painters of the early nineteenth century in America, still following the lead of Europe, may be divided into representatives of Classicism and Romanticism. The cultural soil was too thin for the taste for neo-classic historical painting to take permanent root, so that the failure of a man like John Vanderlyn (1776–1852), an American representative of the David style, was inevitable. Washington Allston (1779–1843), the first American painter of the imagination, is best remembered for his romantic landscapes and figure pieces.

Although landscapes mainly topographical or decorative in character were occasionally painted even in the colonial period, it was not until the second quarter of the nineteenth century that landscape came to rival the portrait as an independent and accepted mode of artistic expression. One of its leading exponents was Thomas Cole (1801–1848), a mystic painter of pretentious allegories, who was the first to

514. Millais. The Return of the Dove to the Ark. 1851. *Oxford University.*
515. Arnold Böcklin. Triton and Nereid. 1875. *Berlin, Nationalgalerie.*

represent the American scene in a manner derived from Claude Lorrain. Among the other artists of this the Hudson River school was Thomas Doughty (1793–1856), a pastoral painter in the bland manner of the Dutch masters.

An even more American form of expression is genre painting, which came into its own in the thirties of the nineteenth century. William Sidney Mount (1807–1868) gave a vibrant interpretation of country activities on Long Island based on the technique of the Dutch Little Masters, and George Caleb Bingham (1811–1879) was the pictorial counterpart of Mark Twain in his chronicling of life on the Mississippi.

The second half of the century witnessed a new period of maturity in American painting. Of the really great artists of this time, Winslow Homer (1836–1910, pl. 516) was a painter of the sea and a monumental illustrator of themes of the active American outdoor life: childhood games, hunting, fishing, and the drama of men against the sea. In Homer's paintings his concentration on a big central theme presented with specific realism transcends the literary content. Whereas Homer realized his seascapes with complete objectivity in an impressionistic technique based on value contrast rather than color, Albert Pinkham Ryder (1847–1917, pl. 517) was a mystic painter of the sea, in his

516. Winslow Homer. Fog Warning. *Boston, Museum of Fine Arts.*

517. Albert P. Ryder.
Moonlight-Marine. *New York, Metropolitan Museum.*

expressionistic distortion a forerunner of the art of the twentieth century: his patternized pictures of moon-drenched waters are the pictorial counterparts of Melville's descriptions of the great deep. Thomas Eakins (1844–1916) completes the trinity of artists with whom American painting came of age. He was a forceful, completely objective painter of portraits and athletic subject matter executed in the broad technique of the great Spanish artists of the seventeenth century.

Among the expatriate American painters were James Abbott McNeill Whistler (1834–1903), whose entire artistic career was passed in Paris and London. He was among the first to be influenced by the newly discovered Japanese prints; his distortion of spatial arrangement and subtlety of occult balance were far in advance of his contemporaries (pl. 518). Mary Cassatt (1845–1927), resident in France from 1879 until her death, worked in a manner reflecting Degas and Renoir. John Singer Sargent (1856–1925) was an artist of international reputation, a painter of superficial fashionable portraits in a facile and dazzling technique that went far to disguise their empty ideality.

Impressionism in America never attained the importance of its European prototype. George Inness (1825–1894), who actually denounced the Impressionist theory, was himself an American follower of Corot and the Barbizon school. Childe Hassam (1859–1935) and John Henry Twachtman (1853–1902), although described as Impressionists, suggested light in terms of value rather than the pure color of Monet and Pissarro.

518. Whistler. La Princesse du Pays de la Porcelaine. 1864. *Washington, Freer Gallery.*

By turning painting into the evocation of a sensation, Whistler freed the English school from Pre-Raphaelitism, and the New English Art Club, founded in 1886, at last absorbed Impressionism. Through Whistler, also, French naturalism and unity of feeling strengthened paintings of the London scene by Walter Greaves (1846–1931) and the intimate canvases of F. H. Potter (1845–1887). Whistler's example was the starting point for early evocations of seaside light and color by Philip Wilson Steer (1860–1942) and W. R. Sickert (1860–1942), a friend as well of Degas and Lautrec, who painted in Dieppe, Paris, London and Venice, and prolonged Impressionism well into our century. Gwen John (1876–1939), pupil of Whistler and friend of Rodin, painted with simplicity and severe penetration the poor, the alms-women, and nuns of Meudon.

In Holland, Impressionism was represented by George Breitner (1857–1923), who painted the Amsterdam canals.

THE MINOR ARTS

The decorative arts went through a progressive decadence during the nineteenth century.

Until about 1820 the Empire style was a dignified version of the ancient Pompeian decoration which had already been imitated but with greater subtlety in the late eighteenth century in England and in France under Louis XVI. The Empire style was introduced under David's influence by Georges Jacob (1739–1814), who in 1789–1790 made a whole set of furniture to be used by David for his classical compositions. This sober style crystallized toward the end of the century into the "Directoire" style, and lasted a while under the Empire in domestic furnishing, parallel with the official style of furnishing. Under the guidance of the architects Percier and Fontaine, Georges II Jacob (d. 1803) and Jacob-Desmalter (1770–1841) acted as furnishers for the national palaces as well as for highly placed dignitaries, under the Directory and the Empire. They were assisted by the bronzeworker Thomyre (1751–1843). They made what was perhaps an excessive use of Greco-Roman, Etruscan and even Egyptian patterns and motifs, which they applied in stucco on walls, and in bronze on items of furniture (pl. 519).

Between 1820 and 1830 the Restoration style evolved from the Empire style, and was more rational, purer and much simpler in its decoration. The severity of this style was softened by the play on

519. Jewel cabinet, made for the Empress Marie-Louise by Jacob-Desmalter. 1809. *Fontainebleau, Palace.*

curved lines, while dark mahoganies were abandoned for light timbers such as beechwood, ash, cedar, maple and citron. Hangings and wall-papers were also in light colors, and voile curtains were fashionable. It was a period of great elegance of form.

Between 1830 and 1850 mahogany returned to favor with the French Louis-Philippe and German Biedermeier styles, both of them a mixture of the two preceding styles (Restoration and Empire), showing also a certain revival of classical forms especially in easy chairs which imitated the Roman magistrate's chair or *curule*. Interiors contained a great deal of upholstery and hangings, bright materials being used in preference to dark, and voile curtains rather than heavy textiles. Under Louis-Philippe there was a vogue for Neo-Gothic interiors which have wrongly been dubbed "Charles X Style." This "troubadour" style produced clocks and fine bookbindings of a highly medieval flavor.

The Great Exhibition of 1851 in London and the Paris Universal Exhibition of 1855 showed the public how far the applied arts had degenerated. Attempts were made to put this right by giving artisans good examples to work from, which were housed in so-called craft or industrial museums set up for their benefit. This only made matters worse, resulting in more copying and eclecticism. Until 1890 or there-abouts it was an understood thing that a dining room should be of the Henry II period, a bedroom Louis XV, a sitting room Louis XVI. In official Second Empire furnishing, under the Empress Eugénie's guidance, eighteenth century styles were most imitated. Interior deco-ration made the utmost use of textiles in the form of heavy draperies and materials for upholsteries, thick, opaque curtains, thick carpets, padded chairs. Dark red was the prevailing color for all these purposes.

*Carved in the living rock, a chaotic stream of images
sweeps along as though impelled by some cosmic power.*

520. Brahmanic art. 7th century. The Descent of the Ganges.
Mamallapuram. Detail.

CHAPTER XI

THE CIVILIZATIONS OF THE FAR EAST

ALL WESTERN WORKS OF ART are intended for a spectator: they are
meant for another man's eyes and mind. They have to be readable;
their parts must be clearly marked while remaining a coherent unity.
They are essentially a defined significant form strictly related to space
and time, as in the rhythmed colonnades of the Greek temple and the
arrangement of its pediments; or as in the gravitation round a central
point that governs a Byzantine church, or the perspective of Romanesque and Gothic naves which later passed into those painted canvases
in which the spectator is invited to advance as down some avenue. The
West worked toward the essential notion of a work of art, as the
product of a specific activity addressed to a few members of an élite
capable of appreciating it. It amounts to a dialogue between artist and
spectator on an aesthetic theme.

In the hands of the artist of the Far East, form emerges as the
manifestation of the being of the world itself, a symbol of universal
powers or forces. It is not the result of a man's thought striving to

403

master some definite aspect of nature. It is "inspired," an artist's imaginative reflection of the eternal play of appearances; it aspires to the infinite, either through portraying an indeterminate flux, or on the contrary through the powerful concentration of its structure. At Mamallapuram, the famous bas-relief of the *Descent of the Ganges,* carved into the rock face, is a river of images (pl. 520). In the same way Far Eastern painting has no use for the idea of a frame, which governs ours: at Ajanta the various themes of the paintings are linked into one continuous action, as in some stage play in which there are no intervals and the last act reintroduces the first. Kept in cylindrical cases, Chinese pictures unfold so to speak *in time;* they have to be read like musical compositions, and they suggest vague landscapes, fragments of the universal, which convey the mystery that runs in fragments through all things. Round the sides of archaic Chinese bronzes there seethes a whole world in gestation, a chaos from which here and there forms seem to emerge, only to vanish before they can give enduring shape to fleeting appearances: they are monstrous shapes, apparitions from a world of fear. All these works are "open" forms; that is to say, they do not oppose their bold outline or definition to the invading fluidity of the universe, but are penetrated by it. They act as conductors to the cosmic flow, whereas Western works act as insulators; but the touch of the infinite is perhaps most intense in those Chinese objects which have naked contours over which the hand and the eye may glide—such as archaic jades with their hidden meanings, or the Sung vases with their slender curves, whose opalescent substance has the blue-green depth of the ocean itself.

This feeling that everything is no more than a moment in the cosmic flux of becoming hardly encouraged the Orientals to develop architecture, which is the major art of the West, where it governs all other art forms, imposing its framework on them and allotting a particular function to each. The Chinese went in for wooden construction only, which they later imitated in brick and ceramics. The Hindus, whose feeling for sculpture gave them a special gift for handling stone materials, did the same as the Chinese as soon as they took to building, bringing to it the primitive methods of timber construction which they perhaps borrowed from the Middle East. Then, being unequal to those abstract calculations which show how solids behave in space, and in which Greek, Roman, Romanesque and Gothic architects were fully

*At an interval of a thousand years, the clash
of a mystical religion and a Western plastic
sense resulted in remarkably similar forms.*

521. Gandhara art. Approximately early Christian period.
Stucco head from Tashkurghan (Afghanistan).
522. Gothic art. Angel, from a buttress of Reims Cathedral. About 1240.

proficient, they raised in corbeled layers colossal piles of blocks. This
rudimentary form of building was primitive man's way of imitating one
of the most impressive sights in the world, the mountain, which for the
East is a symbol of the cosmos.

With its inorganic structure, this kind of monument knows nothing
of the distribution of solids and spaces, or the concentration of decorative features and carved figures at vital points in the building so as to
show off the pleasing completeness of the walls. Rock faces in the
East are profusely covered with ornamentation and carved figures;
Chinese monuments are decked with multicolored ceramics which make
them look like enormous vases, while hundreds of figures swarm like
ants on the pyramidal Hindu temples.

China and India are alike in their conception of a cosmic order in
which man must live through a cycle in order to find his place. But
the two civilizations differ in the meaning they each give to the universal essence.

Few peoples have had so profound an intuition of the divine as
the Hindus. On this earth in which everything is God, in order to find
his salvation man must discover godliness in himself. The sight of end-

less creation unrelieved by seasonal change is a feature of tropical nature that has inspired the Hindu with a profound faith in existence. The Indian aesthetic is therefore "naturalistic" in its essence. In the West, the Christian idea of original sin, the Fall, and the periodic need for revolt against the idealism of schools and academies have given this word "naturalism" a harsh meaning which makes it hard for us to understand all the purity attached to it in the East. The West knows nothing of true naturalism, but is more at home with realism, an analytical attitude which isolates one or other aspect of the world only to fix it into some lifeless form. Perhaps Rubens, and after him Renoir, managed to avoid this trap. But the flux of life runs through all Hindu art, one and indivisible, completely incarnate in all its potential strength, in the least of Hindu works. By a phenomenon which is unique in history, this art seems to have been born already complete, in a state of maturity, without going through all the conventions and

The lofty spiritual quality of early Chinese Buddhist art expressed itself in tapering, unsubstantial forms, in which (as on the Royal Porch of Chartres) bodies are reduced to a fragile, stemlike support for an inspired face.

523. Bodhisattva from Lungmen. Wei Dynasty. 6th century.
New York, Metropolitan Museum.
524. One of the kings of Judah. Statue column from the Royal Porch
of Chartres Cathedral. About 1150.

*The dynamic forms of the Chinese medieval
period (Wei and T'ang Dynasties) are sometimes
very close to those of Western Romanesque art.*

525. Buddhist stele. Detail. Wei Dynasty. Dated A.D. 533–543.
New York, Metropolitan Museum.

526. The Prophet Isaiah. Detail from rear wall of façade of abbey church
of Ste.-Marie at Souillac. About 1150.

stylizations so dear to the primitive mind. Of all the artistic civilizations, the Indian is the least stylized. What for the Greek, Roman and Gothic artists was the fruit of a slow conquest of the external world, achieved only by throwing off primitivistic preconceptions and by dint of an unquenchable thirst for objective knowledge, was given to the Hindus from the very start. Right from the beginning, after a very short archaic period which is hardly noticeable, Sanchi art had come to terms with nature. On the contrary, it was Hellenic influence, brought in through Greco-Buddhist art, which was to strengthen Gupta stylization, though it was soon abandoned once more in favor of a return to more lifelike forms.

Indian naturalism, like Greek realism, was bound to lead to an increasing prestige of sculptural form, since it can express the physical presence of living things better than any other type of art. The Greek experiment in realism was all based on the masculine form, whose sharp edges and distinct planes lend themselves to the Greek sense of measurement and definition. But the Indian aesthetic is feminine. The female body is more suggestive of flesh itself than of volume: the indefinite

407

transitions of its modeling suit the Hindu outlook which refuses or fails to see anything at all definite in the world. Exaggerating the female attributes, the Indian artists stressed whatever is capable of giving and sustaining life, and the bodies they portray seem to sway like fruit-laden trees and are symbols of plenty.

The evolution of Greek sculpture showed a progressive liberation from the wall, a triumph of three-dimensional form. Hindu art was late in producing sculpture in the round. Sculptured forms were not detached from the rock face, nor on the other hand were they completely subservient to monumental values as in Romanesque; but they draw their life from the block of which they are still a part, the Hindus conceiving nothing as distinct from its surroundings, but seeing everything in every thing. In the Mamallapuram carving the surge of figures represents the moment when living form emerges from raw matter: that is why the Hindus have always been fond of drawing their works from the very bowels of the earth, hewing out caves and carving into mountains. The Greek temple, being an expression of victorious humanism, stands on the acropolis like a statue on its pedestal, whereas Hindu works flow like living seed in the matrix of the earth. The powerful biological creativeness that is typical of India produced strange monuments which multiply like cells and which, like a tree in a forest, are fast throwing out new shoots, while all around them swarm other sanctuaries cast in the same image (pls. 527, 528).

Burdened with ritual and formalism of every kind, the life of the "Celestials" is fundamentally little moved by religious aspirations. Chinese theology is another version, though transposed to the level of a very high culture, of a primitive state of mankind which precedes the religious outlook in the proper sense of the term. The Chinese do not worship gods, though they believe in genii and demons which are formal expressions of the principles governing the universe: for them a knowledge of magic rites enables man to intervene in the universal order and attune himself to it. The Westerner prides himself on the free will that he regards as man's privilege and something that makes him the "Lord of Creation," whereas for the Chinese, free will appears to be the root of all evil. Like some sorcerer's apprentice, man upsets the world's natural order, and the gift of intelligence, which he alone of the creatures is blessed with, becomes a failing if he uses it to exploit the world; for man ought to serve the world and make the best of his

Examples of a multiplication of forms comparable with biological reproduction. The plan resembles cellular division, or a crystal formation.

527. The Lingaraj temple at Bhubaneswar (Orissa). 11th century.

528. Half-plan of the shikhara of the Nilakantha Mahaveda Temple at Sunak (Baroda). 13th century. *After Marchal, L'Architecture comparée.*

privilege by contributing to the universal order. Magic enables him to do this. It is remarkable that the highest metaphysical form of Chinese thought, Taoism, has its roots in magic ritual.

In the field of art, creation tends to take place without regard to nature; that is to say, in spite of or against nature's example. Whereas Hindu art is a figure, Chinese art is a stylization. The hidden source of the Chinese soul is to be found in the art of the ancient period, in the bronze caldrons which are drawn from the bowels of the earth, still charged with the magic potentialities of the rites they will be used for. The plastic form of that primitive art writhes with a satanic rhythm, it is the source of that bristling, jagged, cruel style which was to obsess China even in its works of architecture right through its long history.

The wealth of Chinese civilization lies in its many contradictions. The gust of naturalism that came from Steppe art and from Indian art,

the sense of the divine which was brought in by the Buddhist mission-
aries of the *Great Vehicle* (Mahayana), these came into conflict with
their obsession with the chimera. When they came into contact with
Buddhism, the Chinese, who had naturally little sense of the divine, yet
managed to express its sublime spirituality even better than India itself
had done. India, overwhelmed by naturalism, sought to translate the
inner life of the Buddha by taking from Greco-Buddhist art a formalism
which resulted in the somewhat conventional works of Gupta art. The
Chinese stripped the Yün Kang and Lungmen statues of their fleshly,
earthly attributes so that they convey with the utmost dignity the
Bodhisattvas' inward contemplation or compassion. But the warlike
China of the T'ang period turned away from these holy images and
gave themselves to a brutal realism fraught with the more pragmatic
element in Chinese civilization. And to complete the gamut of human
expression, the Sung period produced works full of the philosophical
reverie, fundamentally atheistic, typical of decadent periods in which
strength is ousted by an elegant, intellectual skepticism.

Because the Chinese had an attitude of independence toward
nature, they had more than any other race an exalted sense of essential
form, and language cannot describe something which is as far from
nature as it is from abstraction: those naked objects, those archaic
jades and Sung ceramics, are addressed to the aesthetic sense in all its
purity, so that once again the object becomes symbolic—a symbol of
the absolute.

INDIAN ART
HISTORICAL BACKGROUND

A peninsula of over two and a half million square miles, India is cut
off from direct communication with central Asia by the great ranges
of the Himalayas and the Hindu Kush. Its great gateway is the Indus
Valley, which brings it into contact with Iran and what is now
Afghanistan. Through this gate the Mesopotamian civilization pene-
trated in the protohistoric period, and in the historical period came the
Hellenistic influences of the Greco-Iranian kingdoms, brought in by
Alexander's invasion. The link with China leaves Kashmir to join the
Iranian highways of the Oxus Valley, passing through the Turkestan
oases; it was by this route that Buddhism made its impact on Chinese

civilization. Buddhism also spread eastward through Burma, into Siam, Cambodia and Annam, and by sea along the Coromandel coast toward the Indian Archipelago and Java. This eastern region was the real colonial province of Indian art: Buddhism flourished there after its introduction in the third and fourth centuries, and continued to do so after it was driven out of India in the twelfth and thirteenth centuries.

Excavations have shown that the Indus Valley (Mohenjo-Daro, Harappa) had a civilization that depended on Mesopotamia. It is difficult to date (perhaps 2000 B.C.) and its relationship to the native civilizations of which works have survived is obscure. The latter are relatively recent and are confined to a fairly short era (second century B.C. to seventeenth century A.D.). The Moslem invasion which swept into India in the eleventh century and penetrated deeply into the subcontinent in the following centuries sterilized and gradually impoverished the native art, though it managed to retain all its spirit in the miniatures of the Rajput, Sikh and Delahani schools. A most surprising fact about India is that no trace remains of the period when the Indian mentality was formed, no doubt because their monuments and other works were made of timber. Between 1500 and 800 B.C. an Aryan invasion filtered into the peninsula via the Indus, driving the Dravidian natives down to the southern tip. These invaders gave India its earliest religion, Vedism, which is not unlike the other Iranian religions such as that of Persia. Vedism later took on more marked native characteristics and developed into Brahmanism. This religion is based essentially on the belief in a universal soul (Brahma) in which all individual souls find their fulfillment. But in order to rejoin the primordial Being the individual soul is condemned to move upward through the scale of creatures by means of transmigration of souls (*samsara*) until it has attained the way of salvation and broken the chain of rebirths, when a final disincarnation ensures its identification with God.

The Aryans brought a language with them, Sanskrit, which shares a common origin with the languages of the other Aryan peoples who invaded Europe and which form the Indo-European language group (Sanskrit, Persian, Greek, Latin and Germanic). Treatises were composed in Sanskrit which serve as the basis of the Indian religions. These are the Vedas, composed between about 1500 and 1000 B.C. and written down in about the sixth century B.C., then metaphysical speculations

529. Brahmanic art of the Deccan. 12th century.
Nataraja, or Shiva as Lord of the Dance.
Amsterdam, Aziatische Kunst.

(Brahmanas and Upanishads), precepts (the Sutras), and finally two great epic poems, the Mahabharata and the Ramayana. Perhaps the reason why Vedism left no form of art was that, like the religion of the Persians, it must have been very spiritual and opposed to the making of images. Vedism was later paganized to some degree, in the stage known as Hinduism, and on the contrary began to represent gods who were formerly conceptual but were now personified. The main gods are: Brahma, the least individualized and the least often portrayed; Vishnu, a messianic god who returns to the earth in successive incarnations (*avatara*); Shiva, a cosmic deity who is both creative and destructive, the god of life and death, whose mystic dance created the world and whose most famous representation shows him as lord of the dance (Nataraja, pl. 529).

Meanwhile, when Brahmanism with its polytheistic pantheism was being developed, another religion, Buddhism, which began as no more than a moral teaching, was founded in the sixth century B.C. by the son of a Rajah of Nepal (eastern basin of the Ganges), Prince Siddhartha, known as the Buddha or Enlightened One. He believed that the way of salvation lay in the suppression of the desire or thirst for existence, so that the soul may break free of its predestined transmigrations and efface itself in the state of Nirvana. Legend gives every detail of the life of Prince Siddhartha, from his previous incarnations (*jatakas*), his noble birth, his youthful sensuality which he renounced in order to become a monk, when he took the name of Sakyamuni. After attaining wisdom (the Bodhi or Enlightenment) in spite of the attacks of the demon Mara, he went about preaching the truth until he died after achieving Nirvana. His ashes were distributed in eight funerary monuments or stupas. Buddha's disciples set up monasteries, where they followed an ascetic life according to their rule. In the first or second century a doctrinal schism arose and the religion split into two branches, Hinayana or Theravada Buddhism (the Small Vehicle of Salvation), and the Mahayana (Great Vehicle). The Hinayana conforms to the basic doctrine of the Buddha, regarding him as a superman but not as a god; it seeks personal salvation through the exercises leading to Nirvana. The Mahayana deifies Buddha and is a religion of redemption and love, comparable with Christianity; it brought hope and appealed to millions all over Asia. The redeeming divinities of Mahayana are the Bodhisattvas, or future Buddhas, who are so touched by compassion for human suffering that they renounce Nirvana until all the other beings in the world are saved.

India has had a strange destiny, for after creating in Buddhism the most spiritual of Eastern religions, she lost sight of it in the eighth and ninth centuries, falling into the paganism of an idolatrous renewal of Brahmanism, in the form of Hinduism. After reaching China in the sixth century, Buddhism found its strongest hold in the cultural colonies of India, that is to say Indochina and the East Indies.

530. Greco-Buddhist art. Head of the Buddha.
Paris, Musée Guimet.

EVOLUTION OF INDIAN ART

The early history of India is complicated by the fact that the country was always divided into a number of kingdoms or principalities, except in one or two periods when political unity was more marked (Maurya Empire, about third century B.C. and Gupta Empire in the fourth and fifth centuries A.D.). In spite of these divisions India's artistic civilization shows a genuine unity because of the common cultural outlook imposed by the Aryans and the consistency of the tropical climate.

The first Indian art was of Buddhist inspiration, for primitive Vedism and Brahmanism left few works, or at least few have survived. It was the Maurya Dynasty which helped this early art to spread all over India. In the third century B.C. the Emperor Asoka, who has been called the Constantine of Buddhism, built memorial columns (at Sarnath) in the Ganges Valley and stupas in the places associated with events in Buddha's life, and his example was followed by his successors.

If we set aside India's protohistoric civilization, which has no obvious connection with what followed, the artistic history of the country may be divided into the following periods:

1. *Primitive period. Introduction of Buddhist art. Third century* B.C. *to first century* A.D.

The kings of the Maurya and Sunga Dynasties built memorials (at Sarnath) and stupas in the Ganges Valley (at Bharhut and Sanchi) which show the life of the Buddha in narrative form and with lavish naturalism though he himself was never represented in person (pl. 531). The stupa is a stone version of an older timber construction, and shows belated Achaemenian influence in its ornament. The same features are to be found in sanctuaries and convents carved in the rock in central India, in the Deccan (Nasik; Karli, pl. 533; Bhaja).

2. *Buddhist art. The early Christian era to fifth century.*

Indian art now developed on three different planes:

(*a*) In the northwest provinces, bordering Iran, and in Gandhara (province of Peshawar) and Kapisa in what is now Afghanistan (sites excavated at Hadda, Bamiyan, Kapisa), an art called Greco-Buddhist appeared under the Kushan Dynasty between the first and fifth centuries, and is so called because it shows the application of Hellenistic

531. Buddhist art. 2nd century B.C. to 1st century A.D.
The Great Stupa at Sanchi (Bhopal).

principles to Buddhist statuary (pl. 521). Large numbers of sculptures in blue schist or slate as well as in stucco have been found in the small stupas in the Hadda monasteries. There the Buddha was shown in person for the first time, dressed in a Grecian type of mantle or pallium with clinging folds or swags, and in various symbolic postures which became typical of Buddhist iconography. The idealized face is of the Apollo type, though with some Indian traits: the lobe of the ear is lengthened, the *urna* or "third eye" between the brows, the *ushnisha* or cranial protuberance disguised as a topknot resembling that of the Greek sun god (pl. 530). Demons and genii are also found in this very figurative or representational iconography.

(*b*) Parallel with Greco-Buddhist art, the native naturalistic aesthetic that had appeared earlier developed between the first and third centuries A.D. in the form of the Mathura or pre-Gupta style, representing the Buddha, and perhaps with some influence from the Greco-Buddhist idealist manner which gradually affected it. The architecture of central-Indian caves showed the same features as in the preceding period.

(*c*) In the south of India between the first and fourth centuries, that is to say in the Deccan, at Amaravati in the Krishna Valley, a sculptural style developed which, perhaps owing to Greco-Buddhist influence, lost something of the native, naturalistic heaviness and sought to portray movement; the figures became more elongated, while the ritual *tribhanga* pose of the body, moving in three ways simultaneously —a pose introduced in the Sanchi period—found a graceful suppleness.

415

3. *The Gupta period. Fourth to sixth century.*

The Gupta period saw the triumph of idealism over the naturalism and vitalism of the previous periods. In the sculptures in the round of the Ganges Valley, and in the frescoes and bas-reliefs of the Ajanta caves in central India, artists sought to express a divine serenity, detachment and mystic love through forms that have a great classical poise and that have a precise canon behind them. Buddhist iconography was now fixed into several types which spread to overseas Indian territories. Rock architecture was still carried on, but there were also some outdoor temples.

4. *The post-Gupta period. Seventh and eighth centuries.*

The academic impoverishment of Buddhist sculpture in the post-Gupta period was made up for by a revival of Brahmanism, resulting in a renewed native taste for a wealth of forms, and a new tendency to the colossal in an effort to express the greatness of the deities. Artists had the courage to carve enormous rocks (*Descent of the Ganges* at Mamallapuram in the southeast, pl. 520; the cave temple on the island of Elephanta). Sometimes they gave these blocks an architectural form (*Raths* of Mamallapuram, seventh century, pl. 532), and did not shrink before tremendous labors of excavation (Kailasanatha temple, sculptured in the eighth century from a single block excavated at Ellora). This period begins to show examples of open-air architecture

532. Brahmanic art. 7th century. Raths (temples) carved out of rocks at Mamallapuram.

(as distinct from caves) executed in durable materials. Starting from the elements of timber construction showing Iranian characteristics, architecture now became more and more Indianized.

5. Development of Brahmanic art. Ninth to seventeenth century.

While the Indus and Ganges regions were invaded by Islam and ceased being the great creative center, the Indian spirit survived in the northeast (Bengal and Orissa) and the Deccan. Cut off from the external influences which might have been profitable, Indian art became self-centered and quickly exhausted its creative potential. This period saw the development of temples, from simple *cellae* into structures of a more complex plan. In the north, the cella was given height, becoming a bulb-shaped *sikhara* (Lingaraj temple, at Bhubaneswar, Orissa, about 1000), while in the south it became the pyramidal *vimana* (Tanjore, eleventh century). Multiplied in the form of *gopuras* or porch towers, with concentric halls (pl. 536) this pyramidal type of structure gave the design of the great Temple of Shiva at Tanjore which later, in the fourteenth century, was enriched with a columned ambulatory or *mandapa* (Madura, the greatest temple in India, dating from the seventeenth century). Decoration lost all its plastic value, becoming no more than a monotonous ornamentation which in the state of Mysore assumed tormented, "flamboyant" features. However, from the eleventh to the fourteenth century, Dravidian art still produced admirable bronze statues made in the round, of moderate size and in which the sense of poise handed down from the Gupta aesthetic gives an elegant restraint to the intense urge to movement: the Nataraja or dancing Shiva is, thanks to its subject, the finest expression of this equilibrium (pl. 529).

ARCHITECTURE

The Hindu architecture made in durable materials is entirely for religious purposes. The ancient lay buildings, made of timber, have not survived. The Buddhist undertakings were of three types: the chaitya, the vihara and the stupa. Outdoor buildings (stupas) or those excavated in rock (chaityas and viharas) are a literal stone reconstruction of wooden architecture. The *stupa* or reliquary (pl. 531) is a tumulus or dome, of masonry, topped with one or more stone "parasols"— symbols of dignity—and surrounded by a circular balustrade with four heavily carved gateways which open to the four cardinal points. The *chaitya* or Buddhist church, whose form perhaps originated in the West, is a basilica with a nave and ambulatory, ending in an apse which contains a small stupa or dagoba (pls. 533 and 534). The *vihara* or monastery consists of cells grouped round a square courtyard containing a sanctuary, and can be hollowed in rock as at Ellora.

The Brahman temple strongly resembles the Egyptian temple. It consists in its essentials of a square cell or vimana which is the sanctuary holding the idol, entered by a vestibule to which a columned hall or *mandapa* was added for the worshipers. In its definitive form, one or a number of enclosures, pierced by towers or *gopuras*, were set round this nucleus, and they contained columned halls (pl. 536), extra sanctuaries and sacred pools bordered with arcades or galleries and steps (pl. 535). As is the case with Egyptian temples, Brahman temples were subject to indefinite extension, by the process of adding more and more and ever larger internal sections.

533. Buddhist art. Early 2nd century B.C. Interior of the Chaitya-hall at Karli.

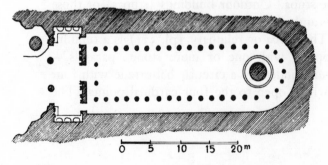

534. Buddhist art. Plan of the Chaitya-hall at Karli.

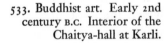

0   5   10   15   20ᵐ

India did not develop the keyed arch or vault, so that the exclusive use of corbeled vaulting led the architects to build in tiers, arriving at a pyramidal structure (pl. 535). The successive tiers were decorated with smaller versions of the edifice itself, which, as it were, bud all over the building or even swarm all round it as at Bhubaneswar (pl. 527). In the Dravidian temples the composition follows a diminishing pattern, the gopuras becoming smaller and smaller toward the central vimana, which is the smallest of the towers. As a result, no over-all view of the temple can be had except from one of the gopuras.

Indian architecture has not succeeded in creating any original decorative code. The decorative principles of the earliest monuments consisted of nothing more than taking over into stone the same forms as were used by the carpenter, and borrowing freely from the old Achaemenian system (bell-shaped capitals ending in a bulbous form (pl. 538), sometimes topped with a flat supporting beam, or with animals back-to-back: the plinths are often in the shape of an animal —fabulous beasts, gryphons, sphinxes, fishlike or birdlike sirens, centaurs; or jointed patterns, palm-leaf molding, garlands). Among those forms which persisted for a long time from the early timber structures one might mention the pillar surmounted by a beam or bracket which supports the entablature, and above all the *kudus* or projecting skylights which are one of the pervading features of the decoration (pl. 532). In the last period of Dravidian art, the entire temple was overrun by

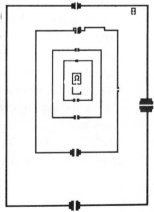

535. Brahmanic art. 15th century. Gopura, vimana and sacred pool of the Shiva temple, Tinnevelly (now Tirunelveli, Madras).

536. Brahmanic art. 16th century. Plan of the enclosures, gopuras (porch towers) and sanctuary of the temple at Srirangam.

537. Buddhist art. 2nd century B.C. Yakshi, or tree spirit.
A pillar from the balustrade of the Bharhut stupa. *Calcutta, Indian Museum.*

538. Brahmanic art. 7th to 8th century. Ellora. Pillars in Cave 31.

539. Buddhist art. 2nd century A.D. Yakshi.
Pillar from the balustrade of the Mathura stupa. *Calcutta, Indian Museum.*

figures sculptured in the round which tended to oust ornamentation of other kinds. The cornice work was overdone and gave a confusing impression.

By comparison with sculpture, which evolved to a very high level, Indian architecture never outgrew its archaism. Like the primitive civilizations, India sought to convey an impression of strength, either through immense excavatory works or through colossal piles of materials. The inclination which was shown from earliest times for direct carving either in the form of excavation (crypts) or in the round (rock temples of Mamallapuram) shows that the Hindu temperament tended to think of architecture as something closely related to a sculptured form: the Indian pantheistic genius discouraged the labor of geometrical, abstract calculation that architectural composition demands. With its ever increasing number of enclosures and its decorations as recklessly plentiful as the growth of a virgin forest, the Hindu temple, gathered round its vimana as though round a pivot, none the less answered the needs of the Oriental temple, that had to be an image of

420

the cosmos which was thought of as having the form of a mountain. But the Khmers on the other hand were able to carry out the same program in a way that implies a more proper conception of architecture.

THE FIGURATIVE ARTS

Sculpture is the major art of India. Her genius for naturalism expressed itself most completely through the carving of stone. The development of sculpture from the Bharhut bas-reliefs to Dravidian bronzes shows a thorough exploitation of the formal possibilities of this art. Although it was not the main tradition and shows many signs of the Hellenistic aesthetic, yet Greco-Buddhist art finds a natural place in this development, for, in introducing the Greek example into Hindu sculpture, it quickened the evolution away from that archaism which stunted Indian architecture.

Hindu plastic art, however, never lost the mistrust of carving in the round which dated from early times: related to low-relief, it is a monumental form and it resembles that of the French medieval period rather more than it does Greek sculpture. But its function was not decorative, it was not applied to the building or monument, but on the contrary absorbed it: indeed buildings became no more than a piece of sculpture carved on every side, without a single blank space on their walls.

With the summary planes of its modeling, its frontalism with figures so flattened on the block of stone that the spectator has no side view to consider, the Bharhut style (pl. 537) has all the strength of an art in the first stages of its vitality: the forms recall the early Romanesque works in the ambulatory of St.-Sernin at Toulouse (pl. 636). The perspective is shown by means of tiers or rows as in all ancient civilizations, whose first concern is the readability of forms (pl. 540). The art of the stupas at Sanchi has all the luxuriance of Romanesque art in its first flowering: as in the twelfth century in Europe, the genius of the artist is seen reveling in its creative capacity, and inventing new variations on old themes borrowed from the Middle East; but now a rich sap, that of tropical life, flows into and rounds the forms. In the *yakshi* the canon of feminine Hindu beauty, which at Bharhut was still rather stiff, finds its full suppleness and sensuality, with the three-way movement of the body (*tribhanga*) expressing the rhythm of the dance, and the fullness of the breasts, the narrow waist

540. Bharhut art. 2nd century B.C. The dream of Maya. (The conception of the Buddha, who descends to his mother's breast in the form of a young elephant.) *Calcutta, Indian Museum.*

and a broad pelvis. Plastically, the flattened modeling of the planes, avoiding profile, that was perhaps taken over from ivory-carving, is sometimes accompanied in the animal and feminine figures by a tendency toward a rounded modeling, sensual and heavy like a ripe fruit. But—as in the finest Romanesque compositions, for instance at Moissac—the sculptor continued to respect the wall surface, bringing it alive with the chisel rather than trying to produce a jutting relief. This final stage was reached in the Mathura style (first to fourth century A.D.), in which the voluptuous curves of the modeling have a fleshly quality that India was never to surpass (pl. 539). Parallel with the Mathura school, the Amaravati school (second to fourth century A.D.) conforms more strictly with the wall's plane surface and flattened modeling, but in its sinuous movement recalls the feverish Romanesque of Burgundy

541. Buddhist art. 2nd to 3rd century.
Women kneeling at the throne of the Buddha. Bas-relief from Amaravati.

(pl. 541). The smiles that grace these faces, the dancing rhythm of the figures both at Mathura and Amaravati, convey all the optimism brought by the gospel of salvation.

The Gupta aesthetic put an end to this feverishness, and may be compared with early Gothic, which shares the same moral and plastic significance. Like the Gothic, it sprang from a desire to create holy images and to convey divine serenity and compassion through restrained postures and the simplified modeling of a classical style: just as the Gothic created the typical Western image of Christ, Gupta art determined the image of the Buddha. Orientalists disagree as to whether the classical development happened spontaneously or whether, as seems likely, it was helped by Greco-Buddhist art. The art of Hadda was certainly more attuned to the West than to the East, and is perhaps the last smile of Greek art, surviving in an outpost on the very edge of the Ancient world: the extraordinary likeness between Hadda figures and those of thirteenth century Gothic in France, proves the existence of enduring laws in the creation of forms (pls. 521 and 522), for at an interval of ten centuries the meeting between a mystical religion and the plastic sense of the West resulted in very similar forms.

The urge to abstractness gave Gupta statuary a rather dry stylization which might be called pseudo-Byzantine (frontal presentation, conventional modeling of draperies, facial impersonality, pl. 542). Perhaps Gandharan influence was also responsible for introducing an alien formalism which arrested the development of the native temperament. The mural paintings of the Gupta period were spared this influence (Ajanta caves), and in them we see the highest expression of Buddhist spirituality (pl. 543). These works, which are now worn down and difficult to decipher, have even more of the traditional Indian suppleness of movement than the statues. The gracefulness of the arabesque here assumes a mystical tenderness. In keeping with the Oriental aesthetic, which sees everything unfolding or flowing, the different scenes shown in the same room or cave are all linked one to the other by figures or personages who play a part in two neighboring subjects.

Brahmanic art had a means of expression at its disposal that had been enriched by centuries of experiment. It avoided Gupta abstractness and in its masterpieces at Elephanta (seventh century, pl. 544), Mamallapuram, seventh century and Ellora, seventh, eighth centuries,

542. Buddhist art. 4th to 5th century. Standing Buddha
from Mathura. *Mathura, Museum.*
543. Buddhist art. 4th–5th century. The Great Bodhisattva.
Wall painting in Cave I, Ajanta.

it rediscovered the strength that works of art always have in early
phases of development while at the same time profiting from the plastic
achievement of a mature classical art. But the evangelistic enthusiasm
of Buddhist humanism gave way to the superhuman images common to
primitive religions. In the tenth and eleventh centuries, at Orissa, the
Hindu plastic system seems to have returned to the origins of Mathura

544. Brahmanic art. 7th century. The sleep of Vishnu.
Cave temple at Elephanta.

545. Brahmanic art of Mysore. 12th century.
Krishna playing the flute. *Calcutta, Indian Museum.*

art in works of overwhelming sensuality, while in the twelfth century, in the overladen bas-reliefs of Mysore, the feverishness of a declining art became exasperated in the same way as Flamboyant Gothic (pl. 545). After this, the major monumental sculpture withered into a decorative craft. However, from the tenth and almost into the seventeenth century, the Deccan produced admirable bronze statuettes in which an unexpected sense of arabesque restrains the usual lush roundness of the volumes. The firmness of line, the inner energy of the intense modeling, the depth of symbolism, together with an expansive feeling of life make some of the Nataraja of the twelfth century—representing Shiva's cosmic dance—works of a formal perfection not often found in India, and which can be set beside the most refined creations of the Italian Renaissance or of Chinese art (pl. 529).

REPERCUSSIONS OF INDIAN ART

The cultural expansion of India by way of the sea routes of the East Indies and through Indochina has been compared with that of Greece. It is true that a similar phenomenon is to be seen in both cases. India brought to the countries it influenced, not only religious forms of expression but also a classical vocabulary of images that was Aryan in spirit; that is to say, profoundly naturalistic. But the native temperaments of the peoples concerned reacted on the imported culture, so that the Indian aesthetic was "orientalized": as it lost some of its original character its forms finally became Asiatic and inclined toward expressions that were not far removed from the Chinese. Generally speaking, Hindu naturalism found itself opposed by the tendency toward stylization which characterizes the mentality behind all Asiatic civilizations—always aspiring to the abstract.

JAVANESE ART

The evolution described above is particularly noticeable in the art of Java. In the first period, which lasted from the eighth to the tenth century, the artistic civilization that developed in the east of Java remained obedient to the Indian aesthetic, while imposing an even more purified classicism upon it. The temples, sanctuaries and pyramids (pl. 546), while being of modest dimensions, were restrained and balanced compositions in which a monumental conception imposes its own strict laws on sculptural form, whether it be Buddhist as at Borobudur, or Brahmanic as at Prambanam: the sculptor was pursuing the Gupta ideal of naturalism, while being held back by his impulse to idealize. The finest monument in Java is the Borobudur stupa (second half of the eighth century), a structure unique of its kind, with its rising terraces surmounted by open bell-shaped *dagobas* or stupas, and

546. Javanese art. 8th century.
Temple at Candi Pawon.

547. Javanese art. Second half of 8th century.
The conception of the Buddha. Borobudur stupa.

with some 504 statues of the Dhayani Buddha set in niches, and bas-relief friezes telling the story of the Buddha in extraordinary detail, forming 2000 pictures which stretch over more than 3¾ miles. If the Dhayani Buddhas are suggestive of Gupta idealism, the friezes make one think more of the Ajanta frescoes: the mystical tenderness of the Great Vehicle was never expressed anywhere with greater humanity and sweetness than in these youthful forms which have none of the lushness of the Indian canon but show a very graceful elongation (pl. 547). At Prambanam this art developed toward refinement and worldly preciosity. After a certain gap, due no doubt to a period of political upheaval, Javanese civilization revived in the west of the island in the eleventh century, in a renaissance which produced its finest works in the thirteenth and fourteenth centuries. The Indonesian tendency became the stronger and showed itself in hieraticism, a fanciful stylization similar to the Chinese, and a taste for the monstrous. After the Moslem invasion this type of Javanese art retired to Bali, where it persists to this day.

Richly endowed with an imagination unusually prolific of forms, and which seemed unable to conceive of anything except at the prompting of what can be seen in nature, India was impotent when it came to making anything like a genuine architecture. The countries that depended on India and inherited a ready-made canon of ideas and imagery were capable of some speculation in the monumental field. Java pro-

427

duced some exquisitely pure monuments which were worthy of its own aesthetic, that seek gracefulness rather than mere size. The Khmers built the most beautiful and impressive monumental works to be found in the East.

KHMER ART

If the Khmer kingdom seems to have existed since the third century, the earliest remaining monuments date from the sixth to the eighth century (so-called pre-Angkor art). The great achievements of the kingdom date from the eighth century. In 802 the king Jayavarman II inaugurated on a mountain the cult of the divinized king, lord of the world, from which no doubt sprang the notion of the temple-mountain which remained dear to the Khmers. Between 893 and 910 Yashovarman chose the site of Angkor for his capital, later to be enriched with more and more imposing monuments, of which the finest are the Angkor Wat temple (first half of twelfth century) and the Bayon temple (thirteenth century) at Angkor Thom. Decadence set in rapidly after the Siamese invasion.

Of all the Oriental peoples, the Khmers alone showed a true genius for architecture. They understood how to plan cities according to definite principles, and how to make them into a harmonious monumental whole, and created a type of temple which may be compared with the finest architectural conceptions of the West. Being more positivistic than the Indians, who avoided any precision which might hinder their flights of thought, the Khmers took quite literally the idea that the temple should be an image of the cosmos, and therefore invented the temple in the form of a mountain. Taking the Indian gopuras, they had the idea of setting these out symmetrically and setting them in tiers on terraced pyramids, in such a way that the whole architectural composition rose gradually toward the central vimana which contained the effigy of the king-god and the king's soul in the form of the "royal lingham." From this pivot of the mountain-temple other sanctuaries radiated, these being dedicated to ancestors (pl. 548). This central plan with its series of enclosures recalls that of medieval keeps and castles, and is a perfect symbol of the monarchic theocracy invented by the Khmers. The possibility of dedicating a temple to themselves led to competition between the sovereigns, and explains the prosperity of building in that country.

548. Khmer art. First half of 12th century.
Aerial view of Angkor Wat, Cambodia.

All the elements of composition were ordered according to architectural requirements and principles. The towers were built in the shape of a cross to a coherent design: in some cases all the sides of a tower would be decorated with a gigantic head of monumental effect; these heads are a powerful symbol of the king, identified with the Lokeshvara Bodhisattva and thus asserting his entry and fitting place in the pattern of the skies and of the kingdom. Inside the enclosures, galleries which served as libraries or halls of worship were arranged with a fine sense of perspective, and crowned with corbeled "false vaulting" which gave the effect of a pointed barrel vault. The Khmers worked out a system of ornamentation, whereas in India decoration never rose above an accumulation of heterogeneous forms; they also restrained the carving and molding of cornices which ran riot in Hindu architecture; they knew the proper principles of molding, best calculated to enhance monumental effects. Such was their sense of the logic of architecture that in the pillars of the Angkor galleries they unwittingly reinvented the essential feature of the Doric column (pl. 549).

The Khmer sculptors spread their work almost as lavishly as in

429

549. Khmer art. First half of 12th century. Temple of Angkor Wat. Capital in the gallery of the first enclosure.

the Indian temples, but with a proper regard for the needs of architectural design. The Khmers covered the walls inside the galleries with immense, flat bas-reliefs which respected the wall surface but brought it to life (pl. 550). In these works, the forms follow a rhythmic pattern unknown to Indian art (pl. 551). The repetition of the same form in an indefinite series is a characteristic feature of the Asiatic mind. The flamboyant suppleness of contours and predominance of the arabesque

550. Khmer art. First half of 12th century.
Column of troops of King Suryavarman II. Temple of Angkor Wat, Cambodia.

551. Khmer art. Second half of 12th century. Bayon style.
Frieze of apsaras, or flying deities. *Paris, Musée Guimet.*

(frieze of apsaras) in Bayon art show the increasing expression of the Asiatic temperament and a strengthening of affinities with Chinese art.

Khmer art produced admirable statues in the round. The hieraticism of the frontal attitudes, the stylization of a summary type of bas-relief result in works that part company with Hindu naturalism and recall Egyptian art: they have an architectonic dignity and balance. In the Bayon period the famous "Angkor smile" graces the faces which, with closed eyes, express the fervor and bliss that the soul can achieve through the Buddha. This smile is to be found not only on Aryan and Indian faces, but also on faces which are more Asiatic, with almond-shaped eyes, waving eyebrows, thick and arched lips. An imagination given to the creation of monsters (*nagas, garudas,* stylized lions) also related the art of Angkor to that of China: it was no doubt the Siamese invasion which prevented a more pronounced Asiatization.

The forms developed by the Tchampa (Annamese) are close to those of Khmer art. As for Siam, its main creation was its bronze sculpture, strongly hieratic, in which an Asian stylization was taken farther than in Java or Cambodia; its best pieces were produced in the thirteenth to the sixteenth centuries.

CHINESE ART
HISTORICAL BACKGROUND

Although its immense coast line opens China to the Yellow Sea and the China Sea, yet its civilization is of the continental type. Cut off from the rest of Asia by the high Tibetan plateau, China has always been focused on the interior owing to the constant need for defense against the nomad peoples of the steppes who poured southward

431

through Mongolia. China only communicates with difficulty with the West by means of the oasis of Turkestan, the meeting point of two different worlds through which the silk route ran, a route which went through the Kashgar passes via Afghanistan to end at the gates of China at Tun-huang. The emperors were always concerned with holding the nomads at arm's length in the North and keeping the road open through Turkestan in the West. China is a fertile land, consisting of the alluvial plains of three great rivers stretching from north to south—the Yellow River (Huang Ho), Blue River (Yangtse), and West River (Si Kiang). This huge area, which at times came under a single emperor and was often divided into many states, has a great racial and religious unity which are ensured by a common language and method of writing. The history of China is one of alternating contraction and expansion. Whenever a dynasty managed to unify China under a single ruler, the need for quelling the barbarians resulted in an expansionist policy; but sooner or later an invasion of nomads, helped by internal strife, would come and shake the structure of the empire. Then the native dynasty would retreat to some internal province (Szechwan) or down to the South, while the barbarians, rapidly taking to Chinese ways, would give up their nomadic habits and found a settled state which might even work for the reunification of China. This perpetual state of alarm and readiness has favored Chinese civilization, since it discouraged the tendency to inertia rising from its respect for tradition while infusing China periodically with new blood and strength and keeping it in contact with the outside world. The area of Chinese expansion stretches by sea toward Japan, and overland into Burma, Indochina and the Indian archipelago, where it made contact with Hindu civilization.

Chinese religion is essentially based on a belief in the magical harmony between the human and universal orders, a harmony maintained by a ritual laid down by the emperor as head of the state. This religion, which is a rationalized form of a very early stage of human beliefs, sets man at the mercy of cosmic Heavenly Powers which are also delegated to the emperor who rules on earth. Ancestor worship contributes to this universal harmony because the souls of the dead become intercessors. The moral code of this practical religion is also a civic code, formulated by Confucius, whose thought inspired all the theories of the state developed by the intelligentsia or mandarins who followed him. It resulted in a philosophical humanism which underlies and cements the continuity of Chinese civilization. However, the Chinese mind has also been tempted by various mysticisms which sharpened its more spiritual instincts. Taoism, attributed in its origins to Lao-tse, who lived in the sixth century B.C., urges that the soul must put off all material sensation so as to find in itself the principle of its pure essence, which is in harmony with the principle of universal order. This is the *Tao*. This mysticism, which had great influence on painting, was practiced by monks. Introduced into China under the Han Dynasty, in the first century of our era, Buddhism took root and was proclaimed the state religion by the Tatar Dynasty of the Wei in the fifth century, in the form preached by the Great Vehicle. To the highly sophisticated Chinese, Buddhism brought the corrective of a religion of love based on a belief in the mercy of the Bodhisattvas, Maitreya, the Lord of infinite Light and ruler of Paradise, and Avalokitesvara, who in China became the goddess Kuan Yin, the very spirit of compassion. The so-called contemplative sect (*dhyana* in Sanskrit, *tch'an* in Chinese) linked up with Taoism and sought the essence of the Buddha in the human heart by intuitive means. Thus through its various approaches Chinese thought always tends toward a kind of monism; that is to say, a belief in the unity, the oneness of all beings and all things in the universal essence, while regarding all differences and individualities as being no more than appearances, illusions of the senses. This intellectualism, together with an extreme refinement of the senses, makes the Chinese more inclined than any other race to prize purity of form above all else: for the Chinese the highest artistic pleasure is to be found in handling a jade piece whose extremely simple form and smoothness of touch, together with its supernatural meaning, uplift the soul in a kind of ecstasy which takes it beyond the world of appearances.

552. Ancient Chinese art. Middle Chou period. Crouching tiger. Bronze. *Cambridge, Fogg Art Museum.*

EVOLUTION OF CHINESE ART

1. *Prehistory.*

A number of sites in northern China give proof of the existence of a neolithic pottery whose spiral decorations recall those of Aegean or central-European pots. This confirms that there was some continuity in neolithic civilizations.

2. *Ancient China. Shang or Yin (sixteenth to eleventh century* B.C.) *and Chou Dynasties (eleventh to third century* B.C.).

The excavations at Hsiao-t'un in northern Honan, and at An-yang in northern China, have brought up bronze vessels, inscribed and carved bones, jade objects, and a few marble figures of animals dating from the Shang period, the oldest historical dynasty. This symbolic art continued under the Chou Dynasty (pl. 552) which ended in a feudal anarchy with the period known as the Warring States period (fifth to third century), until Shih Huang Ti, who founded the short-lived Ch'in Dynasty (221–207 B.C.), established a United China for the first time. The emperor was responsible for the building of the famous Great Wall of China, which served as a barrier against the Mongol tribes. The art of this period may be considered as a highly cultured expression of the Bronze Age civilization, which at that time spread all over the Eurasian continent with the exception of the Mediterranean. The artist's activity was essentially bound up with a magic function, the objects he made being used for ritual purposes. These include bronze caldrons or kettles of a strictly defined design and use, being reserved for libations and sacrifices (pl. 553); inscribed bones used for divining; jade pieces for various uses, some being amulets, others symbols of power or strength (axes, knives, halberds) which were given to officials; the most remarkable were cosmic symbols used for sacrifices (a pierced disk meaning *pi*, a symbol of Heaven (pl. 554), or a cylinder inserted in a rectangle meaning *tsong*, a symbol of the earth; a rectangular plaque standing upright and engraved with the Great Bear, or *kuei* symbolizing a mountain). These articles have no decoration and owe their beauty to their purity of form and the quality of the jade, a hard stone which for the Chinese was a symbol of pure Essence. The caldrons are covered with a stylized decoration with a ritualistic, propitiatory meaning. The concentrated energy of these patterns makes itself felt in flamboyant curves in the Warring States and Ch'in periods.

553. Chinese art. Shang Dynasty, 12th century B.C. Ritual kettle in bronze, animal shape. *Washington, Freer Gallery.*

3. *Medieval China.*

Medieval China saw the vicissitudes of the great empire founded by the Ch'in. It began with the strong monarchic, theocratic and cultural centralization of the Han emperors (202 B.C. to A.D. 220) which collapsed beneath barbarian invasions and gave way to a divided and chaotic China until the T'ang Dynasty (618–906) managed to restore the empire. After a short period of anarchy (907–960) the Sung Dynasty again unified the country, but only for a short time (960–1126) because it was soon conquered in the South by the Mongols (1127–1279). The Mongols again unified China but to their own advantage (Yüan Dynasty, 1280–1368).

(*a*) *Han Dynasty* (202 B.C.–A.D. 220). It was the Han Dynasty which established the political and cultural unity of the Chinese Empire. This achievement meant the restoration of dynastic traditions as well as of Confucian philosophy, which had both been abolished by the Ch'in, according to a characteristic rhythm, since China always progresses by renewing its inspiration from the past. The Han policy of expansion into Asia opened China to the outside world and, through the North, brought in the influence of the animalistic art of the Steppes (which had previously penetrated in the time of the Warring States), and, through Turkestan, which General Pan Ch'ao had overrun, influences from Iran as well as the Buddhist religion. The Han capital cities were Ch'ang-an (formerly Hsi-an-fu) and, later further east, Lo-yang, also in Honan, on the Yellow River.

After the long period of magic and symbolism of the Ancient period, the Han period allowed some relaxation which showed in the

435

beginning of an art portraying figures (pl. 554). Han art tried to make great syntheses of forms freshly taken from nature, especially in terracotta sculpture for funerary use.

(b) *Political division. Period of the Six Dynasties*, A.D. 220–618. The Han Empire fell owing to revolution, and the Turco-Mongols invaded North China where they created new kingdoms, while national dynasties in the South carried on the native tradition. In the North the Tatar Wei Dynasty, which came to regard itself as fully Chinese, made Buddhism the state religion in the fifth century (453). Buddhism brought with it a demand for idols which produced great monumental sculptures, whose themes and style were borrowed from Turkestan Buddhism, which in its turn sprang from a mixture of Greco-Buddhist, Iranian and Gupta styles. It was then that the caves of Yün Kang in Honan were sculptured (453–515), followed by those of Lungmen (495–515). In these rock carvings and the Buddhistic styles of the same period, the feverish energy of the Chinese mind is sweetened to express only bliss and mystic ecstasy: it is the only time in Chinese art when a smile appears on the human face. The last supreme flowering of this mystic art occurred in the Sui period (589–617) under a dynasty which unified China for thirty years.

(c) *T'ang Dynasty* (618–906). The sense of the divine was crushed by the realistic outlook of the T'ang period, which produced the most naturalistic art known to China. The positivism of this triumphant dynasty, which kept China in a state of political unity for a period of two hundred years, thanks to its military strength, expressed itself in the cult of sculpture in the round which now became the dominant art medium (pl. 555). This form imposed its style on all other art, and for instance the decoration of mirrors in bronze is completely unbalanced by a powerful modeling out of proportion with the object. Painting also developed in this period. Generally speaking the T'ang aesthetic, strongly marked by outside influences as a result of imperial conquests, was rather foreign to the native Chinese genius.

4. *Sung* (960–1279) *and Yüan Dynasties* (1280–1368).

After a period of anarchy the Sung emperors unified China, but not for long. Under the pacifist, traditionalist influence of the educated class, the Sung emperors gave up the T'ang policy of defensive aggression and were soon left with only South China, where they made

Hangchow their capital in 1127. These emperors had little sense of political realism and were dilettantish aesthetes, "crowned dreamers" who gave all their time to poetry and painting. The decadence of the arts of carving in relief is a sign of the decay of energy and realism, but painting, which now came to the forefront, offered a ready form of expression to intellectual, metaphysical speculation (pl. 565). In the capital at K'ai-feng-fu in Honan, and later at Hangchow, the emperor and his courtiers accumulated rich art collections, while art critics wrote the history of the artists of the past and showed their esteem for those of the present, there being a Fine Arts Academy (with sections for painting and calligraphy) to pay honor to the most famous artists. Subjects for paintings were given out for competition.

Softened by social refinements and the enjoyment of life, this society lost grip on its own future preservation. The formidable hordes of Genghis Khan found it easy to sweep away this effete empire, to unify the land once more under the rule of Mongolian emperors (the Yüan Dynasty, which for a time brought China back to a more realistic art, with animal and military themes).

554. Chinese art. Han period, 202 B.C.–A.D. 220. Pi, a symbol of Heaven. *Private Collection.*

555. Chinese art. T'ang period, 8th century. Head of a Bodhisattva, from T'ien-lung-shan. *New York, Metropolitan Museum.*

5. *Modern China. Ming* (1368–1644) *and Ch'ing Dynasties* (1644–1912).

The really creative period of Chinese art ended with the Sung Dynasty. The native dynasty of the Ming emperors, who overthrew the Mongols, brought back a Restoration spirit with an emphasis on tradition resulting in an academic outlook in art which was only further strengthened under the Manchu Ch'ing Dynasty. The European demand for Chinese pieces now hastened a decline by encouraging a tendency toward picturesque trinkets. Ceramics were the favorite art in the Ming and Ch'ing periods. Almost all the great Chinese monuments date from these dynasties, since few survived from the previous periods. In 1421 the Ming emperors transferred the capital from Nanking to Peking, a city which was founded in the tenth century by Mongolian settlers.

ARCHAIC ART

As can be seen from the various articles and bronzes of the Shang, Chou and Ch'in periods, ancient Chinese art is a most remarkable example of the strength of expression that can be achieved in a range of forms extremely stylized in order to raise the image to a symbolic level. The characteristic Chinese genius for inventing nonrepresentational shapes is found here at its highest intensity (pl. 553). These bronzes have a decoration whose purpose was to give the ritual utensil a magic power: the principal decorative features were the *t'ao t'ieh*—a horned, jawless monster with popping eyes derived from a mixture of the ram or bull, the owl and the tiger (pl. 556), the *kuei* or dragon, and the snake, the bird, various types of spiral (some of which suggest the *lei wan* or thunder pattern which symbolizes rain, pl. 557). These signs could be transformed or combined in a thousand ways: some-

556. Drawing of the *t'ao t'ieh*, after a bronze of the Chou period.

557. Drawing of the *lei wan*, after a bronze of the Chou period.

times they are grouped symmetrically, though they consist of distinct elements which could be arranged like pieces of a jigsaw pattern, on a uniform background of carved spirals or *lei wan*. They seem to spring out suddenly, threateningly, from the primordial chaos of matter, and in this maze the human mind finds no natural feature on which it can rest, and thus feels itself snatched into a demoniacal world devoid of human meaning: the broken stylization of line strengthens this impression of a merciless form of art. Made in a period of bloodshed and torture when human lives seemed worthless, these works are the most eloquent messages of the archaic periods when mankind lived in fear of cosmic powers. In spite of the temptations offered by realism, mysticism and humanism which it was to feel later, this sense of the power of a universe intent on crushing man is rooted deeply in the Chinese soul. The evolution of their bronzes shows a gradual weakening of this will to supernatural expression. As is usually the case, the artist's hand is most expressive when it is busy inventing, and the virtuosity that comes with experience weakens the value or impact of the message. The strongest examples of this style are thus the oldest, those of the Shang period (pl. 553). Though they were still powerful in the Chou period (pl. 552) the forms tend gradually, at the end of the dynasty, to decline into a purely decorative stylization, being only superficially inscribed on the bronze surface. This trend was completed in the Ch'in period, when the figures of animals carved in the round, inspired by Steppe art, reached a further stage by giving the eye the reassuring shapes of living things.

SCULPTURE

The Chinese have never given sculpture much importance in the scale of artistic values. Whereas from the Han period onward historians have piously recorded the names of painters whose works have long since vanished, the arts of relief have remained anonymous. They were practiced by artisans who were all the less honored because most of their works were at once hidden away in tombs. Sculpture had no place in the Chinese house, and as for the temples, it was only with Buddhism that any demand was felt for sculpture. However, all the arts of relief were practiced successfully in the period of the great empires which created China. This sense for the most realistic of the arts, which exists and works in real space, is like a symbol of the positive outlook and energetic policy of the great dynasties. The animal and human forms taken by the funerary ceramics of the Han period show a fresh and bold desire to bring forms to life in space: the Chinese modeler shows only the essentials of his volumes without lingering over detail. In the Wei period the funerary statuettes became hieratic under the influence of the massive Buddhistic sculptures. The first Buddhistic works, the bas-reliefs of Yün Kang (453–515), still retain something of the naturalistic vision of the Indian carvings that inspired them (pl. 558). But the Chinese gift for stylization set to work on the Indian data, showing a complete transformation of the Indian into the Chinese plastic code, in the art of the Lungmen caves (pl. 559). The modeling loses its roundness and is summary, and the draperies fall into conventional folds that reach down to the feet in sharp waves while the bodies are set in a frontal symmetry that eliminates natural movement, all the forms being withdrawn and elongated in a hieraticism that gives symbolic expression to the internity of the Buddha. These highly spiritualized works have been compared with those of Romanesque art; but perhaps they are even more like those of early Gothic,

558. Chinese art. Wei period, 5th century.
Figures from the Yün Kang caves. *Boston, Museum of Fine Arts.*

559. Chinese art. Wei period, 6th century.
Bodhisattva from the Lungmen caves. *Boston, Museum of Fine Arts.*

such as the statues on the Royal Porch of Chartres Cathedral, in which the dematerialized bodies are reduced to little more than a fragile stem supporting an ecstatic face (pls. 524 and 560). The Sui period brought this style to its highest perfection, by detaching the figure from the wall and making it a work in the round. A hint of aristocratic mannerism which reminds one of the Gothic statues at Reims tends, however, to slacken its spiritual intensity a little (pl. 561). The T'ang period's will to power shows itself in an ostentatious fullness of the forms, a heavy vigorousness in the volumes (horsemen from the tomb of the emperor T'ai Tsung, pl. 562). The realism in the portrayal of animals, handed down from Sassanian art, came in by way of Turkestan, as did the growing taste for virile or warlike themes such as horsemen, warriors, guardians of tombs or *lokapala*. The way in which muscles are accentuated (pl. 563) and the complete lack of stylization show that the triumphant China of the T'angs was given over to foreign influences, most of which filtered through from Turkestan, which China was then occupying. The Buddhist sculptures of T'ien-lung-shan, copies of Gupta art, amount to a rejection or betrayal of the national

560. Chinese art. Wei period, late 5th–early 6th century.
Head of a Bodhisattva. *Private Collection.*

561. Chinese art. Sui period, late 6th–early 7th century.
Head of a Bodhisattva. *Private Collection.*

562. Chinese art. T'ang period. Warrior drawing an arrow
from his horse's side. Relief from the tomb
of the Emperor T'ai Tsung (*d*. 647) near Tsingkien (Shensi province).
Philadelphia, University Museum.
563. Chinese art. T'ang Dynasty, 7th to 10th century.
Figure of Dvarapala (a gatekeeper). *Cambridge, Fogg Art Museum.*

temperament (pl. 555), and it is the terra-cotta ceramists, producing funerary works, who seem to have been in closest touch with the traditional Chinese sense of arabesque (pl. 567). The Sung period marks the sharp decline of sculpture, when the image maker strayed into a mass of mere picturesque detail, such as jewels, delicacy and softness of draperies, which have more to do with painting. The huge statues of animals which line the avenues leading to the tombs of the Ming emperors are clumsy versions of chimeras and beasts, and merely served to show where emperors lay buried.

PAINTING

It is difficult for the public to appreciate Chinese painting—which along with the ancient bronzes best conveys the essence of the Chinese mentality—because so few good specimens from the best periods are to be found in museums and galleries, as well as their poor state of preservation, and the piecemeal presentation that becomes necessary for reproduction in books. When Chinese painting was not set on walls, it was done on rolls of paper or silk which were kept in special cases. According to whether they opened horizontally or vertically the scrolls were called (in Japanese) *makimono* or *kakemono*. The paintings were not intended to be seen at one glance, but to be read through systematically in the same way as handwriting.

Although the mural paintings that adorned the Han palaces no longer exist, we have some idea of them from the engraved funerary slabs that were copied from them: there is a feverish energy in those silhouettes which recall the black-figured Grecian vases (pl. 564). The scroll of Ku K'ai-Chin in the British Museum, which is a T'ang copy from the work of that fourth century artist, is evidence that the Chinese style of painting was already formed at that period. To make up for the scarcity of specimens up to the T'ang period, we have the large group of Buddhist mural paintings in the oasis of Tun-huang in Turkestan. These date from the seventh to the tenth century. Those which have been found in other oases (Turfan in Sinkiang, Miran, Dalan-Viliq) do not give a proper idea of the Chinese style, as they are strongly marked by Greco-Roman, Iranian and Indo-Gupta influences.

It was in the T'ang period that Chinese painting came into its own, at the same time as poetry, to which it was closely related. To judge from the few surviving examples, the artists seem to have been intent on defining forms by means of very precise outline both in landscape and figure painting, as might be expected of the realistic outlook of their age.

In the Sung period, at the capital K'ai-feng-fu and later at Hangchow—a city beautifully situated in the hills—the Taoist and Zen mystics had an influence which helped landscape toward a kind of metaphysical impressionism which was also reflected in poetry. Artists were trying

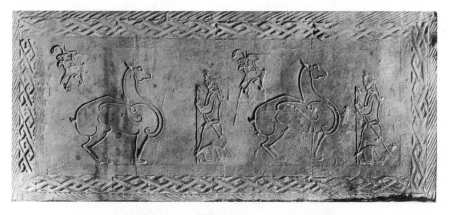

564. Chinese art. Han period, 202 B.C.–A.D. 220.
Tombstone. Detail. *Philadelphia, University Museum.*

to express the moods nature inspired in them, and the contemporary philosophy inclined them to feel the impermanence of things when they considered the world, and to probe behind appearances into the mystery of the universal Essence into which everything merges. This "cosmic dream" led them to compose landscapes of mountains and water, in which the mist-drenched forms seem to belong to a dissolving world (pl. 565). The grounds are shown one above the other in the kakemono in which they are treated as distances, the landscapes—shown vertically—being viewed from a very high point by the artist: when the human figure is shown it is no bigger than some insect, except when the painter is trying to suggest the meditations of some Taoist or Buddhist in the seclusion of his mountain hermitage. Through this naturalistic form produced by a decadent period, the paintings somehow share the cosmic meaning of the primitive bronzes: the shapes of things float as though dissolved in space, just as in former times symbols were scattered across the sides of bronze vessels, and the steaming mists play the part of the diffused background that in former times was filled by monotonous series of spirals. In the foreground, the

565. Attributed to Mi Fei (1051–1107). Landscape.
Ink on silk. *Washington, Freer Gallery.*

566. Liang K'ai. About 1200. The poet Li T'ai-po.
Ink on paper. *Japan, Private Collection.*

Sung landscapes often have some tormented outline of a tree that recalls the cruel, bristling arabesque of the monstrous visions of the Shang period. The painters, in their efforts to represent immateriality, gave up the naturalistic coloring of the T'ang artists and ultimately handled landscapes in a monochrome wash, relying on nothing but tone values. In their treatment of human figures or the shapes of flowers and animals very often a brief arabesque, indicated by the merest stroke of the brush, suggests the presence of some evanescent form.

A great number of artists, whose names have been piously handed down by Chinese art critics, devoted themselves to painting, an art which was held in such honor at court that some of the emperors such as Hui Tsung (1082–1135), who was overthrown by the barbarians, did not disdain to practice it. Among the most famous of the painters were Li Lung-mien, Ma Yüan, Hsia Kuei, Liang K'ai (pl. 566) and Mu Ch'i, the last two being Taoist painters. This glimpse of a dream world fell into a set formula in the Ming period, when artists were so lost in admiration of their ancestors that they merely followed the old recipes.

CERAMICS AND LACQUERS

The industrial arts took an increasingly important place in Chinese civilization, which is one in which our distinction between major and minor arts loses all meaning. A taste for pure form naturally led the Chinese to love ceramics, a field in which they undertook endless experiments.

It was in the Han period—long after its first use in the Mediterranean—that the Chinese took to the potter's wheel. The Han artists, moved by that gift for synthesis that had already inspired the early sculptors, began to throw their clay into very beautiful contours which they covered with a yellow or green glaze, sometimes adding a relief or incised decoration on the shoulder or neck. Equally gifted with a plastic sense, the T'ang potters worked on the same lines but introduced polychrome decoration in bright colors, green, yellow, reddish brown, cobalt blue. In the Sung period these refinements in coloring were followed by those in materials and shapes (pl. 568). The paste was ever thinner and finer, approaching porcelain, taking ivory-white tones or a milk-white, a reddish gray; but the so-called *celadon* tones are the loveliest with their light bluish-green glazes, whose indefinable sea-

567. Chinese art. Figurines in terra cotta, showing a princess and her handmaidens with musicians and dancers. T'ang period, except for the two smallest figures, which are perhaps of the Wei period. *Philadelphia, University Museum.*

568. Chinese art. Sung period, about 12th century. Celadon green bowl. *Boston, Museum of Fine Arts.*

like softness has a mysterious depth. The glazing often has a delicate incised decoration with a sweeping but simple effect. The way in which celadon lost its charm in the Ming period, when it became a stereotyped, stiff enamel, is enough to prove the Ming artists' loss of feeling for materials. They now replaced refinement of substance by a stress on effects, such as burnt glazings, "shot" with streaks of color, violent monochromes in *sang-de-boeuf* red, turquoise blue, aubergine, peach yellow and the like. The finest vases are those with a blue decoration on a white ground which were imitated by the makers of Delft ware. Under the Ch'ing emperors the sides of vases, which were made in larger dimensions than before, were too readily used for figured decoration in polychrome: these vases are classified into "families" according to the dominant tone. These are usually given in French, *famille verte, famille rose, famille rouge*. Little figurines and trinkets were also made in biscuit, the porcelain sometimes reaching an extraordinary egg-shell thinness. The popularity of Chinese ware in Europe certainly helped to ruin this art by quickening the production of fanciful images and knickknacks.

The same taste governed lacquered furniture, which was enlivened with decorative motifs or scenes from Chinese life from the late seventeenth century onward. Chinese lacquers were even ordered for furniture made in Europe.

ARCHITECTURE

In any study of the Chinese arts, architecture can be treated only as secondary, as a minor art. The Chinese are more deficient in architectural powers than in anything else, for they tend to think of forms in isolation as "objects" and have little or no aptitude for making a whole or groups of wholes with an underlying composition governed by a rational distribution of forms. Their habit of building in light materials such as brick and wood means that no buildings earlier than the Sung period remain, and even Sung buildings are few and far between. China—unlike India—knew the principle of the vault and was thus able to erect important public works such as city gates, bridges and colossal walls or ramparts. The Chinese temple or pagoda is essentially a tower made of superimposed stories, whose roofs are tilted up-

569. Chinese art. Ming period. Pagoda, Palichuan, near Peking. 1578.

ward at the corners. Like the palace, the temple may be surrounded with annexes which stand in the enclosure without any apparent logical arrangement. From the Ming period onward the buildings became covered with a garish polychrome ceramic (pl. 569), and architecture became practically a branch of decorative art. The Chinese have attached less importance to their houses than to their gardens, which are laid out like small images of the universe, having miniatures of various natural features such as mountains, rocks and lakes. These gardens were imitated in Europe in the eighteenth century, first in England and later in France.

THE EXPANSION OF CHINESE ART—JAPAN

In its spread southward, Chinese art found itself checked by Indian art, which followed the preaching of Buddhism across the East Indies and Indochina, in which territories Chinese art was obliged to come to terms with Indian art. The same happened in Tibet, whose position made it a meeting place for both influences. In the eighth century Tibet took to a rather inferior form of Buddhist mysticism known as Tantrism. Its sensuality and demoniacal drive are still felt there to this day. Annam fell into the Chinese sphere of influence.

In the Pacific, on the other hand, Chinese civilization found in Japan a field where there was no danger of rivalry from other sources. The great religious and aesthetic currents which reached Japan, including those from India, all came by way of China, so that Japan became a kind of terminal of the Eurasian continent.

Japan emerged from its prehistoric state only in the sixth century, at the time when Buddhism found its way there and was at once absorbed by this awakening people, whereas China merely adapted it to her own traditions. The Buddhistic aesthetic, known to Japan through the art of the Wei and Sui Dynasties, resulted in statuary of a high level of mysticism, but its rather studied perfection of form robs it of depth (seventh to ninth century). The finest works of that time are the Nara period statues (eighth century) and the Horyuji frescoes, which are like a belated echo of those of Ajanta (pl. 571). Meanwhile the aggressive realism of the Japanese temperament was already showing in statues of the four Deva Kings (pl. 570). In the medieval period when Japan was split by feudal wars, the people discovered its warlike,

570. Japanese art. Nara period, 8th century. Head of a Deva King
(guardian of the Buddhistic paradise).
Temple of Shinzakushi.

571. Japanese art. Nara period, early 8th century.
Head of Bodhisattva from the Horyuji frescoes.

chivalrous nature and began to break loose from the Chinese example in art; but Japan never ceased turning to China for inspiration, while tending to modify all that it borrowed in accordance with its national outlook. The worship of Amida or Amitabha—the compassionate Buddha—and the influence of the mystical Zen sect gave Japan some inkling of Chinese philosophical pantheism, but this influence was too weak to make much impression on an art which was moving closer and closer to realism (Kochi sculptures, late twelfth century, painted portraits of the Tosa school). In the fourteenth and fifteenth centuries Japanese painting felt the rather tardy influence of the Sung aesthetic, but however skillfully the painters handled their washes of Chinese ink and overlaid their landscapes with mist, their firm, energetic draughtsmanship was out of keeping with their contemplative intentions (Sesshu, about 1420–1506; Sesson, end of fourteenth century). From the seventeenth century onward Ming formalism also affected Japanese art, which was now awakening to color; the painters took readily to lacquer technique (Korin, 1658–1716, pl. 572). This kind of reverse interpretation of the Chinese aesthetic ended when the Japa-

449

572. Korin. Lacquer painting. *Private Collection.*
573. Utamaro. Young woman holding a cage. Woodcut color print.

nese found a technique really suited to their temperament, a hard dia-
grammatic use of line, a preference for the concrete, a taste for bright,
clearly defined colors, all of which fitted the Japanese for prints and
engravings. Black and white engraving was in use in the sixteenth century, but the discovery of color printing in 1742 gave this form of art
full scope. Torii Kiyonaga (1742–1815) brought ease of line and a
freshness of color to a sensuous art which portrayed feminine gracefulness. Utamaro (1754–1806) added a touch of eroticism in his studies
of courtesans (pl. 573). Hokusai (1760–1849) was leader of the realist
school. He brought a sharp eye to scenes from Japanese life and his
country's magnificent landscape, which he portrayed with a tense dry
line. In his *Thirty-six Views of Mount Fuji* he began the "record" or
chronicle of a single site which goes even farther than Monet's mere
variations on atmosphere. Hokusai's unquenchable curiosity also made
him a keen observer of every gesture of everyday and working-class
life (pl. 574). He published fifteen books of drawings, the *Mangwa,*
which are a kind of journal of his life as an artist. Whereas Hokusai
interpreted nature with a somewhat romantic, violent draughtsmanship,
Hiroshige (1792–1858) was a poet who rid landscape of anecdote and
abandoned himself to a dream of light and vastness, like an Impressionist
(pl. 575). The Japanese print, incidentally, was to have a considerable
influence on French painting in the second half of the nineteenth
century.

450

Japan also depended on China for its architecture, and although stone materials were plentiful on the island, building was almost entirely carried out in wood, on account of earthquakes. For the same reason the paper-partitioned Japanese house is extremely flimsy. However, the Japanese have a wealth of fine materials and they outstripped the Chinese in their skillful use of timbers. The Japanese decorative arts, which are so admired in the West, are very unlike those of China, which tend to the fantastic. The Japanese craftsman, with great skill, takes his ideas from nature, cleverly exploiting some natural shape for decorative purposes while respecting its objective truth: always clinging to realism, the Japanese search for style shows itself in a certain formalism unknown to Chinese art, which is always open to the mystery of things.

In some respects the Asiatic situation of Japan is a paradox. Thanks to its strict realism, Japanese art, which began at the same time as Western art—with which it has a parallel historical development—is much nearer to modern European art than it is to Chinese, and it is to Japan rather than China that the West has turned for inspiration.

574. Hokusai. Street scene. Wash drawing. *Boston, Museum of Fine Arts.*

575. Hiroshige. A shower on a bridge. Woodcut color print.

576. Matisse. The Joy of Life. 1906. *Private Collection.*

CHAPTER XII

ART NOW

A GLANCE at the artistic atlas of the world today shows that the only regions that have remained creative artistically are those in which a scientific civilization has developed, in other words the Western countries. Asia is sterile, after being a fertile source of forms for thousands of years. European colonialism cannot be blamed for this decadence, for the vast country of China, which was never subdued, is no less poor in artistic genius than its neighbors. Japan is the only part of Asia which has shown a lively interest in our contemporary plastic arts, though it has nothing to contribute; but Japan deliberately adopted the mechanized civilization of the West, the Japanese showing remarkable affinities to our mentality while the rest of Asia pursued its own dreams.

Thus the accusation that science is fatal to art can be maintained only when art is too narrowly defined. Equally valid in all its activities, the genius of man at any given time makes its mark in the realm of facts in the same way as in works and ideas. Scientific creation and artistic invention are expressions of the same vital energy in our time.

Scientific civilization has produced a crop of new forms in a world that was rapidly becoming static. The revolution in building methods

452

brought about by technical invention means the end of a time-honored
system of proportions based on the resistance of stone or wood. The
conflict between old and new is particularly noticeable as regards
classical architecture, limited by the use of the flat arch and the consequent need for numerous supports and the predominance of solid
masses over empty spaces. By allowing wider spans, reinforced or ferroconcrete has brought architecture back to speculations on space that
were the subject of experiment in the Middle Ages, thanks to a skillful
handling of the vault and arch that freed the structure from its own
weight. Architecture has become vertical again, after being horizontal
for a long period: the skyscrapers of New York recall the competition
for height that was so marked in the French cathedrals of the thirteenth
century. The building has again been converted into an immense work
of glass; it no longer rests on a solid foundation but on piles as slim as
the pillars of Soissons Cathedral. Reducing the weight-carrying features
to a few riblike girders, bridging immense gaps without visible support,
suspending structures over empty space, the modern architect seeks to
surprise us by the airiness and daring of his colossal works. Like the
thirteenth century master builders, he seems to take pride in defying
gravity and proving the superiority of mind over matter. Moreover,
history confirms the conclusions we draw from such an analysis of
forms. Contemporary architecture, created by the use of steel and reinforced concrete, has taken lessons from the Middle Ages in its reaction
against academic convention. Was it not an archaeologist who formulated the theory of functionalism? Until very recently the New York
skyscrapers, "cathedrals of business," were vying with the towers of
Gothic churches (pls. 577, 578).

However revolutionary it might appear, when the human mind
invents it always starts from some hint given by works that only a generation ago were despised. The creators of the modern aesthetic took
themselves for iconoclasts, and the war cry of the Fauves and Cubists
was "Burn the museums." But before the holocaust, the fire raisers
had a quick look round the museums to feast their eyes on their ancestors' works. If they pretended to walk scornfully past those of Raphael
and Rubens, on the other hand they were passionately interested in
China, archaic Greece, the medieval Romanesque, Pre-Columbian America and also Negro art (pls. 579, 580). The critics vied with the
painters, and no art was more anxious to justify itself by pointing to

ANCIENT AND MODERN SKYSCRAPERS

*The Gothic spirit had its final flowering in the
United States, where the first skyscrapers took
not only their vertical thrust, but also their
crown and decoration from the medieval tower.*

577. Ralph Walker. The Chicago Tribune Tower, Chicago. 1928.
578. The "Butter Tower," Rouen Cathedral, begun in 1487
by the architect Guillaume Pontifs.

INFLUENCE OF NEGRO ART

*The Negro fetishes "discovered" by Vlaminck and Derain
helped the Cubists to compose in geometrical terms.*

579. Pablo Picasso. Head of a woman. 1908. *Private Collection.*
580. African sculpture. From Gabon, French Equatorial Africa.
Private Collection.

the past than this modern art which was denounced as lunacy. Of course this "past" had on no account to be that of classical antiquity, for contemporary art was based on the destruction of the aesthetic that Europe had lived on for four hundred years: its appeals were made both to the medieval genius for formal invention that was never hide-bound by realism, and to popular or folk art (pls. 583, 584).

The modern world has to be credited with the discovery of the true value of artistic forms, a discovery that no other period managed to make, not even the China of the Sung period, which had such a subtle capacity for aesthetic analysis. The language of forms had become a learned language with its own vocabulary and syntax, and art historians pored over a dead medium. The Fauves and Cubists were intent on achieving the "pure" work of art, and tried to make it a living language. But at the same time an opposite current wanted the work of art to express the human passions—no longer, as in the past, by illustrating a "subject," but in a modern manner, through the eloquence of forms alone. The revelations of recent psychology, by showing the human mind to have an irrational substructure, led certain artists, the Surrealists, to invent a new style of imagery whose symbolic process owed something to the Middle Ages.

EXPRESSIONISM AND STYLIZATION

Rouault aims at a violent, expressive schematization of line and modeling. He consciously imitates Fayum portraits, Coptic textiles and medieval stained-glass.

581. Georges Rouault. Head of a woman. *Private Collection.*
582. Coptic art. Portrait of a woman. Fayum.
First half of 4th century. *Paris, Louvre.*

The creation of the plastic language in use today was a cosmopolitan event. Perhaps this sharing of all the nations of the West in a
common cultural endeavor heralds the political unity toward which we
are painfully striving? Until now all the main stages of our artistic
civilization were dominated by some particular nation that gave the
lead to others: France, Flanders and Italy took turns in playing that
part. France emerged from the nineteenth century proud of having
kept her creative faculties intact while the arts were at such a low ebb
in the rest of Europe. The Paris school has produced three groups
of artists, France's lucid genius showing itself in the creation of movements—Fauvism, Cubism and Surrealism—which are all based on intellectual speculation. On the other hand Expressionism, which was the
main contribution of the Slavic and Germanic countries, had a more
emotional, passional basis. The emergence of the Slavs is a remarkable
event that must be related to the awakening of Russia, which passed
overnight from the Middle Ages into the modern world. Thrown into
exile by an official doctrine which demanded a dull realistic imagery,
the Russian artists are none the less genuine representatives of their own
people, which no doubt will reclaim them sooner or later. It is the first
time that Slavic artists have thrown off their moribund Byzantinism to
take part in the Western art movement. Finally, Spanish romanticism

was to provide its shock troops, pioneers who brought a revolutionary violence into every movement they touched. Spain gave the world a man who has been astonishingly sensitive to all the forces animating his period. Pablo Picasso's work, so prolific and many-sided, would be enough in itself to interpret our age to future generations.

Even through the worst tragedies of modern times—to which she was always the first to be exposed—France has never failed to maintain that *sense of unity* which she draws from her confidence in the supremacy of thought over all other human activities. Ignoring the terror of modern existence, Bonnard, Matisse, Braque, each in his own way pursued an art of contemplation whose aim (as Matisse consciously formulated it) is to reconcile man to himself by means of aesthetic harmony. The sense of urgency brought about by the most recent world conflict was necessary before younger French artists could create a tragic style which they are already beginning to forget, while in his poetic tapestries a Jean Lurçat is celebrating the victory of light and life. Spaniards, Slavs and Germans, on the contrary, gripped by a consciousness of drama, were expressing the stampede of demoniacal powers in the human soul, through an art of breathless cruelty. Picasso, the greatest of them all, carried this expressionistic language to its highest intensity of horror, and in those years of slaughter he was the conscience of a tortured world.

Expressionism is an instinctive form of art which, more than either Fauvism or Cubism, lends itself to the infinite variety of men's temperaments: it has therefore encouraged the revival of national schools which, together with the creation of the Paris school, is the main event in twentieth century art, especially for the northern European countries. Spreading to Latin America, a region once so tragically inspired by the bloodthirsty religions of the Indians, it has produced vigorous offshoots in Mexico and Brazil.

The United States, full of confidence in human progress and refusing to take a dramatic view of the world, was bound to absorb Cubism and Surrealism, which are the plastic and psychological expression of our time. The New York school is perhaps the nearest there is to the Paris school.

If the creative qualities of a period are to be judged by variety of expression, no period has been so rich as ours. We are witnessing no less than an artistic inflation. The feverish pursuit of change which originated in scientific development and competition has now affected art. This need for advance has condemned the artist to an endless renewal of style, and the individual is always producing new variants out of the plastic language invented by the pioneers of contemporary art, sometimes with the addition of features taken from the past. Our period, far from being sterilized by the abstractions of science, is one that thirsts for images. The forms of the past, as well as those that are being invented daily, are being consumed at an enormous rate, by a civilization that rapidly devours everything, including time, in its efforts to achieve the world of the future which scientific progress is constantly putting out of reach.

THE REVOLUTION IN ARCHITECTURE

The principle of architectural rationalism which makes the layout, appearance and decoration of a building depend entirely on its function was formulated for the first time by the archaeologist and architect Viollet-le-Duc, who believed that this formula was demonstrated in Gothic architecture (*Entretiens sur l'architecture*, 1863–1872). A new material, steel, now allowed the rapid construction of the enormous covered spaces required by industry, such as stations, factories, stores, exhibition halls, which could be built by processes not unrelated to those of the Gothic cathedrals, since they resulted in a nerved or ribbed architecture in which the wall, deprived of its weight-bearing function, could be replaced by partitions or glass. Steel construction had been extensively used in England for bridged and industrial buildings ever since the end of the eighteenth century (Coalbrook Bridge over the Severn, 1777–1779). It came into domestic architecture with the Brighton Pavilion by John Nash, in which steel was used with brick (1815–1820). The famous Crystal Palace, built for the 1851 exhibition, made entirely of glass with a steel framework, already fulfilled the modern ideal of transparent architecture (pl. 585). This work was built by Joseph Paxton, who, however, profited from a plan entered for the competition by the French architect Horeau and disallowed because it was submitted by a foreigner.

Horatio Greenough (1805–1852) was the first American to suggest that in architecture, as in nature and the machine, beauty resides in function rather than superficial or symbolic decoration. His ideas found an

585. Paxton. The Crystal Palace, London. 1851 (since destroyed).

eloquent illustration in the span of Brooklyn Bridge, the famous suspension bridge first conceived by the engineer John Roebling in 1857 and brought to completion by his son in 1883.

Practiced occasionally before 1850 (Pont des Arts, Paris, 1803; the Mint, Nantes, 1825), steel architecture developed in France at about that date. Baltard built the Grandes Halles (market), Paris, in this style in 1855, Labrouste the framework of the Ste.-Geneviève library in 1843 and the main reading room of the Bibliothèque Nationale in 1854. In 1866 Baltard began building the St.-Augustin church, a steel structure with stone revetments. Stations, factories and bridges bene-

586. Henry Hobson Richardson. The Marshall Field Wholesale Store, Chicago. 1887.

fitted at once from the use of this new material, outstanding works being
the Galerie des Machines (147 feet 6 inches by 382 by 1355 feet) by
the architect Dutert and the engineer Cottancin at the International
Exhibition, 1889, and the Eiffel Tower (984 feet high). By his shrewd
calculations and technical inventiveness, together with the remarkable
simplicity and boldness of his methods of erection, the engineer Gustave Eiffel gave a sharp impetus to steel construction. Between 1877 and
1879 he built several such bridges and viaducts in Portugal, and from
1880 to 1884 he built the admirable Garabit Viaduct in France, perhaps
his masterpiece (with a span of 541 feet, 8 inches, 400 feet elevation).
The Eiffel Tower, erected quickly, 1887–1889, was his crowning
achievement. It was intended as a kind of triumphal arch for the International Exhibition, celebrating the triumph of industrial civilization.

Meanwhile, public and private buildings continued to be built in
stone, in a composite and overdecorative style which was usually Greco-
Roman for civic and Gothic for religious purposes. The Palais de Justice at Brussels (1883) by Polaert, and the Petit Palais in Paris, built by
Girault for the 1900 exhibition, are among the most pretentious of
these efforts; but toward 1890 the Belgian architects Henri Van de
Velde, Victor Horta, and Hankar formulated the principles of "functionalism" which forced the architect to show the structure of his
building: while not condemning decoration, they wanted ornament
to be based on nature as it was in medieval architecture. This idea led
to the short-lived modern style or Art Nouveau, a kind of baroque with
undulating forms and vegetable decoration, which at that time seduced
Guimard in Paris and Antonio Gaudí (1852–1926) who, in Barcelona,
produced fantastic architectural works inspired by rock movements
and swamped in lavish decoration (unfinished church of the Sagrada
Familia, 1878 onward, and the Milá apartments, pl. 587).

The renewal of architecture was to be accomplished by a further
step in steel construction with the help of reinforced concrete. The
process consists of casing steel girders or steel frames in concrete, thus
preventing oxydization of the metal. The elasticity of this material,
which allows great spaces to be bridged without supports, was to upset
all the traditional rules of proportion based on flat-arch and vault construction. The new process began to be used in England and France
toward 1850; but it was in France that it was developed rationally and
had its greatest success. The first attempts were made by the engineers

587. Antonio Gaudí. The Milá block of apartments, Barcelona. 1907–1910.

François Coignet (from 1852) and Joseph-Louis Lambot, who at the 1855 Paris exhibition showed a ship built according to this technique, and the gardener Joseph Monier. Together with steel, concrete was readily used for industrial buildings and artistic enterprises (road bridges, viaduct bridges), thanks to such daring engineers as Hennebrique, Bouissiron and Freyssinet. The 1900 exhibition gave its blessing to concrete, just as the 1889 exhibition had established steel. In 1900 the architect Tony Garnier scandalized the Institute by sending, from the Villa Medici, a plan for a whole industrial city in reinforced concrete. However this new material, which was widely used for industrial purposes from 1900 onward, was slow in invading "architecture." From 1894 to 1904 Anatole de Baudot, a pupil of Viollet-le-Duc, built the church of Saint-Jean de Montmartre, in Paris, with reinforced concrete and brick. The brothers Auguste and Gustave Perret gave a final impetus to reinforced concrete in their architectural programs (house, rue Franklin, 1903; Théâtre des Champs-Elysées, 1914; church at Le Raincy, 1922, pl. 589); but they still observed the old system of proportions based on classical architecture. In 1904 a bold aesthetician, Paul Souriau, in his work *La Beauté rationnelle*, formulated the principles that would combine industrial efficiency with aesthetic value.

Meanwhile other architects both in Europe and the United States were concerned with freeing architecture from its Gothic and Greco-Roman trammels through a disinterested study of the function of materials and their logical use. In Britain this tendency was particularly marked in domestic architecture. As early as 1859 William Morris

461

588. Adolf Loos. A house in Vienna. 1910.

(1834–1896), whose aim was to revive the domestic arts according to the principles laid down by Ruskin, commissioned Philip Webb to build him the "Red House" at Bexley Heath (Kent), based on traditional English rural design. Norman Shaw and C. F. A. Voysey followed this lead at the close of the century, as did the Scottish architect Charles Rennie Mackintosh, whose Glasgow School of Art was conceived in the same spirit in 1898. This revival of domestic architecture, with its reaction against eclecticism, was soon followed elsewhere. It caused a stir in Germany, thanks to a book written by Hermann Muthesius in 1904; while it brought in its wake an entirely new outlook on town planning, first outlined in theory by Ebenezer Howard in his book *Garden Cities of Tomorrow*. Influenced by Ruskin's idea, Howard called for the spreading of residential areas on the outskirts of towns, so that the population would live in detached houses on estates ringed by "green belts." In Holland, H. P. Berlage carried out in the national material, brick, a work of satisfying plainness in the Amsterdam Stock Exchange (1897–1903) and was followed by a new school whose most outstanding representative was Michael de Klerk. Functionalism was introduced into Germany by the Belgian savant Henri Van de Velde, who was given the Chair at Weimar University. German architects created the *Deutsche Werkbund* at Darmstadt in 1907 in reaction against the *Jugendstil*, the German equivalent of the "modern style." From the aesthetic point of view, however, the most striking innovator was the Austrian Adolf Loos, who early in the century began building flat-roofed houses with plain boxlike walls, the façade relieved only by horizontal recesses (pl. 588). The German Walter Gropius took Adolf Loos's methods still farther in the glass cagelike design of his Fagus works at Alfeld, near Hanover (1911–1913).

In the United States, Chicago became the center of the reaction against the eclecticism which was even more marked in America than elsewhere. Pioneers in the new movement were Henry Hobson Richardson, who built the Marshall Field Wholesale Store (pl. 586, completed in 1887), but was not one of the Chicago school; John Nellborn Root, and above all Louis Henry Sullivan. Using traditional materials, the Chicago school initiated a method of construction based on the framework without supporting walls, applying it with particular success in the first skyscrapers (Home Insurance, Chicago, 1885, by Jenney and Mundie; Auditorium, Chicago, 1887–1889, by Adler and Sullivan; Shell-Singer-Mayer Building, Chicago, 1894–1903, by Louis Sullivan; Call-Spreckels Building, 1897, at San Francisco, by Jervanos Reid). The first building in reinforced concrete was a Protestant church in Chicago designed by Frank Lloyd Wright in 1905–1907. With astounding foresight, Wright had already discovered before 1914 the normative principles and forms of contemporary architecture, much as Walter Gropius (who founded the Bauhaus at Weimar in 1919) and Le Corbusier were to formulate

589. A. and G. Perret. Church at Le Raincy (Seine-et-Oise). 1922–1923.

590. E. Freyssinet. Hangar at Orly Airfield, Paris. 1924.

them later. Wright, an artist of independent outlook who specializes in designing private residences, argues that every house must have its own individual character and be fully expressive, thanks to the wide range of materials that go to its construction, while fitting harmoniously into the natural surroundings among which it is built (viz., Kaufmann House at Bear Run, Pennsylvania, which is built across a stream, 1936).

The need for strict economy in the use of restricted sites in the business areas of great cities led American architects, from the late nineteenth century onward, to build skyscrapers whose colossal dimensions were made possible by the invention of elevators in 1852. The highest building at the time, built in 1889, had only ten stories. The Woolworth Building, New York, built by Cass Gilbert (completed in 1913), had forty-five stories. The two highest, the Empire State Building, which was finished in 1931, and the Chrysler Building, are 102 stories and 77 stories respectively. This vertical architecture, built in superimposed stories, has produced no distinctive form and derives from the Gothic cathedral tower; indeed some of the first skyscrapers were capped with an amortizement in the form of a spire (Woolworth Building) or a crown (Chicago Tribune Tower, 1928, pl. 577).

The first experiments in "modern" architecture before 1914 were not entirely free from the habit of ornamentation, or from traditional proportions. It was after the First World War that a strictly applied functionalism established a truly modern art by creating new forms deduced from a rational study of technical needs; such as hospitals, banks, museums, factories, civic and administrative buildings, bridges,

464

blocks of flats, private houses, town-planning. This movement developed simultaneously in Germany and France. In Germany Walter
Gropius founded the Bauhaus in Weimar in 1919 for this purpose (it
was subsequently transferred to Dessau). Gropius, who is now in the
U.S.A., was inspired by a certain socialistic missionary zeal, and thought
in terms of standardized production of buildings answering all the
needs of great communities. In France, Le Corbusier, a Swiss of French
extraction, expounded his ideas in the review *Esprit nouveau*,
which he founded in 1920 with Ozenfant. Le Corbusier is an inexhaustible theorist, who coined the famous term "a machine for living in" to
define a house. In spite of this he saw beyond engineering and was
not content with a purely materialistic functionalism as Gropius was:
he gave proper attention to architectural form, while basing it on
strictly mathematical proportions. Le Corbusier's fundamental technical process is to rest his building on piles and girders that support
flooring, though there are no solid walls, only glass surfaces shaded by
sun screens (pl. 593). This architect is driven by a kind of mystical
cult of sunlight and open air, and has drawn up plans for what he calls
villes radieuses, sunlit or radiant cities which would house a dense

591. Frank Lloyd Wright. The S. C. Johnson and Son, Inc.,
Administration and Research Center, Racine, Wisconsin. 1936.
Courtesy of Johnson's Wax.

population while having only five per cent of the area built over. He has completed his *unité d'habitation* or housing unit at Marseilles, the first specimen of a thorough application of the idea of a functional dwelling based on a system of proportions depending entirely on the human body and its needs; this he calls *le modulor* (from *module* meaning standard or unit). The *modulor* was first known as the "proportioning grid."

Since 1914 French architects and engineers have vied with each other in their bold experiments. E. Freyssinet exploited the properties of parabolic curves in the aeronautical hangars at Orly (1924, pl. 590), while Tony Garnier has built a number of civic buildings at Lyons. Mallet-Stevens, Roux-Spitz and André Lurçat make full use of the devices and proportions of the new architecture.

Functionalism is now universal. One of the most flourishing schools of architecture in Europe is in Holland, where J. J. P. Oud, Jan Wils and Willem Dudok, who built Hilversum, combine reinforced concrete and brick with a simple but pleasing effect. In Brazil, Le Corbusier's visit in 1936 aroused great enthusiasm for architecture, which is being stimulated and satisfied by such artists as Lucio Costa, Burle-Marx, Oscar Niemeyer. The first great undertaking to incorporate Le Corbusier's principles was the Ministry of Education Building at

592. Oscar Niemeyer, Lucio Costa and Burle-Marx,
after a design by Le Corbusier. Ministry of Education Building,
Rio de Janeiro. 1936–1945.
593. Le Corbusier. Block called the "Housing Unit,"
Marseilles. 1945–1953.

Rio de Janeiro, an immense stretch of glass fourteen stories high, built by a group of Brazilian architects. Made of glass bricks, with sun screens, the design was completed by Le Corbusier in 1936 (pl. 592).

All over the world ferroconcrete has outstripped steel building in the twentieth century, though it has not entirely replaced it. In the U.S.A. in particular, steel coated with concrete to prevent rust is commonly used. Such gigantic buildings as the Empire State Building, New York (1931), and the group of skyscrapers composing Rockefeller Center (1931–1940) are steel-built.

The American architects were drawn to the Gothic through the Anglo-Saxon tradition, and have tended to remain faithful to it. Manhattan, with its forest of towers and vertical rows of windows, suggests some greatly enlarged Tuscan town of the fourteenth century. As late as 1932, in such a functional building as Cornell University's New York Hospital the central part has all the appearance of a keep, and the high strips of glass, like lancet windows, recall the machicolation of the Papal Palace at Avignon. But more recently this Gothic verticalism has been given up in favor of the system created by Frank Lloyd Wright, Gropius and Le Corbusier, which is to build in horizontal strata or layers. The U.N.O. Building at Lake Success, erected by an international team, and the Brooklyn Veterans Administration Hospital, New York, built by Skidmore, Owings and Merrill (1950), are obvious examples of the return to horizontal design.

THE PARIS SCHOOL

PAINTING

The renown achieved by the French school of painting in the nineteenth century attracted artists from all over the world after 1900. The invention of the plastic language of our age was thus a matter of universal rivalry in which the Spaniards, Slavs and central-European artists played an important part. The exasperated individualism which urges modern artists to create a personal style makes it hard to analyze contemporary art, for groups are now no sooner formed than scattered.

The first great movements in modern painting were, once more, of purely French origin. The Nabis (about 1890) and especially the Fauves (1905), were violently opposed to Naturalism but none the less derived from Impressionism since they both thought of the painting

594. Henri Rousseau.
Monkeys in the Forest
of Orange Trees.
Private Collection.

as *pure color:* it demands little effort for us to pass from Gauguin and
Van Gogh to Matisse and Vlaminck. The essential principle of modern
painting was formulated by the painter-aesthetician Maurice Denis,
when he wrote in 1890, "Remember that before being a warhorse, a nude
or some story or other, a picture is essentially a flat surface covered
with colored pigments arranged in a certain order." The moderns dis-
carded any dependence on subject or nature and made it their business
to create "pure painting." Even when they wanted to translate some
definite emotion, it was the form itself that had to be expressive, and
not the representation or evocation of some touching theme. This aim
was still not very noticeable in the group of painters who between

595. Pierre Bonnard. Nude. *Private
Collection.*

1890–1900 went under the name Nabis (Prophets): Pierre Bonnard (1867–1946, pl. 595); Edouard Vuillard (1868–1940); K. X. Roussel (1867–1944) and Maurice Denis (1870–1943). Bonnard's entire work was dedicated to the lyricism of appearances; Vuillard's to *intimiste* interiors; while Roussel and Maurice Denis tended toward applied decoration. They all contrived to keep on good terms with nature. The movement that because of its uncompromising program was nick-named *Fauve* (wild) by Louis Vauxelles at the Salon d'Automne in 1905, on the contrary, broke completely with the whole naturalist tradition. Deliberately distorting the models which they continued to take from nature, all those connected with Fauvism sought to produce a shock effect on the spectator by sheer color and brushwork. The numerous artists who began as Fauves were not long in deviating according to their own temperament. Only Henri Matisse (1869–1954) remained faithful to the original doctrine of pure painting (pl. 576), and in his old age even tended toward increasingly subtle colored abstraction (pl. 583). Others like Manguin (1874–1945), Camoin (b. 1879), Puy (b. 1876), Friesz (1897–1949), Marquet (1875–1947)—who painted some atmospheric scenes of seaports (pl. 596)—moved imperceptibly toward an art of sensation like Impressionism itself. The Dutch painter Van Dongen (b. 1877) borders on Expressionism; after a short Fauve stage André Derain (1880–1954) returned to a neo-traditional con-

596. Albert Marquet. The Port of Algiers. 1941. *Private Collection.*

ception of painting. Marie Laurencin managed to make a graceful
stylization out of Cubism. Others used extremes of color to express
tragic feeling, as in the case of Rouault (b. 1871), a painter haunted by
Christian anguish (pl. 581), and the dramatic landscape painter Maurice
de Vlaminck (b. 1876). The instinctive painter Maurice Utrillo
(1883–1955) interpreted disillusioned suburbs, although he had
no historical connection with Fauvism and his tone scale is quite
different, being nearer the typical French feeling for "values" (pl. 597).
Instinctive or intuitive painting enjoyed great popularity after the discovery of Henri Rousseau, known as the Douanier (1844–1910), a
self-educated painter who belonged to the Symbolist generation (pl.
594). Numerous self-made painters from the working classes were to
follow his example, with a naïve awkwardness in which the public
thought they saw a return to the frankness of the primitives: they formed
a group supported by Wilhelm Uhde, a German critic who had settled
in Paris (Bombois, Vivin, Jean Eve, Boyer, Bauchant, Seraphine Louis).

The Cubist movement insisted still further on the independence of
the painted work. Cubism, which received its name from Henri Matisse
at the Salon d'Automne in 1908, was the joint creation of the Spaniard
Pablo Picasso (b. 1881, pl. 579) and the French painter Braque (b. 1882,
pl. 598), who both quoted Cézanne's constructivist aims in support of
their own. The first, Picasso, gave this common effort his revolutionary
violence, while Braque contributed his methodical approach. Between
1907 and 1914 they set out doggedly to invent a purely formal language. To the objects or figures they took from nature they brought
an increasingly geometrical analysis which in the end reduced the

597. Maurice Utrillo. Church
at Deuil (Seine-et-Oise).
1912. *Private Collection.*

598. Georges Braque. Man with a Guitar. 1911. *Private Collection.*
599. Juan Gris. Chessboard, Newspaper and Glasses. *Private Collection.*

painting to an interplay of surfaces and lines in which abstraction was deeply emphasized by ascetic color, in which a grayish brown predominated.

With the support of the poet Guillaume Apollinaire's forceful publicity, Cubism developed a host of offshoots. The Spanish painter Juan Gris (1887–1927, pl. 599) and the Pole Marcoussis (1883–1941) were alone with Braque in remaining faithful to orthodox Cubism. The Frenchmen André Lhote (b. 1885), Roger de la Fresnaye (1885–1925), Jacques Villon (b. 1875), Metzinger (b. 1883) and Gleizes (1881–1953) created a "color cubism," starting from a stylization of the real rather than breaking it down analytically. Robert Delaunay (1885–1941) gave this color cubism a more abstract character by making the canvas a chromatic variation on contrasted colors, an aesthetic which Apollinaire labeled *Orphism.* Certain artists, the *musicalistes,* used this technique in an effort to translate auditive sensations in painting (Valensi, Bourgogne, Blanc-Gatti, Belmont and others). The Futurist movement, which originated in Italy (Marinetti) and tried to portray forms in motion on the canvas, was Parisian in its first and purest phase and learned something from Cubism.

600. Raoul Dufy. The Paddock at Deauville. Water color.
Paris, Musée National d'Art Moderne.

The fifteen years before the 1914 war were marked by a remarkable mental tension, provoked perhaps by the desire to create a plastic language suitable to our times. After 1918 this new vocabulary was to be exploited for many different expressive purposes. There was a noticeable relaxation among all the prewar pioneers, during the decade 1920–1930, perhaps owing to the feeling of well-being after the Armistice. This resulted in a more conciliatory attitude to nature. This was Matisse's "sensual" phase, while Braque went through a period of realism. Raoul Dufy (1877–1953) gave Fauvism a genial, picturesque tonality (pl. 600). As for Picasso, between 1918–1928 he adventured

601. Fernand Léger. Woman with a Vase. 1924. *Private Collection.*

into experiments in harmony which sometimes he expressed in Cubist idiom (*The Three Musicians*, 1921), at other times in a naturalistic vocabulary (*Portrait of the Artist's Wife*, 1918).

It was also after the war that Fernand Léger (1881–1955), who created the *Effort moderne* movement, and Amédée Ozenfant (b. 1886), the inventor of Purism, began drawing a new plastic language out of Cubism. They aimed at creating a genuinely modern imagery, adaptable to the machine-age and capable of being mass-produced. Propagandist pictures and images, commercial art and advertising, window dressing, stage settings, all the spheres of modern life that call for visual forms, were profoundly influenced by Léger's art (pl. 601), while interior decoration and posters also owe much to Ozenfant.

But there were some artists—mainly from Slavic countries and some of Jewish origin—who brought a sense of pathos to the postwar world. This they conveyed in different ways: through melancholy (Moïse Kisling, a Pole, 1891–1953; Amedeo Modigliani, Italian, 1884–1920, pl. 603; Jules Pascin, Bulgarian, 1885–1930), or else convulsive methods of expression (Chaïm Soutine, Lithuanian, 1894–1943, pl. 602). This expressionist tendency, which in Germany rapidly became a kind of school but which in Paris had only appeared haphazardly before 1914, came to a head in France between the wars. The Russian Jew Marc Chagall (b. 1887) gave the Parisian school something of the Slavonic uneasiness of mind, in a kind of supernaturalism which blends the

602. Chaïm Soutine. The Old Actress. 1924. *Private Collection.*
603. Amedeo Modigliani. Seated Nude. 1917. *Private Collection.*

604. Marc Chagall. The Funeral. 1909. *Private Collection.*

worlds of dream and reality (pl. 604). The name *Expressionist* was
also given to a generation of French painters who were all born in
about 1890 (Henri Le Fauconnier, 1881–1946; Edouard Goerg, b. 1893;
Amédée de la Patellière, 1890–1932; Marcel Gromaire, b. 1892). These
painters are closer to Flemish folk expressionism than to the "pathetic"
expressionism peculiar to the Slavs and central Europe.

In its reaction against the demand for the autonomy of painting
so typical of the prewar movements, the decade 1920–1930 therefore
shows a tendency to relate the picture to some inspiration outside itself,
whether the external source or referent be the material world or human
sensibility. The Surrealist movement, which is the most original school
to have emerged since the First World War, and which is as important as Cubism, points in the same direction. Surrealism derived from
Dadaism, an ephemeral movement of absolute negation, a protest
against reason itself, which sprang from the feeling of anguish created
by the 1914 war and appeared during it simultaneously at Zurich
(Tristan Tzara, a Rumanian poet, Hans Arp from Alsace, the Germans
Huelsenbeck and Hugo Ball) and in New York (Picabia from Spain,
Marcel Duchamp from France), as well as in Cologne and Berlin. They
came together in Paris in 1919, but through the efforts of Louis Aragon
and André Breton, two French poets, Dadist nihilism was soon liqui-
dated. On its ruins they founded Surrealism, a word derived from Guillaume Apollinaire's early play, *Les Mamelles de Tirésias*. Taking over
from Dada all its hostility to rationalism, but drawing on the Freudian

474

theory of psychoanalysis, literary and plastic Surrealism tries to grasp
elements of the subconscious depths of the human mind and bring
them to the surface, by expressing them in forms or words with a suitable symbolic apparatus. Far from being an abstract tendency, Surrealism is on the contrary an "imagery" in all its essentials, and perhaps its
mistake lies precisely in having often neglected the purely plastic values
of its works by sacrificing them to the symbolic power of the image.
This movement so deeply reflected the sensibility of our time that it
united artists from all over the world: Swiss (Paul Klee, 1879–1940);
German (Max Ernst, b. 1891, and Wolfgang Paalen, b. 1905); French
(Marcel Duchamp, b. 1887, Yves Tanguy, 1900–1955, pl. 605, and André
Masson, b. 1896); Spanish (Joan Miró, b. 1893 and Salvador Dali,
b. 1904); Italian (Giorgio de Chirico, b. 1888, pl. 606); American (Man
Ray, b. 1890); and Cuban (Wilfredo Lam, b. 1902).

Now a world-wide movement, this new symbolism is being constantly renewed by the contribution of new generations of artists.
Owing to the upheaval caused by the war, its principal center now is
perhaps New York, although André Breton has returned to Paris.

While Matisse, Braque and Picasso seemed to be showing a more

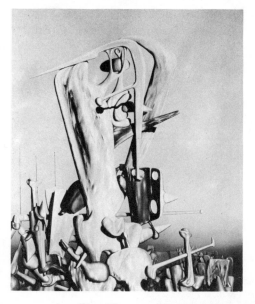 

605. Yves Tanguy. Ma Vie Blanche et Noire. 1944. *Private Collection.*
606. Giorgio de Chirico. The Disquieting Muses. 1916.
Private Collection.

indulgent attitude toward nature during the twenties, other artists who had already taken up that position before the 1914–1918 war continued to maintain it—Dunoyer de Segonzac, b. 1884; Luc-Albert Moreau, 1882–1948; Boussingault, 1883–1943. The young artists who were born about 1900 and began to express themselves toward 1930 took courage from this example and tried a pictorial realism which events were soon to eliminate. Some sought to comply with bourgeois tastes by making mild adaptations of Matisse, Bonnard, Vuillard, Derain (viz., Terechkovitch, Cavaillès, Limouse, Brianchon, Chapelain-Midy). Others, with more success, followed their own bent (Aujame, Planson, Oudot, Poncelet, Despierre). Others tried to make an aesthetic out of an austere kind of realism (*Forces Nouvelles* group, founded in 1935: Jean Lasne, Humbolt, Rohner). Under "Neo-Humanism" the critic Waldemar George advocated a sort of pseudo-classicism in which the human form played an essential role. Christian Bérard and others (Berman, Léonid, Joseph Floch, pl. 607, Hosiasson, Helmuth Koll) assembled under this banner.

But realism was rejoicing too soon in its triumph. An international group founded in 1931 under the title *Abstraction-Création* called for an absolutely abstract art which would take none of its data from nature. It demanded "non-representational" forms, whether imaginary or mathematical. This group included Piet Mondrian, 1886–1944, pl. 608, Theo Van Doesburg, Hans Arp, Albert Gleizes, Valmier, Hélion, Gorin, Herbin and Ben Nicholson.

607. Joseph Floch. Intérieur d'Eté. 1934. *Private Collection.*

608. Piet Mondrian. Abstraction. *Private Collection.*

Meanwhile Matisse, after his trip to Indonesia in 1931, and the murals he painted for the American collector Albert C. Barnes (*La Danse*, 1933), began to return to a more "purist" art which he carried increasingly in that direction for the rest of his life (Chapel of the Rosary for the Dominicans, Vence, 1948–1951).

After a short abstract period, Braque made a smooth synthesis of his naturalistic inspiration and his original Cubism (pl. 609). But the sensation of anguish provoked by the Spanish war and the approaching

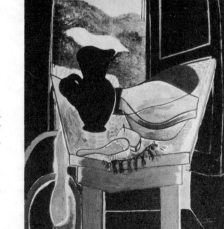

609. Georges Braque. Still Life. 1942. *Private Collection.*

world war drove Pablo Picasso, the painter who has in him the greatest measure of the grieving soul of our age, to invent a new expressionistic style which achieved greater violence than anything had been capable of before. For over ten years this inspired painter expressed the cruelty that had been unleashed on the world, by means of broken composition, jagged line, exasperated color, showing murdered figures whose reassembled limbs result in grimacing monsters (*Guernica*, 1937, pl. 610). Out of this cruel style a new expressionism was to emerge in France during the war, attracting such artists as Bernard Lorjou, André Marchand, Francis Gruber.

However, while these artists emphasized expression, the mental stress arising from the conflict produced an unforeseen revival of pure painting, in the form of violently colored compositions with an abstract bias (Le Moal, Bazaine, Manessier, Pignon) or with a more or less emphatic stylization of reality (Gischia, Fougeron, Tailleux, Estève, Lapicque, Desnoyers, Robin). The blended influences of Delaunay, Villon, La Fresnaye, Matisse and the Romanesque fresco painters all gave something to this movement.

This return to abstract art found itself countered at the same time by another tendency, in the renewal of an old color technique which had been dead for over two hundred years and was now revived by Jean Lurçat (b. 1892). Freed from any allegiance to a school by his experiments in a new technique, Jean Lurçat reinvented a style of imagery which achieves a synthesis of natural forms with the strict

610. Pablo Picasso. Guernica. 1937. *Owned by the artist.*
Courtesy of the Museum of Modern Art.

plastic demands of our time and the pure poetic inspiration that leads from Symbolism to Surrealism. The painter-poet has the multitudinous forms of the world at his disposal, and Jean Lurçat evokes them in cycles of images whose associations are thoroughly motivated by plastic requirements as well as by lyrical metaphor.

To sum up the main features in the complex evolution of the Paris school of painting in the past fifty years, it might be said that the 1905–1914 period tended to restore the prestige of pure *form* which had been weakened by Impressionist naturalism. The post-1914 period saw the *image* exalted once again, whether in an expressionist sense or a symbolic sense (Surrealism), but often at the expense of form. The art of Jean Lurçat, which incarnates the form in the image, suggests the opening of a new era in painting.

SCULPTURE

If contemporary sculpture cannot compete with painting in its variety of expression, this is inherent in the very nature of the art, which demands a costly and painful training and is more dependent on social conditions than is painting. The demand for sculpture has been almost entirely from official quarters, and public authorities have continued to support a school of academic artists who merely prolong the canons of the nineteenth century without the slightest change.

Moreover, rationalistic architecture has discouraged sculpture: it is a paradox that this art should be driven away from buildings at the very time it was rediscovering the monumental sense that it had lost with Carpeaux and Rodin, both of whom were seduced by the fluidity of painting. In the same way as painting, modern sculpture has evolved toward a definition of its true laws, and has therefore sought density of volumes and balanced masses. If Antoine Bourdelle (1861–1929), a pupil of Rodin, belonged to the nineteenth century thanks to his heroic vision, at the same time he tried to find the secret of architectonic poise in the archaic styles of Greece. It was to the Greek plastic example that our sculptors turned in their search for the lost sense of sculptural density. It inspired the meridional artist Aristide Maillol (1861–1944), whose researches were exclusively confined to the female nude. He did not forget Renoir's opulent forms and attained a fine balance between life and beauty. Had he been given more commissions he could have been a great monumental sculptor (pl. 612). Charles

611. Charles Despiau. Eve. *Paris, Musée National d'Art Moderne.*
612. Aristide Maillol. L'Ile de France. Bronze. 1910.
Paris, Musée National d'Art Moderne.

Despiau (1874–1946), another southern artist who turned to Greece, revived a long but forgotten French tradition in his portrait busts, though his method of grasping character was synthetic rather than analytic (pl. 611). Joseph Bernard (1866–1931), unlike Bourdelle and Despiau, sought the gracefulness of the arabesque, not the density of compact forms. Pompon (1855–1933), the Spaniard Hernández (1888–1949) and Joseph Constant (b. 1891) earned a reputation for concentrated, sober reliefs in their animal sculptures.

If the French in painting led the way in the onslaught on nature, they lagged behind in sculpture in this respect, no doubt because in the nineteenth century sculpture had been given up to academicism and romantic sentimentality, and what was now required was a return to the model. Most of the artists who translated Cubism into metal or stone were from other countries. Some went no further than a geometrical stylization of the real, such as the French artist Duchamp-Villon (1876–1919), the Russian Chana Orloff (b. 1888), though others adventured more boldly into the domain of abstract forms. The Frenchman Henri Laurens (b. 1885), who both paints and sculptures, started from a kind

480

613. Jacques Lipchitz. Melancholy. Bronze. 1930. *Private Collection.*
614. Pablo Gargallo. Harlequin. Bronze.
Paris, Musée National d'Art Moderne.

of bas-relief rendering of Braque's pictures to end with compact, involved forms. Constantin Brancusi (1876–1957) has invented smooth, egglike shapes of an absolute simplicity; Ossip Zadkine (b. 1890) breaks up the elements of relief and then fuses them into a solid composition; the Russian Jacques Lipchitz (b. 1891, pl. 613) together with the Ukrainian Archipenko (b. 1887) and Spaniard Pablo Gargallo (1881–1934, pl. 614) are all baroque artists whose aim is to create form vibrating in space. Painters such as Matisse, Braque and especially Picasso have often ventured into sculptural problems, like Degas before them. Hans Arp (b. 1887) and the Swiss Giacometti (b. 1877) do not hesitate to give their non-representational pieces a Surrealist meaning. A revival of non-representational sculpture is in progress in France at the present time, parallel with Neo-Cubism in painting (Adam, Béothy, Brauner, Vitullo). Some of them, such as Jean Preyrissac, go so far as emulating the "mobile" constructions of the American Calder. However, Paris has produced a whole school of representational figure sculptors following on the example of Maillol and Despiau. Wlérick (1882–1944), Auguste Guénot (b. 1882) and the Spaniard Manolo (1872–1945)

481

are Maillol's most faithful disciples. Gimond (b. 1894) is a scrupulous portrait artist; Couturier (b. 1905) is developing a sense of the monumental. Auricoste (b. 1908), Yencesse (b. 1900) and Saupique (b. 1889) all go back to much earlier French traditions.

THE NATIONAL SCHOOLS

One of the most remarkable events of the twentieth century is the revival of national schools. While a cosmopolitan art has been developing in France, but without the French tradition as its stabilizing factor, the other European countries, whose artistic schools were sterilized for over a hundred years by the tyranny of neo-classicism and of French realism, have finally asserted their independence and given expression to their native temperament, pushing it even to extremes. After the 1914 war, the new aesthetic which emerged in France spread to North and South America, where it was quickly absorbed and original talents began to spring up.

The most notable feature in this movement is the awakening of the northern spirit as opposed to the Latin, as can be seen in Germany, Switzerland, Scandinavia, Belgium and Holland.

Nineteenth century Germany was gripped by an academic outlook which was completely hostile to the national temperament, and this is one of the most astonishing paradoxes in the history of art. But during 1890–1900 Germany rediscovered expressionism, a manner which corresponds to something profoundly rooted in the national soul and which had provided the great tradition of Germany's finest period, the Middle Ages and the Renaissance. While the French Fauves and Cubists were busy defining pure painting, an art completely free of contingent elements, Germany sacrificed every consideration of form to the expression of its dramatic, tortured spirit, sometimes with brutal overemphasis. In 1892, at the time of an exhibition of work by the artist Edvard Munch, in Berlin, which was to lead to the so-called Berlin Secession, Germany had abandoned neo-classicism for a kind of realism inspired by Courbet (Menzel, Leibl) which was still not what she needed. The Expressionist lead was given by the surrounding northern countries, by the Swiss Hodler (1853–1918), who painted gigantic epic pieces in clashing colors (pl. 615), the Norwegian Edvard Munch (1863–1944, pl. 616), and the Dutchman Van Gogh. The "Secession"

615. Ferdinand Hodler. Warrior. 1897. *Geneva, Musée d'Art et d'Histoire.*
616. Edvard Munch. Winter night. *Zurich, Kunsthaus.*

painters sought to free themselves from academic convention by turning
to impressionism, but if Max Liebermann (1847–1935) went far toward
assimilating it, Slevogt (1868–1932) and Corinth (1858–1925) interpreted it with a dramatic feverishness that is alien to it. Toward 1905,
when Fauvism was emerging in France, expressionism was becoming
more fully conscious of itself in the *Brücke* (Bridge) group, which was
founded in Dresden in 1904 by artists including Kirchner (1880–1938),
Schmidt-Rottluff (b. 1884), Heckel (b. 1883), Nolde (b. 1867), Pech-
stein (1881–1955), Otto Mueller (1874–1930). By means of harsh color,
rough drawing, dramatic choice of subject and a return to primitivism by
echoing Negro sculpture, these artists unleashed an inward frenzy
which sometimes became irrational. In Austria Oskar Kokoschka
(b. 1886) expressed this anguish in the human face (pl. 617) as well as in
the "face" of nature. While the *Brücke* dissolved in 1913, a new group,
Der Blaue Reiter (the Blue Horseman), founded in Munich in 1911 and
supported by the Sturm Gallery in Berlin in 1912, was approaching
non-representational art, but differently from Cubism, in a manner which
amounts to a negation of appearances: Franz Marc (1880–1916), Macke
(1887–1914), the Swiss Paul Klee (1879–1940, pl. 618), Campendonck
(b. 1889). The most representative artist of this group was Kandinsky
(1886–1944), a Russian artist whose abstracts evoke some strange world
which refuses the limitations of geometry (pl. 619). The Bauhaus, a
Modernist school founded in Weimar in 1919, and which gave a great

483

617. Oskar Kokoschka. Portrait of a Man. About 1910. *Private Collection.*

618. Paul Klee. On the Meadow. *Private Collection.*

619. Wassily Kandinsky. Rays. 1927. *Private Collection.*

impetus to architecture, saw the possibility of a more constructive abstract art, more closely related to Cubism (Feininger, 1871–1956; Schlemmer, 1880–1943; Baumeister, 1889–1955). After the war Germany produced another aesthetic, the *Neue Sachlichkeit* (New Objectivism), which demanded an uncompromising, exasperated realism that was set at the service of a revolutionary imagery related to Surrealism (Otto Dix, b. 1891; Georg Grosz, b. 1893; Oskar Schlemmer, Max Beckmann, 1884–1950). German sculpture was strongly marked by the influence of Maillol and Despiau (Wilhelm Lehmbruck, 1881–1919, pl. 620; Ernst Barlach, 1870–1938).

484

By another paradox, when Nazism appealed to the Germans to rediscover their soul in the name of the "Aryan" tradition, it condemned as degenerate the very expressionism which had been based on all that was most characteristic of the race, and the political movement imposed in its stead a propagandist imagery expressed in terms of puerile realism. The artists fled the country and the modern German movement came to nothing.

Meanwhile impressionism helped Belgium to throw off a stifling realism. Between 1884 and 1889 the *Société des Vingt* (Twenty group) gave exhibitions of the modern French masters in Brussels. With different emphasis according to their temperament, Van Rysselberghe (1862–1926), Vogels (1836–1896), Evenpoel (1872–1899), Oleffe (1867–1932), Opsomer (b. 1878) and the fine painter Rick Wouters (1886–1916) used the Impressionist "rainbow palette" of light tones; the real founder of the modern Belgian school was the English-born James Ensor (1860–1949), who already in 1888 with his *Christ Entering Brussels* (pl. 621) disturbed this sense of rapture with his visionary art, his violent tonality, his grimacing masks which recall Hieronymus Bosch. This tendency to view reality as the outward sign of a hidden world, which at that time could be seen in the Symbolist writings of Maeterlinck, resulted in a coherent movement which has been called the Laethem-St.-Martin school, after the name of the Flemish village where from 1900 to 1910 a number of artists formed a group

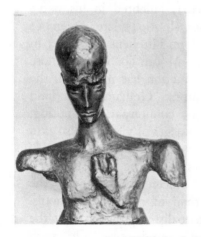 

620. Wilhelm Lehmbruck. Bust of a girl. 1913–1914.
Private Collection.
621. James Ensor. Christ Entering Brussels. 1888. Detail.
Private Collection.

round the sculptor George Minne (1866–1940). Flemish expressionism
has two main streams. First there is the mystical tendency toward symbolism, best represented by George Minne, Albert Servaes (b. 1883),
Gustave Van de Woestyne (b. 1881). Then there is a rustic, folk or
popular tendency with a stress on the health, joviality and robust
physique of the Flemings, or else the grandeur of Flemish landscape.
This stream is composed of Tytgat (b. 1879), Van den Berghe (b. 1883),
Gustave de Smet (b. 1877), Valerius de Saedler (b. 1867) and Constant
Permecke (1886–1951), the last of these creating an elemental, colossal
vision of man and nature out of the Flemish land and its people.

After impressionism (George Breitner, 1857–1923) Holland also
turned to expressionism, with some hesitation over its plastic technique
which rapidly threw Dutch painting into a harsh realism not unlike that
of the *Neue Sachlichkeit* in Germany (Jan Sluyters, b. 1881; Charles
Toorop, 1857–1927; A. C. Willink, b. 1900). England hesitated longer,
after being profoundly marked by Impressionism through the charming
painter Walter Sickert (1860–1942). It interpreted Cubism with a
personal note (Ben Nicholson). The war resulted in a belated Surrealist
and Cubist movement in Sutherland, Hodgkins, Moore. In 1910 and 1912
paintings of the School of Paris were exhibited in London at the Grafton
Galleries. In 1914 Wyndham Lewis (1884–1957), painter and theorist of
a constructive alliance of the "wild body" and the eye as compass of the
intelligence, founded the Vorticist movement. In the late twenties
the Seven and Five group brought together artists of decisive influence
in England: Christopher Wood (1901–1930), indebted in his naïve
landscapes to Fauvist principles, Ben Nicholson (b. 1894), later a member
of the *Abstraction-Création* group in Paris, Ivon Hitchens (b. 1893) in
landscapes influenced by Matisse, and Henry Moore (b. 1898), whose
evolving, inventive idiom of an organic abstraction has made him the
most influential of living European sculptors. Graham Sutherland
(b. 1903) is in some degree Moore's idiomatic counterpart in painting.
Edward Burra (b. 1905) has painted sardonic images of violence also akin
to German *Neue Sachlichkeit*.

The history of twentieth century painting in the United States,
following a trend already established in the nineteenth century, is the
history of many individual artists rather than of groups or schools.
Self-constituted groups or schools do occasionally appear but lack the
solidarity and continuity of schools in the European sense. One such

group was "The Eight," which numbered painters like Robert Henri (1865–1929) and John Sloan (1871–1953), whose art, based on observation of the realities of urban life, was a protest against the academic tradition. A follower of Henri and his ideals was George Bellows (1882–1925), painter of eloquent and sensitive portraits, dynamic boxing subjects, and elegiac landscapes. Post-Impressionism was slow in coming to America. Marsden Hartley (1877–1942) and Max Weber (b. 1881), artists sponsored by Alfred Stieglitz, the distinguished photographer, introduced American variations on Cubism and Expressionism to New York as early as 1910.

The turning point in modern American art was the Armory Show of 1913, a vast array of paintings and sculpture brought together to illustrate the most modern trends in Europe and America. This exhibition, organized by Walt Kuhn and Arthur B. Davies, was a sensation and a revelation to the American public.

So many factors contributed to the transformation of American art into the modern idiom of the Fauves and Cubists that it would be impossible to relate them all. Perhaps most influential of all was Stieglitz and his group at the "291" gallery; new assertions of freedom and defiance of the academicians brought about the first Independent show of 1910 by the Independent Artists, precursors of the later Society of Independent Artists founded in 1917.

Aggressive representatives of artistic isolationism were the regionalist artists of the thirties, Thomas H. Benton (b. 1889), Grant Wood (1892–1942) and John Stuart Curry (1897–1946). Among the artists who gave an American interpretation of Post-Impressionist ideals was

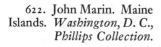
622. John Marin. Maine Islands. *Washington, D. C., Phillips Collection.*

John Marin (1870–1953, pl. 622), who in a very personal calligraphic watercolor style sought to suggest dynamic change in the face of reality. Marsden Hartley (1877–1942) developed into a twentieth century Ryder in his expressionistic painting of the sea and its people. Lionel Feininger (b. 1871), an offshoot of the modern German school, presented a formula of romantic, decorative abstraction.

A group sometimes described as Cubist-Realists includes Charles Sheeler (b. 1883), recorder in sharp focus of the cold face of the industrial landscape, and Charles Demuth (1883–1935), whose sensitive reworkings of Cubism are second only to his very personal flower studies. In his fondness for clean, unencumbered surfaces, the Surrealist Peter Blume (b. 1906) is an outgrowth of this trend.

American landscape painting has its distinguished representative in the twentieth century with Charles Burchfield (b. 1893), whose work, almost exclusively in water color, has been concerned with a romantic interpretation of the midwestern scene and the animation of motifs in nature through expressionistic devices. Edward Hopper (b. 1882) in figure painting as well as in urban landscape reveals the American and the American scene in terms of sharp, cold illumination that intensifies the loneliness of his theme.

At mid-century the division of American painting into the work of many individuals and small, loosely associated groups continued. The so-called New York school, numbering such *avant garde* artists as Jackson Pollock and Robert Motherwell, represents a phase of non-objective expressionism with a complete suppression of any kind of representation. Opposed to this group is the violent coloristic expressionism and social protest of Jack Levine (b. 1915) and Hyman Bloom (b. 1913). Ben Shahn (b. 1898) has given his impressions of the rights and wrongs of democracy in forms combining realism with the simplicity of the primitive. A list of the more interesting American abstract painters would include the pioneer, Arthur Dove (1880–1946), Karl Knaths (b. 1891), Rice Pereira (b. 1907) and Stuart Davis (b. 1894). Magic realism has its representative in Andrew Wyeth (b. 1917), and the romantic visionaries or "Painters of the Inner Eye" number Mark Tobey (b. 1890) and Morris Graves (b. 1910).

In the American sculpture of the early twentieth century, the Renaissance idiom of Augustus St.-Gaudens (1848–1907), without his peculiarly lyric interpretation of form, continued with Daniel Chester

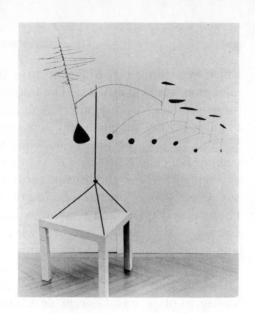

623. Alexander Calder.
Horizontal Spines.
*Addison Gallery
of American Art,
Andover, Mass.,
Phillips Academy.*

French (1850–1931). An archaistic but graceful eclecticism marked the work of Paul Manship (b. 1885). A more original contribution to a medium that has never won the interest of the American public appears in the voluptuous conceptions of form by Gaston Lachaise (1882–1935). John Flannagan (1895–1942) with his vision of the image in the rock was one of the most powerful carvers to appear in the first half of the twentieth century. More conservative, but very moving human figures, realized with great feeling for the texture of stone, typify the work of William Zorach (b. 1887). Alexander Calder's (b. 1898) abstract revolving metal compositions or "mobiles," the artistic counterpart of the American love of the gadget, have won their creator an international reputation (pl. 623).

The Latin countries other than France have had a less impressive artistic period than the Nordic countries. Spain was robbed of a living national school because its best artists went to Paris: the first, "Blue" period (1902–1905) of Pablo Picasso, who is the acknowledged leader of the whole modern movement, may be considered as entirely Spanish. The romantic Spanish temperament lends itself readily to expressionism (José Gutierrez Solana, who recalls Goya), but other artists come close to Cubism (Ismail de la Serna) or Surrealism (Manuel Angelico Ortiz and the sculptor Alberto). Portugal has produced a great sculptor, Franco, who is gifted with a sense of the monumental which is rare in our century. Italy produced a very original movement in Futurism, which was formed in Milan in 1910 by the poet Marinetti. Its first exhibition was held in 1912. The Futurist aesthetic exalted the clear-cut forms produced by machinery, and aimed at expressing dynamism by a kind of plastic "simultaneism" conveying movement and energy (Gino Severini, b. 1883, pl. 624; Prampolini; Carlo Carrà, b. 1881; Balla; the sculptor Boccioni, 1882–1916). When Futurism returned to Italy it lost its original character and became confused with a vague idea of Modernism. Gino Severini became a decorator, Prampolini a Cubist, Carlo Carrà a Surrealist; Tato exalted aviation, which of course was the pet glory of Fascism, with a Realist imagery; Massimo Campigli and Mario Tozzi both sought inspiration in the painting of antiquity. Two great artists springing from the Paris school are the Tuscan Amedeo Modigliani (pl. 603), who had all the sensitive and nostalgic gracefulness of the Sienese painters, and Giorgio de Chirico (pl. 606), who was a forerunner of Surrealism with his symbolic paintings composed of features taken from the antique and from the Quattrocento. More recently, Marino Marini (b. 1901) has found something of the terse energy of primitive volumes.

After 1918 modern art spread into North and South America. The U.S.A. has a flourishing school in which Surrealist and non-representational tendencies (Maurer, Arthur Dove) have become established, particularly in recent years. Expressionism has also proved very successful (John Marin, A. Rattner, K. Knaths). Among the most original recent creations in America are Calder's mobiles, which are geometrical constructions moved by motors or by wind, and which are the artist's

624. Gino Severini. Composition.
Private Collection.

tribute to the dynamism of the machine age. The U.S.A. has made more effort than any other country to help the masses to understand modern art, and the Museum of Modern Art in New York, which was founded for that purpose, is a laboratory of modernism. The Latin American republics have rapidly assimilated the whole plastic vocabulary of modern art, helped by the fundamental richness of the folk tradition which has been revitalized by European contributions. The "Neo-Latins" have produced some most original works. The two schools showing the greatest variety of talents are those of Argentina and Brazil. In Uruguay, Pedro Figari (1861–1938) is an exquisite colorist and a witty reporter of local life. Torres García (b. 1874) has been influenced by Pre-Columbian art. The most remarkable development in the region is the emergence in Mexico and Brazil of a monumental expressionism reflecting the vitality and power of the masses, and which has found its medium in enormous mural paintings. The revolutionary movement in Mexico has inspired a number of painters. Of these, Diego Rivera (1880–1957) developed an imagery of the awakening proletariat in his vast compositions; Orozco (1883–1949) and Timayo (b. 1899) are more expressionistic; Alfaro Siqueiros (1898–1950) found an impressive source of inspiration in the lost Indian tradition. In Brazil, Lasar Segall (b. 1890) has transplanted Slavic melancholy into a new civilization, while Candido Portinari (b. 1903) has created a powerful style suitable for monumental works; during the recent war Portinari successfully took up Picasso's expressionism and with its help gave moving utterance to the anguish that then swept the world (pl. 625).

625. Candido Portinari. Gaucho. 1942. *Formerly in Rio de Janeiro, Radio Tupi (destroyed).*

626. G. Serrurier. Dining Room. 1899.

THE MINOR ARTS

Toward 1890, with Horta in Belgium and Galle in France, a reaction set in against copying classical styles in furniture, in favor of a new style based directly on natural forms. Emile Galle (1846–1904), who founded the Nancy school, designed furniture, vases and jewelry in floral patterns with a latent symbolic meaning, whose lavish curves recall the Flamboyant Gothic. This is what is known as Art Nouveau. Louis Majorelle (1859–1926) developed this style in furniture, and it had particular success in pottery (Delaherche, Emile Lenoble, Emile Decoeur) and in glassware (René Lalique, Daum).

The baroque style fell out of favor toward 1910, when it was simplified by means of purer curves and plainer decoration, the result being a style which became established at the Paris Exhibition of Decorative Arts in 1925 (Paul Follot, Maurice Dufrène, Paul Poiret). This style made great use of textiles, the materials taking their geometrical patterns

627. Paul Follot. Dining Room. 1921.

from Cubism, or having a stylized or geometrical design based on the floral style of 1900. Brandt and Subes made some fine wrought-iron work in this manner. The best pieces of furniture—and perhaps the only ones that are not already dated—were those of Ruhlmann, which have a very pure contour deriving from the Louis XVI and English styles and are constructed of fine timbers.

Shortly after the 1925 exhibition there was a reaction against curves, when Le Corbusier's influence imposed a functional style with straight lines and no decoration. This style was already to be seen in Germany before 1914, and it was shown in Paris in 1910 at the Deutsche Werkbund's exhibition. This sober style was only established in Paris in 1930 (Francis Jourdain, Pierre Chareau, Djo Bourgeois, Louis Sognot). The influence of modern machinery resulted in making furniture with metal tubing (René Herbst). Toward 1937 a further reaction ousted the "architect's" style, producing a "decorator's" style which was less austere, some of the new school (Arbus, Serge Roche) going as far as using stylized rococo shapes.

The first half of the twentieth century witnessed a considerable development in scenic art. This movement began in Paris, with Bakst's scenery for the Russian Ballet in 1909.

Since about 1940 the craft of tapestry, which had for a long time been in a state of decadence, was revived with impressive results at the private workshops at Aubusson. Although Raoul Dufy and Marcel Gromaire were attracted to this craft and created some fine works, the painter Jean Lurçat was the moving spirit. He brought a "modern's" rationalistic outlook to bear on the technical processes and formal laws

628. Djo Bourgeois. Interior.
1932.

of the art of tapestry as they had been in its finest period in the fourteenth and fifteenth centuries, and was finally in a position to impose
his own aesthetic ideals on it. This renovation of an applied art, which
calls for craftsmanship and appeals to a wide public, offers a much
needed change from the modern esoteric tendency which confines art
appreciation to an élite. Several individual styles have found their expression in this adaptable medium, from the lyricism of Lurçat (pl. 631),
Picard le Doux, Marc Saint-Saens to the expressionism of Vogensky and
the pure abstracts of Matégot (pl. 629). There has also been a noticeable
tendency in recent years, among established artists, toward applying
their skill in the field of the industrial arts. Pablo Picasso gave an impetus
to the search for new possibilities in pottery with his pieces fired at
Vallauris in Provence since 1948. Fernand Léger, Joan Miró, Lurçat
and Chagall have all followed his example. Henri Matisse has designed
not only a chapel but all its accessories, from the architecture itself
down to the stained glass and ceramic decorations (Dominican chapel

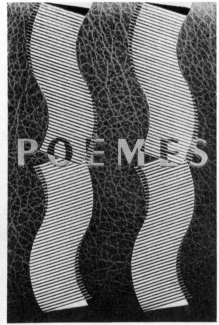

629. Mathieu Matégot. Tapestry. *Private Collection.*
630. Rose Adler. Bookbinding. *Private Collection.*

631. Jean Lurçat. The Sly Dogs. Detail of tapestry.
Private Collection.

at Vence). Two Dominicans, Fathers Couturier and Régamey, headed a campaign to admit modern art into the churches, the most remarkable success of its kind being the chapel at Assy-Passy, where Bonnard, Lurçat, Léger, Matisse, Braque, Bazaine and Germaine Richier all collaborated in the decoration.

632. Emile Decoeur. Stoneware vase.
Private Collection.

CLASSICAL AND BAROQUE

*Static, focused on the center and completely self-
contained, Titian's composition is classical.
Rubens' composition follows the baroque aesthetic
and is cut across by a great diagonal movement.*

633. Titian. Assumption of the Virgin. *Venice, Church of the Frari.*
634. Rubens. Assumption of the Virgin. *Brussels, Musée des Beaux-Arts.*

CONCLUSION

WHILE ART historians have been gradually taking stock of the manifold aspects of works of art in time and place, it is inevitable that they should be constantly concerned with the problem of what a work of art is, and what are the conditions under which art may come into being.

For the first historians, the work of art threw more light than any other human creation on the individual: the Italian, Vasari (1550), and the Fleming, Carel Van Mander (1600), both approached art from the biographical point of view.

However, it gradually began to be thought that the production of a work of art is determined by "the material, moral and intellectual climate in which a man lives and dies" (Taine). Originally suggested

496

to some extent by a belief in astrology, this notion was already to be found in Winckelmann's *History of Ancient Art* and the Abbate Lanzi's *Storia pitturica della Italia* (1789); the Swiss scholar Jacob Burckhardt applied it brilliantly in his *Civilization of the Renaissance* (1860). None the less, Hippolyte Taine in his *Philosophy of Art* (1865–1867) was mistaken in turning it into a systematic approach which swept all before it in the late nineteenth century.

Other historians, by stressing psychological more than geographical or historical factors, have believed the work of art to contain the most significant evidence of the spiritual outlook of a given period. This leads to the idea embodied in the work receiving more attention than the form itself, as in the case of Emile Mâle's *Religious Art from the Twelfth to the Eighteenth Century* (1949). Even more recently the Czech critic, Dvorak (writing in German), defended the same thesis in his study of the formation of baroque.

Since the racial problem caused so much disagreement in the second half of the nineteenth century, it is not surprising to note its repercussions on art. Following on the French writer Courajod, the Austrian scholar Josef Strzygowski thought he found the most fruitful element in artistic creation in the Nordic race. After working for years in the field of Western and neighboring Asiatic art, he astonished the art historians of his time in 1901 with his book *Orient oder Rom?* in which he attributed the development of Byzantine art to the Eastern civilizations rather than to the genius of the Romans. Whereas Courajod gave a psychological and strictly ethnical meaning to the term *race*, Strzygowski also gave it a geographical significance. For him, the history of Western art showed an endless struggle between two centers of world culture; that of the South, which he centered on the Equator; and that of the North, beginning near the North Pole—a zone which would appear to be particularly favorable to artistic creation, thanks to the artistic gifts of the peoples who settled in it and whose origins Strzygowski sought eastward, at first in Armenia, then in the East, and finally in the Siberian steppes. Whereas the South generated "academic" forms which served a temporal or religious hierarchy, the Northern peoples had an imaginative capacity for creating pure forms for their own sake. After defining the psychological make-up of these "Nordic" peoples, Strzygowski tried to show their contribution to the different Mediterranean civilizations which they had fertilized.

By reducing history to such postulates, Strzygowski invented a chronological method which consisted of ignoring historical facts and dating artistic forms according to a supposed logical succession: in particular he saw folk art as a reflection of basic primordial forms and not as the degenerate survival of advanced cultures. Strzygowski's theories have an epic touch which appeals to the imagination; but as they have no proper connection with realities his later views particularly may be dismissed as romantic speculations.

The end of the century showed a weakening grasp on the concrete and on rationality (which is its correlative), and this came to a head in the philosophy of Bergson, deeply influencing both the art and the politics of our time. Art historians, following a certain "finalist" tendency which showed itself particularly in neo-vitalist doctrines, began to seek the determining factors in the work of art no longer in circumstances outside the work, but in the artistic activity itself. They credited this activity with a capacity for development or expansion of its own, to be understood like life in terms of a "creative evolution" working toward a more efficient use of its inherent properties.

It is not surprising that Germany was the first country to think of the work of art in these terms, for whereas French thought in the nineteenth century tended to be positivistic, German philosophy was more idealistic. The *Kunstwollen* formulated by Alois Riegl in 1893 in his *Stilfragen*, that will-to-art which he postulated as the active principle behind all artistic development, is an *idée force* or dynamic theory characteristic of German philosophy. In 1908, in a violent attack on the ideas developed by Semper in *Der Stil in den technischen und tektonischen Künsten* (1860–1863), Alois Riegl argued that the art of the later Roman Empire (Byzantinism) resulted from the appearance of a new form of artistic expression and not merely a decay in technical processes, the latter being themselves determined by a "will-to-art" in the proper sense of the term. This work is one of capital importance, the first to recognize the creative value behind the artistic decline of ancient classical forms that resulted in medieval primitive forms.

Everything happened in a way which suggests that as soon as a new principle was discovered, the successive generations of artists were only concerned with developing it to the full, blindly obeying its implicit laws until they brought it to its inevitable end. Gothic architecture, as the present writer tried to show in a work on Mont Saint-Michel in 1934, is perhaps the most perfect example of an art obeying an unavoidable law of growth.

At the end of the nineteenth century a Swiss professor, Heinrich Wölfflin, made a most valuable contribution to art history, by defining the psychological concepts "classical" and "baroque" for the first time. This he did apart from historical uses or applications of the terms, by confronting and opposing two artistic attitudes that correspond to two mutually hostile attitudes to life. Classicism, which attempts to strike a balance between form as it is conceived by the intellect on the one hand and the direct observation of nature on the other, expresses itself in centered compositions and through a strict arrangement of component parts, each of which retains its distinct unity: classical forms are ponderable and static, and obey the laws of gravity, while movements are governed by rhythms and may be reduced to a harmonic cadence (pl. 633). The baroque, on the other hand, expresses uneasiness and a longing for freedom, and shows itself in open compositions, fragments of the world rather than a world in themselves, which overflow the limits of the frame. Baroque forms are imponderable, weightless, they soar into space, which they cut across with movements that set the eye moving in every direction, far beyond what they actually show: the unity of baroque compositions is not of an intellectual order, but it is organic, living, comprehensive, resulting in a close dependence of the forms one upon the other (pl. 634). In extreme baroque the pursuit of depth leads to forms being completely dissolved into their surroundings (Monet's *Nymphéas*). Classicism means cohesion, it reduces nature to the human scale, it is a state of being; while baroque is a state of becoming, a dispersion, so enamored of nature that it absorbs man into the cosmic rhythm. Baroque tries to depict human passion, grief and pain (pls. 645 to 647), love and death, all the ages of man; whereas classicism is interested only in the mature man at the height of his powers, when all his faculties are swayed by reason. The favorite medium of the baroque is painting or music, while classicism expresses itself most fully in architecture and sculpture. In extreme baroque, architecture tends to abandon abstract principles to assume a "vegetable life" closely wedded to the organic forms of nature (Manueline art, pl. 300).

An archaeologist who developed Riegl's fundamental ideas and took as his point of departure the astonishing parallelism he found between the evolution of Greek and Romano-Gothic sculpture, the

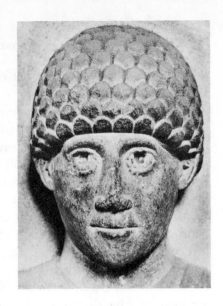

EVOLUTION OF STYLES
PRIMITIVISM

635. Head of the Moschophorus (Calf-bearer). About 570 B.C.
Athens, Acropolis Museum.

636. Head of a cherubim. Late 11th century. *Toulouse, St.-Sernin.*

Hellenist Deonna, director of the Geneva museum, suggested that there are endlessly recurring "artistic cycles." This thesis has been taken up and cleverly developed by two French aestheticians, Elie Faure (*Esprit des formes*, 1927) and Henri Focillon (*Vie des formes*, 1934). These different works have satisfactorily defined the complete evolutionary cycle of a style as passing through the following stages:

1. *Primitive, archaic stage, corresponding to the experimental age.*
In this immature stage man is still unable to make a clear distinction between his own soul and that of the world. The myriad forms of the world appear to him as being in a state of continuous creation and interchangeable with one another. Style is governed by certain mental data that the artist projects into his work. These impose certain schematic and ornamental deformations on nature (pls. 635, 636, and 651 to 654), but they gradually diminish as man's power for observation awakens, as he begins to be aware of the reality of the external world and finds that he can act on it rationally.

EVOLUTION OF STYLES
CLASSICISM

637. Greek statue. First half of 5th century B.C.
Rome, National Museum.

638. Angel of the Annunciation, Chartres Cathedral.
Early 13th century.

2. *Classical stage, corresponding to the age of maturity.*

This stage represents an equilibrium between the soul's receptiveness, now open to the external world, and the creative power of the mind—the mind informing the soul of its concepts and ideas and thus controlling observation and spontaneous sensation. These two currents in the human being, the one so to speak directed upward and the other downward, come together in the imagination, to their common advantage: they help the imagination to respect appearances and at the same time to perceive the harmony underlying their apparent disorder.

3. *Academic and Mannerist stages.*

These two stages may be reached after any great creative period, even after baroque; but they are particularly noticeable after a period of classicism. The soul's former ability to absorb the manifold forms of the world now becomes inhibited by the artist's undue respect for the forms created by the previous generation.

A sense of weariness now pushes the weaker spirits towards academ-

639. Praxitelean Aphrodite. 4th century B.C. *Naples, National Museum.*
640. Virgin. Troyes Cathedral. 14th century.

icism, or a conformity in which they obey conventional rules deduced from the art of the great masters and feel excused from having to invent anything themselves. But the more gifted artists revolt against the feeling of impotence and create what we call the *Mannerist* phase to which all styles are liable. With his mind obsessed and arrested by conventional memorized forms, his soul impoverished by the sudden lowering of vitality that cuts it off from the outside world, the artist can only create a world of his own, a substitute for the real one around him. This anaemia results in artificiality and drives artists to extremes, for instance such deformities as the exaggerated lengthening of the body (pls. 330, 641, 642) or frantic gestures, feverish attitude and caricatural expression.

This sickness of styles is one of the most constant phenomena in the history of art. It is particularly noticeable in the Greek fourth century, in the French fourteenth century (pls. 639, 640) and in the second half of the sixteenth century, when it afflicted the whole of Europe as a result of the nervous shock given by the Renaissance. It can

STYLES: MANNERISM

641. Akhenaten making an offering to the sun disk. From a stele. *Cairo, Museum*.

642. El Greco. The Resurrection. Detail. *Madrid, Prado*.

also be seen in the Florentine school at the end of the fifteenth century, in Chinese sculpture under the Sung Dynasty, or in the Art Nouveau, an artificial style which arose out of exasperation against the conventionality of architecture in the nineteenth century, and which at the same time has none of the powerful rhythm of the baroque. One of the most remarkable examples of the Mannerist crisis would seem to be the eccentric art of the eighteenth Egyptian Dynasty, at the time of Akhenaten (pl. 641).

The Mannerist phenomenon has created works which are by no means negligible and have acted as stimulants to the nervous sensibility of our own period. But the artists belonging to a Mannerist generation rarely manage to break through the circle of impotence in which they are held. The cry that came from the very soul of Alonso Berruguete (pl. 357), the mystical outpourings of El Greco (pls. 359, 360) and the feverish discovery of the truth of things by the artists of Tel el-Amarna none the less show the Mannerist way of feeling may reach sublime heights.

EVOLUTION OF STYLES
BAROQUE

643. Figure (reversed) from a frieze on the Altar of Zeus at Pergamon.
2nd century B.C. *Berlin, Pergamon Museum.*

644. Claus Sluter. Holy Virgin. 1391.
Former Charterhouse of Champmol, Dijon.

4. Baroque stage.

The normal end of Mannerism—its cure—lies in baroque. Once the soul is again in contact with the world, the imagination drinks deeply of its forms, and at the very source, with an eagerness born of long deprivation. The very cosmos seems to be throbbing in the soul, filling it with inspiring emotion.

For Germanic thinkers, the baroque is the essential creative power that animates so many primitive works as well as those of so-called baroque periods. According to them, this originates in the Nordic peoples and their Asiatic ancestors or offshoots, but the Southern peoples are always trying to smother it under their academic mentality. The concept of a baroque style as a *resultant*, a consequence and final expression of stylistic evolution, spelling the declines of certain techniques such as architecture and the minor arts, but on the other hand encouraging painting, holds good particularly with the art of the West. But there is also an *immanent* baroque instinct with its reserves in the East, which is also found in such Western countries as Spain and Ger-

EVOLUTION OF
STYLES: BAROQUE

645. Laocoön head. About 50 B.C. *Rome, Vatican.*

646. Juan de Juni. St. Jerome (inspired by the Laocoön). Detail. 1534. *Río Seco, San Francisco.*

647. Head of Christ. 15th century. *Eu (Seine-Inférieure), St.-Laurent.*

many. The meeting of "resultant" with "immanent" baroque results in ultra-baroque, for example the Flamboyant Gothic or rococo in Spain and Germany, or American art after the Spanish conquest.

In the development of his *Homo ludens* theory (1951), Professor Johan Huizinga of Utrecht produced a general vindication of the "formalist" standpoint of the first half of the twentieth century. To him the work of art appeared as an expression of that "urge to play"

(*Spieltriebs*), whose self-sufficiency and spontaneity form an essential human characteristic. Today, however, there is a tendency to reject this Olympian interpretation of artistic activity, which is now seen as being subject to other influences besides the pure *Kunstwollen*. As long ago as 1872 the German Robert Vischer put forward his theory of *Einfühlung*, or "symbolic sympathy," which was derived from the Idealist aesthetic of Kant and Hegel. According to Vischer this instinctive tendency causes the artist, on the one hand, to evoke those forms from the real world which he feels are analogous to his inner inspirations, and, on the other, to create his own world of forms, a handwriting that exteriorizes and clarifies his deepest feelings.

During the last fifteen years the study of art as a human activity has tended to draw steadily closer to psychology (study of the conscious) or to psychoanalysis (study of the unconscious). Contemporary developments in abstract art show a tendency to render artistic forms independently of their representational, thematic or philosophical content, even of their historical associations. These forms are seen as a system of signs and symbols with almost magical significance, which make the fundamental rhythms of the human soul, individual or collective, well up from the depths to the surface. This tendency, closer to psychoanalysis, which explains hidden meanings, than to psychology, the interpreter of the conscious mind, is shown in recent works by André Malraux, which together form his *Psychologie de l'art* (1947–1950).

In 1946, the present author drew attention in his *Crépuscule des images* to the profound correspondence between the forms of contemporary art and the "morphology" of our times. Moreover, as much in the realms of scientific thought and of poetry as in the world of action, the artist finds himself more often than not playing a prophetic role and anticipating the course of events.

The impossibility of "explaining" the work of art and the fact that it has a language peculiar to itself alone have been strongly emphasized by André Malraux and still more so by André Breton (*L'Art magique*). Breton, the leader of the Surrealist movement, rejects as useless all means of expression which are not derived from magic, and he considers it one of the merits of our times to have rediscovered the sense of this profound message. The theory of archetypes in Jungian psychoanalysis favors such interpretations.

WORLD-WIDE
UNITY OF STYLES

The spiral pattern, which probably originated in Cretan art, spread into Barbarian art, Anglo-Irish art, and survives in contemporary Breton art.

648. Vase. Cycladic. Bronze Age.
Athens, National Museum.

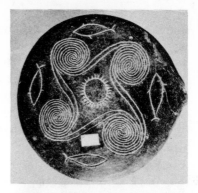

649. Detail from a stele. Vallstenarum (Gotland, Sweden). About 400 B.C.

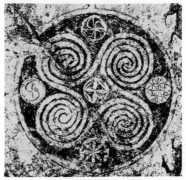

650. Ornamentation, Book of Durrow. Anglo-Irish. 2nd half of 7th century. *Dublin, Trinity College.*

While the historians, aestheticians, psychologists and psychoanalysts have been investigating the work of art along these lines, paying special attention to primitive art, Bernard Berenson, who at the beginning of our century gave the decisive impetus to the discovery of early Italian painting, has remained stubbornly faithful to the assumption of the superiority of classicism and to the traditional interpretations dating back to before Riegl and Wölfflin (*Aesthetics and History*, 1950).

The study of the great laws governing artistic creation was made

by the historians of Western art and of the art of adjacent Asiatic countries. Our knowledge of the arts of the Far East was pursued quite
independently, but if one wants to have an over-all view of the great
styles that have swept the world, it would be advisable to consider
whatever morphology might be deduced from Western and Eastern
art together. René Grousset, in his *Bilan de l'histoire* (1946), wrote
the first great synthesis of the Western and Eastern cultures, taking
works of art into account, though, as evidence of civilization rather
than for their own sake.

There are many analogies of form between the arts of the East and
West, and some aspects of these have already been mentioned. The
principles behind the birth and development of forms are the same all
over the world, but it is apparent that the rhythm of formal evolution as
defined by Riegl, Deonna, Elie Faure and Henri Focillon can strictly
be applied only to the arts of the West. In the Far East many stages
appear to be missing. India seems to have begun straightaway at the
stage of naturalism, without having passed through the ideomorphism
or stylization common to primitive arts. In China the normal evolution
—through primitivism, classicism and the baroque—can be clearly seen
running through the Wei, T'ang and Sung Dynasties, but there is an
inexplicable gap between the primitivism of the earliest periods and the
sudden realistic work of the Han Dynasty.

The resemblance between forms that emerge at immense distances
from each other may have various explanations. However great the
distance may be, it does not cut out all possibility of influence: for
instance Chinese figures could be brought in to the West across the
silk route that crossed Turkestan and Iran, carrying artistic forms to
Byzantium and Islam. Or a remote common origin might explain similar-
ities between peoples who have been separated over a long period of
history: perhaps this explains the strange resemblance between the forms
of Pre-Columbian art on the American continent, and the much older
forms of early China. It has also been known to happen that without
any possibility of influence, similar circumstances produce similar artistic
forms at enormous distances of time and space, the most famous of these
parallels being that of Gandharan Greco-Buddhist art, which anticipated
Gothic spiritually by a thousand years. In sociology this phenomenon
is known as "convergence."

The frequency with which these resemblances recur tempts the historian to see or to seek profound unifying principles in the infinite variety of civilizations all over the world. If we try to take an over-all view of the forms of art created by mankind, we see that after a phase of uniformity common to all the earth in the Neolithic period, the world seems to have become divided into three parts: two zones showing evolved civilizations which are clearly defined in geography, both of them being on the Eurasian continent, the third being a zone of archaic civilizations scattered over Africa, America and Polynesia.

The two zones of evolved civilizations, one covering the East and the other the West of the Eurasian continent, both exploited the plastic arts as far as they could take them. The differences between these two regions should not blind us to the resemblance between their underlying rhythms. In each of these two zones, indeed, two distinct poles are to be seen, based on opposite centers: the first tending to remind man of his attachment to the universe and his submission to supernatural powers, the second urging him, on the contrary, to free himself from those powers and rely on his own strength, so that he might possess the world and himself by means of thought.

In the primitive period of Mediterranean civilization, after the very earliest stage of immaturity Mesopotamia showed itself to be progressive as compared with a static Egypt. Then, in classical antiquity, Asia Minor began to play its part as the enduring "reservoir" of immanent powers as opposed to the Greco-Roman sense of progress. Asia Minor maintained the rights of God against Greek and Roman anthropomorphism, and restored God to the Mediterranean peoples. The Middle Ages saw an opposition between unchangeable Byzantium and the belated but impressive rise of the West. The same struggle was taken into the interior of Western Europe when Renaissance rationalism was checked by the resistance of Gothic irrationalism. At that time Germany seemed to have inherited from Asia its function of serving as a reservoir for irrational forces, in the same way as Spain, which had become strongly marked by Orientalism owing to Islam: the Churrigueresque of the Spanish eighteenth century is of the same stock as the "retarded Gothic" of fifteenth and sixteenth century Germany. The struggle and the mingling of these two forces accounts for the extraordinary wealth of the so-called baroque period.

If we now look to the Far East, the same pattern may be observed there. But before considering that part of the world it is important to

*The urge toward stylization in primitive civilizations
makes them all produce similar formal patterns,
though at considerable removes in both time and space.*

651. Greek vase. Detail. Early 6th century B.C.
Athens, National Museum.

652. Buddhist stele. Wei Dynasty (China). Detail.
Dated A.D. 533–543. *New York, Metropolitan Museum.*

remember that the creative evolution came to a standstill there in the
fifteenth century, for the prolongation of Chinese art thereafter represents a decadent crystallization or fixity, while that of India was arrested
by Islam.

India, a creator of great metaphysical ideas as well as of a philosophy which quickly developed into a religion with universal implications, in the form of Buddhism, India is in a way the "West" of the
Eastern Hemisphere. Compared with India, China has remained cultur-
ally archaic in spite of a highly developed civilization, and may be
called a force for tradition. Were it not for the mystery of Han art,
whose origins cannot be traced, it might be suggested that the influence
of Buddhist India freed China from its prolonged primitivism, so great
and so marked was the effect of Gupta art on the Chinese in the Wei
Dynasty, when Buddhism came to China. Just like ancient Greece, into
a still-primitive world—that is to say, one whose art was ideomorphic
and magical—India brought the awakening of naturalism, a sense of the
concrete, a sense of the figure, in a word a physical, corporeal art, which
perhaps she herself had created under the influence of the last faint
repercussions of Hellenism that were brought across Iran and Bactria

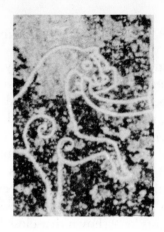

UNITY OF STYLES

653. Christ. Detail. Tympanum of the Church of the Madeleine,
Vézelay. About 1230.

654. Incised rock drawing, Ramsunberg (Norway).
About 1000.

into Gandhara. It was at Gandhara that the two worlds met, the point where the two great cultures, dating back to the antiquity of man, recognized their blood relationship. In his book *De la Grèce à l'Orient* (1948) René Grousset has described the astonishing adventure of Hellenism as it spread its roots and multiplied until at last it reached Japan.

This phase of lively Buddhist progress in India proved to be brief, because it rapidly succumbed to the upsurge of irrational forces provoked by Hinduism, a decadent form of the earlier Brahmanism. Dravidian India may be seen as a denial of Gupta India. The seed of India was to germinate in China. But even in the period of its highest philosophical refinement, China remained deeply committed to its need for magic: its symbol is the chimera, and the dragon that emerges from the broken tortuous patterns of archaic Chinese bronzes leaps from the sky in Sung paintings. It is extraordinary that though they have such a high metaphysical level, Sung landscapes show no sign of *perspective*, which is the particular expression of the Western will to progress. But in the Gupta period (for example, in the Ajanta paintings), India had long since taken perspective to the same stage as it reached in the

Hellenistic period—that is to say, a perspective with several vanishing points.

When the Spaniards reached America at the end of the fifteenth century, they discovered a world at a stage of civilization which must have been much the same as that of ancient China. When we consider the art of the so-called Pre-Columbian peoples, it is surprising that though they had reached a high quality as regards form, they had still not passed beyond the primitive stage in the evolution of styles. The cause for this must no doubt be sought in the isolation of the American continent. Sociologists have shown that closed societies, confined to what are called "segregation territories," become static and die out. Here we put our finger on one of the most profound laws in the evolution of mankind. Man is necessary to man, there is no progress without contact between races and exchanges of influence, for man becomes more aware of himself by the impact of others than by any amount of self-sufficiency. Other races have remained even farther behind in their evolution, perhaps because they were isolated even longer than the American tribes: this is the case with the primitives of Africa, Polynesia, the Polar regions and the Atlantic coast of South America, which are still at the Neolithic or even the Palaeolithic stage. The hunter civilization of the Perigordian Age is still to be seen among the aboriginals of central Australia, who throughout their history had probably never seen other men before the Europeans arrived.

If we now compare the two great zones of the Eurasian continent, the East and the West, it can be seen that altogether they both have a history which shows a tension between the irrational and the rational, and that the internal evolution of each of them has been governed by it. No doubt the artistic manifestations of mankind are countless, but the archetypes toward which they tend are few. The law behind the creation of styles seems to draw its fundamental impulse from a tension between two hostile forces. Thus art history confirms the findings of modern psychology, which tends to see the principle of ambivalence beneath all the manifestations of the individual human being.

BIBLIOGRAPHY

CREDITS FOR PHOTOGRAPHS

INDEX

BIBLIOGRAPHY

THE BIBLIOGRAPHY of art history has now become so vast that it would be impossible to give adequate data, in a small compass, for each chapter in this book. The alternative which has been followed is to direct the reader toward general works which offer fuller accounts as well as the necessary bibliographical information.

HANDBOOKS

LAVALLEYE, JACQUES: *Introduction aux études d'archéologie et d'histoire.* Paris, 1946. A valuable guide for all students of art history, giving an introduction to the methods and techniques of this field of study, with a carefully arranged critical bibliography.

BIBLIOGRAPHICAL INDEXES

LAVEDAN, PIERRE: *Histoire de l'art.* 2 vols. 2d ed. Paris, 1950. I, *Antiquité;* II, *Moyen Age.* Short summaries introducing a considerable critical bibliography, organically classified. The bibliography is comprehensive except in the case of the modern and contemporary sections. The book covers only antiquity and western civilization. Indispensable to any bibliographical study. To be completed by reference to two Indexes published annually in France and the U.S.A.: *Répertoire d'art et d'archéologie*, France (from 1910), and *The Art Index*, New York (from 1929).

GENERAL HISTORIES OF ART
Scholarly Publications

Two comprehensive and scholarly Histories of Art have appeared in French and German: MICHEL, ANDRÉ: *Histoire de l'art depuis les premiers temps chrétiens jusqu'à nos jours.* 8 books in 17 vols. with an important Index. Paris, 1905–29. A collective work, unequal and somewhat dated.

BURGER, FRITZ, and ALBERT ERICH BRINCKMANN: *Handbuch der Kunstwissenschaft.* 27 vols. Berlin, 1912–30. A collective work, more exhaustive than Michel, also broader in scope and showing none of the "classical" prejudices of the former. These two works have become dated and will be superseded by the (English) *Pelican History of Art*, ed. Nikolaus Pevsner, to be completed in 48 vols., of which the first appeared in 1953.

More popular works
IN FRENCH

DEONNA, WALDEMAR: *Du miracle grec au miracle chrétien.* 3 vols. Basle, 1945–48. A comparative synthesis of the evolution of all Western art, compiled by Waldemar Deonna himself, remarkable for its formulation of principles. Contains a very useful critical bibliography, though this is not always easy to follow.

FAURE, ELIE: *Histoire de l'art.* 5 vols. Paris, 1926–27. (English trans. by Walter Pach: *History of Art.* 2 vols. New York, 1948.) An aesthetic study of both personal and literary value.

FOCILLON, HENRI: *Art d'Occident.* 2d ed. Paris, 1952. The best synthesis yet written on the Western Middle Ages (stopping at the fifteenth century).

GROUSSET, RENÉ: *Les Civilisations de l'Orient.* 4 vols. I, *L'Orient;* II, *L'Inde;* III, *La Chine;* IV, *Le Japon.* Paris, 1929–30. (English trans. by C. A. Phillips: *The Civilizations of the East.* 4 vols. New York, 1931–34.) A history of the Oriental arts, set against their cultural and religious background. No bibliography. Original in its ideas, though sometimes factually outmoded, except for the two volumes on India and China which were revised after the author's death.

Réau, Louis: *Histoire universelle des arts, des temps primitifs jusqu'à nos jours.* 4 vols. Paris, 1930–39. Intended for university students, the best available history of art on account of its textual quality, scientific information and soundness of ideas. A comprehensive bibliography. The sections on Western art are all by Louis Réau himself. The volume on the Far East is the only learned and didactic synthesis to be had in French, containing a historical account of the facts and an important bibliography.

Meer, Frederik van der: *Atlas de la civilisation occidentale.* Amsterdam, 1952. (*Atlas of Western Civilization.* Amsterdam and New York, 1954.) Extending from Greek art to the present day, this is a remarkable presentation of the subject in atlas form, with numerous maps. Some reservations are necessary in view of its severely Catholic outlook, which puts no emphasis on secular art.

In German

Die Propyläen Kunstgeschichte. 24 vols. Berlin, 1925–35. Richly illustrated, with thorough interpretative texts; also in Spanish as *Historia del arte.*

Hamann, R.: *Geschichte der Kunst.* 1935. Popular textbook or "guide" presentation: thorough bibliography and list of principal monuments.

In English

Cheney, Sheldon: *A World History of Art.* New York, 1937. Popularization.

Gardner, Helen: *Art Through the Ages.* 3d ed. New York, 1948. Popularization.

Gombrich, E. H. J.: *The Story of Art.* New York, 1950.

In Spanish

Pijoán y Soteras, José: *Summa artis; Historia general del arte.* 15 vols. to date. Madrid, 1931–. An enormous synthesis of world art, written entirely by Prof. Pijoán: at present the fullest, best, and most up-to-date collection of illustrative material. No bibliography.

——*Historia del arte.* 3 vols. Barcelona, 1914. (English trans. by R. L. Roys: *History of Art.* 3 vols. New York, 1927.) Popularization.

Speculum Artis. 3 vols. to date. Ed. J. F. RAFOLA. Founded in 1943.

IN DUTCH

Algemeene Kunst Geschiedenis; Die Kunst der Menschheid van de Oudste Tijden tot Heden. Ed. F. W. S. VAN THIENEN. 5 vols. 1941–50.

HISTORIES OF ART, BY COUNTRIES

GERMANY

DEHIO, GEORG G.: *Geschichte der deutschen Kunst.* 4 vols. of text, 4 vols. of plates. 2d ed. Berlin and Leipzig, 1920–34. A standard work, particularly good on Middle Ages.

ROTHKIRCH, W. VON: *Deutsche Kunst.* Berlin, 1934. Popularization.

ENGLAND

The Oxford History of English Art. Ed. THOMAS S. R. BOASE. Oxford, 1949–. A scholarly work, to be completed in 11 vols., of which five have appeared.

WHITLEY, W. T.: *Art in England,* 1800–37. 2 vols. Cambridge, 1928–30. Popularization.

LAMBERT, RICHARD S. (ed.): *Art in England.* Harmondsworth, Eng., 1938. Popularization.

BELGIUM

FIERENS, P.: *L'Art en Belgique.* 2d ed. Brussels, 1947.

LEURS, STAN (ed.): *Geschiedenis van de Vlaamsche Kunst* . . . Antwerp, 1936–37.

FRANCE

GILLET, LOUIS: *Histoire des arts.* In *Histoire de la nation française.* Ed. G. HANOTAUX. Paris, 1922. Dated.

Encyclopédie générale de l'art français; a collection of works for the general public; excellent statements of the contemporary viewpoint, written by specialists, but lacks a bibliography.

Publications de la Société française d'archéologie consists of (a) *Bulle-*

tin monumental, 111 vols., 1834–1953, archeological scholarship; (b) *Congrès archéologique de France*, 109 vols., 1834–1951, collections of studies in archeology, classified geographically according to the districts in which Congresses met; vol. XCVII (1934, II) contains a general bibliography of French monuments, under period classification; (c) a subject index of the above two publications published in 1930.

SPAIN

LOZOYA, JUAN C. Y LÓPEZ DE AYALA: *Historia del arte hispanico.* 5 vols. Barcelona, 1931–51. A learned work designed for students by a university professor. Considerable bibliography.

——*Ars hispaniae.* Madrid, 1947–. To be completed in 18 vols., 14 of which appeared 1947–58. A very detailed work of scholarship.

U.S.A.

BAUR, JOHN I. H.: *Revolution and Tradition in Modern American Art.* Cambridge, Mass., 1951.

LARKIN, OLIVER: *Art and Life in America.* New York, 1949.

TUNNARD, CHRISTOPHER, and HENRY HOPE REED: *American Skyline.* Boston, 1955.

ITALY

Italian studies are well covered bibliographically. Representative works include: Italian Touring Club: *Attraverso l'Italia*, 17 vols. to date, an enormous compilation of some 15,000 illustrations, geographically classified.

MODIGLIANI, ETTORE: *Mentore, Guida allo studio dell'arte italiana.* Milan, 1946. This well-documented guide, designed for students of Italian art, is a remarkable introduction such as exists in no other country.

MOTTINI, GUIDO EDOARDO: *Storia dell'arte italiana.* 2 vols. 2d ed. Milan, 1949. Popularization.

VENTURI, ADOLFO: *Storia dell'arte italiana.* 11 vols. to date. Milan, 1901–40. The most important work of scholarship on Italian art: not completed. Bibliography. Certain sections dated.

——*A Short History of Italian Art.* New York, 1926.

RUSSIA

ALPATOV, M., and N. BRUNOV: *Geschichte der altrussischen Kunst.* Augsburg, 1932.

BUNT, CYRIL G. E.: *Russian Art, from Scyths to Soviets.* London and New York, 1946.

RÉAU, LOUIS: *L'Art Russe des origines à Pierre le Grand.* Paris, 1921.

———*L'Art Russe de Pierre le Grand à nos jours.* Paris, 1922.

SWITZERLAND

GANTNER, J.: *Kunstgeschichte der Schweiz.* 2 vols. to date. (1st vol. available in French trans.) Frauenfeld, 1936.

ART FORMS AND TECHNIQUES

ARCHITECTURE

CHOISY, AUGUSTE: *Histoire de l'architecture.* 2 vols. Paris, 1899; later revised. The best theoretical treatise on architecture, still a standard work.

GOTTHEIN, M. L.: *Geschichte der Gartenkunst.* 2 vols. 1914.

GROMORT, GEORGES: *L'Art des jardins.* 2 vols. Paris, 1934.

HARTMANN, K. OTTO: *Die Baukunst in ihrer Entwicklung von der Urzeit bis zur Gegenwart.* 3 vols. 2d ed. Leipzig, 1931.

LAVEDAN, PIERRE: *Histoire de l'urbanisme.* 3 vols. Paris, 1926–52. I, *Antiquité et Moyen Age;* II, *Renaissance et temps modernes;* III, *Epoque contemporaine.*

MUGGIA, ATTILIO: *Storia dell'architettura dai primordi ai nostri giorni.* Milan, 1933.

SCHMITT, DURM, ENDE, and WAGNER: *Handbuch der Architektur.* 28 vols. in 52. Darmstadt, 1881–1911. The largest encyclopedia of architecture.

STURGIS, R.: *A Dictionary of Architecture and Building, Biographical, Historical and Descriptive.* 3 vols. New York, 1901–2.

WASMUTH, E.: *Wasmuths Lexikon der Baukunst.* 4 vols. Berlin, 1929–32. *Nachtrag 5* published in 1937.

SCULPTURE

POST, CHANDLER R.: *A History of European and American Sculpture from the Early Christian Period to the Present Day.* 2 vols. Cambridge, Mass., 1921.

PAINTING

DALBON, C.: *Les Origines de la peinture à l'huile.* Paris, 1904.

DRAWING

LAVALLÉE, PIERRE: *Les Techniques du dessin.* Paris, 1943.

MEDER, JOSEPH: *Die Handzeichnung, ihre Technik und Entwicklung.* 2d ed. Vienna, 1923.

SCHÖNBRUNNER, JOSEPH, and J. MEDER: *Handzeichnungen alter Meister aus der Albertiner und anderen Sammlungen.* 12 vols. Vienna, 1896–1908. The most important collection of drawings in facsimile.

ENGRAVING

BARTSCH, ADAM VON: *Le Peintre graveur.* 21 vols. and albums, with checklist. Vienna, 1803–21; another ed., Würzburg, 1920.

LE BLANC, C.: *Manuel de l'amateur d'estampes.* 4 vols. Paris, 1854–90.

PASSAVANT, J. D.: *Le Peintre-graveur.* 6 vols. with catalogue. Leipzig, 1860–64.

ROSENTHAL, LÉON: *La Gravure.* 2d ed. Revised Jean Adhémar. Paris, 1939.

MINOR ARTS

BOSSERT, HELMUTH THEODOR: *Geschichte der Kunstgewerbes aller Zeiten und Völker.* 6 vols. Berlin, 1928–35.

GOEBEL, HEINRICH: *Wandteppiche.* 6 vols. Leipzig, 1923–24.

GUIFFREY, JULES M. J.: *Histoire générale de la tapisserie.* 3 vols. Paris, 1878–85.

MOLINIER, E.: *Histoire générale des arts appliqués à l'industrie, du Ve à la fin du XVIIIe siècle.* 5 vols. Paris, 1896–1911.

ROSENBERG, M.: *Der Goldschmiede merkzeichen.* 4 vols. 3d ed. Frankfurt, 1922–28.

MARQUET DE VASSELOT, JEAN J.: *Bibliographie de l'orfèvrerie et de l'émaillerie françaises*. Paris, 1925.

ICONOGRAPHY

The only works available are on Christian iconography: there is no general work on ancient iconography.

BRÉHIER, L.: *L'Art chrétien*. 2d ed. Paris, 1928. Deals more thoroughly with the medieval than with the modern period.

CAHIER, C.: *Caractéristiques des saints*. 2 vols. Paris, 1866–68. A dictionary of features by which images of saints may be identified.

KÜNSTLE, KARL: *Ikonographie der christlichen Kunst*. 2 vols. Freiburg, 1926–28. Presented in dictionary form. Embraces all the European arts. Very comprehensive: valuable bibliography.

MÂLE, EMILE: *L'Art religieux du XIIe siècle en France*. 5th ed. Paris, 1947.

————*L'Art religieux du XIIIe siècle en France*. 8th ed. Paris, 1948. (English trans. by Dora Nussey: *Religious Art in France, XIII Century*. New York, 1913.)

————*Religious Art from the Twelfth to the Eighteenth Century*. New York, 1949.

————*L'Art religieux de la fin du moyen âge en France*. 5th ed. Paris, 1949.

————*L'Art religieux après le Concile de Trente*. Paris, 1932.

Emile Mâle's works are the finest comprehensive works available on Christian Art, especially that of France and Italy.

MARLE, RAIMOND VAN: *Iconographie de l'art profane au Moyen Age et à la Renaissance et la décoration des demeures*. 2 vols. The Hague, 1931–32.

DICTIONARIES
General

AESCHLIMANN, E.: *Dictionnaire des miniaturistes* . . . Milan, 1940.

BÉNÉZIT, EMMANUEL: *Dictionnaire critique et documentaire des pein-*

tres, sculpteurs . . . 3 vols. Paris, 1911–23. Now under revision, considerably augmented, to be completed in 8 volumes of which 6 have appeared, giving the prices of works at public auctions. No bibliography.

BRYAN, MICHAEL: *Dictionary of Painters and Engravers.* 5 vols. London, 1903–5. Dated.

DARMON, J. E.: *Dictionnaire des peintres miniaturistes* . . . Paris, 1927.

THIEME, ULRICH, and F. BECKER: *Allgemeines Lexikon der bildenden Künstler* . . . 37 vols. to date. Leipzig, 1907–50. An exhaustive work with very full bibliography. Standard work of reference.

National
GERMANY

SCHMITT, OTTO (ed.): *Reallexikon zur deutschen Kunstgeschichte.* Stuttgart, 1933–. Unfinished.

ENGLAND

REDGRAVE, SAMUEL: *A Dictionary of Artists of the English School: Painters, Sculptors, Architects, Engravers and Ornamentists.* London, 1874.

BELGIUM

BAUTIER, PIERRE, R. CAZIER, R. L. DELEVOY, C. DE MAEGER, P. FIERENS, E. GREINDI: *Dictionnaire des peintres flamands.* Brussels, 1951.

U.S.A.

FIELDING, MANTLE: *Dictionary of American Painters, Sculptors and Engravers.* New York, 1945.

FRANCE

BELLIER DE LA CHAVIGNERIE, EMILE, and L. AUVRAY: *Dictionnaire général des artistes de l'école française* . . . 2 vols. and Index. Paris, 1882–87.

LAMI, STANISLAS: *Dictionnaire des sculpteurs de l'école française.* 8 vols. Paris, 1898–1921.

HOLLAND

WURZBACH, ALFRED VON: *Niederländisches Künstler-Lexikon* . . . 3 vols. Vienna and Leipzig, 1906–11.

ITALY

COLNAGHI, DOMINIC E.: *A Dictionary of Florentine Painters from the 13th to the 17th Centuries.* London, 1928.

GALETTI, UGO, and ETTORE CAMESASCA: *Enciclopedia della pittura italiana.* 3 vols. 1951. The most complete and up-to-date work available, with a bibliography.

PREHN, I. E.: *A Short Lexicon of Italian Painters.* Florence, 1938.

GLOSSARIES

GAY, V.: *Glossaire archéologique du Moyen Age et de la Renaissance.* Paris, 1887–1928.

RÉAU, LOUIS: *Dictionnaire polyglotte des termes d'art et d'archéologie.* Paris, 1953.

————*Dictionnaire illustré d'art et d'archéologie.* Paris, 1930.

SERRANO DE HARO, AGUSTÍN: *Terminologia scientifica, industrial y artistica.* 2d ed. Madrid, 1929.

VOLLMER, HANS: *Kunstgeschichtliches Wörterbuch.* Leipzig and Berlin, 1928.

WEALE, JOHN: *Dictionary of Terms Used in the Fine Arts.* London, 1876.

AESTHETICS AND METHODOLOGY

BAZIN, GERMAIN: *Le Crépuscule des images.* Paris, 1946.

BURCKHARDT, JAKOB: *Der Cicerone.* 3 vols. in 1. 2d ed. Leipzig, 1869. (*The Cicerone: or, Art Guide to Painting in Italy.* London, 1873.) Published and translated in many languages.

————*Die Kultur der Renaissance in Italien.* Leipzig, 1869. (English trans. by S. G. C. Middlemore: *The Civilization of the Renaissance in Italy.* New York, 1945.)

BRUYN, EDGAR DE: *Esquisse d'une philosophie de l'art . . .* Brussels, 1930.

CROCE, BENEDETTO: *Breviario di estetica.* 2d ed. Bari, 1932. (French trans. Paris, 1925.)

————*Aesthetic as Science of Expression.* Trans. by Douglas Ainslie. 2d ed. London, 1922.

————*La Critica e la storia delle arti figurative.* Bari, 1934.

————*Ultimi saggi.* Bari, 1935.

DEONNA, WALDEMAR: *L'Archéologie, sa valeur, ses méthodes.* Paris, 1913.

FOCILLON, HENRI: *Vie des formes.* Paris, 1934. (English trans. by C. B. Hogan and G. Kubler: *The Life of Forms in Art.* 2d ed. New York, 1948.)

GHIKA, M. C.: *Esthétique des proportions . . .* Paris, 1927.

GROUSSET, RENÉ: *Bilan de l'histoire.* Paris, 1946. (English trans. by A. and H. Temple Patterson: *The Sum of History.* Hadleigh, Eng., 1951.)

GUYAU, J. M.: *L'Art au point de vue sociologique.* Paris, 1889.

JIRMOUNSKY, MIRON MALKIEL: *L'Amour de l'art.* 1932. A critique of the work of Josef Strzygowski, referred to in Chapters II and IV, and an account of his great theses, with comparative illustration, will be found on pp. 77–94.

JOSEPHSON, RAGNAR: *Konstverketsfödelse.* Stockholm, 1946.

LAGUÉ, A.: *Le Monde des formes.* Paris, 1948.

LALO, CHARLES: *Le Sentiment esthétique.* Paris, 1910.

MALRAUX, ANDRÉ: *Psychologie de l'art.* I, *Le Musée imaginaire;* II, *La Création artistique;* III, *La Monnaie de l'absolu.* Paris, 1948–50. (English trans. by Stuart Gilbert: *The Psychology of Art.* 3 vols. New York, 1949–51.)

————*Les Voix du silence.* Paris, 1952. (English trans. by Stuart Gilbert: *The Voices of Silence.* Garden City, N.Y., 1953.)

MARANGONI, MATTEO: *Come si guarda un quadro.* Florence, 1954. (French trans.: *Apprendre à voir.* Paris, 1948.)

MARITAIN, JACQUES: *Art et scolastique.* Paris, 1935. (English trans. by J. F. Scanlan: *Art and Scholasticism.* London, 1943; New York, 1947.)

ORS Y ROVIRA, EUGENIO D': *Tres horas en el Museo del Prado, Itinerario estético.* 2d ed. Madrid, n. d. (French trans.: *Trois heures au Musée du Louvre, itineraire esthétique.* Paris, 1927.)

———*Las Estructuras barrocas.* Madrid. (French trans.: *Le Baroque.* Paris.)

———*Las Ideas y las formas.* Madrid, 1928.

RIEGL, ALOIS: *Stilfragen.* Berlin, 1893; 1923.

———*Kunstgeschichte und Universalgeschichte* in *Festgaben für Max Budinger.* Innsbruck, 1898.

———*Die Spätrömische Kunstindustrie nach den Funden in Oester-reich-Ungarn.* Vienna, 1927.

———*Die Entstehung der Barockkunst in Rom.* Vienna, 1907.

SEMPER, GOTTFRIED: *Der Stil in den technischen und tektonischen Kunsten.* Munich, 1863.

SOURIAU, ETIENNE: *Pensée vivante et perfection formelle.* Paris, 1952.

TAINE, HIPPOLYTE A.: *Philosophie de l'art.* 2 vols. Paris, 1865–67. Widely translated. (English trans.: *The Philosophy of Art.* Variously reprinted.)

TIETZE, HANS: *Die Methode der Kunstgeschichte.* Vienna, 1911.

VENTURI, LIONELLO: *Storia della critica d'arte.* 2d ed. Florence, 1948. (French trans. of 1st ed., Brussels, 1935. English trans. by Charles Marriott: *History of Art Criticism.* New York, 1936.)

WAETZOLDT, WILHELM: *Du und die Kunst, eine Einführung in Kunst-betrachtung und Kunstgeschichte.* Berlin, 1938.

WÖLFFLIN, HEINRICH: *Renaissance und Barock.* Munich, 1888.

———*Kunstgeschichtliche Grundbegriffe.* Munich, 1915. (English trans. by M. D. Hottinger: *Principles of Art History.* New York, 1932.)

———*Die klassische Kunst.* Munich, 1924. (English trans. by Peter and Linda Murray: *Classic Art.* New York, 1952.)

On Wölfflin's theories, see HANNA LEVY, *Henri Wölfflin, sa théorie, ses prédécesseurs,* Paris, 1936, and LIONELLO VENTURI, *Gli Schemi del Wölfflin,* in *Prestiti di critica,* 1929.

Revue d'art et d'esthétique.

CREDITS FOR PHOTOGRAPHS

Numbers refer to plates, not pages.

A.C.I. Brussels, 391, 634

Alinari, 70, 72, 74, 85, 95, 96, 100, 103, 114, 117, 120, 122, 128, 130, 131, 132, 134, 136, 137, 149, 154, 159, 221, 222, 223, 224, 226, 227, 228, 257, 259, 260, 265, 266, 276, 281, 303, 314, 317, 322, 328, 329, 330, 332, 378, 379, 380, 381, 382, 384, 385, 428, 449, 470, 637, 639

Victor Amato, Washington, 498

Anderson, 79, 92, 105, 121, 129, 143, 150, 231, 232, 233, 234, 250, 253, 258, 261, 262, 263, 264, 267, 270, 271, 272, 273, 277, 279, 287, 309, 312, 313, 319, 321, 326, 331, 333, 339, 359, 360, 371, 383, 386, 390, 401, 402, 403, 415, 453, 508, 513, 633

Annan, Glasgow, 435

Archives Photographiques, 6, 30, 33, 39, 106, 107, 108, 161, 168, 170, 176, 180, 183, 193, 194, 195, 244, 288, 293, 295, 338, 367, 395, 459, 463, 464, 466, 489, 560, 578, 600, 608, 640

Arvix Mas, 9, 190, 355, 398, 587

Germain Bazin, 97, 188, 203, 237, 297, 301, 356, 400, 645

B.C.C., 49

Bibliothèque Nationale, 110, 111, 155, 162, 209, 247

Bijtebier, 393

Boissonnas, 48, 89

Braun, 94, 133, 239, 286, 318, 341, 344, 350, 369, 372, 392, 421, 422, 427, 448, 452, 455, 456, 458, 462, 476, 477, 484, 487, 499

British Museum, 16, 43, 55, 98

Brogi, 225, 269, 275, 308

Brunner, Côme, 115

Bulloz, 184, 186, 294, 353, 389, 425, 432, 451, 454, 478, 483, 491, 524, 614, 653

J. Buyens, 343

Byzantine Institute, Paris, 174

Calavas, 46

W. A. Call, Monmouth , 214

Carnegie Institution, Washington, 60

Carria Carrabella, 399

Cauvin, 597

Chevojon, 245, 296, 589

Chicago Architectural Photographing Co., 586

Chicago University, Oriental Institute, 127

Colten, New York, 607

Compagnie Aérienne Française, 442, 548

Compagnie des Arts Photomécaniques, 181, 185, 199, 200, 201, 202, 336, 340, 346, 441, 444, 461, 482, 518

Country Life, 431, 471

Deutscher Kunstverlag, 289

Robert Doisneau, 631

Echo Foto, 419

Ecole Française d'Athènes, 90, 109

Editions du Chêne, 246

Flournoy, 439
Marc Foucault, 445
Freer Gallery of Art, Washington, 230
Frequin, The Hague, 396
Frobenius, 2

Galerie Louis Carré, 601
Galerie Maeght, 619
Garabella, Valladolid, 357
Gasparini, Gênes, 388
Gemeente Musea, Amsterdam, 504
Gesellschaft für Wissenschaftl. Lichtbild,
    Munich, 413
Giraudon, 3, 7, 18, 19, 40, 45, 71, 82, 123,
    153, 157, 171, 205, 208, 210, 254, 256, 274,
    284, 285, 334, 335, 337, 342, 366, 450, 485,
    486, 488, 492, 526, 550, 618
Greater Boston Chamber of Commerce, 438

Harvard University, 440, 511
W. Hege, 81, 84
Lucien Hervé, 593
Hess, Rio de Janeiro, 411
Hoursch und Bechstedt, 217
Hunt, 538
Hurault, 282
Hürlimann, 206

India Office, London, 535, 537
Institut Archéologique Allemand, Rome,
    145

S. C. Johnson & Co., 591

Kaufmann and Fabry, Chicago, 577
Kazys Vozylius, Rio de Janeiro, 625
W. Kessels, Brussels, 64

Larkin, London, 529, 545
Noel Le Boyer, 169
Linck, Winterthur, 510

Dora Maar, 610
W. F. Mansell, London, 28, 41, 67, 93, 211,
    507
Marburg, 78, 164, 165, 191, 192, 218, 219,
    220, 251, 316, 348, 352, 397, 412, 414, 475,
    509, 515, 636
Gianni Mari, 606
V. de Mestral, 21
Metropolitan Museum of Art, 119, 517, 525,
    652 (Tet Borsig)
Gebhardt Metz, Tübingen, 11
Mohsen Moghadam, Teheran, 36, 37
Moreira, Oporto, 408, 409
Musée des Antiquités, Istanbul, 68
Musée Archéologique, Teheran, 36, 37, 126

Musée d'Art et d'Histoire, Geneva, 573
Musée d'Art et d'Histoire, Vienna, 235
Musée des Arts Décoratifs, Paris, 243, 363,
    474
Musée de Cassel, 73
Musée Guimet, 52, 53, 240, 248, 520 (Gol-
    oubew), 527, 530, 531, 532 and 533 (Gol-
    oubew), 540, 541, 542, 543, 544, 547
    (Goloubew), 549, 551, 558 (Chavannes),
    566, 570, 572
Musée de l'Homme, 65
Musée du Louvre (Laboratoire), 582
Musées Nationaux Bavarois, 494
Musées Royaux des Beaux-Arts de Bel-
    gique, 394
Museo National de Arte Antiga, Lisbon,
    300, 302
Museum of Fine Arts, Boston, 141, 424, 430,
    503, 517

National Gallery, London, 216, 429, 512
National Gallery of Art, Washington, 175

Panajou-Sautier, Bordeaux, 446
Philadelphia Museum of Art, 125
Phillips Academy, Andover, 623
Photo Club Burgos, 298

Charles Ratton, 63
Rijkmuseum, 423, 468
Rodriguez, Toledo, 358
Royal Academy of Arts, London, 539

Walter Scott, Bradford, 10
Sebah, Istanbul, 147
Emile Séraf, Athens, 91
Service des Antiquités, Cairo, 13, 31
Service Archéologique Néerlandais, 546
Sougez, 66, 204
Spreng, Basel, 252
Studio Lorelle, 443, 447

Trosley, 590

Universitetets Oldsaksamling, Oslo, 54
University Museum, Philadelphia, 59

Pierre Verger, 56, 57, 58, 410
A. Vigneau (Editions Tel), 12, 14, 26, 27,
    29, 32, 42, 44, 76, 101, 102, 112, 113
Roger Viollet, 469
Vizzavona, 25, 323, 368, 420, 467, 479, 500,
    501, 502, 503, 594, 595, 598, 599, 612

Wallace Collection, London, 433
Fernand Windels, 1
Wolfrum, 365

Zani, Milan, 387

INDEX

All references are to pages. Numbers in italics indicate illustrations on text pages. Roman numbers followed by an asterisk indicate text reference to a work which is illustrated on the same page.